Dark Shamans

NEIL L. WHITEHEAD

Dark Shamans

KANAIMÀ AND THE POETICS OF VIOLENT DEATH

Duke University Press Durham & London

2002

© 2002 Duke University Press

All rights reserved

Printed in the United States

of America on acid-free paper ∞

Designed by C. H. Westmoreland

Typeset in Carter & Cohn Galliard

with Pelican display by Tseng

Information Systems, Inc.

Library of Congress Cataloging-

in-Publication Data appear on

the last printed pages of this book.

FOR KENNETH, MY FATHER

Contents

Acknowledgments ix

Introduction 1

1. The Ethnographer's Tale 11

2. Tales of the Kanaimà: Observers 41

3. Tales of the Kanaimà: Participants 88

4. Shamanic Warfare 128

5. Modernity, Development, and Kanaimà Violence 174

6. Ritual Violence and Magical Death in Amazonia 202

Conclusion: Anthropologies of Violence 245

Notes 253

Works Cited 285

Index 299

Acknowledgments

There are many people whose direct and indirect help have contributed to this work, but those who imparted information about specific acts of violence or killing cannot be named. I thank those individuals and acknowledge their bravery in being prepared to speak out. I am able to openly thank Roger Edwin, Clarence Edwin, and Alfred Edwin, as well as Matteson Williams, Robinson Williams, and Sharon Williams for their consistent help. Matilda Sago, John Aldi, Roy Edwin, Calvin Simon, Rodney Nazio, and Persaud Jonas also were generous in their concern for me and in offering their knowledge. Anna Benjamin, Janette Forte, Derek Leung, John Miles, Rupert Roopnaraine, Terence Roopnaraine, George Simon, Dennis Williams, Jenny Wiseheart, and Brigadier Joe Singh (ret.) all were gracious in enabling my research in Guyana, and I warmly thank them for that.

Funding for my field research was provided by the Wenner-Gren Foundation and by the graduate school of the University of Wisconsin-Madison. The National Endowment for the Humanities awarded a fellowship to assist in composing this work.

Many colleagues both wittingly and perhaps unwittingly influenced this work, and I would like to express my gratitude for their patience and indulgence in listening to my earlier attempts to make sense of the experiences I went through. In particular Brian Ferguson, Jonathan Hill, George Mentore, Darrell Posey, Terence Roopnaraine, Anne-Christine Taylor, and Johannes Wilbert were important in that process. I also benefited from professional reaction to papers I presented at the American Anthropological Association, Oxford University, and the University of Wisconsin-Madison.

Introduction

The term *kanaimà* refers both to a mode of ritual mutilation and killing and to its practitioners. The term also can allude to a more diffuse idea of active spiritual malignancy, in existence from the beginning of time, that consumes the assassins. This book is about those killers and the reasons they give for their actions. It is also about their victims.

Kanaimà as an ethnographic issue is complex to research because it is a discourse that operates at a number of levels, referring simultaneously to the dynamics of the spirit world, physical aggression by individuals, the tensions and jealousies between villagers and family members, and the suspicions of distant enemies and outsiders. This means that any ethnography of kanaimà necessarily involves a broad appreciation of cultural life and social organization, not least because one of kanaimà's key characteristics is that it is regional, not just local, in its practice. It is therefore part of the cultural repertoire of a number of Amerindian groups, and is known of and suffered by their closest neighbors as well. As a result, one is simultaneously dealing with convincing case histories, wild rumors, considered attributions of blame, false accusations, ungrounded gossip, and justified suspicion.

This pervasive and profound discourse of kanaimà is a central ethnographic fact of the lives of the people of the Guyana Highlands.[1] Both dramatizing the human condition and indicating its futility, kanaimà is a daily subject of conversation and closely influences the decisions that people make with its vision of a cosmos filled with predatory gods and spirits whose violent hungers are sated by humans. Decisions to go to the farm, to make a journey with someone else or not, to carry a gun or not, to pass by the spirit abode of a famed killer, or to walk by a longer route are thus woven into the texture of everyday life, influencing its practical aspects as much as the ideational. For those that participate in this discourse there is also the distant but steady drumbeat of the killings that are the discursive proof of the malign nature of the cosmos and the enmity of others.

For these reasons the following study examines the discourse of kanaimà as well as the histories of the killings. This is not just for the good theoretical reason that acts and ideas cannot properly be treated as separate realms, but also because our notions of causality and facticity are challenged by the nature of kanaimà. Such has been the case in the study of magical and spiritual phenomena worldwide, particularly where the possibility of dark shamanism, "witchcraft," and assault sorcery is under discussion. While this is not a unique problem, however, this book is not about the philosophy of causation or the conceptual conflicts between "science" and "magic" but about the way in which such issues are woven into the fabric of everyday life; that is, this book looks at the poetics of kanaimà and the violent, mutilating death it envisages. This poetic is neither a system of empirical observation nor a fanciful embellishment of the inexplicable—it is both. The term *poetic,* in this sense, suggests that the meaning of violent death cannot be entirely understood by reference to biological origins, sociological functions, or material and ecological necessities but must also be appreciated as a fundamental and complex cultural expression. Such cultural expression itself, if it is to be understood, must necessarily involve competence in the manipulation of signs and symbols. Any particular act of manipulation—that is, any given cultural performance— is therefore akin to the poetical in that it involves discursive forms of allusion and implication that are highly specialized, albeit rarely textual.[2] In short, I am not concerned with the formal properties of signs, symbols, and rituals—semiotics—but how those signs are used performatively through time—poetics.

I have been researching kanaimà among the Patamuna since 1992. Because the Patamuna and Makushi frequently intermarry, some of my information is derived from Makushi informants; however, as kanaimà is fundamentally a supra-ethnic phenomenon and is practiced by Amerindian groups throughout the Guyana Highlands, this regional perspective actually helps delineate the nature of kanaimà.[3] Numbering around 5,000, the Patamuna are distributed in villages whose populations range from 50 to nearly 1,000 people, the latter being the case for Paramakatoi, where I was largely based. However, many individual family *benab* (houses) or settlements of several benabs are strung out like beads along the main trails through the forest. De-

MAP I. Map of the Guyana Highlands and Surrounding Region.

spite their tiny populations, these lone settlements may also have a deep historical resonance (e.g., Wandapàtoi). Such relatively isolated settlements once provided the context for kanaimà activity, but periodic warfare might sometimes have led to the formation of larger villages. Such aggregations would have split up eventually as the threat of raiding faded and people reverted to the "ideal" household context of forest seclusion. Today, even in a large settlement like Paramakatoi, the houses stand apart, placed on low hills surrounding the small savanna rather than being clustered in an overtly organized relationship to one another. However, particularly in Paramakatoi and a few other central settlements like Kato and Kopinan, during the recent period of rapid change following the arrival of the missionaries and the spread of the government's presence, larger villages have aggregated around landing strips, schools, medical posts, police stations, and stores. In addition, mining, logging, and the cross-border trade with Brazil have all served as dynamic influences in the social-structural changes. The Guyana Highlands comprise the upper reaches of the Essequibo River and its tributaries to the north (Mazaruni, Cuyuni, and Potaro) and are bounded by the Ireng River, the border with Brazil, to the south. At the heart of this region are the Pakaraima mountains, so named for the *pakara* (basket) shape of the *tepui* (granitic uplifts) that characterize the region. At the center of this mountain range and forming the point where the borders of Brazil, Venezuela, and Guyana meet is Roraima mountain, rising to an elevation of nearly 9,000 feet. Mount Kowa, which overlooks Paramakatoi, rises to about 3,000 feet, and there are numerous smaller elevations, "bumps," that are in the 1,000- to 2,000-foot range. Patamuna *asanda* (paths) use such bumps to cross from one valley to the next. Communication between villages involves walking these asanda, and most major settlements are about a day's walk apart, with smaller clusters of houses sometimes occurring in between.

Regions of Patamuna settlement are usually in the heavily forested valleys, such as the Yawong to the north of the Ireng, which to its south gives way to vast savannas of low scrub and grasses. The Patamuna and Makushi see themselves as primarily oriented to one or other of these ecotones and as a result the Patamuna are known to the Makushi as a people preferring the cool wetness of the forest to the hot, dry savannas. Both the Patamuna and Makushi are Cariban speakers, and their languages are somewhat related, although the Patamuna are linguistically closer to the Akawaio to their north. The general lifestyle of the Patamuna is well known from the many descriptions of tropical forest manioc farmers that already exist, although no particular ethnographic study of the Patamuna has been made so far. As will be evident from chapter 1, this work is not intended to be a general ethnography of the Patamuna but rather an ethnographic and historical study of kanaimà, in the context of the contemporary Patamuna. Socially the Patamuna also broadly conform to other, better-known Cariban groups of the region, practicing cross-cousin marriage, which is ideally combined with a uxorilocal residence. However, Patamuna society is very much in flux, and kanaimà itself plays an important role in the construction and persistence of particular forms of sociality.

Kanaimà is a form of dark shamanism, and one purpose of this work is to disaggregate our concept of "shamanism" and to show how it has obscured important differences and purposes in the range of shamanic techniques, as in the case of the Patamuna. This work identifies three distinct but related shamanic complexes: *piya, alleluia,* and kanaimà. Piya shamanism, most often described in general anthropological literature, refers to individuals who have the power to cure and kill but who are primarily sought after for the former purpose. At the end of the nineteenth century a new form of shamanism, influenced by contacts with missionaries, was invented in the Guyana Highlands and involved a direct relationship with *Katú/Akwa* (God). The key ritual technique of this complex is the possession of chants; these chants make use of certain non-Patamuna words or phrases, such as the term *alleluia* for which this ritual practice is named. The nature and meaning of kanaimà, a form of assault sorcery, and how it relates to these other shamanic complexes is the subject of this work.

Kanaimà involves the mutilation and lingering death of its victims and as such clearly involves criminal activity. Therefore, I have changed or obscured personal names, and occasionally places, in order to protect those who confided information to me.[4] These informants included the families of victims, as well as avowed killers and kanaimà practitioners. These latter individuals were extremely difficult, as one might imagine, to interview. The interviews with killers in particular were both complex to arrange and expensive, though not all such interviewees were as knowledgeable as they sometimes pretended. I also interviewed practicing piya, *alleluia'san* (chant owners), and *kàyik* (eminent men) who have an excellent contextual knowledge of kanaimà. More difficult was to produce a statistical profile of kanaimà killing. My own assessment, based on the situation in Paramakatoi, was that such killings were regular but infrequent, amounting to around one per year. In any case, Guyanese law does not recognize the category of "kanaimà death," so cause of death is sometimes falsified to satisfy this bureaucratic nicety, as the interview with a government nurse indicates (see chapter 3). Such inattention from the Guyanese govern-

MAP 2. Map of the Patamuna Region.

ment and police led in part to the exceptional support I received from Patamuna in making this study. At the same time, no one would wish to inflict a campaign of "law and order" on the people of the Highlands, for such exercises are themselves apt to become indiscriminately lethal. Given this, kanaimà has become somewhat accepted and is endured as a mark of Amerindian autonomy. Since the politics of ethnographic representation in Amazonia are complex, this work was not written as promptly as it might have been, the issue of how it might be used beyond the anthropological community needing careful assessment; in other words, I wanted to avoid using anthropological representation in service of the state.[5]

This work falls into six chapters. Chapter 1 details the chronology of my own fieldwork in the Pakaraima mountains and explains the circumstances under which I first learned of the kanaimà complex, how I was myself threatened by kanaimàs, and how I went on to interview avowed killers and their victims. The purpose of this will be to reflect on the entanglements that fieldwork involves, the ethical duties we have to our informants, and the unforeseen consequences of close ethnographic engagement. Chapter 2 gives a history of kanaimà as far back as it can be reconstructed, since sixteenth-century materials also point to the presence of the kanaimà complex. I give particular attention to the way in which kanaimà was presented by colonial, anthropological, and literary authors, especially those who claimed direct experience of kanaimà.

Chapter 3 opens with a synthetic account of kanaimà ritual practice, derived from the result of all the interviews. Patamuna testimony on the kanaimà is then presented, and such materials appear in all the subsequent chapters. Where possible I have reproduced verbatim narratives of kanaimà and the interviews with both killers and the families of their victims. All testimonies and stories were recorded on audio or video tape. If Patamuna was spoken, then the testimony was translated orally by a Patamuna and taped by myself. The resulting translation is reproduced verbatim, as are all materials originally spoken in Guyanese English, according to my transcription of the tapes. Synoptic accounts of events or persons derive from my field notes or conversations held in both English and Patamuna. I hope in this way to allow a fairly direct presentation of native voices, though clearly my acts of translation and editing necessarily obscure that aim to some extent. These materials are then discussed in terms of their thematic and empirical contents

Paramakatoi, Region 8, Guyana.
Looking north with Kowatupu to the east.

with a view to delineating the nature of kanaimà ideas and practices among the Patamuna and neighboring peoples.

Chapter 4 presents further ethnographic and historical materials relevant to shamanic warfare between kanaimà, piya, and alleluia prophets, as well as the Christian missionaries. This analysis of the war for the souls of the Patamuna is intended to draw out the historical changes in the meaning and practice of shamanic rituals and how those changes were connected to, and reciprocally influenced by, Christian evangelism and other forms of colonial intrusion. I also present an account of a particular shamanic battle between a piya and a kanaimà.

Chapter 5 then moves consideration of occult violence and its cultural meanings to a global stage. I suggest that, however unique South American kanaimà shamanism may be, it is still comparable to other resurgent forms of occult violence, assault sorcery, and even state-led campaigns of terror. The way in which the state itself co-opts occult magic is thus an important theme in the discussion, as is the way in which the advent of modernity relates to the expression of hypertraditionality in the form of kanaimà. In particular, I argue that kanaimà violence is an authentic and legitimate form of cultural expression and is mimetically linked to the violence of economic and political "development." The ethnographic materials for this chapter include accounts of alleluia, discussion of the mining frontier and its effect on the practice of kanaimà, current representational practices, and the making of a "snuff film" dealing with kanaimà.

Chapter 6 provides a comparative ethnological discussion of kanaimà and other forms of assault sorcery and also reviews current literature on warfare and violence in Amazonia, thus bringing together two bodies of theory—that of European and that of North American anthropologists—that have in large part developed independently. Examination of the kanaimà presents opportunities for both forms of analyses that makes use of the strengths of both schools of thought.

CHAPTER I

The Ethnographer's Tale

As I got off the plane in Paramakatoi in 1992, I had not a thought of kanaimà in mind. The purpose of my journey was to make, in collaboration with the Walter Roth Museum of Anthropology, a preliminary survey of archaeological sites, in particular cave occupation sites, urn burials, and old villages. I hoped with that survey to begin to counter the exceptionally negative view that the region was sparsely populated and devoid of cultural time-depth, a view that had been promulgated in the archaeological literature outside of Guyana.[1] I was accompanied by a Lokono man from the Mahaica River who was a highly experienced field archaeologist. He had been through the region a couple of years previously and had already examined the kinds of sites—old villages, burials, battle sites—that we were now interested in documenting as systematically as we could. We planned to walk out from Paramakatoi, south toward the Ireng River, then follow the north bank of the Ireng to Puwa village, turn north to Kurukabaru and then south again to Kato, where we would be able to catch a flight to Georgetown. Logistically and physically this was a difficult itinerary since we would have to carry most of what we needed over a terrain that features numerous mountains covered in dense tropical forest alternating with savannas. However, with the aid of various Patamuna who were enthusiastically behind the project, it seemed feasible to accomplish within the six to eight weeks we had planned to be away.

I want to emphasize the active participation of Patamuna individuals, both at the outset of this project and in subsequent ethnographic investigations. I do so to indicate not only their interest in my work but also the way in which my research was shaped by their priorities. While this may sound ideal, it meant that my research risked becoming partisan as it became more closely identified with the interests and ambitions of certain individuals, albeit that they were legitimate leaders

The Pakaraima Mountains showing the *tepui* (granitic uplifts).

of the community. This is not to suggest that there can be any "unpositioned" viewpoint; clearly any researcher is necessarily part of one kind of social network and therefore not another. However, the public authority of the individuals involved—or, later, their lack of it—became a particularly significant factor in the history of my fieldwork in the Pakaraimas between 1992 and 1997. It also fundamentally influenced my ability to gain otherwise relatively obscure, and even dangerous, knowledge.

Although this was not my first visit, Guyana had been relatively off-limits to anthropologists and most outsiders during the years of the Peoples National Congress government. Policies of self-reliance and an understandable antipathy to intellectual colonization by the United States and United Kingdom meant that foreign researchers were often judged superfluous. However, the Walter Roth Museum, under the directorship of Denis Williams, provided invaluable support for my field trips into the Pakaraimas, and without that assistance it is doubtful I could have worked in Guyana at all.[2] I was therefore doubly pleased to not just be in Guyana but to have the opportunity to reach an interior region that was largely unknown in recent archaeology or ethnography.[3]

Unknown to me at the moment the plane touched down, but soon

Kowatupu (Kowa Mountain).

apparent, the kanaimà would come to dominate that trip's research, as well as subsequent fieldwork in the region. Within thirty minutes of landing, we were visited by the Nurse for Paramakatoi, who politely listened to our plans, then launched into a startling account of what we "should really be investigating"—the kanaimà, especially because of the interest (not all of it favorable) that the earlier work of my Lokono companion had aroused.

It is hard now to reconstruct how much I knew or had heard of kanaimà before that moment, as it has come to dominate my thoughts over nearly the whole of the last decade. However, being reasonably well read in the anthropological and historical literature of northeastern South America, I had certainly heard the term. I had also at some point read Walter Roth's classic synthesis of materials on the kanaimà and so vaguely recalled kanaimà as some peculiar revenge cult that was probably in substance a colonially projected idea of native savagery. I had even referred to Brett's account of an "unappeased" kanaimà in a publication on Karinya warfare, but only as a possible example of the results of colonial suppression of warfare in the nineteenth century (Whitehead 1990b). I was therefore intrigued and surprised to find kanaimà being almost the first topic of conversation, since I had assumed that the phenomenon had simply faded away, which had seemed to be the implication of Roth's account. I could not have been more wrong.

The sequence of my own intellectual interest in kanaimà seems, as an anthropological issue and category of ethnographic description, to closely reproduce the history of anthropological debate about "cannibalism." As will become evident, nonnative ideas about kanaimà, as with cannibalism more widely, cannot be taken as simply reflecting impartial results of an encounter with some objectively present form of native savagery or exoticism. Rather, our interest in the savagery of others, in particular when it appears to take the form of cannibalism, clearly has served an ideological purpose in both politically justifying and morally enabling violent conquest and occupation of native South America (Arens 1979; Hulme 1986, 2000; Hulme and Whitehead 1992; Whitehead 1988, 1995a, 1995c). Nonetheless, ideological agendas aside, some cultural practices are undeniably challenging to interpret, in that they apparently give meaning and value to acts that we might abhor or simply deny as "real." However, this lack of "reality" often reflects our own lack of understanding, and what we actually mean is that those acts are "incomprehensible."

Kanaimà perfectly instantiates such a category, for the term invokes truly strange and troubling acts. In both the colonial literature and native oral testimony, kanaimà refers to the killing of an individual by violent mutilation of, in particular, the mouth and anus, into which are inserted various objects. The killers are then enjoined to return to the dead body of the victim in order to drink the juices of putrefaction.

> The . . . victim will first become aware of an impending attack when the *Kanaimàs* approach his house by night, or on lonely forest trails [*asanda*], making a characteristic whistling noise. . . . a direct physical attack might come at any point, even years thereafter, for during this period of stalking the victim is assessed as to their likely resistance and their suitability as "food." . . . In some attacks the victims may have minor bones broken, especially fingers, and joints dislocated, especially the shoulder, while the neck may also be manipulated to induce spinal injury and back pain. This kind of attack is generally considered to be a preliminary to actual death and mutilation; . . . fatal attack will certainly follow but, informants stress, many months, or even a year or two, later. When a fatal physical attack is intended, victims are always struck from behind and physically restrained. . . . A variety of procedures, intended to produce a lingering death, are

then enacted. The victim has their tongue pierced with the fangs of a snake, is turned over and either an iguana or an armadillo tail is inserted into their rectum so that the anal muscles can be stripped out through repeated rubbing. Then, pressing on the victim's stomach, a section of the sphincter muscle is forced out and cut. Finally, the victim's body is rubbed down with astringent plants . . . and a thin flexed twig is forced into the rectum, so that it opens the anal tract. Packets of herbs are then rammed in as deeply as possible. This is said to begin a process of auto-digestion, creating the special aroma of *Kanaimà* enchantment, rotting pineapple. . . . As a result of the completion of these procedures, the victim is unable to speak or to take any sustenance by mouth. Bowel control is lost and the clinical cause of death becomes acute dehydration through diarrhoea. . . . the *Kanaimàs* will try and discover the burial place of their victim and await the onset of putrefaction in the corpse that usually occurs within three days. . . . [When] the grave site is discovered, a stick is inserted through the ground directly into the cadaver, then the stick is retracted and the *maba* (honey-like) juices sucked off. . . . If the corpse is indeed sufficiently "sweet," it will be partially disinterred in order to recover bone material and, ideally, a section of the anal tract. The use of previous victim's body parts is necessary to facilitate the location and killing of the next victim. (Whitehead 2001b)

One can readily appreciate, then, how issues of "representing others" are brought forcibly to mind by apparently "objectively encountering" such a ritual complex not as a textual remnant from colonial days but as the earnest testimony of living individuals. Moreover, I was to learn that the idea of kanaimà exercises a constant and intense influence over the cultural imagination of the Patamuna and their neighbors, the Akawaio and Makushi. However, my initial reactions to the Nurse were to try to fold her testimony into that more general discourse on "witchcraft" and to see her declarations as a performance of Patamuna alterity and desire to differentiate and distance themselves from others, especially white anthropologists.

However, the Nurse's—and later other's—absolute insistence on the physical reality of kanaimà, coupled with her sophisticated acknowledgment of its wider discursive properties, was unsettling;[4] it challenged me to truly confront a kind of cultural difference that it had been easy to assume had been eroded by the long histories of colonial contact in this region, even if the Patamuna had not been in the forefront of that process. Indeed, I found that my hesitation to immedi-

Patamuna *asanda* at the head of the Yawong Valley. Facing east toward Aluatatupu.

ately acknowledge the reality of kanaimà put me alongside the British missionaries who had, according to the Nurse, assumed that kanaimà was just part of the "superstitious nonsense" cooked up by "primitive" peoples. The missionaries, lacking cultural competence, simply dismissed kanaimà as some kind of spirit, an example of Wittgenstein's observation that "Wherever our language leads us to believe there is a body, but no body exists, there is a spirit" (1953, 1:36).

Nonetheless, if I had not then encountered something more "real" than "just talk," presumably I, too, would have remained within the standard view of the anthropological literature, that is, that whatever may have been true in the past, accusations of kanaimà exemplified the social functions of belief in witchcraft as a mechanism for community inclusion/exclusion. So they may be, but that by no means exhausts the matter—and not just because such a discourse might serve as a rich realm of cultural performance and signification, but because people actually die in ways consistent with the notion of kanaimà attack. I

The Yawong Valley. Looking south towards the Ireng River, the border with Brazil.

have never witnessed such an attack, nor have I attempted to do so, even though the lack of eyewitness accounts has rightly been adduced as an ethnographic weakness in anthropological discussions of cannibalism. Nonetheless, a moment's reflection should indicate that to witness physical violence is in itself extremely dangerous and necessarily entails complex ethical judgments as to how (and whether) such events should be described or published. Yet it is equally clear that the only difference between my position and that of the missionaries would be a willingness to take seriously what was so evidently being impressed on me—that kanaimàs are real people who do real killing of specific and identifiable individuals.

We were due to leave Paramakatoi early the day after next in order to keep to our itinerary, and though I made copious notes of that first conversation, I did not yet seriously entertain deviating from our original plan. So we walked from Paramakatoi, which is on a small savanna at the top of a mountain at the end of the Yawong River valley, down into the valley to search for our chief Patamuna collaborator, whom I call "Waiking." It was on this day that archaeology and kanaimà came together in a startling way. We learned that, at the head of the valley, there was a small cave, Kuyali'yen (Macaw Cave), in which an urn

Kuyali'yen
(Macaw Cave).

burial had recently been found. This was exactly the kind of information we had hoped to gather, and it immediately justified our decision to organize the research in a way that directly involved Patamuna. To have uncovered this site through physical survey would have been much more time-consuming and uncertain. We decided to visit the site immediately so that we could walk out of the valley, as planned, the following day.

When I first saw the "burial" I was disappointed as it was evident that the "burial" vessel was very small, not nearly large enough to contain a complete human set of remains. It was accompanied by a small *tumi* (offering bowl). It had not been my intention to collect archaeological materials; we not only wished to be alert to Patamuna sensitivities about the handling of ancestral remains, but we were also in no position to carry heavy and fragile ceramics for the remaining six weeks. However, what happened next was to become, both in my mind and that of others, a defining moment: as the Patamuna with us would not "trouble" the pot in any way, my Lokono companion moved the pot to the cave mouth where I could photograph it—and where I, too, without thinking, touched it.

This act came to define my identity to many Patamuna in many ways. Indeed, I believe I was to some degree manipulated into this "archaeological discovery," since I was not the first non-Patamuna to see it.[5] It also transpired that the reasons for showing it to me were substantially more connected with contemporary conflicts than with the archaeological past, for the pot was in fact a ritual vessel still being used by a kanaimà, as was evident from the contents of the pot—it contained human skeletal and tissue material that appeared, and was later verified to be, very recent indeed, not at all archaeological.[6] As yet, though, none of this was apparent.

At the time, and despite the obviously ethnographic nature of the context, we nonetheless had given an archaeological commitment to the Walter Roth Museum, which we honored by measuring and photographing the pot and, unfortunately, by removing a sample of the bone material to determine its age. I say "unfortunately" because this act, as far as can be said with certainty, may have been the immediate reason for an apparent attempt to poison me. The less-than-favorable light in which the earlier archaeological survey was held by some Patamuna thus came to have a real and definite consequence.

On our way back from the cave, my Patamuna companions suggested that this was something "kanaimà" and that we should return via the benab of an individual whom I call "Pirai." At that moment, I presumed that this was because Pirai was living the closest to the cave, but it transpired that he had a much more substantive connection with the vessel. I could not follow the initial part of the conversation with Pirai on arriving at his benab, but it was obvious that he was very excited and upset about something, and the word *kanaimà* occurred a number of times. We climbed back up the bump to Paramakatoi to find that news of the "discovery" was already in the village and that, in the opinion of those villagers who spoke to me about it, it was an excellent development and should enable the museum "to let everyone know the truth of those kanaimàs." But, whatever the intriguing ethnographic aspects, the implications of the ritual vessel seemed to be

Kanaimà ritual vessels. Ossuary containing human remains with appliqué snake coiled around the rim in foreground, *tumi* (offering bowl) in background.

something I could better pursue on a subsequent visit and that anyway might not please the museum, on which I was reliant for future permissions to work anthropologically in the interior. All that was changed dramatically by the events that followed.

We were lodged at the boarding school for the duration of our visit, since it was still the Christmas vacation and the children had returned to their home villages.[7] We also had use of the refectory, and while we were starting to prepare some food that evening, a Makushi woman came in and offered to cook for us. As she did so she started to talk animatedly about kanaimà, although we had not raised the topic, but neither of us spoke Makushi and her English was fragmented. I must confess that I had had quite enough of the topic for one day and was more concerned with how I was going to physically meet the challenges of six weeks of hard trekking. I knew that, among other things, eating properly was a basic rule, and I wished that she would simply serve up the rations that we had given her to prepare. The food was execrable. Although it was simply rice and a few dried shrimp, she had managed to make it taste absolutely horrible. My Lokono companion suggested that it was just the *casareep* (manioc juice) that she had used to flavor the dried shrimp and that I was being a typical "white boy" in my excessive delicacy of taste. But I had eaten casareep before and so just concluded that she was a lousy chef.

I have no proof otherwise and make no accusations, but I started feeling extremely ill within a few minutes of finishing that meal, and the symptoms got steadily and acutely worse during the next few days. I was quite unable to sleep that night because of a high temperature and incessant vomiting. I was feeling very weak by sunrise when, nevertheless, we set off back down the Yawong valley to rendezvous with Waiking. Thinking that my illness was a reaction to some form of food poisoning, I ignored my physical state as well as I could. However, in the general conversation we had while redistributing our loads at Waiking's house, the matter of my "illness" came up, as the *droghers* (carriers) were concerned about taking me into the bush while in such a condition.[8] When I jokingly blamed the poor culinary arts of the Makushi woman, someone, I don't recall whom, remarked that to have let her cook for us was "a stupid thing to do, boy. Don't you know she lives by Pirai?" Of course we hadn't known, but with that strange luminosity that comes with feverish thought, I suddenly appreciated that what was being suggested was not poisoning *by* my food but *of* my food.

During that day my condition got worse and worse until, when we were almost at the summit of Aluatatupu on the other side of the Yawong valley, I collapsed with severe retching and stomach cramps. I had never ever lain down on the forest floor before, for the obvious reason that it is home to many voracious biting insects, but neither can I recall having felt quite so grim, even though I have had malaria, hepatitis, and pneumonia, as well as "normal" food poisoning. My companions carried me to the summit, about a half mile farther on. I was laid down and I cried by the waters of Akaikalakparu. In the crossing place of this creek is a small, submerged stone; carved on it is the face of a *totopù* (spirit guardian) who died right there, from exhaustion, as he couldn't make it down into the valley. We eyed each other balefully.

Everyone was thoroughly alarmed at the prospect of having me die, for it was acknowledged that even Patamuna could simply "fall down on the line [asanda]," that a fear of "not making it" would kill you as certainly as any accident or other misfortune. Of course, the Patamuna regularly walked this route and could easily make the next village, Taruka, from Paramakatoi. However, as the petroglyph of the totopù's face at Akaikalakparu suggested, longer journeys were always a challenge for small parties or lone individuals, given the food shortages that could occur if the bumps weren't walked in sufficient time. It was not that people had no food, or indeed would refuse to share it if someone were desperate, but there was not necessarily enough food to buy or trade, and what there was had become extremely expensive due to the mining activities throughout the region. We had planned to reach Taruka in one day and Monkey Mountain in one or two days after that and so had only minimal rations with us. These were immediately exhausted by meals that night and the next morning. I slept for a few hours and actually felt better, if weak, the next day. My load was distributed among the others: Waiking; his brother, Yabiku; and Hashiro, my Lokono companion.

It took us all of that day to reach Taruka. On the line we had another uncanny experience when Pirai passed us in the company of two adolescent boys. What was peculiar was that he, as well as his companions, simply refused to address anyone. They emerged right behind us on the trail as we stopped by a creek to drink, and while Pirai made eye contact with us all, he responded neither to greetings nor to the insults shouted after him as he proceeded up the mountain trail. When we finally arrived at Taruka we were greeted politely and offered bowls of *cassiri* (manioc beer), but only one of my companions accepted, which I knew to be a real breach of etiquette. Taruka was a Makushi village at that time, and the conviction that the Makushi were kanaimàs was certainly part of Patamuna ethnic prejudices, but refusal of cassiri seemed to imply a very particular judgment about this village. Perhaps unsurprisingly, then, no one had food to sell us. This was a serious matter, as we had no food left and the only place to buy it would be Monkey Mountain, which we could clearly see some twenty miles away toward the Brazilian border.

We were stuck. We could not go on, or at least I couldn't, because I could hardly walk to the latrine, let alone Monkey Mountain, and my symptoms now became far worse, developing into a constant diarrhea and nausea. All that night I had to keep leaving the house we were lodged in. On one occasion I staggered some twenty yards from the house, squatted, and looked out over the savanna toward Siparuni mountain. The moon was bright, and as I tried to enjoy the beauty of the scene I saw in the distance some movement that appeared to be two distinct figures moving along the ground toward me. My first thought was that they were dogs, but as they turned to flank me they appeared instead to have the shape of anteaters because of the elongated head and tail. As I pulled up my pants, I looked away, then could not find the figures again when I looked back. Although that seemed odd, I reflected that, all other things considered, perhaps this was to be taken seriously. I would not recount this incident at all were it not for the unpleasant effect it had on everyone else, who immediately took the distant figures to have been kanaimàs and who were now convinced that the interest of the kanaimàs was centered on us. It was rather unsettling to be sick, to be a long walk from the next village, and to feel menaced by something I could not easily understand or explain away.

The next morning it had become vital that we either try to go on or go back, and we were fortunate that someone did finally sell us three eggs and some pieces of *tasso* (dried meat). We were not technically starving as yet. It was fortunate also that Waiking had been able to persuade someone to fetch a horse, Sharon, so that I could be carried down the trail to Monkey Mountain. Since everyone was now weak and tired from hunger, our progress was slow. Although I do not think we ate the whole of that day either, we did occasionally find wild cashew trees in fruit, which inhibited my diarrhea. As we finally reached Monkey Mountain early the next morning, we passed the remains of a crashed aircraft, a token of the mining frontier, once used by a Brazilian diamond trader who had been flown in to buy up stones. In Monkey Mountain we were able to purchase food, and we also met Johnny Roth, the great-grandson of Walter Roth.[9] Having eaten at last, everyone was feeling better, including myself, and we planned to continue toward Puwa with a good store of rations. It was not to be.

I have taken some pains to depict the palette of events and ideas from which each of us constructed our pictures of what happened next, and I am not suggesting that we were necessarily all in perfect accord. I can therefore only speak to my impressions, but that certainly does not exclude suggesting the motivations present in others—that being the essence of any attempt at anthropological explanation or cultural interpretation. The pervasive nature of kanaimà as a cultural discourse and the manner in which I had entered into it—by inviting enmity as a result of "troubling" the vessel in Kuyali'yen—entailed certain consequences that were beyond my control.

I was lying in my hammock while the others had gone to the shop at Monkey Mountain, when, to my surprise, one of the youths who had been with Pirai on the line into Monkey Mountain appeared in the doorway. He said not a word at first and didn't respond to my questions. He then began to speak rapidly but deliberately in Patamuna, which I couldn't clearly follow. Waiking, Yabiku, and Hashiro saw the youth as they returned and they let out a loud shout, at which he bolted off. When I explained what had happened they suggested that he had been sent to "check you out" and that he had been threatening me. Whether or not this was the case, and I certainly don't like to think it was so, this at least suggested that we should abandon our original itinerary. It had been a key aspect of the project that it should be done with Patamuna cooperation and, although I was receiving support from some of them, it seemed that my presence was simply not welcome to others among them. Since this was actually the inference of my Patamuna companions, I also took this to mean that persisting at this point was likely to be a cause of further trouble for them.

In retrospect it is clear that tension was building with Pirai and that Hashiro and I were unwittingly increasing that tension, since we must have seemed intent on uncovering kanaimà pots as much as burials. Nonetheless, we all had the sense that we were being forced to give up something that was important and useful. Waiking and others in Paramakatoi, such as the Nurse, believed that a key aspect of future political and economic opportunities for the Patamuna was to possess a recognizable and distinct external ethnic identity. Archaeology and ethnography were seen as part of the means by which that could be achieved. In addition the Walter Roth Museum itself had been making a series of efforts to more adequately inform the Guyanese about the interior populations.[10] The aim was to establish the antiquity of the Amerindian presence in Guyana through excavation and also to document the little-known highland peoples through broad archaeological and/or ethnographic surveys, such as the one we were conducting, as well as through longer term fieldwork.

At that moment it seemed to me that the best way to return to this survey, or another project in Paramakatoi, would be to leave now before the suspicions of kanaimà grew out of hand and something worse happened. In any case I was still very ill. I discussed the possibility of leaving with both Hashiro and Waiking, and we agreed that we should do so but that we would return and make the kanaimà itself the focus of investigation—not least because it was evident that the ritual vessel we had disturbed was very significant. To answer why that should be and to find further the physical evidence of kanaimà activity seemed feasible, if risky, given our own direct encounters with those held to be kanaimà. Moreover, to leave and then return, rather than continue on, seemed preferable at that point, not just because I was very sick but also because it would allow us to plan properly and let things calm down a bit. In addition, Waiking was adamant that it would be possible to interview piya on the matter, since there was a general feeling that the "work of the kanaimà had to be better known," and setting up those interviews would take time. The Nurse's testimony was further evidence of this appeal for openness about ritual practice, and I was intrigued to find myself already cast in the role of "ethnographer." Usually an ethnographer is expected to justify and explain that role as a precondition of extended research. So I was very impressed by the sophistication of Patamuna in exploiting the interest of outsiders for their own benefit. In fact, I came to understand that this theme had been very deeply inscribed on their historical consciousness, as the "fetching" of both alleluia and various missionaries into Paramakatoi, which I discuss later, clearly showed. In this sense it was not me as such but the need for a certain kind of external connection that made me appropriate and useful in the political aims of Patamuna.

So that was it. We used the police radio at Monkey Mountain to contact the bush-pilot Derek Leung who extracted Hashiro and myself the following morning. We had promised Waiking that we would return at a future date.[11]

Once in Georgetown we decided to utilize the remaining weeks with a survey of archaeological sites on the Berbice River which proved to be highly productive.[12] But with time and distance I found myself more and more intrigued by what had "really happened" in Paramakatoi, and the kanaimà remained for me a continual topic of conversation, reflection, and inquiry. I had felt a bit better when I returned to Georgetown, with only intermittent fever, vomiting, and diarrhea, but I became alarmed again when I started urinating blood after a couple of days in Berbice. I had now begun to be persuaded that whatever the cause of my sickness it was not routine, as the symptoms did not match readily with any particular cause. Hashiro then had the suggestion that I fight "fire with fire" by consulting someone on the Berbice who had knowledge of bush-medicine. This we did and I swallowed what I was given. I stopped passing blood.

It was only then that Hashiro told me something which he had not previously mentioned—his own father had been killed by kanaimàs. According to Hashiro, his father was working as a woodcutter at the time and had gone upriver to Mahaica, only stopping at St Cuthbert's, where they lived, to collect pineapples. He returned unusually late, around 6:30 P.M., saying he couldn't remember why or what had happened. His wife began to worry about him, but he bathed as usual. He then started feeling very sick and from then on his condition deteriorated rapidly. Despite seeking medical help in Georgetown the very next day and being given a clean bill of health and a release form, he died suddenly on the third day. As he was being prepared for burial the family noticed finger marks and bruising on his arms and back. For the family this was evidence of the *yawáho* (kanaimà) but they insisted that this was actually a case of an attack gone wrong, in that the man who claimed the killing had mistakenly identified Hashiro's father as the intended victim.[13] According to Hashiro, they also pointed to the fact that the killing was "not done that way," implying that the attackers had actually realized their misidentification and had therefore stopped short of enacting the full kanaimà ritual. However, Hashiro further surprised me by making an explicit connection between his own earlier work in the Paramakatoi region, the possibility that his father's death might have been intended for himself, and the menacing circumstances we had just encountered. In short, Hashiro felt that I was becoming involved in an active contest between the kanaimàs and those who would "expose" them.

I was not able to return to Paramakatoi until 1995 as I had accepted a post in the United States, at the University of Wisconsin. The demands of migrating from England to a new country with a wife and two small children, none of whom had visited the United States before, had meant I could not visit South America in 1993. Prior to this, on my return from Paramakatoi in 1992, my father had been diagnosed with inoperable colorectal cancer, on top of which my maternal uncle died just before Christmas of that year. I will say that this deeply affected me, as the loss of a father in particular would affect anyone, but that it also affected my view of the events in Guyana. In that time of stress it was hard not to recall that Hashiro's father had been "mistakenly" killed for his son and to not let form the idea that the anal wounding of the typical kanaimà victim was somehow being recalled and reduplicated, first in the rectal pain I had suffered as a consequence of being continually sick, and then in the fatal rot that was eating away my father's insides. He did not go quietly into that long night, and my family situation meant that it fell to me to nurse him in his last weeks of life in the spring of 1994. Again, then, I was unable to return to Paramakatoi, although I had kept the connection with Waiking active with the help of the museum and Hashiro.

In 1995, however, I was able to plan my return to Paramakatoi for the summer months. By that time, having had many reasons to contemplate the cultural forms of death and dying, I was also resentful and angry toward those who, it seemed, had tried to poison me—for on my return to Guyana I found that this was the story being told. This story was heard not just in Paramakatoi, where anthropologist Duncan Kilgour had recorded it in 1994, but it also had spread right across the highland region to Lethem and eventually even as far as Dominica in the Caribbean.[14] My return to Paramakatoi was thus considered highly significant, both because it signaled a refusal to be intimidated by the possibility of kanaimà and because I could be of definite use as an ethnographic recorder. In fact, it was my work on historical themes that proved the most important, as the textual recording of oral history was, for the Patamuna in Paramakatoi, the principal benefit of my presence. The investigation of kanaimà was certainly a secondary consideration for some Patamuna and was therefore always going to be the more provocative and divisive subject of research. However, there was also strong support for bringing kanaimà "into the open," to publish accounts of their practices, to "collect" their ritual equipment, and to interview avowed kanaimàs directly so that their "reality" could finally be established in the minds of outsiders and so that their violent criminality, as it was then pictured, might somehow be curbed.

During 1995 I collected both oral histories about the Patamuna generally and about Paramakatoi in particular (Whitehead 1996c). I was also able to interview piya on the subject of kanaimà and, eventually, a powerful kanaimà himself. The centerpiece of the oral historical materials was undoubtedly the testimony on warfare, alleluia, and the arrival of the missionaries; such testimony was given in rather a formal way. I was not encouraged to ask questions as such, but rather to be as faithful a recorder as possible. Testimony was always given in Patamuna, tape-recorded, then translated and transcribed into English by myself and an English-speaking Patamuna. The Patamuna also insisted on the adoption of particular spellings for Patamuna words, since they felt that misspelling was a particularly damaging form of misrepresentation by outsiders, given their overall commitment to resisting language loss.[15]

As a result of achieving the aims of addressing Patamuna wishes for a record of key events in the history of both Paramakatoi and the initial occupation of the Yawong Valley by the Patamuna ancestors, I then received full support for researching the issue of kanaimà. The key interviews with piya and kanaimà occurred during my 1995 research trip. Without the assistance of Waiking, the initial interviews could not have been easily achieved, but once I had identified the key kanaimà, I then made independent approaches. These interviews were hard to broker, but the lure of money and the sense that, whether or not they granted interviews, I was going to say or do something which might affect them did encourage some kanaimàs to speak with me. This in turn built a momentum such that more senior kanaimàs, their ritual tutors, finally also agreed to speak directly with me. I avoided Pirai, however, because of a suspicion that he was behind the problems I had experienced in 1992. The younger kanaimàs were often braggarts and sometimes really quite ignorant of ritual matters, but they did allow me to form a picture of possible motivations for becoming involved in kanaimà practices. The older kanaimàs were much more intimidating, less given to freely explaining their motives or procedures, and physically wasted in appearance. Interviews with piya were also complex to arrange and conduct but were not tinged with the same air of menace. The most forthcoming of the older kanaimàs, whom I call "Emewari," probably supplied the bulk of the information I had from these sources, and other interviews were really confirmations (or not) of what he said. The other key interview was with a piya who is known widely across the region, and it was he who made a shamanic attack on a kanaimà while I was present, though I think not at my behest.

The interview with Emewari was of course invaluable, not just for the detailed information he gave but also because the conviction that kanaimà lacked "reality" had arisen in part from the absence of anyone avowing to be a killer. I should note that Emewari asked for, and got, a considerable sum of money for information on the kanaimà.[16] Although I was initially suspicious of the fact that such knowledge would be "for sale" at all, I found that for the kanaimà, as for the piya, material rewards serve as tokens of spiritual eminence and power. I would also add that, as with all the other avowed killers I have encountered, Emewari had a marked tendency to boast about what he could achieve.

Since most avowed killers admit to no specific killing and allusions to killing are often given metaphorically—as when it is said "we tied a cow" to mean "trussed up a victim"—it is perhaps unsurprising, then, that Emewari was extremely difficult to interpret, speaking of certain events through allusions to individuals I could not identify and using words that were not of Patamuna origin.[17] Although I had linguistic assistance from a Patamuna, who I cannot name for obvious reasons, the results of this much-anticipated encounter were still frustratingly incomplete—one always thinks of the best questions only with hindsight. However, what I did understand was illuminating, even if still somewhat inconclusive, which I'll discuss in chapter 3.

As mentioned, I was able to supplement this interview by seeking out alleged kanaimàs in more distant villages, and even in Georgetown, the capital of Guyana. None of these individuals would admit to any specific incidence of violence, but most were grimly keen to "educate" me in generalities. For this, I had to play my role as one who was morbidly fascinated with kanaimà and with "manly" violence more generally, and who was quite ready to recount my own "experiences" of inflicting pain and violence in return for theirs. The catalog of violence in and by Western cultures from which I could draw such "experiences" is sufficiently replete and shocking to have made kanaimà appear quite tame at times. In particular, I remember that tales of Nazi atrocities and the refinements of modern "antipersonnel" armaments, such as the Claymore mine, particularly captured the imagination of one of these individuals.

The reasons that these interviews were possible at all were, I believe, closely connected to the political positioning that was going on in Paramakatoi in 1995 with regard to promised, or at least rumored, development schemes. I think the Patamuna felt that, if it were to be the subject of an ethnography, kanaimà would no longer be merely a "cultural problem" for the Patamuna but could be repositioned as a political and law enforcement "problem" for the government. As various interest groups vied for the scarce resources of the Guyanese state, the issue of kanaimà, it was supposed, would politically dramatize the situation of the Patamuna and therefore encourage attention to their overall situation.

Operating on a subtler level were the more local conflicts that led some individuals to see my "research" as a way of getting back at those boasting of their kanaimà connections or knowledge. If such supposedly "secret" knowledge could be made available to all, through writing about it and publishing the results, then the "real story" of kanaimàs could be told and their influence undermined.[18] It is certainly the case that the very vagueness, yet pervasiveness, of the presence of kanaimà allows it to assume a central place in indigenous imagination. Given this, the kind of "documentation" that outsiders are particularly good at producing serves to make exact and particular what otherwise can be elusive and uncertain. In this sense kanaimà is a joint and mutual cultural production not just by practitioners but by victims, bystanders, and outsiders, as well.

Nonetheless, community support resulted in interviews not only with avowed kanaimàs but also with many of the victims' families, as well as with piya who had experienced spirit battles with kanaimàs. The atmosphere in Paramakatoi, however, began to intensify as more people learned that we had been "troubling" kanaimà and, worst of all, had recovered some ritual paraphernalia used by a killer (see page 89 and plate III). As a result I received a very alarming note from Wai-king, warning me off further inquiry into the topic and withdrawing his hitherto vital assistance and protection. This was quite understandable under the circumstances, but it left me feeling very exposed and uncertain—perhaps I had been too successful and thus was inviting attacks on those who had helped me, or even on myself?

Such thoughts were not dispelled by the various warnings I then began to receive, sometimes from individuals with whom I had never spoken, warnings to the effect that I had "gone too far," that I should not have troubled such things. It was therefore particularly unsettling to be visited, on three successive nights, by an unidentified person(s). I was lodged in Paramakatoi in a four-room concrete building next to the clinic.[19] The windows had firmly locking shutters, and the only door was also secured by a strong lock, although there were, of course, gaps in the fit of both windows and doors. I was alone, since only other visitors would sleep there. Although I had assumed that, whatever the case in 1992, the passage of time and my apparent ability to culturally negotiate interviews with kanaimàs had rendered me irrelevant or external to the politics of ritual assassination, those illusions were ended over those three nights. Each night, I would clearly hear the approach of one person, maybe more, followed by the sound of a deliberate scratching at the doorframe and windows. I would call out but receive no reply. Then, once again, I would hear scratching that moved in a circle round the building, ending back at the doorway each time. I might have taken this as a (not very funny) prank by the young men had it not been that on each occasion I found afterward a *yamali-wok* (coral snake) somewhere in the house.

I would have been much happier to think of these incidents as co-incidence and overactive imagination—and I admit that my imagination had been put into overdrive by that point. However, the very unwelcome news soon came that "Bishop," held to be the most adept kanaimà from the Kopinan River, had already left there five days before to come over and "check me." The bearer of these tidings was particularly alarmed because that meant that he must already be "in the bush outside PK [Paramakatoi]," as he had not come into the village. I was also visited by one of my most knowledgeable informants, whom I call "Acoori," as well as by the village *Tushau* (chief), who both warned me quite strongly to now desist as "bad things were happening."

With only about ten days left in my planned time in the Paramakatoi region, I decided that this was definitely the moment to go, but only after having first promised to return when the oral historical materials were in a published form. Around that time, I also began to get high fevers in the night, which I could not separate in my imagination from the alleged presence of Bishop and the unsettling events around my own house. In fact these fevers continued for about two months after my return to the United States. The doctors were unable to identify a cause as such, but while investigating all possible angles they discovered that I had incurable hepatitis C, probably contracted from contact with a large amount of infected human blood when I went to the aid of someone accidentally who had severed an artery with a cutlass while working on his *mùloka* (farm). So it felt as if the kanaimà's had gotten me anyway!

The Walter Roth Museum responded magnificently to both the historical materials and the desire of Patamuna leaders to see them published. Denis Williams suggested that I put the materials into order and that the museum would then print them up in pamphlet form for distribution as widely as possible among the Patamuna villages. The result was published in 1996, and I returned in 1997 to carry the 5,000 pamphlets up to Paramakatoi and help with their distribution.

When I returned to Paramakatoi in the summer of 1997, various Patamuna expressed a great deal of satisfaction with the outcome of my previous visit and held a parade and ceremony to hand over the "little history" that had been made. At this point I also hoped to be able to reinterview some people as, inevitably, there were many aspects to kanaimà magic and ritual that remained obscure. However, interest and support for this had waned, and those who had previously supported the research were now quite hostile to me. I found out that the reasons for this were threefold. First, a strong suspicion had developed that all along I had only been trying to initiate myself as a kanaimà. This threw me somewhat, as quite the opposite had always been the basis of our collaboration, but it was sufficient indication that I should not look to the same set of individuals for more assistance with this. Nonetheless, I very much needed to dispel this suspicion, which had been "proven" by a sequence of deaths that had occurred since my last visit, among them the wife of Pirai and the father of the family that lived next to him. I countered that the deaths of my uncle and father were equal proof that I was not the origin of the "magical death" sent against them.[20] In addition, some argued that the white man was probably trying to steal kanaimà, just like he stole cocaine from the Amerindians, and that he would put kanaimà to use against the Amerindians, just as he had done with cocaine. On this occasion I countered that the white man had no need of kanaimà, that the whole of the Yawong valley could be made a desert if the white man called in an airstrike, so that we had no need of kanaimà. I don't know how convincing this ultimately was, but it abated talk of my "becoming kanaimà." Connected to their suspicions was also the charge that I had stirred up trouble between Paramakatoi and neighboring villages by having published, in the oral history pamphlet, Patamuna accounts of warfare that featured a well-known raid by the Kopinan on Paramakatoi. Unfortunately my protestations that I had only faithfully done what I had been asked to do could not overturn the impression that this might be another example of my "kanaimà-like" propensities for conflict.

A second reason for hostility was the emergence of a new antipathy to external researchers in general and the threat that such researchers might steal from or otherwise exploit indigenous people for their cultural knowledge. The figure of the ethnobotanist, I must say, rather than the ethnographer was the chief villain of the piece. The debate around intellectual property rights, quite rightly, had become a big issue with all the Amerindian people in Guyana, but the effect for me was to have to continually explain why the notion that I could "make millions" from my research was unfair, if not entirely inaccurate in relative terms. Clearly I was better off materially than all the Patamuna, so I could certainly pay them for assistance at a rate that reflected that relative wealth, but unfortunately not at the level that the rhetoric of the foreign nongovernmental organizations suggested.

A third reason for encountering new difficulties may have stemmed from the "magical force" of the pamphlet itself. By this I mean that the mere fact of the pamphlet, whatever its particular contents, stimulated excitement because of an association, initiated in alleluia shamanism, between texts and divine power. Alleluia thus comprises both alleluia'san and *iwepyatàsak* (prophets) and, as will later become clear, such prophetism has often been evidenced through the possession of special texts. That may also be the reason why I was told that both the pamphlet and my presence had been prophesied. Either way, that was not a recommendation for those already becoming ill-disposed to the research.

Given these obstacles, the opportunity to interview kanaimàs further seemed unlikely, if not foolish. I therefore decided to examine the relationship between kanaimà and alleluia more closely, since it had struck me that there was perhaps a ritual and a historical connection. I also knew that alleluia had gone "underground" in Paramakatoi after the arrival of the Pilgrim Holiness missionaries but was not by any means extirpated. Unfortunately, those who had formerly assisted me were not only now reluctant to speak out about kanaimà but also showed a similar disinterest in discussing alleluia. I therefore got to know Alfred Edwin one of the still-practicing alleluia singers, and his son, Roger. From Alfred, and with the translation assistance of Roger, I recorded both alleluia songs and a whole series of mythic tales and historical accounts. In particular Alfred guided us to many of the alleluia places in the Yawong valley that had fallen into disuse. This was the happiest of times, and the materials we gathered will certainly be the subject of further publication, but the practice of alleluia also carries political implications. Neither did we ignore the subject of kanaimà ignored, and it was precisely the disinterest of my earlier collaborators that now encouraged other Patamuna to relate their experiences and even act them out.[21]

These changing orientations of my research directly replicated some of the social and political divisions in Paramakatoi itself. No longer being exclusively involved with one extended family, I was now able to be much more involved with others, like the Edwins. They did not have a high status in Paramakatoi, and this was partly connected to their obdurate practice of alleluia. Alfred's brother, Roy, is a lay pastor in the village and therefore gave up being an alleluia singer against Alfred's wishes, evidence that even close family ties were affected by decisions to abandon, or not, the practice of alleluia. Roger wanted his father's songs to be heard again in the village and to have a film record made of the event. The idea thus evolved that I would sponsor an alleluia event that would enable Alfred to sing alleluia in Paramakatoi for the first time since the 1960s. Roger therefore spent an enormous amount of time and effort to build an "Alleluia House" as a venue for this rather subversive event, which was simultaneously a snub to those who had withdrawn their support for my researches. The resulting event was filmed, but what the film cannot adequately communicate was the background conflicts that were played out that day and night.

People began assembling at the Alleluia House the day before the singing was to begin, and I was surprised to see that people had traveled up from as far as Lethem to join in the event. This did not mean that all who had come had come to see it succeed, and my heart fell when a group from Lethem wired a boom box to a car battery and started playing Brazilian samba and passing out bottles of rum. Given the sacral nature of alleluia, such behavior would ruin the possibility of the event vindicating alleluia in Paramakatoi. The next day was to be the commencement of the alleluia singing, but the following morning the samba party was still in full swing. A showdown had to be engineered to eject the interlopers, if not quiet them. As the day wore on, more and more people from Paramakatoi arrived at Roger's place, and it became clear from the reactions of the crowd, that the "moral majority" was definitely in favor of hearing "real" alleluia, and the loutish elements were quickly quelled.

So it was that the first alleluia songs were heard in Paramakatoi for over forty years, and I can only say that it was a true privilege to have been there. Indeed, those who had abandoned me so suddenly were now insisting that I return with video equipment as soon as possible in order to record "proper" alleluia. These same individuals had boycotted Roger's event, considering it too much of a "spree" (drinking party), just as the outsiders from Lethem had wanted. Indeed, the disruption by the outsiders from Lethem may have been directly encour-

aged by these individuals, since a younger brother of one was prominent in the attempt to wreck the event.

This was the closing scene from that 1997 trip, and I returned to
Georgetown and again received the enthusiastic support of the Walter
Roth Museum for a publication containing all the materials on alleluia and kanaimà I had just gathered, which would then be distributed among Patamuna villages, as had happened with my first set of
materials. But I should have known that such things cannot be easily
repeated. Even as I was rushing to complete the manuscript for the
museum back in the United States, Denis Williams, the director of the
museum, was dying of what had become symbolically potent to me:
colorectal cancer. While Williams did review and approve my manuscript before he died, which was a comfort to me, he was not always
an easy person and was therefore a controversial figure in Guyanese
political life. The Ministry of Culture, which took over the administration of the museum after Denis died, saw only a minimal academic
product in my manuscript and so declined to publish the work, even
though the galleys were already at the printer. Unlike Denis, the ministry saw no political value in the production and donation of this text
to the Patamuna. The Patamuna themselves, I later learned, had come
to suspect the museum of selling the earlier work at a great profit, since
there was a nominal cover charge for tourists or visitors who purchased
a copy at the museum itself.

On top of this I was given a final "sign" that the project, so pre-
cipitously begun in 1992, was probably at an end. Derek Leung—the
bush-pilot without whom not only my fieldwork but more important
the daily life of the people in Paramakatoi would have been infinitely
more difficult, for want of emergency medical assistance and supplies
of gasoline, tools, and the like—was killed. His plane lost instrumen-
tation just outside Mahdia, his base of operations, and, according to
air-traffic control, his last words were, in that inimitable terseness that
was his hallmark, "Ooooh fuck." The logistical and political obstacles
to my return seemed insurmountable, and the writing of this book is
partly a symptom of that frustration.

The way in which ethnographers might become enmeshed in the beliefs and desires of those they study has been addressed before in the
anthropological literature, and the book that I read in 1995 that seemed
best to provide an analogy with my own situation was Paul Stoller's
and Cheryl Olkes's (1987) account of their time with Songhay sorcer-

ers in the Republic of Niger. What struck me about the account was that, in seeking to understand Songhay sorcery more closely, Stoller was sucked in as an unknowing agent of sorcery, even to the extent of possibly having been responsible for someone's death. This story is still, strangely, something of a comfort, as I remain anxious as to the reason for the shamanic assassination of a particular kanaimà, since its occasion was so conveniently timed to satisfy and so closely tied to my intense interest in such shamanic warfare, as I discuss later.

In South American ethnology in general, the topic of violent and aggressive shamanism has rarely been broached, and I made a point of canvasing colleagues as to whether or not they had had any similar experiences, or even experience of killing shamanism at all. I was surprised, and somewhat relieved, to find that this phenomenon was more common than I had thought, though it was not part of my colleagues' research projects at the time. Darell Posey, an anthropologist of the Kayapó, wrote the following to me in 1996: "I REALLY enjoyed our brief encounter in Madison. Your research is certainly interesting and, well, frightening. I have seen so much of this stuff up close and from around the edges . . . and, frankly, one of the reasons I left the Kayapó was that I was learning too much about these things. The other dimensions (death-shamanism) have a physical component, but the visible is only the mask."[22]

Terry Roopnaraine, a fellow anthropologist born in Guyana, wrote to me in June 1997, just after my departure from that country. He had returned from the Pomeroon, where he had decided to make inquiries about kanaimà, being intrigued and perhaps a little skeptical of my reports from Paramakatoi since he had himself done his doctoral research in Monkey Mountain:

> "This is pretty much everything I have on kanaima. I believe that there is more information to be had, but frankly I got too nervous to pursue the matter. As I said on the phone, I had three successive nights of identical nightmares. For about a week, I was very edgy and quicktempered. All in all, I had the feeling that there was something awful crawling in my head. Sometimes, for no apparent reason, all the hair on my arms would stand up. On a couple of occasions, I just started crying, apropos of nothing. So I am sorry, but I am very reluctant to continue these inquiries in the field. There are some things best left alone. I was getting genuinely worried about you in the Pakaraimas, and I am very glad you're OK."

Terry expressed well the emotional state that dealing with kanaimà generates, and certainly a daily focus on kanaimà meant I often felt I was just "getting through it." Both Darrell and Terry were also right to raise the possibility that such things might be better left alone, but, as I related, the intensity with which an investigation of kanaimà was initially supported and the genuinely affecting stories of those who had suffered from their attacks had caused me to persist. Of course, these were not the only reasons; no academic can help being seduced by the prospect of discovering what has previously been secreted or hidden, of making that original contribution to the ethnographic literature of the region, so I suppose that motive must have been in there, too, crowded out though it was at the time by the sheer vividness and immediacy of kanaimà violence. I also think that a certain anger, connected to my grief after the death of my father, was focused into my research on kanaimà and that such anger led me to persist in the face of difficult or trying circumstances.[23]

Despite my personal rage, there has also been a wider mythopoetic dimension to my experiences, in that they at times seem to uncannily recapitulate the experiences of other outsiders who encounter kanaimà. Graham Burnett (2000, 183–89) provides a nice discussion of the reactions of various nineteenth-century travelers to the "demon landscape" of the interior of Guyana, pointing out how the discovery and desecration of native spirit places, as well as their occasional defacement, served to enable the possession of that landscape through a mapping and surveying that exorcized the genius loci. In a less literally geographical sense, ethnography also, through its explanations, undoubtedly robs cultures of some of the force of their performative expression. In this sense, knowledge itself becomes colonial (Whitehead 1995b). However, as Burnett also notes, the very "recognition of the hallucinatory power of the landscape placed the explorer at risk; it was a short step from empathy to the kind of collapse—the 'going native' (or mad)—that disqualified the explorer," and also the ethnographer, no doubt.[24]

In the hallucinatory landscape of kanaimà, tales or allegations of whites poisoned or killed by the kanaimà are of particular interest for the way in which they reveal the nature of kanaimà as a cultural discourse. As such, kanaimà is not just directed toward other Amerindian groups, nor only toward co-villagers, but also toward the agents of eighteenth- and nineteenth-century "colonial" and twentieth-century "modernizing" development. The colonial development of the interior, principally under the Dutch, was intended to occur through trade for forest products, which included slaves. By 1750 it was already apparent that such trade had indeed had a considerable effect on the peoples of the interior, particularly in the Essequibo–Rupununi–Rio Branco corridor. In his report of that year to the Dutch West India Company, the colony's *commandeur*, Storm van's Gravesande, noted that the traders "act so badly towards the natives that several have already been murdered by the latter; others get poisoned and expose the Colony to danger of war with the savage tribes" (Harris and Villiers 1911, 260). Van's Gravesande also noted that the trade in "red slaves" from the upper Essequibo region was "fairly large" and that some of the traders "do not hesitate even to go with some tribes to make war upon others . . . and selling them as slaves, and abusing Indian women. Hence it was that in the year 1747 the rovers G. Goritz and H. Bannink were murdered by the Indians [in upper Essequibo], some others poisoned, and others forced to flee" (Harris and Villiers 1911, 269).

Colonial development under the British administration of the nineteenth century was at best "absent minded" (Rivière 1995) and so largely devolved into the missionary effort that I describe later. At the forefront of evangelical progress in the highlands was the British missionary Thomas Youd. His case is examined more fully below, but the tale of his poisoning by kanaimàs has become notorious. Although there are reasons to question the accuracy of this tale, its place in the discourse of kanaimà is undeniable. Lesser known in twentieth-century literature but equivalent to the case of Youd was that of one Pastor Davis. Theodor Koch-Grüneberg described Davis as having died in a village by Roraima "from a hemorrhage, as it was described, and was buried here" and indicated that it was a killing enacted by Patamuna or Makushi kanaimàs (1979, 1:103, 109, 114; 3:186).[25]

Either way, the notion of the susceptibility of whites to death by kanaimà is not just a particular claim about the forensic causes of death in any given instance but a wider attempt to bring whites within native categories in a way that renders them less powerful and threatening. This is how I have come to understand the "legend" of my own poisoning by kanaimàs, as well as that of other whites, about which I was carefully and deliberately informed.[26] In particular, the case of Bengi, eventually shotgunned in the late 1960s, was related to me on a number of occasions by different persons, so as to firmly impress it on my thinking, as a relatively recent example of how avaricious whites might fall victim to shamanic attack. Bengi and his brother were known as practicing kanaimàs who went to work for a white man in a *balata*-bleeding (rubber-gathering) operation on the Siparuni. However, the white man got angry because he thought they were being lazy. They in turn demanded a payment of cigarettes, but when the confrontation ended, they were smiling. Everyone in the balata camp wondered if the white man would try to chase them out of the camp, and everyone thought that since he had a concrete house that could be closed up tight he was safe.[27] But it is said that Bengi and his brother must have gotten into the white man's house, because they left the next morning and he was sick on waking. He died within a week. Clearly other forms of assault sorcery are not being distinguished from specifically kanaimà attack in the way these events are narrated, but the point for those who recount this incident is to suggest the susceptibility of whites to Amerindian occult forces.

The cultural contextualization of specific histories like these thus allows us to see that such multiple versions erode the authority of the idea of History itself. How can we say "what happened" if the cultural meanings of a story (*histoire*) diverge in such a way as to appropriate the key events, which are registered in all versions but in culturally specific ways? Probably only by counting all versions as relevant and legitimate historiographical expressions. As a result, whatever such kanaimà deaths may have involved, including the clear possibility that they were not examples of ritual violence, they should not be interpreted as we once thought they might be, as opportunities for the destruction of the Mythical by the Historical. This was the notion that drove the colonial occupation and exorcism of the "demon landscape" in the nineteenth century.

A more adequate response, in the light of nearly a hundred years of ethnographic engagements, must be to recognize the discursive origins of apparently empirical claims and that the proof of such claims is established by reference to the discourse from which they emerge, not by a suprahistorical procedure in factual verification. In one sense it really does not matter if I, or anyone else, was clinically poisoned—it is the claims made to that effect that are anthropologically significant for our understanding of the histories and historicities of others. As with Hugh Goodwin's death on the Orinoco in the sixteenth century, or the death of Captain Cook which has exercised the anthropological imagination more widely, the "apotheosis" of whites in the cosmologies of others, their relevance to the cultural discourses of history, reflects not their historical importance as we understand it but precisely an attempt to negate that potential. The effort, then, to disprove or prove kanaimà deaths becomes the vehicle for the colonization of the historical experience of others by bringing it within an external model of historiography. It remains important to ethnographers to know who did or didn't die and how, but our knowledge of the cultural plurality of notions of death, individuality, and agency also teaches us the limits of our own notion of history.

The purpose of this chapter has been, among other things, to illustrate the entanglements that fieldwork involves, the ethical duties we have to our informants, and the unforeseen consequences of close ethnographic engagement. My experience is not presented as an example of how those difficulties might be avoided, but rather to suggest that, even with the best of intentions, they are inevitable. At the same time, if the classic injunction of ethnographic fieldwork—to be a participant observer—is not to be taken as a mere tautology, then it must mean that our manner of "participation" should be no less an object of our theoretical and methodological reflection than the issues of "observation" that have been the focus of discussion since the early 1990s.

In the case of the kanaimà, participation has, of course, been fraught with difficulty, if not outright danger, but it has resulted, I believe, in a distinct and new view of kanaimà as a shamanic practice. Moreover, in negotiating the sometimes contradictory and shifting attitudes and statements that are made with regard to kanaimà, it becomes apparent that its "reality" as conceived of within an empiricist and rationalist tradition of thought is quite different from its "reality" for those who live kanaimà and its consequences. This is why the matter must be approached as a form of discourse whose practice is simultaneously and in varying degrees verbal, emotional, psychological, sociological, and cultural—in a word, *real*. Kanaimà, therefore, is not just a matter of "forensic" evidence, although the following chapters certainly contain such evidence, since it is certainly the more culturally satisfying to minds trained in the traditions of rational empiricism. Nonetheless, as I will attempt to show, kanaimà is much more than the poisoned and mutilated bodies it produces.

CHAPTER 2

Tales of the Kanaimà:
Observers

By referring to "Observers" in this chapter title, I do not intend to set up a complex theoretical argument but to contrast the colonial gaze that engendered the materials presented here with the largely untextualized voices of Amerindians whose status as "Participants," which I turn to in the next chapter, alludes to the inescapable and culturally pervasive nature of kanaimà for them. In both cases I use the notion of "Tales" to suggest that there is an epistemological equivalence in these sources, to the extent that the oral accounts of the Patamuna are no less "hard evidence" than the literary production of outsiders. At the same time, I mean to suggest that all such accounts must be critically interrogated and that myth will become "history" just as "history" is composed of myth.

In the imagination of the Patamuna and other peoples of the highlands, kanaimà is from the first time—a primordial force that has structured the universe and formed the world as we know it. Kanaimà is more ancient than warfare and more ancient than society itself; it may even be more ancient than the other forms of shamanism and magical action, piya, *talen* and alleluia. As a result, kanaimà itself almost becomes outside history, or it is at least a universal and constant human possibility that is only contingently realized in the course of human history. In this way one may say that, while there is a history to the ritual practice of kanaimà, kanaimà as a way of being in the world is beyond time.

The temporal and spatial dislocation of kanaimà is therefore an integral part of its ritual and symbolic force, for practitioners are both able to travel vast distances in a short space of time and are able to expand their life-time and life-space by the means of the ritual practices that are involved in being kanaimà—that is, they have access to the plane of shamanic encounter and exploration (*kalawali*), as well as being directly nourished by the production and consumption of the "honey" of necrosis (*maba*), derived from the bodies of their victims. As a result, there is not, as it were, an oral history of kanaimà by its practitioners; there are no synthetic accounts of the deeds of powerful killers and sorcerers except as they relate to the historical testimony by the uninitiated, both native and colonial. The kanaimà therefore act in a ritual space that is both then and now, simultaneously both here and there, and the paradox and contradiction that appear in accounts of kanaimà reflect this conflation of ritual and historical practice—for although the enactment of ritual categories may be historicized, in actuality the "timelessness" of ritual is part of the historicity of the Patamuna themselves.

Kanaimà has been narrated within nonnative sources since at least the early nineteenth century. However, it was assimilated in these works to revenge more generally. As a result, any instance of revenge became one of kanaimà, and certainly native discourse might allude to kanaimà in cases of violent or unexpected death. But the assimilation of kanaimà to all revenge killings meant that a vast array of different kinds of death were attributed to kanaimà although they might not have been ritual killings at all. Inevitably, the nature of kanaimà deaths appeared to be quite obscure. The claim that a killing was the work of kanaimà was therefore seen as more the superstitious invocation of a spirit-ghoul than a reference to a distinct and ritually significant mode of death. Thus, as more systematic ethnographic observation began, since the native discourse of kanaimà certainly would have raised the possibility of action by kanaimàs in all manner of death and injury, it might have appeared that a kanaimà killing was no more than a vague attribution of sickness and injury to an all-encompassing evil force.

When considering the external meanings and representations of kanaimà it will be apparent that this latter idea, of kanaimà as a native "Satan" or other Manichaean construct, was central to the ethnological and literary production of kanaimà. At the same time, there was a symbolic convergence and mimetic elaboration of the category "kanaimà" in both native and colonial discourses.[1] This meant that the wider projection of kanaimà in the written sources served mostly to exemplify the savagery of the native population. Moreover, since kanaimà was seen as a "skulking" way of war, it also stood in clear contrast to the ideal modes of military display and combat practiced in Western cultures of war.[2] However, in ethnographic discourse, kanaimà transmuted over time into a functionalist mechanism for sustaining social order, and the killing became a kind of "jungle justice" that, in the absence of the Hobbesian state and its police, regulated and punished the "criminal." As a result, the symbolic and ritual meanings of kanaimà were effectively ignored, or understood as merely an unfortunate welling up of Amerindian savagery.

The question then arises as to the nature of the colonial gaze that produced this ethnological and literary view of kanaimà and the extent to which it may have been linked to or otherwise served the project of colonial administration. The issue is, of course, complex and relies ultimately on consideration of the motivations of specific authors, who are considered below. Kanaimà practice and its meaning were not accurately portrayed, but this was as much a function of the limited kinds of interaction that missionaries and others might have had with the interior peoples as it was a conscious attempt to misrepresent what otherwise was evident. However, even if the cultural importance of kanaimà was vividly represented as the "oppressive nightmare" of the highland peoples, the cosmological significance of kanaimà as a shamanic practice was persistently overlooked. Colonial representation always emphasized apparent juridical features to kanaimà, picturing it as a codified system of revenge—a *lex talionis*. This resulted principally from a failure to discriminate among the various forms of shamanism and magical action. Although the piya, especially for the missionaries, was seen as the key figure standing in the way of rapid and complete conversion, only a limited understanding of such "weedy entanglements of evil" was required for its suppression. The highly physical nature of kanaimà killing and its connection to notions of revenge—or, more exactly, its reputation as a rebounding violence in the face of challenges to social norms—therefore obscured its occult meanings for the colonial commentator. In this way kanaimà served as an answer to the puzzle of how native society might regulate itself in the absence of formal institutions of law or criminal justice.

As Nicholas Thomas (1994, 127) has pointed out with regard to British missionary efforts elsewhere, each mission "field" was apt to dramatize certain key cultural practices—head-hunting, cannibalism, widow-burning—in order to provide an index of growing evangelical success. As a result, such representations tended also to suggest that the cultural practice in question was on the verge of extinction.

This was very much how shamanism generally, including both piya and kanaimà, was presented. Nonetheless, kanaimà proved so elusive that it could not become a basis for the campaigns of cultural extirpation that have been associated with other dramatized cultural practices, such as cannibalism. This elusiveness, coupled with pervasive native reference to kanaimà, meant that kanaimà still required some codification, so the legalistic interpretation was pursued by major missionary and ethnological writers—Brett, Im Thurn, Walter Roth, and Gillin.

The ferocity and horrific mutilations of a kanaimà attack were nonetheless impossible to ignore, but they were seen as an almost laudable aspect of the rigor of native "justice," provoking some authors to favorable comparison with "tribal" Saxon and Judaic ideas of retaliation and recompense. The beneficial effects of kanaimà in producing social order were identified in both its protolegal functions and its supposed consequences for sustaining social distance and the particularity of "tribal" identity. This perspective was emphasized to the point that kanaimà became, to the colonial mind, merely an example of a legal system founded on retribution and punishment, the only distinction with "white society" being that kanaimà was the retributive force of government and society, rather than that of the family, which was being expressed in the case of "white society." In twentieth-century imaginings of kanaimà, this notion has been further expanded as the secular State supplants Religion and the Justice of Law supplants the Mercy of God. In this context the inevitability of vengeance, exemplified by kanaimà, becomes a token of the necessity for discipline and the certainty of punishment in an otherwise insouciant cosmos. The profound spirituality of kanaimà was simultaneously erased by its presentation as a folkloric belief, akin to the vampire or werewolf.

Unlike sixteenth-century Spanish attempts to delineate "cannibalism" or nineteenth- and twentieth-century British attempts to determine the "reality" of African witchcraft, kanaimà was not the subject of "official investigation." However, as in Evans-Pritchard's (1937) classic work on Azande sorcery, the ethnology of kanaimà shamanism "revealed" a system of justice and legality. In this way the cultural force of kanaimà, which so manifestly entranced and troubled the colonial imagination, was portrayed as an expression of the ineffable and irrational nature of colonial subjects. That primitive mystery was then made less threatening through the "science" of ethnological description, which sanitizes barbarous practice through its selective re-presentation in familiar, intelligible, and comforting terms—as a form of law and order. Literary and observational processes were also under-written by a high degree of intertexuality among the colonial authors. Certain key accounts, especially those of the Schomburgks, have been constantly recycled, thereby progressively constricting the interpretive space for subsequent descriptions or information. As a result, by the end of the nineteenth century, the colonial imagining of kanaimà had become embalmed in the textual record and later accounts have largely failed to escape this rendition.

In sum, kanaimà was clearly misrepresented in the colonial sources in ways that enabled the progress of colonial administration, primarily through missionary evangelism but also through the imposition of colonial legal codes. A number of the authors I discuss below de-pict kanaimà as an institution of primitive law, thereby also laying the groundwork for a later appeal to colonial justice as an improvement on this primitive, if somewhat admirable, law of blood-revenge. Tales of whites killed by kanaimà and the possibility that whites might be susceptible to the physical mutilations, though not the occult mean-ings, of kanaimà attack were addressed by the reassuring suggestion that the "white man" might act as a final court of appeal in the jungle justice of the blood feud. Such an ethnological presentation also al-lowed the "naturalization" of retributive law and capital punishment, so that kanaimà in fact aided the cultural project of government in the metropolitan setting as much as in the colonial. However, an exclusive focus on kanaimà was precluded by the manifest importance of piya as an obstacle to the spiritual and political dominance of the native popu-lation. At the same time, the intense interest in both piya and kanaimà signaled the significance of spiritual practice for the colonial regime and so encouraged the expression of resistance or opposition through these practices. The colonial attitude in itself connoted kanaimà's im-portance to the world outside the Pakaraimas, an external importance that has fed into its current resurgence.

SATANIC MAJESTY:
ASSAULT SORCERY AND DARK SHAMANISM, 1500–1800

The earliest European source that relates to kanaimà derives from the Orinoco in the sixteenth century. In his account of his 1596 journey to Guiana, Walter Ralegh (1997, 80) says that he left behind two English youths, Francis Sparry and Hugh Goodwin, in order to continue his "discoverie" and learn the local languages. The subsequent killing of Goodwin, who "going out into the country in English dress, was attacked by four jaguars who tore him to pieces" (BL ADD. 36317 f. 62; my translation) has naturally perplexed many subsequent commentators. This strange incident has been taken as evidence of the cruel abandonment of Goodwin or even as an indication that he was not in fact killed. The various accounts appear to make no sense, since jaguars (*tiguere*) do not hunt in packs and are not known for their sartorial prejudice (Ralegh 1997, 29–30).[3] Harlow (1928, 120) therefore suggests that this was a story spread around by Sparry and the natives to discourage Spanish efforts to capture Goodwin.

However, there are cultural circumstances in which "jaguars" might become enraged at European clothes. The four tiguere who dismembered Goodwin may have been "were-jaguars" or kanaimàs. Contemporary kanaimàs are hypertraditionalists and refuse all tokens of contact with outsiders, such as metal tools, guns, matches, and, particularly, clothing. Kanaimàs also often hunt in "packs" of perhaps up to five men. Any suggestion as to why kanaimàs might have killed Goodwin is speculative, but both the political situation in the lower Orinoco at the end of the sixteenth century and the otherwise enigmatic description of the attack suggest that this incident might reasonably be interpreted this way. Ralegh certainly appeared to offer a substantive challenge to Spanish imperial designs in this region, and subsequent native testimony makes clear that his political influence on native leaders and promises of return were taken seriously (Ralegh 1997, 45–52). This did not preclude pro-Spanish sentiments among the indigenous population or the possibility that other native leaders might be interested in alliance with either of the colonial contenders.

In such complex circumstances, the killing of Hugh Goodwin—who was the living token of Ralegh's return—was a forceful political statement, since his death was politically significant for both those who might approve and those who might refuse alliance with the English.

Likewise, when the Dutch were initiating their own attempts to make alliances on the lower Orinoco and Guyana coast, their presence was a subject of native prophesy, indicating that European intrusion was as much the occasion for native ritual performance as it was for the realization of material gain or the political ambition of indigenous leaders (Ralegh 1997, 23, 67, 111). In short, the European entanglement in native cosmologies is to be expected, but the historiographical complexities of such events persist even where our textual evidence is much more copious than this.[4] Nonetheless, conflict about the adoption of colonial cultural items has remained a constant in native political calculation, and the native semiotics of English clothing persist to the present day in Guyana, such that the long trousers of the English colonial are preferred over the short trousers of the American peace-corps.

There are no further unambiguous references to kanaimà forms of ritual violence until the nineteenth century, which marks the inception of the term *kanaimà* into European cultural consciousness and the production of increasingly detailed descriptions of its practice. This absence in the literature does not, of course, mean that kanaimà did not exist; what it does clearly illustrate are the limits of ethnological description in the absence of sustained ethnography or missionary work. Kanaimà certainly has its precursors and analogs within the wider history of shamanism and assault sorcery in the region, but it remains open as to whether or not it is possible to reconstruct its historical emergence as a distinct ritual complex and to suggest reasons for that change in shamanic practices. Ritual practices, as I present later, are very much part of historical change, even though their timeless and perpetual aspects dominate the forms of their expression.

A claim to great antiquity, such as is made by kanaimà practitioners, is not evidence itself of antiquity; such statements are, however, vitally important to a proper appreciation of the meaning of historically contingent ritual practices—and kanaimà provides a good example of this. Neither should claims of such antiquity in the practice of kanaimà be dismissed out of hand as a reference to "mythic time," for there are many discussions in the colonial literature as to the practice of assault sorcery and associated predatory cosmologies. Kanaimà, even if its particular ritual forms were an innovation or radical disjuncture in shamanic practices, still did not appear out of nowhere. It was these cultural repertoires, these discourses of aggressive shamanism, that were a crucible for the formation of distinctly kanaimà modes

Aygnan and Kaagerre, aggressive spirits of the Tupi (Léry 1580). *Courtesy of the John Carter Brown Library at Brown University.*

of ritual action. The emergence of kanaimà can thus be reconstructed to some degree, especially since the tenor of much nineteenth-century discussion of kanaimà was to see it as a peculiar, pathological excrescence on an otherwise admirable native simplicity. In turn this meant that the historical contingency of kanaimà was very much part of the external commentary on its practice.

In the colonial literature of the sixteenth, seventeenth, and eighteenth centuries there was little disaggregation of the forms of shamanism that were encountered, but the literature does contain repeated references to various "evil spirits" that were adversaries of the curing shaman, or piya, and hints of a separate ritual complex dedicated to managing human relationships with such a divinity. They even refer on occasion to mutilation and assassination as a shamanic technique (Drake Manuscript 1996, f.III, see color plate 1; Barrère 1753, 206; Crevaux 1883, 119; Stedman 1988, 304, 314; Waterton 1825, 110). In addition, there are copious references to Tupian, Karipuna, and Karinya cosmologies that describe an aggressive spirit-being, called respectively Aygnan/Yuruparí, Mapoya/Opia, or Wattopa/Wattipa.[5] This spirit-being was conceived of not as simply an ethereal presence but as physically manifest as a lurking assassin, whom "they feare, and hate him much . . . for hee will often times (to their great terror) beat them blacke and blew" (Harcourt 1613, 26). This allusion to physical beating, especially the fact that it is bruising, is suggestive of the kinds of description that are currently given of kanaimà attacks, which involve the dislocation of the neck and shoulder; in such descriptions heavy bruising to the arms and chest is seen as diagnostic of kanaimà attack.

For the Karinya, Wattopa was also endowed with oracular properties (Ralegh 1997, 23, 67, 111) and referred to ritual techniques of physical transformation that were used as part of assault sorcery (Civrieux 1974, 17–18). Mapoya of the Karipuna, Opia of the other Antillean cosmologies, and shamanic techniques among the Karipuna were described in the *Dictionnaire Caraibe-Francois* of the Jesuit missionary Raymond Breton. *Eremerícaba láo eroútou* was the phrase to describe the invocation of the cannibal-spirit, and *Leremerícayem bóye lóubara aráli racati* was the chant of the shaman to call down the spirit beings (Breton 1665, 216–18). Breton also suggested that the melancholy and taciturn nature of the Karipuna was related to the way in which they were perpetually oppressed by Mapoya, "who sends black smoke into their brains causing dark and horrible dreams." Sorcerers who specialized in communication with Mapoya and who used him to attack their enemies were called *nharomán mapoyanum* (341–42). That kind of assault sorcery was distinguished from *ierénapoue* (war magic), which consisted of disease and epidemics sent by the *boyé* or piya (375).

In Tupian cosmologies were also recognizable analogous divinities and spirits, in particular Aygnan, or Yuruparí, appeared as an aggressive, evil force who physically attacked people through forest demons such as Kaagerre and if he "were to find no other meat nearby, he would unearth the body and eat it. So that from the first night after a body has been buried . . . , they put out . . . well cooked food, along with some *caouin* [fermented drink], on the grave of the dead person . . . until they think that the body is entirely decayed" (Léry 1990, 136, 176). This description is reminiscent of how the kanaimà seeks out the grave of the victim in order to taste the corpse. Viveiros de Castro (1992, 68–69) also describes the Āñĩ (Aygnan) spirits of the forest as "ferocious, cannibalistic, kidnappers of women, and assassins of men." Another name for Yuruparí is also given as Ouaioupia (Evreux 1985, 213), which suggests a link to Mapoya/Opia of the Karipuna, who were actually settled along the Atlantic coast as well as the Antilles and show other points of contact with the Tupian groups to the south (Whitehead 1995a, 95). Reichel-Dolmatoff (1996, xxvi), in discussing the historical ethnography of the term *Yuruparí,* rightly notes how native cosmologies were usually forced into the binaries of Christian religion, so subtle distinctions in the meaning of spiritual concepts such as Yuruparí were conflated across cultures and historical time. This is an important point and applies as well to the interpretation of kanaimà; in the search for the ideational repertoire from which kanaimà emerges, the archaeology of all these concepts essentially forms the subject matter of this and following chapters. Suffice it to say here that Reichel-Dolmatoff notes that Yuruparí has been understood and practiced as, among other things, a "secret society" of men.

I do not introduce these other shamanic complexes in order to suggest a direct relationship with kanaimà, although that remains a possibility, but rather to show the existence of a variety of shamanic practices in which some of the symbolic and ritual elements of kanaimà are already present. Kanaimà has been represented in contradictory ways. On the one hand it is considered external or marginal to social reproduction, a kind of aberrant welling up of a savage and unquenchable desire for vengeance, but on the other as a mechanism for producing social order. This analytical contradiction stems from the failure to historicize kanaimà ritual practice. As recent work on Tupi societies has demonstrated, vengeance was not simply a mode of social distancing nor evidence of the uncontrollable political passions of the natives, but in fact a legitimate means of social contiguity and personal fulfillment. Consequently, the native theory of cannibalism was not an unfortunate and reprehensible means to achieve ends that would otherwise be realized through more civilized social mechanisms, which were unavailable to those who were "sin Loi, sin Foi, sin Roi," but a fundamental expression of Tupian political cosmology (Combès 1992; Carneiro da Cunha and Viveiros de Castro 1985; Viveiros de Castro 1992).[6] Combès (1992, 62) also notes that a stick was inserted into the anus of those destined for consumption, just as de Bry's depiction of the aftermath of battle and the taking of human body parts among native groups in Florida, to illustrate the account of Rene Laudonnière, suggests that the meaning of anal penetration was important to the magic of mutilation elsewhere, as it is for kanaimà.[7]

Within this context of widespread ideas about predatory and can-

Evisceration of Enemies by the Soldiers of Outina (Laudonnière 1591, plate xv). *Courtesy of the Albert H. Small Special Collections Library, University of Virginia Library.*

nibalistic spirits that make themselves physically manifest as men, it is important to note that Grillet and Bechamel (1698, 42) wrote that when traveling with the Karinya one night

> they heard the cry of a bird, and said to one another in the Galibis tongue, "hark how the Devil cries"; I reproved them, telling them they were mistaken and that the Devil had no body, but was a spirit as our souls are, which they confess to be invisible and immortal, which yet they do not say of the Devils, but pretend that their Physicians or piaies kill them with great clubs. The Nourages of one cottage made the figure of a man in the way that they thought the Devil came to their cottage in the night, to make them sick, that so while he stopped at this phantom and took it to be a Nourage, the piaies that watched for him might have their opportunity, when they saw him, to knock him on the head.[8]

In this passage, as with many historical accounts of demons, there is an insistence on the physical actuality of such demons, just as is the case with kanaimà today. The bird they heard was undoubtedly the goatsucker (*Caprimulgiformes steatornithidae*), which is the herald of the kanaimà and other malignant forces, and the stratagem for killing the spirit-assassin is echoed in the contemporary Patamuna tale of Kanaimà Hill, which I discuss later. The killing of "demons" or kanaimàs with clubs is also borne out in current Patamuna practice. The "Kangai special," is a form of club made specifically for killing kanaimàs (228). It is distinguished from the *taikek* (war-club) proper, which is more spatulate and blade-like, sometimes with toothed edges.

Barrère (1753, 206), writing about the Karinya, also mentions that, "Our savages further subdivide the Devil into many kinds and encounter them in various forms, such that it would be useless to record their names here. Him who they fear the most is called Chinay. This Chinay, these poor people imagine, is a real eater of Indians. He eats nothing but their flesh: & he sucks all their blood." This vampiric imagery is often used by the Patamuna to describe the kanaimà, and it is tempting to speculate a relationship between the terms *canayi* (used by Bernau 1847, 57), *chankon* (mentioned by Sifontes 1982, 31), and *chinay* mentioned by Barrère.

Whatever the wider valence of the idea of kanaimà in both the colonial literature and in the native imaginary, its locus has always been in the northeastern part of Amazonia, in particular the region of the Rio Branco and Essequibo River systems. Ethnologically, the Karinya, Pemon, Makushi, Akawaio, and Patamuna are most constantly associated with the practice of kanaimà in the literatures. Descriptive accounts of killings, the presence of kanaimàs, and the invocation of ideas associated with kanaimà, also occur in the areas proximate to these groups' locations. The Waiwai, Wapishana, Ye'kuana, Wayana, Warao, and Lokono therefore all know of and discuss kanaimà but claim they are not practitioners. This seems largely borne out by their lack of highly specialized knowledge of the shamanic complex, which is definitely not to suggest that forms of assault sorcery are unknown to them.

Therefore, the absence of the term *kanaimà* from the colonial sources until the nineteenth century does not necessarily indicate its absence from native practice. There is in fact reason to suppose a florescence of the kanaimà complex at this time and continuing to this day. This florescence of kanaimà is linked to the relationship between assault sorcery generally and the conduct of warfare. Shamanic assault was invariably a prelude to, or part of, physical attack. However, the *kwayaus* (warriors) were also a social force that could inhibit the operation of kanaimàs and even physically eliminate particular kanaimà practitioners. As the colonial regimes of the region suppressed indigenous warfare and enslaved and decimated the native population, the kanaimàs found themselves relatively unopposed either physically or spiritually. As a result of this ritual and military power vacuum, the kanaimàs rapidly took a prominent role in the predatory imagery that suffused both village and family relationships, and that was clearly evident in the nineteenth-century materials.

KANAIMÀ: VENGEANCE AND
THE MIASMA OF EVIL, 1825–1881

The first unambiguous mention of kanaimà is made by William Hilhouse in his 1825 publication *Indian Notices*. Hilhouse advocated, if not always successfully, closer relations between the indigenous population and the British colonial government that had succeeded the Dutch administration in 1814 (Whitehead 1988, 170–71). Although he was continually frustrated at the indifference of the coastal colony to the human and natural resources of the interior—a theme that remains in Guyanese political consciousness to this day—his interest and knowledge of the interior was unsurpassed at that time. Hilhouse (1825, 7, 37–38) thus provides the first direct reference to the "Paramuni" or Patamuna people as one of the nations of the far interior, along with the "Attaraya" and "Attamacka." He wrote, "These three nations are too far in the interior to be of any service to the Colony. They may be called mountaineers, and have all the propensities peculiar to highlanders, being always at war, or engaged in predatory expeditions. All the information we possess concerning them is derived from the Accaways (Akawaio), who sometimes purchase their slaves; but they are described by them to be warlike and ferocious, and determined against the admission of any white person into their country" (38). Hilhouse continues to the effect that these peoples are not, however, cannibals and that even the "Caribisce" (Karinya), though making flutes from the bones of their enemies, "abhor the idea of either eating their flesh or drinking their blood, and this abhorrence is general" (38).

Whether or not Hilhouse was correct to so characterize native ideas about the ritual significance of human flesh, what is interesting is both the need he felt to offer this observation and that he should so explicitly confront the standard ethnological prejudice of the region—that the Caribs were cannibals. Although, kanaimà does entail acts of a cannibalistic nature, it has not been treated in the literature as an exemplary case of that phenomenon. The prevalent regional representation of cannibalism by Hilhouse's contemporaries, as for example in Humboldt 1907 (2:392, 411–13), pictures the cannibal moment as the collective expression of a barbarous form of revenge, or even the corrupt individual propensity of the powerful as well as (paradoxically) the socially marginal. The cultural meanings of kanaimà, when it finally appears in the literature, are much more focused on its secretive and even spiteful nature. In this way kanaimà comes to represent a declension in the integrity of Amerindian society and so opens the hermeneutical door for the subsequent interpretation of kanaimà as expressive of native disempowerment in the face of stabilized colonial administration throughout the region. Whatever the merits of these analyses, they do show that kanaimà must be understood as historically changing, not frozen in "mythic time."

This relative disconnection between kanaimà and cannibalism is, then, clearly reflected in the fact that it is the Akawaio, neighbors to the fierce but noncannibal Patamuna, who are the first to be directly associated with the ritual complex. Hilhouse (1825, 22) wrote of the Akawaio that once they had secured the basic material necessities they "set to work manufacturing warlike implements of all kinds" and if they "can muster a cargo of European goods" will set off on long-distance trade expeditions. So, given the fine line between trading and raiding, if they encountered weakly defended villages they would attack them rather than trade. "Their audacity on these predatory excursions is astonishing. If a party can muster eight or ten stand of fire-arms, it will fight its way through all the mountain tribes, though at open war with them; and by the rapidity of their marches, and *their nightly enterprises, which they call Kanaima,* they conceal the weakness of their numbers, and carry terror before them" (23; my emphasis). Apart from the way this passage shows us the effect that access to fire-arms could have on patterns of native warfare, it also nicely illustrates the connection between kanaimà and warfare.

Hilhouse also offers the first definition of "Kanaima" (sometimes "kenaima") as "a self-appointed avenger of evil, a man to whom the

Indians attributed all evil, illness and death, hence he was greatly feared. The kanaima never rested until he had killed his victim, usually by poison which was his particular weapon" (1825, 17). This passage presages the key tropes of kanaimà as they appear in subsequent accounts: the pervasive yet elusive threat of kanaimà as explaining all ills and evils, the fear and respect in which alleged kanaimà practitioners are held, the secret and persistent nature of his pursuit of the victim. Crucially, though, the relationship of kanaimà to Amerindian society and culture remains mysterious, for the kanaimà is characterized as a "self-appointed" avenger, and the reasons and means by which any individual might seek or achieve such an "appointment" are left open, as is the case with subsequent accounts. Hilhouse refers to this as a lex talionis that is "observed rigidly. . . . But in this respect, the influence of the European is productive of the happiest effect: for though an Indian will hear of no compromise from another Indian in a blood feud, he will yet faithfully abide by the determination and award of a favorite European, and will consent to a commutation, even for the life of the dearest relative" (14). Subsequent authors question neither the intensity of the desire for revenge nor the legalistic force of the obligation to seek such revenge.

Importantly, Hilhouse also characterizes the difference between Karinya and Akawaio warfare in these terms and suggests the policy that the British might follow with regard to them: "The Caribisce differ materially from the Accaways, in that they never go to war for the purposes of traffic, or procuring slaves. Their disputes are either on account of *personal affronts, or infringement of territory, and their wars are always wars of extermination.* On the Portuguese frontier, they do sometimes make prisoners and sell them. . . . it is the undoubted duty of Government if not to prevent the occurrence of the wars themselves, at least to endeavor to render them less bloody. For this purpose, the Government should itself become the purchaser" (29–30; my emphasis).[9] This is actually a crucial insight, for it presages the decline of intercommunity warfare under the British administration and the corresponding florescence of kanaimà killing itself. Although I later discuss links between kanaimà, warfare, and the colonial suppression of violence, it should be noted here that kanaimà is strongly associated with the practice of warfare and that with its suppression the cultural meaning and social consequences of kanaimà underwent important transformations during the nineteenth century. Since colonial commentators were not at all concerned with historicizing native cultural practice, which was seen as timelessly primitive, efforts to understand and explain the persistent indigenous interest in the discourse of kanaimà were bound to fail, since the practice was changing even as it was being more fully encountered.

Despite his extensive travels in the interior between 1835 and 1839, Robert Schomburgk (1931, 74) hardly mentions kanaimà at all, except as the name of a "Macusi Chieftain" in the village of Anai (see also Richard Schomburgk 1922, 1:351). Robert Schomburgk's work (1931, 59) also contains a brief allusion to kanaimà as the "arch-enemy of the human race" and as a cause for village abandonment on the death of "the more influential members of the settlement." Likewise, the no-less-well-traveled Alexander von Humboldt, who as Schomburgk's mentor who wrote a preface to the 1841 *Travels in Guiana*, does not mention kanaimà either. However, Robert Schomburgk's brother, Richard, did allude to the practice and elaborated some of the basic ritual elements of kanaimà, even though he still saw it as basically a persistent style of revenge.[10] This relative absence of references to kanaimà in the work of both Alexander von Humboldt and Robert Schomburgk, juxtaposed with the series of references to it in Richard Schomburgk's account is intriguing and justifies a brief consideration of the three men's various attitudes to native customs.[11]

Although it would be facile to suggest that Humboldt and the elder Schomburgk, as accomplished travelers and scientists, simply rejected the whole notion of kanaimà as an example of preposterous native superstition, their silence on the matter may also be related to the manner and purposes of their journeys. Both Humboldt and Robert Schomburgk were engaged in scientific and geographic projects of collection and delineation, both also possessing significant government connections and having established reputations as scientific observers. Robert Schomburgk was often aggressively dismissive of many aspects of native tradition.[12] He was even censured by both Humboldt and the editors of the *Journal of the Royal Geographical Society,* in which his travel accounts first appeared, for his defacement of petroglyphic inscriptions at Waraputa on the Essequibo River. Fortunately this vandalism was limited by the fact that "I was so exhausted with fever that the blows of my heavy axe could not split it" (Robert Schomburgk 1931, 14, 55).

Richard Schomburgk was of a different character, much more the writer of travelogue; his scientific and geographical investigations were far more haphazard, nor were they directly shaped by wider political policy or intellectual dispute, despite his "commission" from the King of Prussia. In the preface to his account, he readily admits his dependency on the good-will of both his brother and Humboldt, as well as his lack of training for the purposes of botanical and geographical observation (1922, ii). Equally, the inclination to observe and question people about kanaimà may simply not have been present for Robert Schomburgk and Alexander von Humboldt, given that their tours of the interior were dedicated to the more important work of Science; their accounts were heavily larded with precise geographical, zoological, and botanical observation. Richard Schomburgk, avowedly more idle in his motives for journeying, tended to produce a record of the exotic, bizarre, and outré.

It seems significant, then, that aside from Humboldt and the Schomburgks, accounts of kanaimà in the nineteenth century derive almost completely from the writings of either missionaries or long-term residents in the colony, with the sole exceptions of Henri Coudreau and Theodor Koch-Grüneberg. The traveler thus had little chance of encountering kanaimà other than as a vague reference to "evil spirits," not least because its ritual practice is both regional in scope and often takes place over time. Unless a traveler came on a particular incidence of killing and mutilation, there would have been nothing but the poetics of the native discourse to observe. Equally, a claim to have encountered kanaimà in some form could serve to authenticate the traveler's tale by serving as "proof" of having reached the outer limits of a colonial world bounded by savagery. Accordingly, Richard Schomburgk did encounter what he understood to be a kanaimà victim. His references to kanaimà also represent the first attempt to systematically understand the practice by relating it to ideas of social conflict and innate or fundamental human proclivities—at least amongst the native population. This framework for understanding kanaimà has persisted to this day, since the crucial connection between kanaimà and other forms of shamanic practice has never been made.

In Richard Schomburgk's account of his journeys in Guiana during the years 1840–44 he discussed both kanaimà and piya, though he recognized only the latter as a shamanic practice, interpreting kanaimà as

> an evil invisible, demoniacal essence and also in many cases an individual personality, though always in the nature of the avenger of

known or unknown wrongs. Who and what Kanaima is they could never tell us, but they explained every death as his effect, his doing. Out of all the confused conceptions, this much seemed to me to stand out clear that the manner and method by which the Indian satisfies his revenge—for he never approaches his transgressor face to face, but seeks to overcome him by ambush, and satisfy his revenge by guile—is the chief creative cause of this delusive belief in Kanaima which, like an oppressive nightmare, everlastingly pursues his every act and deed, makes him bar the door at the day's close, and induces him to believe that he recognizes its presence in every unusual noise of the night. (1922, 1:251)

This vision of the kanaimà as the "hereditary enemy of mankind" (II:142–43) was partly prompted by an encounter with a party of Makushi at the Waraputa mission, among whom there was a ten-year-old boy, apparently dying from the effects of a kanaimà attack. This detail in itself makes Schomburgk's supposition as to revenge appear unlikely, as it is hard to imagine what kind of offense a child could have committed to have earned the enmity of a kanaimà. Certainly revenge may have been visited on entire families, as Schomburgk points out, but the relative youth and gender bias toward females and children in contemporary kanaimà killings is no accident of statistics. Nor would it be the result, in Schomburgk's analysis, of a "savage" style of revenge that is unbridled by social mores or excessive and indiscriminate in its choice of victims, since it is otherwise represented by him as being sneaky and cowardly. Nonetheless, Schomburgk's brief excursion into the poetics of kanaimà, the "oppressive nightmare," is effective in communicating the (still) pervasive preoccupation in identifying and preempting kanaimà attacks. The idea of kanaimà thus becomes suffused throughout the landscape, and various rocks and caverns become associated with the reality of kanaimà. Along the Cotinga and Zuruma Rivers, for instance, Schomburgk's Makushi paddlers fell silent at two places where kanaimàs had bored through the riverbank of the Cotinga to emerge some twelve miles distant on the Zuruma, both places being marked by a water spout some fifteen feet above the river (2:142–43).

Schomburgk continues his description of kanaimà by speculating on the poison used, which he identifies with the term *Wassy* (1:251). He acknowledges that he was unable to identify the main ingredient, although Robert Schomburgk had correctly identified the genus from its description. In fact, it is known as *koumi* by the Patamuna and is a kind of bulb (*Arum venenatum*). Richard Schomburgk then suggests a typology of the kanaimà assassin's techniques. The first mode of attack would be a poisoning delivered by sprinkling the wassy on the mouth and nostrils of the sleeping victim, who then suffers various symptoms, including a burning in the intestines, wasting fever, and thirst, which Schomburgk suggests would give the victim "the terrible knowledge that his days, yea even his hours, are numbered. Within four weeks the sick man is reduced to a skeleton, and dies in the most frightful agony" (1:252). However, should that strategy fail, then a more underhanded method would have to be found, so the kanaimà would attempt to cultivate a "pharisaical friendship" in order to deliver the poison.

If even that should fail, then the kanaimà would disappear from the village and "goaded on by the burning desire for revenge that ever more and more inflames his breast, he strides through the forest up hill and down dale, and does not return until he has killed his man or wounded him with a poisoned arrow" (1:252). Since the kanaimà would also now be considered an outlaw by all, he would become "the bugbear, the demon of the neighbourhood" and with no need to hide his "criminal intent" would paint his body and wear an animal's pelt. He would then confront his victim in the forest and fight him; in this confrontation, the kanaimà "wounds him with his poisoned arrow, and transfixes his tongue with the fangs of the most venomous of snakes" (1:252), thus handily forestalling the identification of perpetrator by the victim. Schomburgk later adds that the kanaimà would seek the grave of the victim three nights later so that he could taste the blood (2:397). If the victim could manage to return home and be buried there, so that the kanaimà could not taste the corpse, then the kanaimà himself would be put in mortal danger.

Schomburgk then relates two incidents: first, how Misseyari, a Makushi man who had accompanied his brother, Robert, back to England, had a vision of his own sister's death by kanaimà while staying in Schomburgk's house; second, how the relatives of the young boy whose death he had witnessed attempted to divine the location of the kanaimà who had killed him (I, 253). In the latter incident, the boy's fingers and heels were cut off and put into a pot of boiling water. Wherever the bubbling water first caused the pot to overflow and deposit a piece of the fingers or heels was taken to be the direction from which the attack had come.[13] The boy's body was then broken and squashed into a tin box for burial, in a manner redolent of contemporary burial practice for the victims of kanaimà (Butt Colson 1958). Schomburgk later notes in another burial the inclusion of palm-fronds and leather strips "to tie the kanaimà to a tree with, should he chance to meet him on the way, for this individual was likewise the cause of death" (1:368).

Schomburgk's account certainly reflects aspects of kanaimà shamanism, but the ritual practices described are divorced from their cosmological and ritual context and so appear contradictory, if not simply unlikely. The question one might ask Schomburgk, as well as subsequent authors, is why such a complicated and apparently self-destructive form of revenge would be undertaken at all. The more so since earlier in *Travels in British Guiana* he had described a case of revenge killing that should have been an exemplary case of kanaimà, but in which it is clear there is no hint of such a procedure (1:122–25). As a result, even if one for a moment takes seriously the idea that kanaimà represents no more than a culturally particular and highly intense form of revenge, one is still left with the question as to why it did not occur in that particular case. As presented by Schomburgk, kanaimà not only lies outside "normal" society and personality but is also utterly disconnected from piya shamanism, despite the emphasis given in descriptions of the latter to the prevalence of "evil spirits" and the piya's role in combating them and controlling them (1:131–33, 329–31). Thus dislocated from the rest of native cultural practice, kanaimà becomes, for Richard Schomburgk, mimetically imagined as a free-roaming spirit power that is behind all "evil." Neither can Schomburgk resist partaking of that cultural power engendered by kanaimà, so his revolving pistol becomes "the evil ones' wonderful weapon" when he and his brother undertake an impromptu shooting match (1:288).

During his travels Richard Schomburgk encountered a fellow German—"and that a Prussian born" (1:72)—the missionary J. H. Bernau whose account of *Missionary Labours in British Guiana* contains scant but significant mention of kanaimà. In particular, Bernau (1847, 51) suggests that the idea of propitiation of "the evil spirit" by the offering of human flesh was current at the time, though specifically among which peoples is not indicated. This information links earlier reports of shamanic propitiation of predatory divinities with the core of modern kanaimà practice, which envisages the victim partly as a propitiation of the jaguar-sprit (*kaikuci'ima*). Nonetheless, Bernau also notes that if the death of a relation is considered the work of a poisoner (the term *kanaimà* is not employed), then "the Indian considers himself bound to revenge the death" (51), thus further entrenching the idea of lex talionis as first enunciated by Hilhouse. Bernau (54–59) also discusses the role of piya among the Makushi, which serves as a backdrop for presenting material on kanaimà . Bernau directly incorporates Richard Schomburgk's description of kanaimà divination (quoted above) and makes this appear a general practice of the piya. Although this was not how Schomburgk originally had written it, there are contemporary accounts of this practice among the Xinguanos and Waiwai that suggest it may have been more widespread, as Bernau implies. However, the rest of Bernau's account both adds new details and casts the practice of kanaimà in a somewhat different light.

First, the term *kanaimà* is given as *Canayi,* and the fully legal nature of the lex talionis that drives, in a social sense, the insatiable desire for revenge is presented as a matter of genealogical relatedness: "one of the nearest relations is charged with the execution of the direful deed. The 'Canayi,' the avenger of blood, forthwith puts on a *curiously wrought cap,* takes up his weapons, and pursues his path in search of his victim" (57; my emphasis). Bernau adds that the avenger will subsist on only what the forest supplies. He then goes on to raise the question of gender in the mode of kanaimà killing, suggesting that a man, because he is always armed, will be shot through the back—a mimesis of the invisible poison arrow of the kanaimà, which leaves only a telltale blue mark at the point of entry. If the victims are women or children, they are forced to the ground and the fangs of a venomous snake driven through their tongues. The kanaimà then buries his victim in a shallow grave, returning after three nights to insert a stick into the cadaver, and if blood appears when he retracts the stick he tastes it "in order to ward off any evil effects that might follow from the murder. . . . if he taste not of the blood he must perish by madness" (58).

This account introduces important new elements—the cap and the tasting of the grave—which are certainly also present in current kanaimà ritual practice. However, the highly individualized and legalistic nature of the supposed motivation for becoming kanaimà remains unquestioned. But, as with Richard Schomburgk's account, one wonders in reading Bernau why women and children are being attacked, since they are unlikely killers in the first place. This question remains unanswered in all subsequent accounts, except by reference to the rigors of a supposed lex talionis that would allow any member of the genealogical group to be an appropriate object of revenge. This sounds quite plausible, of course, until one reflects on the way in which the intensity of native desire for revenge at the time Bernau wrote his account may well have been related to the inability to act out such grief in other modes, such as collective warfare or marriage, just as was hinted by Hilhouse in his discussion of Karinya warfare. Contemporary Patamuna narratives of the days of warfare clearly link grief and violence, which may be enacted against those who are physically proximate, not just those who are genealogically distant, in the absence of the actual killers. In other words unsocialized violence has no legitimated object and so challenges the established order. In this way kanaimà violence may be seen as perpetually transgressing such boundaries and so always confusing to external interpreters as they struggle to fit it solely within a framework of legalistic revenge. "Verily," Bernau concludes, "the dark places of the earth are full of the habitations of cruelty" (59).

Bernau's account is also important as the earliest textual source for the curious story of the death of the missionary Thomas Youd, apparently poisoned by an Akawaio kanaimà. Whatever the truth of this suggestion, there can be no doubt that it has exercised a deep influence on the European imagining of kanaimà. Bernau himself makes no specific connection to kanaimà in his account, which he derived from native informants, but tells us that Youd had been instructing two Amerindian boys for a period of ten months, when the father of one summoned him home for a festival, telling Youd of this and to which Youd made no objection. The boy, however, refused to go, because of the "dire consequences of attending such revels," and the father, believing that the boy was influenced by the missionary in this, "swore that [Youd] should pay for it with his life." Both Youd and his wife ate a leg of deer that was sent the next day by the boy's father and were taken ill. Although Thomas recovered through the use of an emetic, his wife did not. Apparently there were two more attempts to poison Youd, the last being successful, and he died on his passage home to England. However, the supposed poisoner was himself killed when, in celebration of the news of Youd's death, he fired off his gun and the barrel exploded, causing a fatal wound to the artery of his left arm. Bernau adds that he questioned Youd's cook and "found too good grounds for suspecting the cook was aware of all that had passed, but, fearing her life would be required for that of the Missionary's, she did not reveal it to him" (127–29).

Although, as Rivière (1995, 117–18) persuasively points out, Youd himself makes no reference to poisoning in his own account of his wife's death, nor in his letters and journal more generally. However, Rivière also recognizes that such a tale is perfectly consistent with native ideas about misfortune and death as emanating from some form of "anthropomorphic agency," and kanaimà functioned in just this way for both colonial and native alike. One feature of the account that Bernau derived from his informants that is worth noting is how three attempts were made to kill Youd, who has a bottle of medicine—the emetic—that counteracts the poison. This eerily echoes the account of the first prophet of alleluia—Bichiwung. Bichiwung may have been a piya before his vision of a new shamanism was stimulated by his contacts with missionaries, as certainly other early prophets were, some of whom were even kanaimàs. The kanaimàs tried three times to kill Bichiwung, and on each occasion, except the third, he was brought back to life by drinking from a special bottle of medicine that he had received from God. The meaning of Youd's death, whatever the forensic circumstances, therefore lay in how it exemplified the power of "native magic" against "colonial religion" and that the kanaimà at that historical juncture began to emerge as a killer of white men as well as of Amerindians. Youd, of course, was not the last white man to be portrayed as a victim of kanaimà, and stories of kanaimà attacks on whites figure prominently in contemporary discourse.

The missionary William Brett (1868, 222) also mentions Youd and is the first to identify the alleged poisoner as an Akawaio, "the other tribes telling terrible stories of them as poisoners and night murderers." He repeats this in a later work (Brett 1881), giving more but no new details, although, as Rivière (1995, n. 17) notes, none of this appeared in Brett's first work (1851). Im Thurn (1883, 34) also repeats this tale and adds his own account of an attempted poisoning.[14] Whatever the meaning of Youd's death for the Amerindians, then, it was no less significant for European imaginings of kanaimà. While Brett does not explicitly cite Youd's death as an example of a kanaimà killing, it would have been easy, given the Akawaio's reputation as assault sorcerers with intimate knowledge of poisons, to infer that the boy's Akawaio father might have used kanaimà knowledge or had access to those that did (Bernau suggested that the father was not physically present in the locations where Youd received the last two doses).

Brett (1868, 288) also describes his own encounter with a kanaimà on the Demerara River: "Two Indians passed us in a very light canoe.

One was unadorned; but the man who steered wore a handsome tiara of feathers, and had his skin covered all over with bright red spots, like those of the jaguar, save in colour. His eyes gleamed widely through circles of the same paint; and both himself and his companion were paddling with all their might against the stream." He adds in a footnote to this passage: "One of our Indians recognised that spotted man as one whom he had seen watching a group of Indians from the corner of a street in Georgetown ten days before. He had not then assumed his paint. He probably tracked his intended victim from the remote interior to the city, and afterwards back to the forest, where he accomplished his deadly purpose of *Kanaima.*"

Brett continues with a general account of kanaimà that further codifies the materials discussed above on the following basis. Given the Amerindian "proneness to blood revenge," the death of a family member is always suspected to be the work of some enemy in the spirit realm, and a piya is asked to divine the source of the attack. A family member is then "charged with the work of vengeance" and he becomes a "Kanaima," that is he is possessed by the spirit thus named. If the family member cannot kill his victim face to face, then he will shoot him from behind, although such vengeance "is considered imperfect, the manes [spirits of the ancestors] of the deceased being supposed to demand more cruelty in the appeasing sacrifice." Accordingly, if possible, the victim is forced to the ground and serpent fangs thrust through the tongue, or a poisonous powder, prepared from a plant called *Urupa* and carried in a Powis's wing-bone in the kanaimà's hair, is forced into the mouth: "Horrible agony and inability to speak, followed in due course by death, are the inevitable result" (357–61).

This account, especially its emphasis on the idea of a legalistic revenge, clearly derives directly from Bernau 1847, as do both Brett's description of the search for the victim's grave so that the kanaimà may taste the blood and the suggestion that tasting the blood is intended to appease the kanaimà spirit by which he is possessed. However Brett (1868, 360) does add some additional details, in particular that the family of the victim may try to defend the grave against the kanaimà by placing some *ourali* (curare) poison on the body or by removing the liver from the corpse and replacing it with a red-hot axe, which will cause the kanaimà to perish as he sucks the intense heat into his body. Brett also recognized that there were systems of poisoning other than those associated with kanaimà. Most strikingly he describes his own encounter with an "unappeased" kanaimà.

> An Indian, reduced almost to a skeleton, and in a dreadful state of exhaustion, was picked up in the forest by some Arawaks [Lokono] and brought to the Pomeroon Mission. He had lost a portion of his scalp and had his lower lip torn down at each corner. This, he said, had been done by a small "tiger," which had sprung on him while lying in the forest. Those wounds were in a most loathsome condition. The Acawaios at the mission took care of him at first, but afterwards judged, from his refusing certain kinds of food and other signs, that he was a devotee and victim of an unappeased Kanaima, and the murderer of a man killed some time before. From this, and his savage ungrateful demeanour (though Mr McClintock, aided by myself, cleansed and dressed his sores to encourage them), we had some difficulty in getting him nursed till his strength had returned, as they feared lest they should become his future victims. (359)

The reference to a "small tiger" recalls Hugh Godwin's encounter with the tiguere on the Orinoco—but, then, Godwin was the victim. For Brett, it seems, the just avenger is even somewhat morally superior to the guilty victim. In that vortex of vengeance imagined in depictions of kanaimà, the victim and victimizer are sometimes conflated, as in Brett's representation of the devotee as victim, leaving only the intimacy of killing as the enduring social relationship—such is life in a cosmos of deathly predation. In the colonial imagination, the dance of devotee and victim is choreographed by the theoretical paradox of fitting kanaimà into ideas of legalized revenge in which the aggrieved, through his manic pursuit of vengeance, becomes transformed into the aggressor—a jaguar of rebounding violence—but may yet return to civil society if his spiritual inversion is total and if he recovers intimacy with the victim through ingesting him as a jaguar. The wider literary deployment of kanaimà thus reflects precisely these poetics of violence and death originating in the colonial ethnology.

Brett (1868, 374) therefore is the first to make a link between kanaimà and human transformations into jaguars. He notes that kanaimà is both a man and "the murderous spirit under whose influence he acts," continuing, "Some of their legends describe the destructive deeds of *animals* of which the same spirit, or a human soul under its influence, has taken possession. A jaguar which displays unusual audacity in approaching men will often unnerve even a brave hunter by the fear that it may be a *Kanaima tiger*. 'This,' reasons the Indian, 'if it be but an ordinary wild beast, I may kill with bullet or arrow; but what will be my fate if I assail the man-destroyer—the terrible Kanaima?' " And in a footnote Brett writes: "Many of the Indians believe that those 'Kanaima' animals are possessed by the spirits of *men* who have devoted themselves to deeds of blood and cannibalism. To enjoy the savage delight of killing and devouring human beings, such a person will assume the shape, or his soul animate the body, of a jaguar, approach the sleeping-places of men, or waylay the solitary Indian in his path." Brett goes on to compare this to the classical story of Lycaon, the original European werewolf: "It is strange to find a superstition so closely resembling that of the '*were-wolf*' or '*loup-garou*' of the European races in full force in the forests of Guiana. The dreaded jaguar in those parts takes the place of the wolf, which is unknown. There is no superstition more prevalent among the Indians than this, and none which causes more terror." Apparently, one is bound to say, causes terror even for William Brett himself, since this is praise indeed. Just how strong an influence the kanaimà had on Brett's creative imagination is shown by a most remarkable inclusion in his work of poetry, *Legends and Myths of the Aboriginal Indians of British Guiana* (1880), a book that versifies various indigenous "myths." In the section devoted to the "Legends of the Acawoios" appears the following.

KANÁIMA

From the base of high Roráima
To the widespread Eastern sea,
Votaries of dread Kanáima
Track their victims secretly.
Deadly vow must each fulfill,
Real or fancied foe to kill.

He who that dread vow is taking,
Family and friends must leave;
Wife and children all forsaking,
No discharge can he receive.
Still around his victim's way,
Hovering night and day to slay.

If the victim warned of danger,
To some other place should fly,
Soon th'assassin, though a stranger,
Will to that retreat draw nigh,
Patiently he bides his time,
Waiting to commit the crime.

Stealthily each step he traces,
Hiding till he strikes the blow.
Poison in the mouth he places
Of his victim, lying low.
Then if found with swollen tongue,
None will know who did him wrong.

When the grave has closed upon him,
The destroyer hovers round:
Dread Kanáima's spell is on him;
By it he must still be bound,
Till he pierce, with pointed wood,
Through the grave, and *taste the blood.*

Stern Kanáima thus appeasing,
Who withdraws his direful aid,
All his horrid influence ceasing
When that off'ring has been made.
Uncontrolled, the votary then,
Goes, and lives with other men.

One who passed us on the water,[a]
Had his victim lately slain;
There triumphant, fresh from slaughter,
He was hast'ning home again.
Feathered crown adorned his head—
Bright red spots his skin o'erspread—

Spots, to show that, nightly ranging
(So do their sorcerers declare),
He, into a jaguar changing,
Could his victims seize and tear.[b]
As the 'were-wolf' of the East
Prowls, on human flesh to feast.

*　　*　　*　　*　　*

Should the victim 'scape him living,
Or, if dead, be borne away;

He, no horrid off'ring giving,
Finds Kanáima on him stay.
Still the spell upon him lies;
Mad, he wanders till he dies.

One, who sank with forests round him,
To our Mission hill was borne;
First, an ocelot, which found him,
Horribly his head had torn.
Head and hands he raised in pain,
Scared the beast, then sank again.

Sank—for life no longer striving,
Christian Indians found him then.
Arawâks, his strength reviving,
Bore him to his countrymen.
Healed and fed, Kanáima still,
Christians all he vowed to kill!

In note a, Brett writes: "Archdeacon Jones and myself, on the Upper Demerara, in 1865. That 'Kanáima' murderer, we found, had followed his victim and friends from the vicinity of Roráima to Georgetown and back, killing him on his return." In note b, he writes: "A set of jaguar's claws, hung up in the sorcerers hut, have the same threatening signification" (152–54).

As an example of poetical art, the work is fairly excruciating, but the window it provides onto the colonial imagination of kanaimà is extraordinary, and the imaginary has quite real consequences. The poem intellectually crystallizes, theoretically codifies, a view of kanaimà as a particular form of cultural practice, principally a lex talionsis, but also an expression of pre-Christian, if not anti-Christian, sentiment and spiritual value. The exoticism of the mutilating cannibalism is balanced by the nobility of primitive, authentic vengeance made morally acceptable and spiritually profound by the rigorous consequences that ensue for both victim and assassin. Kanaimà is also demystified and drawn into the gamut of colonial experience by reference to the European werewolf, and its natural justice is shown in the rebounding violence of the killer, who becomes victim to another killer, who also may become a victim in turn. This view has since gone largely unchallenged.

Brett returned to the theme of kanaimà in his *Mission Work in the Forests of Guiana,* mentioning again the death of Thomas Youd at the hands of "an old Indian sorcerer" (1881, 23). Despite the fact that in the earlier version he was neither "old" nor a "sorcerer," it seems that Brett himself was keen to dramatize his own situation through the story of Youd's death. He writes, "At times I was warned that they were going to 'piai' me, that is, to cause sickness or death by their art; information which gave little uneasiness. For though the Obiah men of the negroes, and these Piai sorcerers of the aborigines, do often cause sickness and sometimes death by the terror their threats inspire, they can only have those effects on minds imbued with a belief in them. In order to injure others they must resort to actual *poison,* as in compassing the death of Mr. and Mrs. Youd" (53). Brett may not have intended it, but this distinction between "belief" and "actual poison" foreshadows Im Thurn's ethnological characterization of kanaimà as either "imaginary" or "real," the irony here being that in doubting the former Brett cites the latter, whereas as Im Thurn doubts the latter while citing the former. Brett makes it clear that it was primarily the piya that had to be persuaded to "renounce the devil and all his works" (52), and he was proud of the fact that already three of the five Lokono shamans he proselytized had "destroyed their marakkas." But it was the Akawaio who Brett saw as the originators of kanaimà, and so Youd's poisoner now becomes "an old Acawoio sorcerer" (195).

Brett introduces one further distinction in his understanding of kanaimà—between an avenger who becomes kanaimà in order to accomplish that vengeance and a "wicked man, of cannibal propensities, [who] by devoting himself to kanaimà" can then transform into a jaguar and so "waylay and devour" his victim. Brett suggests, as in the poem above, that a set of jaguar's claws suspended in the piya's hut is a notice of this propensity (1881, 144). The shape-shifting phantasm of kanaimà thus continually transforms itself in the colonial mind, doing the cultural work then that Hannibal Lecter does now. However, this volume by Brett also represents a terminal point of the preanthropological era in the ethnology of the region. In 1883 Everard Im Thurn, future President of the Royal Anthropological Institute of Great Britain and Ireland, wearing his glittering credentials as "M.A. Oxon.," brings the withering eye of Science to the fanciful poetics of kanaimà.

Two works that appeared between Brett's volumes of 1868 and 1881 merit attention for the information they added to the growing ethnological compendium on kanaimà.[15] In 1877 Charles Barrington Brown, retiring as Government Surveyor, published *Canoe and Camp Life in British Guiana*. The work is replete with references to kanaimà killings, and also refers to the counter-sorcery of the piya (139). Brown's first encounter occurs in the Akawaio village of Cicimong by the Puruni River, where he enters a hut and finds a young man "worn away to a mere skeleton, the effects, he said, of some poison secretly administered by an enemy. His eyes were large and preternaturally bright, and it cut one to the heart to see such a fine fellow like that patiently awaiting his early doom at the hand of the most cowardly of all murderers, the Kanaima or secret poisoner" (32).

The next case also concerns the Akawaio, involving a series of killings over a number of years. At Fort Island in the Essequibo, Brown met a young Akawaio man, William Adams, whose father had been killed (presumably by kanaimàs) when he was a child living along the Mazaruni River. His mother had therefore taken him down to the Essequibo, where she married a creole. Adams told Brown that his father had been murdered by the Akawaio chief Captain John, who had since moved from the Mazaruni to Macedonia on the Essequibo in order to avoid retaliation. When he met Brown, Adams had just heard that his elder brother had also been killed at Cabunie village: "it appeared that he had been induced to join a fishing party, and then had been set upon by a number of men, who, with a refinement of cruelty only practiced by savages, had forced his limbs out of joint, rubbed his body over with a white powder made from a species of wild tannier, and then pulled them into their sockets again. He managed to reach home with great difficulty, and take to his hammock, where he was seized with vomiting and died in a few hours" (1877, 54–55).

In this account Brown introduces new elements of kanaimà ritual violence—the dislocation of joints and the rubbing down of the body with a powerful astringent—but does not here refer to the other elements familiar from earlier accounts. Brown's next mention of the kanaimàs also sheds new light on their social position, since he refers to a case in which a Makushi "peaiman" had been clubbed to death. This might indicate the killing of a kanaimà, since contemporary testimony refers to a similar manner of dealing with kanaimàs, although nowadays such collective action is rarely feasible. In any case, Brown does not appear to question the ethics of this killing but still accepts the assumption made with regard to the legalistic nature of the role of kanaimà, emphasizing that access to "this system of poisoning, amongst people who have no protective laws, prevents the strong from oppressing the weak, but works badly in every other way." He also stresses the mercenary nature of adept poisoners who then hire themselves out to "rid their employers of any obnoxious individuals" (141). What Brown seems to envisage here is a justice system based on revenge murder, but equally accessible to all. It is far from clear, though, even from the case histories that Brown himself presents, that the "system of poisoning" and the kanaimà's ambiguous role in it actually did or might have functioned in quite this "democratic" way. For example, Brown cites the case of a Makushi kanaimà who was living in a Karinya village near Apoterie for protection, having killed both his wife and father, although this seems to be a poor example of a system of revenge that stopped "the strong from oppressing the weak" (146). Likewise Brown encountered on the Burro-Burro River "an Ackawoise Indian, who said he came from the Potaro river, and was fleeing the Kanaima. It was evident that he had committed an evil deed in his own territory, and was fleeing from punishment" (186), but why this was evident we are not told.

This is not simply idle criticism of Brown's attempts to grasp a confusing and exotic practice but an attempt to draw out the different explanations for kanaimà, how they reflect colonial mentality, and so how one might read through such sources to recover the cultural practices that stimulated these descriptions. Moreover, contemporary testimonies about the kanaimà have been produced from a cultural context that has been exposed to precisely these kinds of text and their popular renderings in magazines, schoolbooks, and the like. My expectations as an ethnographer, as well as the expectations and explanatory forms of those Patamuna who colluded in that ethnographic attempt, may thus have overlapped to some degree. This mutual production of the idea of kanaimà is an inevitable consequence of sustained contact between British colonial administration and the peoples of the interior since the mid-nineteenth century when these texts were produced. Moreover, the Patamuna do appear in Brown's account in a number of chapters, and it is also in these chapters that a number of reports of kanaimà are clustered. In particular Brown (1877, 179) records that his Makushi guides, when passing a southern tributary of the Burro-Burro, mentioned that "some Kanaimas of the Partamona tribe, a branch of the

Ackawoise, lived far up it, who only came out to kill or *kanaima* members of the other tribes." At Cara-Cara village, toward the Ireng and on the borders of Patamuna country, Brown was told

> that a few days before our arrival they discovered three strange Indians lurking about the village at night, and knowing that they had come to kill some of their people they had hunted about and started them from their hiding place in some bush. Giving chase they had come up with one fording the river, and as he landed on the opposite side sent a shower of arrows after him, one of which pierced his side, and he fell. Springing quickly up, he broke off the shaft of the arrow and made off.
>
> Before reaching the village we met a band of Indians, twenty in number, all fully armed and painted, going south, who said they were hunting: but I imagine the object of their journey had something to do with the above-mentioned Indian Kanaimas, whose place of residence they had probably discovered. (188–89)

As Brown and his guides approached the Echilebar River farther north, "we saw an Indian coming along the path about half a mile before us. Suddenly he paused for an instant, and then made off like a deer towards the hills on the left. It was evident that he saw our party and had received a scare from our numbers. The Indians with us said he must be a Kanaima, and on reaching the spot from which he made off, went in search of him but without success" (194). It turned out, however, that the man was not a kanaimà, as he later joined their party in order to lead them to his village. Whatever the "facts" of a given case, then, the cultural force of kanaimà partly derives from the pervasiveness of its discourse, as expressed by colonials and natives alike.

In a later journey to the Makushi village of Mora, again on the border zone between Patamuna and Makushi territories, "We came up with a party of Mora Macusis, with whom was the guide who had taken me to the Ireng river in 1869. Amongst this party was an unfortunate woman, whose attenuated body formed a most shocking sight. She was a living skeleton, being nothing but skin and bones, with the exception of the face, which was not reduced in proportion to that of the rest of the body. They told me that this woman had come to them from the Ireng river district, where she had been poisoned by Kanaimas, and that this accounted for her wasted condition" (258).

Colonial sources indicate that the area of the most intense kanaimà practice was in the region of the Ireng River and its northern tributaries, precisely the frontier between Makushi and Patamuna that persists to this day. The connections between the shamanic cults of kanaimà and alleluia reflect this historical geography of interethnic relationships across the Ireng River and are still the subject of both oral history and prophecy. It is also evident from the colonial commentators that, while awareness of kanaimà was present in the coastal regions among the Karinya, Warao, and Lokono, its practice emanated from the highlands of the Makushi, Patamuna, Akawaio, and Pemon. Henri Coudreau (1887, 2:236) also inferred another distinct region in which kanaimà was prevalent—at the headwaters of the Jauapiry and Taruman-Assu, tributaries of the Rio Negro, east of the Rio Branco.[16] He notes,

> These tribes are not wild in the sense of making war on civilized and quiet peoples, they are *tribus canaémés,* as the Indians of the upper Branco say, which means they are tribes which are assassins by profession, raised from generation to generation in murder and theft, killing for the pleasure of killing, not even eating their enemies but using their tibias to make flutes, their teeth as necklaces. All who are not part of the tribe or the association of tribes is killed (*immolé*) by the *canaémés* whenever they wish. It is the way among them to understand patriotism and apply the ancient precept: stranger, enemy. These *canaémés* think like some of the Shiva sects of India. The peaceful tribes have great fear of these wild beasts, with whom they have no communication, unless it is to be the victim of an assassin. The Indians of a dozen different tribes, affirm to me that there exists among the *canaémés* a body of *pagets* (priest-sorcerers) wielding great influence.[17] The thing seems very probable as it is known that the various *tribus canaémés* are allied and more or less united. (236)

Such accounts reflect the adaptation of kanaimà practice to the advent of gun-warfare in the highlands. In the coastal region the Reverend Charles Dance (1881) cites a case of assassination along the Berbice River, where he was curate of St. Margaret's Church, Skeldon. Although he assimilates this killing to kanaimà, it bears no trace of the ritual violence usually associated with a kanaimà attack. It does, however, suggest a context for understanding Coudreau's remarks on the *tribus canaémés,* as seen from a more northerly location. Dance narrates (15–18) how a Lokono chief, Mekro, living on the Ituni Creek, Berbice River, "was a piaiman . . . quarrelsome, boastful, and revengeful in the extreme, and was a terror to both his tribe and the neighbourhood. He is said to have been a great poisoner. . . . It is not to be wondered then that he became obnoxious to the law of Kanaima or retaliation which is sacredly observed. . . . But hitherto the strength of Mekro's 'piai' or his good fortune had prevailed over the machinations of his enemies, who now were numerous. . . . Those who tried to poison him he poisoned: he wrestled with Kanaima and with the coup de grace affixed the deadly-feud mark that was intended for himself."

As a result, the "poisoners" of his own tribe sent a delegation to the Arecunas (Pemon) in Roraima district with presents of guns, cloth, and earrings in order to solicit his assassination. Dance tells us that "the messengers of 'kanaima' surrounded the benabs [houses]. A double discharge of firearms was made. . . . Gun and cutlass did the work of destruction, till not a soul of the settlement was left who was not supposed dead or mortally wounded." But while this is certainly an example of contract killing inspired by vengeance, it is not specifically kanaimà in its character (see also Brett 1868, 261–62). For commentators such as Dance, having decided that kanaimà was a sacralized system of revenge, all cases of vengeance or contract killing, which are also assumed to be the same, become cases of kanaimà. It therefore becomes easy to doubt the reality of kanaimà, as some of the cases of vengeance killing do not conform to the specific modes of ritual violence that define a kanaimà killing in initial reports and that are important today in distinguishing kanaimà attacks from other kinds of murder or violent assault.

However, Dance (1881, 271) emphasizes kanaimà as a legalistic form of revenge, suggesting that it is actually a formal part of the mourning ritual and must be initiated before completion of funeral rites. He embeds this opinion in a synthetic version of a number of mythic narratives he entitled *The Story of Macona-Ura and Anua-Naitu: An Indian Tale Illustrating some of the Customs and Opinions of the Indians* (259–79). This compilation centers on the fortunes of Macona-Ura and his wife, Anua-Naitu, who is part of a sinister family headed by a man-crocodile, her stepfather. This family murders Macona-Ura and so his relations prepare themselves for revenge as "Kanaimas." Dance's "Indian voice" in this chapter also suggests that the whites have kanaimà as well, "only that it is the retributive force of a society or government, and not of a family," a comparison that serves to further enhance the idea of kanaimà's legalistic social status. Nonetheless, some of the exotic character of what would otherwise be reduced to a lex talionsis is preserved by a definition of kanaimà as the "Spirit of Revenge." This vengeful spiritual entity is then used by Dance to account for the other meanings found in the discourse of kanaimà, and in particular the advent of premature death in a world that otherwise would see human life run a natural course of longevity.

The story continues that, following the agonistic *macuarie* dance that tests Macona-Ura's uncle and nephew for the task of revenge, they depart as kanaimàs—nearly naked but painted and subsisting only on *beltiri* (cassava bread)—for the village of the crocodile-family.[18] At this point kanaimàs may adopt the guises of animals, and Dance mentions the jaguar and the boa constrictor, suggesting that the mode of attack reflects the manner of their transformation—a jaguar using sharp blows, the boa wrestling his victim. Macona-Ura's uncle and nephew arrive at the village to find a *paiwarri* (drinking party) under way to celebrate another betrothal of Anua-Naitu. Under cover of the paiwarri, the killers approach and dispatch with gunfire the murderers of Macona-Ura, as well as all the rest of the crocodile-family, except Anua-Naitu. To this point, Dance seems to have merely assimilated another case of revenge killing to kanaimà, but he then adds a most important detail with regard to the death of the suspected actual killer of Macona-Ura, a detail that distinguishes this account from that of the killing of Mekro in important ways. Dance (1881, 277) writes, "The brother alone was singled out for the destructive *death mark* of Kanaima. His bowels were dragged out by means of a forked stick, and knotted; and his tongue was twisted and poisoned so that it was instantly swollen and hung down from his mouth. . . . In that state he was left to die." A footnote continues,

> Formerly the Indians over the Great Falls of the Demerara [Akawaio] were employed by the Arawaks [Lokono] of the lower district to work their vengeance as Kanaima mercenaries. A beautiful Indian woman was, like Helen of Troy, the notorious object of deadly jealousy. Whomsoever she accepted for her husband dies sooner or later with the marks of Kanaima. First Cassimá was killed; then her second husband, John Lambert; and lastly, her third husband, Simichi Lambert, a powerful man, had escaped on several occasions; but at last was entrapped in his own field at Mablissi creek. There was evidence of a great struggle around a large tree. The man was found the day after in a posture of all-fours, disentrailed, and insultingly muti-

lated, and parts of his body misplaced in fiendish mockery, distinctly symbolizing the cause for which he was so cruelly treated.

Lambert's first name, "Simichi," indicates he was also a famed piya, termed *semicici* in the Lokono language. Here one can begin to sense, as from the accounts given by Brown and Hilhouse, something of the interplay between collective revenge, individual and familial retribution, the war-culture of the Patamuna—and the Akawaio—and the way in which the separate purposes of kanaimà may have played into such contexts.[19] The issue of vengeance thus obscured the other purposes and meanings of kanaimà, even if revenge murder and collective raiding and warfare did provide a context in which kanaimà could be performed.[20] That vengeance does not fully explain kanaimà is also evident from the fact that contemporary kanaimà killings do not necessarily follow a pattern of personal dispute, for even if that remains a possibility, it is the *arbitrary* nature of the victims that most concerns the Patamuna today.

THE LAW OF THE JUNGLE:
KANAIMÀ AS ANTHROPOLOGICAL CATEGORY
AND LITERARY TROPE, 1883–1950

Although a missionary like William Brett and Charles Dance, Everard Im Thurn had far more pretension to systematic ethnology than either of his contemporaries. He was also of a new generation that intellectually heralded the advent of professional anthropology itself. Accordingly Im Thurn is here considered with authors of the twentieth century, and his relevance to the advent of modern categories of anthropological thought is somewhat perversely demonstrated by the fact that his synthesis of material on kanaimà was totally ignored by Walter Roth in his otherwise definitive compendium of materials on the native peoples of the region. One can only presume that some "professional" consideration was involved here, just as Im Thurn himself makes an unacknowledged, and prominent, borrowing from Jules Crevaux, who he had personally met in British Guiana.[21] While Crevaux (1883) had not mentioned the kanaimà specifically, he had referred to jaguar-shamans, jaguar-chiefs, piya combating the "devil," assault sorcery, and the spirit guardian of poisons, *Yalock* (197, 201, 242, 254, 269, 299).

In 1883 Im Thurn published *Among the Indians of Guiana,* which, while it contained a standard travelogue of his journeys into the interior, also provided "anthropologic" sketches of the native population. These comprised eleven out of the sixteen chapters and synthesized many of the works I have discussed above. It is therefore important to consider the nature of his borrowing, as well as what was left out, and the kinds of anthropological arguments he makes (see Im Thurn 1883, 328–40). First, Im Thurn firmly locates kanaimà as an aspect of shamanism, treating both kanaimà and piya in the same chapter and depicting the piya as in constant combat with the forces of "kenaima" understood as the source of "very nearly all bodily evil" (328). He goes on to explain that the native idea of a separation of body and spirit allows for men to transform into or enter the bodies of animals, insects, and birds. Im Thurn also insists that "kenaima" is not a murderer as such but a "slayer" "who is bound to slay by a fixed and, in a certain stage of society, undoubtedly salutary custom" that "fully suffices to keep crime in check amongst them" (329). However, he cites Richard Schomburgk's report of the boy who avenged his father's death, but that case actually showed none of the characteristics of a kanaimà killing, the "mark of kanaima" as Dance vividly suggested. Nonetheless, the appeal of the idea of law and order emerging from primitive anarchy via a rigid system of vengeance is reflected in Im Thurn's comparison of kanaimà to both the "Israelitish law of retaliation" and the "Saxon system which resulted in the law of blood-money or were-gild" (330).

"Kenaimas of this kind are realities," says Im Thurn, who then goes on to address those of an "imaginary nature . . . who to the fanciful Indian are equally real" (330), suggesting that this is because Indians believe that all disease and death has a moral not natural origin. Im Thurn refers to Richard Schomburgk's account of the Makushi ritual for divining a kanaimà killer, then suggests that "real kenaimas" and "imaginary kenaimas" also work in different ways—the former indefatigably seeks to club or poison his victim, rub him down with astringent powders, and dislocate his limbs. The latter appears as an animal, bird, or insect and enters the body or attacks it in this form" (331–32). Im Thurn also mentions a "small bird" (332–33) that is especially distrusted, but he fails to identify or describe it. On the other hand, Im Thurn does make the important point that some purportedly kanaimà-related deaths may have been due to "buck-sickness," an unidentified wasting disease that was then common among the native population; indeed, this may have been likely in some of the cases I have related. Finally, Im Thurn suggests a social structural role for kanaimà, it being "partly the cause of the strict retention of the distinctions between the many tribes which live side by side in British Guiana. The kenaima— the real one—*is probably rarely of the same tribe as his victim;* and the imaginary kenaimas who mysteriously cause every death, are naturally thought of as of a tribe different to their victims" (333; my emphasis).

Im Thurn is quite wrong to make the suppositions he does. According to current testimonies, kanaimàs do attack co-ethnics, fellow villagers, and even household members; Brown (1877, 146), for example, cites the case of a Makushi kanaimà who killed both his wife and father. Nonetheless, Im Thurn's codification is useful, for it makes the crucial distinction between physical kanaimà and the wider discourse of kanaimà without sole reference to the issue of vengeance.

In 1915 Walter Roth, that doyenne of Guyanese ethnology, published *An Inquiry into the Animism and Folk-Lore of the Guiana Indians.* Significantly, although he had collated and (presumably) read all reports extant at the time, he did not in fact choose to represent kanaimà as anything more than a principle of revenge that was carried out with more alacrity than might otherwise be. His references to the poetics of kanaimà mutilation were largely confined to observations of injuries to the mouth, to the use of poisons, and to the shape-shifting proclivities of kanaimà assassins—this, despite the fact that Roth had reviewed materials that contained considerably more information than that. He did not, for instance, take up kanaimà's connection to shamanic ritual power at all. Roth's collation therefore represented a lackluster attempt to order the data. He apparently never interviewed a kanaimà practitioner directly, nor (unlike many of the earlier commentators) did he encounter any victims. As a result he was unable to synthesize and weight the various elements of ritual practice that he had collated in a way that might have reflected the relationship of kanaimà killing to the wider field of cosmology, myth, and ritual. This is the more surprising since he placed all these materials on kanaimà in his 1915 Bureau of American Ethnology volume, *An Inquiry into the Animism and Folk-Lore,* not in the 1924 volume on the arts, crafts, and customs of the Guiana Indians.

No less curious, as already indicated, is his failure to mention Im Thurn's (1883, 328–40) extensive discussion of "kenaimas." Given

Roth's subsequent high reputation as a legitimate "forefather" of current ethnology, as reflected in the naming of Guyana's archaeological and anthropological museum after him, and given that it is far easier to obtain a reprint of Roth's collations than it is to obtain one of Im Thurn's volume, it is therefore Roth's work that has become the starting point for many discussions of the native people of the region. As a result, subsequent ethnographic interest in the kanaimà was minimal, even when it was reported. However, Gillin (1936) made much of kanaimà, but for all the wrong reasons, as given in the accounts of Roth and Im Thurn.

Roth (1915, 359) did collect some new information from the Pomeroon Karinya on the use of *massi* poison by kanaimàs, but seems to have conflated his materials with ideas about kanaimà initiation techniques. Overall, by separating his discussion of kanaimà from that of piya, Roth ends up with a less-convincing account than that of Im Thurn, who appears to have appreciated the importance of this connection. Roth simply assimilates kanaimà to modes of vengeance, thereby missing its much more important shamanic dimension. In short, where accounts of particular kanaimàs were available, he treats them as examples of mercenary vengeance killings, and so the image of the kanaimà as a free-ranging, if "legitimate," assassin becomes the key anthropological motif for kanaimà in the regional literature.[22]

However a work of major ethnographic importance appeared just after Walter Roth's classic compilation for the Bureau of American Ethnology: Theodor Koch-Grüneberg's 1924 *Vom Roraima Zum Orinoco* (translated in 1979 as *Del Roraima al Orinoco*). Although Koch-Grüneberg only skirted the region to the east of Roraima and north of the Branco—the enduring zone of kanaimà activity—he does refer to kanaimà on a number of occasions. Unfortunately, his information on its forms, purposes, and modalities seems to be almost exclusively derived from the earlier sources already reviewed herein (Koch-Gruneberg 1979, 1:62; 3:185–87). Koch-Grüneberg does record particular cases of kanaimà attacks and generally notes the way in which the prevalent suspicion, that all misfortune and calamity was due to malevolence expressed through kanaimà attack, served to sustain ethnic and political boundaries (1:62–64, 77, 89, 97, 109, 145, 269, 314), much as Im Thurn had suggested.

Koch-Grüneberg (1979, 1:73, 131, 317) also mentions a famed kanaimà, Dschiawó, the chief of a Pemon (Taulipáng) village near the

Venezuelan mission of Alto Surumú, "separating from his body as he sleeps and taking charge of all the evil spirits that are in the form of jaguars, boas, etc., doing evil to people." He reports (1:170), as Coudreau had, a legendary kanaimà "tribe"—the Pischaukó—a Makushi group living in the Sierra Töpekíng. They were mortal enemies to the Pemon (Arecuna and Taulipáng), though Pemon legend also related earlier times when they had killed many Pischaukó. To the south and east of the Sierra Töpekíng were more peaceful Pischaukó, but to the north they were fiercer, trading with the whites in Venezuela and British Guiana for guns. They did not fight openly, preferring "Kanaimé" by night, wearing the skins of jaguars and deer. They were also enemies to the Shirishana (Yanomami) on the Uraricapará (Uraricoera) River. Sifontes (1982, 190–92) has also recorded an account of the Pichaukok among the contemporary Pemon. Finally, Koch-Grüneberg (1979, 1:317) mentions magical countermeasures that could be taken against the kanaimà, using the plant *woi,* which he identifies as being like a rhubarb. This observation in turn hints at, for the first time in the literature, some of the cosmological ideas that are relevant to understanding kanaimà, particularly the myth-cycle of Makunaim and Piai'ima, its narration of the origin and historicity of shamanism, the use of plant magic, and the meaning of kalawali (that being both "the star-ladder" and where it leads, that is, the plane of shamanic encounter) (2:17–37).

In 1924 the ethnographer William Farabee published his work *The Central Caribs,* which took him among the Makushis and other peoples in the far south of British Guiana, where kanaimà appears as a persistent element in native attitudes, for the Makushi in particular. Farabee (1924, 15, 18) mentions "kenaima" twice in the first pages of his ethnography, describing the precautions taken at night to secure the house against kanaimàs, a habitual nocturnal scene in Patamuna houses as well. Farabee (74–76) also gives explicit consideration to the topic later in the volume. However, he clearly has his doubts for his account is rather lazily constructed. First, he writes that kanaimàs are "little people," forest sprites that come out to make mischief, but then that they are also "real men," although no one has ever seen one. He continues by outlining the mutilations to the mouth and rectum, suggesting the former is to stop a victim from identifying his attacker, and concludes that the "piazong" has no power over the kanaimà. Farabee nonetheless understood that ideas about kanaimà had to be interpreted in the context of wider notions that the origins of all disease and death emanated from potential enemies. He then quotes (again) the account by Richard Schomburgk of Makushi divination using the victim's body parts, but says he could find no evidence that it was then in use. Farabee's only other references (81, 172) to kanaimà record the idea that with kanaimà came the possibility of death, that without kanaimà people would live forever, or at least much longer.

Farabee (1917) also reveals in his account of ascending the Kuyuwini a most interesting fact about Robert Schomburgk.[23]

> Half way up we began to see hills and low mountains. One of these, Mount Kenaima, is the abode of evil spirits of the same name. These spirits take the form of little men and attack the lone traveler at night. They will not attack two persons, even if one is a small child. The deep pools contain great spirits who come up and catch men in canoes. All these places are known and every day we had to make detours to avoid them or wait to pass at a certain time of day. Schomburgk, who traveled up the river in 1837, had so much trouble that he made an image of a young woman and sacrificed it to the spirits. He does not record the incident, but the story has come down among the Indians to the present. The place was pointed out to us and we passed in safety without fear because of this offering. (72)

In contrast to this diffuse spirit landscape and the evanescence of Farabee's "kenaima"—though possibly reflecting differences in kanaimà between the Karinya and Makushi (see also Henry Roth 1950) —John Gillin (1936, 99, 140–52) in his ethnography of *The Barama River Caribs* (Karinya) sees kanaimà as having a crucial role to play in the ordering of society. Gillin strongly takes up the idea of kanaimà, present in the earlier sources, as a form of criminal justice, and the kanaimà "avenger" becomes the agent of society as a whole, despite his outsider status.[24] The majority of Gillin's discussion of kanaimà therefore appears in the chapter on "Crime and Punishment." Gillin nonetheless disaggregates kanaimà from the other forms of shamanism, particularly piya, but also *aremi emu,* a form of Karinya assault sorcery based on drinking pepper juice rather than tobacco juice. There are techniques of magical assault, *talen,* known to the Patamuna, that are similarly distinct from both piya and kanaimà, making this an important comparative observation.

Gillin's account also adds some new details, specifically, that not all kanaimà attacks have the same intent, that kanaimà lead a generally abstinent life with specific dietary restrictions, and that banana leaves are deadly to the kanaimà and therefore are wrapped around the dead body of a victim at burial. Gillin concludes his discussion with a note of skepticism, suggesting that the belief is real but the existence of practitioners is unverifiable because they are killed on sight. However, "on the theory that where there is so much smoke there must be fire, I am inclined to believe that there is such a cult of avengers, voluntary outcasts who, with the aid of black-magic, devote a period to vengeance and possibly to purely malicious mischief. . . . In any case, the mere fact that they are believed to be effective agents of punishment justifies a consideration of the subject in a discussion of Carib penology" (1936, 152).

Kanaimà had become a substantive category not just of regional anthropological theory but also of the colonial imagination. However, external literary representations of kanaimà contrast to its portrayal by "old colonial hands," which, for example, clearly emerges in a comparison of the writings of Evelyn Waugh and Henry Roth. Evelyn Waugh (1934, 182–85), in his travelogue through the interior of "Guiana and Brazil," does not fail to notice kanaimà, but does so only as an aspect of his skepticism toward anthropology as a whole. For him, the credibility of anthropology itself rests on its ability to distinguish "real" from "imaginary" kanaimà. He calls kanaimà an "indefinable dread" that afflicts a wide range of Amerindians, and he sarcastically notes its apparent prevalence in everything. However, while such lack of logical consistency is to be expected of the Amerindians, Waugh seems more exasperated by the way in which "popular 'Outlines' of culture" were fostering all kinds of poorly researched anthropological opinion.[25]

Waugh was also "highly skeptical of all statements made about primitive beliefs" (183), both because of the insurmountable nature of language barriers and because Amerindians were apt to tell inquirers what they thought they wanted to hear. There was also a sectarian dimension to his skepticism. As with most educated Catholics of the period, Waugh disliked the comparative religious claims often made by anthropologists and the way in which particular ethnology was used to generalize the human condition. Bertrand Russell had used the work of Bronislaw Malinowski in his pioneering *Marriage and Morals* (1929), as had Floyd Dell *In Love in the Machine Age* (1930), and Margaret Mead was simultaneously earning her reputation as a founder of the "sexual revolution" (Gallagher 1997). Waugh (1934, 173–75) contrasts the Wapishana's belief in the relevance of the male role in procreation with the Trobriand Islander's "ignorance of paternity," according to Malinowski's *The Sexual Life of Savages* (1929), and so questions ideas about the cultural nature of sexuality that such works purported to elucidate. In discussing "Kenaima" Waugh thus makes full use of the inability of the ethnographer to definitively resolve the "real" or "imaginary" status of the phenomenon, mentioning that he had questioned two Europeans "who had exceptional opportunities of studying Indians," one of them probably Iris Myers, who "gave me completely contradictory explanations of the belief" (1934, 184). Waugh concludes that "I quote the two confidently definite explanations as being noticeable contributions to the general scepticism that is one of the more valuable fruits of travel." As an exponent of the colonial imagination Waugh is perhaps unsurpassed, but his actual engagement with Amerindian people, rather than their "anthropologists," was minimal.

Henry Roth (1950), grandson of Walter Roth, fittingly provides a brief piece of writing that exemplifies the other kind of link between the "colonial" idea of kanaimà and its anthropological expression, this time grounded in a long-term residency in Guyana. Henry Roth, writing for the Guyanese journal *Timehri* as a government officer in the Rupununi district in the period after John Gillin's fieldwork, eschewed all pretense at anthropological expertise, although "I think I can say I should know the subject 'as much as the other man.'" His article, "The Kanaima," is a matter-of-fact summary of all the salient features reviewed above and an untroubled affirmation of "real" kanaimà, since "Any 'Old-Timers' from the Demerara and Berbice rivers can vouch for the corporeal existence of the Kanaimas" (25). Indeed, this is certainly borne out by the biography of Matthew French Young (1998, 25–26), a white Guyanese who remained after independence from Britain and who characterized kanaimà as a "machinery for keeping the peace through FEAR." Henry Roth goes on to make the very important point that, before the worldwide flu pandemic of 1919–20 "decimated the Amerindian population of these rivers," the kanaimàs were "bold and audacious in their activities." As a result, "The Kanaima" also becomes truly disembodied, a textual nightmare with a fading reality as both native bodies and native souls expired in the shamanic smoke of metallic modernity—the black-smoke of disease, industry, and progress.[26]

This was also the way in which the colonial idea of "The Kanaima" was used as a literary trope by Rómulo Gallegos, one-time president of Venezuela, in *Canaima* (1935,1984), a novel set in the Caroni and Yuruari Rivers during the 1930s. Apart from Gallegos's stature as a literary figure, the importance of this work lies in the effect it has had on Venezuelan self-identity, for it has been required reading for many generations of Venezuelan schoolchildren. It also speaks to how to interpret the local meanings of kanaimà in a political culture of Magical States in which the State itself has become but another predatory god in the pantheon of the South American cosmos (see Coronil 1997; Taussig 1997; Vidal and Whitehead forthcoming), even as kanaimà haunted the colonial imagination of Henry Roth and other "old-timers" like Victor Norwood in his adventure novel, *The Skull of Kanaima*.[27]

In Gallegos's *Canaima* we find no longer the lone "Indian avenger" but the very spirit of the deep forest itself, not the elfin spirit of eco-fantasy, but a malignant "goblin" whose realm we enter only with "temerity" (*temeridad*, in Gallegos 1935) toward the forest, an idea also strongly imprinted in the Schomburgkian writings.[28] The result is to risk a loss of humanity, or going "bush" in the "demon landscape," such that it becomes an "inhuman jungle." "Those who ever penetrate it begin to be something more or something less than men," while "The grave and taciturn Indian . . .The jungle goblin" moves through the "green hell" until the intruder utters "the words that set madness free—We're lost!" (Gallegos 1984, 177–79). Gallegos defines Canaima as "the devil of the Waikas [Akawaio] and Makiritares [Ye'kuana], the frantic god, principle of evil and cause of all evils, disputes the world with Cajuña, the good. The demoniac without a definite shape, and able to adopt any outward appearance, old revived Ahriman in America . . . sets free in the heart of man the tempest of infrahuman elements" (181).[29]

In this way "Canaima" for Gallegos acts as the trigger that unleashes an already formed human nature that contains the capacity for violence, whereas native theory sees kanaimà as a means to produce such violence. Gallegos also speaks of "the obsession of penetrating it [the forest], errant as a goblin," and so identifies "Canaima" with both a spirit in the forest and the spirit that draws men to it. In this sense he imagines Marcos Vargas, the protagonist of the novel, as entering the forest "with temerity," despite coming from a land of "unpunished violence" (1984, 204). Vargas himself calls it "this land of Canaima" (206) and mimetically assumes its forms as he acquires "the barbaric experience of feeding himself with a piece of the prey . . . unsalted and half roasted . . . and later raw and bleeding" (207)—so like a jaguar.

For those who do not choose to initiate themselves in this way, the pernicious influence of Canaima is expressed in more petty ways: "The dehumanizing influence of the savage loneliness was producing in those men a somber tendency characteristic of the jungle, . . . a certain frenzy of cruelty, not ardent and impetuous as the one produced by open spaces, but, on the contrary, frightfully calm, of bestial abysses. Crimes and monstrosities of all kinds, narrated and commented with sadistic details, were almost the exclusive subjects of conversation. . . . Several of them, applying these crazy experiences to themselves, had self-inflicted wounds to become unable to work. . . . it was the tempest of subhuman elements stirred by Canaima in the hearts of men" (220). And so, by invoking *The Tempest,* Gallegos conjures up that vivid Carib cannibal of the European imagination—Caliban—thus closing the poetical circle of savagery where it began.[30]

Since *Canaima* inaugurated the metaphorical use of the indigenous notion of kanaimà as a literary trope of wildness, savagery, and supernatural malevolence, there have been increasing references to kanaimà as a backdrop for the imagination of the Guyana Highlands (Petit 1998) and as a literary device for suggesting the welling up of atavistic and ancestral forces into the "modern" world. Such usage is apparent in Wilson Harris's (1995) short story *Kanaima*. The story tells of the brief stay of a party of "Macusis," trekking to escape the malevolent forces of "Kanaima," at the mining encampment of Tumatumari on the Potaro. They arrive to find that "Kanaima been here already," but "He gone so—that way." The key idea that Harris employs is that kanaimà is a diffuse and malevolent force that wastes crops, brings drought, and eventually causes people to die. Harris also gives kanaimà a physical reference through the suggestion that "it came suddenly running along the already withered spaces of the savannahs, leaving great black charred circles upon the bitten grass everywhere, and snaking into the village compound where it lifted its writhing self like a spiritual warning in the headman's presence before climbing up the air into space" (148). This serpentine imagery for the "lord of death" is

Kanaima as
Werewolf by
Mario Alberto.[31]

then continued through the story to its denouement, in which one
of the party of Macusis unadvisedly leaves the benab that night. The
"headman" of the party, whose wife it is who has left, then realizes the
presence of "Kanaima" in the very texture and shapes of the sky and
landscape. The presence then pursues the woman to a waterfall where
she slips and in trying to climb out of the gully is closely menaced
and watched by the ethereal presence of "Kanaima," who "alone knew
whether she would reach the cliff top." Here the story ends.

Harris's work has been widely discussed, and through his literary influence the imagery and notion of "Kanaima" as used by Harris is also
part of later usages, especially in Caribbean literature, as an image of
Death itself (Bachinger 1986). In Pauline Melville's *The Ventriloquist's
Tale* (1997) one of the chapters is titled "Kanaima." The chapter sets up
some interesting historical resonances with the case of Thomas Youd,
since the character of a white missionary to the Waiwai, Macusi, and

Wapishana, Father Napier, is "poisoned" and finds relief only in drink-ing milk. Milk is itself the culturally quintessential item of diet for "white-men" and also recalls the bottle of "white medicine" used by Bichiwung, as well as the "emetic" used by Youd, in trying to counter-act the effects of a kanaimà attack.

Less informed by the actualities of Guyana but still entranced by the trope of "Kanaima," Eugene Orlando (2000) offers a web-based collec-tion of "Victorian 'romance' and adventure" that includes one entitled *Kanaima*. To quote the author's own abstract, "Kanaima—British law conflicts with native Amerindian law in 1884 British Guiana. Alleen Lambeth discovers for herself which prevails when she finds her Vic-torian values stranded in the wilds of one of Queen Victoria's 'crown' colonies, set in 1884." The tale is something of a "bodice-ripper" and is of interest here for its use of the notion of "Kanaima" to dramatize cultural opacity.

Nonetheless, none of these literary renderings quite escapes the old colonial trope of "Kanaima" as indigenous, vegetal, evil, miasmic, and ever present—for it is a mimetic reading of Amerindian thought itself. As such "Kanaima" negotiates cultural opacity through a mimetic pro-duction of indigenous kanaimà that has been growing since the late nineteenth century. This in turn means that the notion of "Kanaima," just as that of the "Cannibal," has its own cultural resonance aside from that of its Amerindian creation.[32]

CHAPTER 3

Tales of the Kanaimà: Participants

To allow a fairly direct presentation of native voices that diverge from colonial constructions of kanaimà, I now present current testimony and recent ethnographic information collected mainly among the Patamuna, including a number of indigenous narratives of kanaimà, interviews I conducted with both avowed killers and the families of their victims, and previously published Amerindian testimonies that bear on kanaimà as it affects and is practiced among other groups (Foster 1993; Guppy 1961; Forte and Melville 1989).

KANAIMÀ ATTACK AS VIOLENT RITUAL

While many elements of kanaimà's violent ritual had been described in the literature by the end of the nineteenth century, it was not possible to weight the relative ritual importance of those elements or to understand attacks that were less than fatal according to the model of "persistent vengeance" by which commentators had sought to comprehend both their own observations and the testimony of others. In the account given below, I will attempt to achieve those ends in the light of current testimonies.

An intended victim probably will first become aware of an impending attack because a kanaimà will repeatedly approach the victim's house by night. I have experienced the tension inside a house when one of the overt signs of approaching kanaimà is identified—perhaps the call of the *bokoboko* ("night-owl," *bubo virginianus scotinus*) or *kururukuru* ("goatsucker," *caprimulgus*), or perhaps a whistling noise, a movement along the base of the walls of the house, or, if a window or crack in the wall is left open, a slight tugging on the strings of a hammock. Moreover, the infallible sign that such intimations are in earnest is the invariable presence of one or more venomous snakes *inside* the house the following morning. After each occasion in which I experienced the night signs, either a *yamaliwok* (coral snake) or a *saloloimà* (labarias/bush-viper) was found within the house the next day. I stress this because it seemed very remarkable at the time and I supposed that they had been deliberately placed there.

However, kanaimà attacks generally are not anticipated within the house, but occur while alone in a garden or while walking an asanda. A number of signs may occur in these contexts, including the same whistling sound that is heard by night. A waving leaf is another common sign. A large leaf on a small sapling or ground plant that is growing along the trail, at about a distance of twenty yards from the observer, will begin to sway or shake in a manner that is contrary to the normal movements caused by breezes along the forest floor. The motion is quite distinct and is achieved by tying a thin string to the plant or using a long twig and manipulating the leaf with short tugs from the string or pushes from the stick. I have clearly seen this happening on two occasions while walking with a group of men. On both occasions we stopped to discuss the meaning of this, and once someone even ran forward in attempt to catch the supposed kanaimà—without success, although both a wicker headpiece and feathers used for camouflage were found in my presence on that occasion.

If a man or woman is walking alone or with only one or two companions, a kanaimà may make a direct appearance, usually either as a man, as a jaguar (in the forest), or an anteater (in the savannas). Such figures can appear first at a distance to the front and then, more quickly than would be expected, appear close by or behind you. I had precisely this experience with one man we were going to interview. We saw him along the trail, cutting wood in a small area of bush just at the savanna edge. Somewhat jokingly my companions remarked that we should keep a "good-eye" on him because of his reputation as a kanaimà. We continued toward the place where he was working, though he was momentarily out of sight. Coming on his cutlass and some cut wood, we appeared to have reached the spot where we had first seen him. I assumed he was simply out of sight in the thicket or had gone farther down the trail until someone pointed him out, coming along the trail behind us. He merely grabbed his cutlass and continued down the trail. We walked on but did not overtake him again that day. On our return

Kanaimà headpiece.

four days later, the cut wood was still where he had left it. Another stratagem of the kanaimà: a group of men lure a potential victim away under the pretense of going fishing or hunting, the "pharisaical friendship" noted by Richard Schomburgk (1922, 1:252; Charles Barrington Brown 1877, 54–55).

Following these signs, a direct and more complete physical attack and mutilation might come at any point, even years thereafter. During this period of stalking, the victim is being assessed as to their likely resistance and their suitability as a ritual "food." The notion of this process directly contradicts the main plank of interpretation in all previous accounts. Kanaimà, of course, was traditionally pictured as a form of vendetta or vengeance and the victims were portrayed as, in some sense, offenders of social norms; but there were many cases, even some cited directly as examples of a kanaimà attack, that did not on examination bear that interpretation (see Richard Schomburgk 1922, 1:122–25). It is therefore critical to appreciate that the selection of victims is ultimately a matter of indifference, in the sense that anyone will do, but obviously not in the sense that the killing of all potential victims has the same consequences in the political or social sphere. The phraseology repeatedly used by kanaimàs is to the effect that they are "hunting for their food" and that means, as with any subsistence hunter, they will take the easiest opportunity. This does not rule out at all "trophy" hunting, as it were, for part of kanaimà's history is how it connects to the constitution of society itself and conflicts with the interests of village chiefs (tushau), village shamans (piya), and regional prophets (alleluia'san or *iwepyatàsak*).

As a result of this framework of ideas, the victim is poetically assimilated to the category of prey, and so actively "hunting" kanaimàs become jaguars, tracking, listening, sniffing, tasting, and touching the intended victim's footprints and spoor. Moreover, although they conceive of themselves as hunting for their food in the guise of and by using the sensual modalities of the jaguar, kanaimàs also use hunting *binas* (charms) in just the way a human peccary-hunter might. In addition to such binas, in which *chiwi* (ginger) is used to enhance scents, kanaimàs also use talen magic. Talen magic is a form of incantation and ritual blowing in which the form of words used is the source of the magic's effectiveness. Anyone, if they possess the right words, can successfully use talen, and it is quite separate from either piya or kanaimà. However, an emphasis on word forms and oral performance shows conceptual connections with other forms of ritual action such as alleluia, where again the forms of songs are key. It is said that kanaimàs use talen to hide like jaguars. Talen magic is also associated with the stealth and rapid movement of the kanaimàs. Ground birds that can hide or move fast, such as the dokwaru or Powis (*Odontophorus g. Guianensis*) are thus associated with kanaimà magic.

In addition to binas and talen the kanaimà is said to be particularly adept at using herbs, which are carried in an *ubi* (gourd). The main plants mentioned repeatedly as key to kanaimà techniques are *kobita* (kanaimà plant), chiwi, and *kowak* (arrowroot), which are used in order to feel aggressive "against everyone," as well as *malimá*, a plant that "you must not trouble or you die." Koumi (a reed-like *Araceae* with a bitter, bulbous root) also plays a central role in kanaimà plant magic, as does the spirit force Koumima, originator of gardening magic. Koumi is an ingredient in wassi poison, but it is also the plant that the kanaimà chews and rubs on himself so he can "go far and come back quick." This dangerous control of the plant koumi is said to be the key shamanic technique of the kanaimà'san, and some of the imagery of killing and death borrows from that of plant nourishment. In order to locate their prey ordinary hunters might use a kobita-based bina, but not of the

Kobita, the Kanaimà plant (*Philodendron canaimae*).

same type as the kanaimàs, which is actually a bina for "taming wild things," and it is this that the kanaimà uses for getting his victim. The kanaimà may also use other tracking devices, particularly a frame affixed with dokwaru feathers that is worn like a hat (see also Bernau 1847, 57).[1] This headpiece has a feather suspended on a long string at the front and the direction in which that feather points is the direction that the kanaimà follows. Kanaimàs also place in the crook of an elbow two short sticks that are sensitive to the direction of the "prey." Like humans but unlike the jaguar, kanaimàs invariably hunt in groups, not as the lone assassins they were pictured to be in the colonial record.

When the kanaimàs find their prey it is a "cool" not "hot" killing for they are producing their food, like any other hunter, not murdering an individual;[2] but the "hunger" of the kanaimà builds inside and heats him as he does his work of mutilation. Ritual techniques are therefore directed toward de-individuating the person and rendering the body in its physical substance edible and nourishing. As a result, if vengeance is achieved on behalf of a supplicant, or even as a satisfaction for a kanaimà, it does not exhaust the meaning of the practice but rather only exhibits its public face and political dynamic. Thus, understanding the arbitrary nature of the victim and the irrelevance of the revenge dynamic to kanaimà allows a better interpretation of the forms and intensities of attack, not all of which are fatal in the first instance. But having once been attacked certainly increases the likelihood of further attacks.

In nonfatal attacks the victims may have bones broken, especially fingers and ribs, as well as joints dislocated or cut, especially in the shoulder area. The neck may also be manipulated so as to induce some kind of spinal injury and back pain. The purpose here seems to be to induce in the victim a "stillness" or passivity that makes them less resistant to further attack. Therefore, this kind of attack is generally considered to be only a preliminary to actual mutilation and death. A frequent reason for these nonfatal attacks is that they function as training sessions for initiates. It was suggested by Bernau (1847, 57–58) that there was possibly something systematic in the varying forms of attack; although his notion that the attacks were gender-based has some merit in that women and children undoubtedly suffer most from these nonfatal attacks, the actual reason is that women and children are simply easier to get at and physically overcome. Most people will recover from such attacks, as they are intended to, but clearly undergo a humiliating and painful procedure with possible physical complications in the longer term. The victims also bear the constant stress of being aware that the kanaimàs "know" them and will revisit them with fatal consequences. (This is currently the case with the Nurse's husband, which may well have been part of her motivation for speaking out.)

Attacks that are meant to be final, that are intended to produce ritual food, are extremely violent but not instantly fatal, nor are they intended to be so, according to the perpetrators. Ideally a victim is first confronted suddenly by a single kanaimà from the front, then struck from behind with a special club—the *yé* stick—and physically restrained, if not already unconscious from the blow. The victim is treated with a powder made from astringent plants, usually koumi, after which their tongue is pierced with the fangs of a venomous snake or, sometimes, with a splinter of greenheart wood.[3] An iguana or an armadillo tail is shoved into their rectum and the anal muscles stripped out through vigorous rubbing. By pressing on the victim's stomach, the kanaimàs also force out a section of the sphincter muscle and sever it. Finally, they force a thin flexed twig into the rectum, so that it opens the anal tract. Packets of herbs, including kobita, koumi, or wassi, are then inserted into the anus as far as possible, which begins a process of autodigestion, creating the special aroma of kanaimà enchantment, *akaikalak*.[4] The sweet odor of pineapple is therefore a sign of kanaimà attack for the victims, and the spoor by which their attackers will be drawn to their bodies after burial.

As the victim is then unable to speak, eat, or drink, and bowel control is lost, the clinical cause of death, for medical certification procedures, is given as "acute dehydration through diarrhoea." I only saw one such individual, a small boy about four or five years old who was brought into the village. It was extremely difficult to get access to him as none of his relatives wanted me, or indeed any other nonrelative, to see him — in case we were acting on the behalf of the attackers. However, I did, in a rather prurient manner that was on reflection quite reprehensible, literally "steal" a glimpse of him. His mouth was extremely swollen, with puckered lips, and as he shifted in his hammock I noticed a large stain on the hammock in his bowel area. I made no actual examination, so I suppose that such injuries could have had other causes, but their consistency with the forms of kanaimà attack was chilling and, judging from the behavior of others, kanaimà was quite obviously a sufficient explanation for them.

The ritual play of the kanaimàs with their victim does not by any means end with their deaths, for the purpose of killing was not the victim's demise but the ritual production of the body as food. Therefore the kanaimàs will try to discover the burial place of their victim and await the full onset of putrefaction in the corpse, which usually occurs within three days. During this time the kanaimàs are understood to be magically vulnerable; as they try, literally, to smell out the first stages of putrefaction, the kanaimàs can be intercepted and killed by the dead person's relatives. Nineteenth-century literature contained a number of references to this idea of the "unappeased" kanaimà, most dramatically in William Brett 1868 (359), and this remains a dangerous possibility. However, in the revenge model, the concept of unappeased kanaimà was seized on only to maintain the notion that the kanaimà was in some sense a just avenger — because they undertake a mission at risk to themselves — and not merely a skulking murderer. In any case, relatives of the victim are acutely aware that, unless the soul (*ekati*) of the dead person, having been "driven away" by the physical and magical force of the attack and denied "reentry" through the muti-

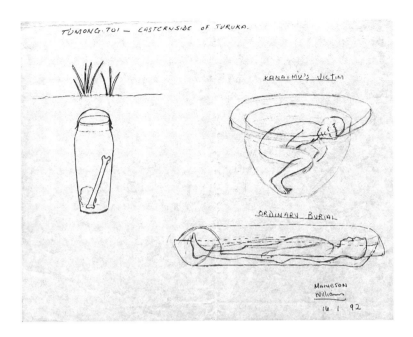

Patamuna burial modes and Kanaimà ritual ossuary.
Drawing by Matteson Williams.

lating ritual procedures to mouth and anus, can find the grave, then
this bodily mutilation will have become truly ontological.[5]

The colonial sources did mention some magical protections that
could be enacted to stop the kanaimà from revisiting the corpse, but
none of them were mentioned to me by the Patamuna or Makushi I
interviewed, except the observation that the kanaimà doesn't like the
sounds of the crow calling, "co-co-co." Rather, the need to ward off
the kanaimàs and protect the body from further interference leads to
a type of burial of the victim's corpse distinct from that usually practiced. This may involve placing the corpse in a rock-niche, covering the
gravesite with large boulders or in a sealed ceramic jar, and/or keeping the location secret. The figure above shows a contemporary Patamuna view of the matter, indicating the physical characteristics associated with burials of human remains in various contexts and vessels.
It is also the case, according to current testimony, that if the kanaimàs
cannot discover the body then they will become overheated (*sopanéy*),
that is, mad or enraged.[6] From the cases I have reviewed, it would

seem that the relatives invariably feel they have succeeded in this purpose.[7] At the same time, kanaimàs say that finding the corpse is easy for them, partly because of their shape-shifting abilities, which enable them to approach as butterflies or small worms. In either case, the figure of the "unappeased" kanaimà seems to have stemmed rather more from the vivacity of Brett's account than from the actual ritual practice of the Patamuna. In short, the relatives must hide the corpse ritually and literally, although not from its own soul, while the kanaimàs must find that corpse or the purpose of the ritual performance will not have been achieved. That purpose is as follows.

When the gravesite is discovered, a stick is inserted through the ground directly into the cadaver, then the stick is retracted and the juices, or maba (honeylike food), sucked off. The juices of putrefaction are said to taste like honey both because of their *tepusine* (sweetness) and because the grave is "tasted" with the help of the yé (ritual stick) in the same way as a stick is used when eating honey from a hive. Other metaphors also are used by kanaimàs to explain this key moment: that of anteaters licking and sucking ants and termites from their mounds, or of plants sucking up food through their roots (a reference to Kou-mima). All these images are striking for their emphasis on the sensuality of licking and sucking, as opposed to the tearing and chewing of jaguar prey. This seems to be related to the way in which the production of maba, not the killing of the individual, is symbolically central to the ritual action of the kanaimà. In a less generic but equally powerful image, a Patamuna kanaimà also referred to the Makushi's *menéné*, anthills into which the dead are directly inhumed so that the ants will pick their bones clean. The image of the anteater sending his long, sticklike tongue into a menéné is thus strongly redolent of the kanaimà divining for his maba with the yé stick. Finally, there is the akaikalak aroma of kanaimà, that smell of rotting pineapple that the corpse of the victim is said to give off and that is honeylike to the kanaimà.

The properties of maba are both significant and mysterious, for that is the nature of this ritual performance of kanaimà. It is hard to get a clear picture of its role in other aspects of kanaimà shamanism, and it often seems as if the production of maba is an end in itself. Those who claim to have drunk it say that the effect of maba is both psychotropic and morphic. The heated kanaimà is cooled by tasting it, and at the same time he wards off the avenging spirit of his victim. This also means the kanaimà has to return to his own humanity, and it is this mundane condition that seems to operate as an incentive and goad to future killing, for initiates at least. Thus, the experience of killing and getting "high" on the maba is represented as intrinsically exciting and powerful, as well as shamanically potent. In this transition the metaphor of Kaikuci'ima (Lord Jaguar) is used to represent the condition of the killer. A kanaimà will not eat "human-food" after a kill until he has tasted the "divine-food" of the grave, and indeed he *must* taste the maba if the dangerous divine forces inside him, represented as the spirit emissaries of Kaikuci'ima, are to be purged and a return to the domain of the human achieved. The maba is also pictured as the gift of the killers to their kanaimà'san (kanaimà adept). They make an offering of their prey to the shaman who leads them and directs their attacks. In this exchange, the kanaimà'san sorcerer becomes identified with the ferocity of Kaikuci'ima, who will only be assuaged by tasting this "honey of the dead" (Whitehead 1990, 2001b).

If the corpse is indeed sufficiently "sweet" on tasting, it will be partially disinterred in order to recover bone material and, ideally, a section of the anal tract. The use of previous victim's body parts is necessary to facilitate the location and killing of the next victim and may also be used to "cool" a killer who is otherwise unable to get access to his victim's gravesite. These body parts are then secreted in special vessels, often kept in caves such as Kuyali'yen. These "gifts of death" from the kanaimàs to their kanaimà'san are part of and historically drive the unending exchanges between divine animals and mundane humans in the guise of hunter and prey. It is this relationship that the kanaimà'san claims to sustain or influence through his special access to Makunaima, ultimate creator of animals and plants. This key role in the creation and management of the predatory interrelation of humanity, animality, and divinity through koumi-based magic is why the kanaimà is the source of powerful shamanic techniques. In an analogous way the divine gift of *kawai* (tobacco), carried by the *kumalak* (swallow-tailed kite), is the source of piya or shamanic curing.

KANAIMÀ AS SHAMANIC PRACTICE

Rather than being a revenge complex, then, kanaimà is a form of shamanism. Once this fundamental aspect of kanaimà has been appreciated, then much that was otherwise obscure falls into place. This is not

to say that I am able to present a full and complete account of that shamanic practice or its theory, for there are formidable obstacles in the
way of realizing such an ambition, not least the secretive and violent
nature of kanaimà practitioners themselves. However, in interviews
with avowed kanaimàs, a slightly clearer picture of kanaimà ritual practice emerged, and comparison with other groups enabled a minimal
delineation of this ritual complex.

In order to appreciate the meanings of kanaimà shamanism we must
begin with the creation of the world itself, and in particular the accounts of Makunaima and Piai'ima, brothers and children of the sun.
These cosmological heroes feature in the myth-cycles of many of the
peoples of the Roraima region, and, like the brothers Wanadi and
Odosha who are described in the *Watunna* of the Ye'kuana (Civrieux
1980), their deeds set the framework and conditions for human society
and individual destiny. Makunaima has conventionally been interpreted as a senior brother; he was even given the characteristics of
the Christian God, because of his role as creator of plants and animals, when the missionaries were undertaking their first evangelization and translating the Bible into native languages (Brett 1868, 59; Im
Thurn 1883, 365; Walter E. Roth 1915, 130–36). This was something of
an error, as Dance (1881, 236) recognized, for the name Makunaima
more properly translates as "great evil" (*makui* means evil, bad; '*ima*
means great, ultimate) and implies "one who works in the dark" or "by
night," as the piya and kanaimà do. Today many, probably most, Patamuna would not translate the name Makunaima as "God." Extant Bib-
lical translations into the Patamuna language (American Bible Society
1966) use the terms *Katú* for "God" and *Makui* or *Setan* for "Satan,"
and the other connotations of the spirit Makunaima are well understood.

Makunaima has many disputes with his brothers, but especially
Pia'imà. He emerges from the oral literature as sneaky, malicious, and
the author of many of the woes of people, particularly of such things
as venomous snakes, scorpions, and stingrays. According to the Patamuna today, Makunaima was the first man, who with Piai'ima originated the world. He made the first woman out of one of his brothers;
although the woman had a vagina, she had no breasts. Makunaima was
a trickster, and he is recalled for having made the stingray out of an
eddo leaf, one of the araceous plant family, like koumi. He created all
the animals and fish, and in this aspect is connected to the Master of

TABLE 1 Forms of Shamanic Practice and Performance

	KANAIMÀ	PIYA	ALLELUIA
Sensual Modes	Smell, Hearing, Sight	Vision	Song, Smell
Sensual Performance	Running, Tracking	Soul Flight	Song, Dance
Magical Resources	Plants, Animals	Birds, Plants	Words, Text
Magical Equipment	Yé Stick	Leafy Rattle	Voice, *Gobi* *
Magical Substances	Koumi, Maba	Tobacco	Cassiri
Ritual Performance	Shape Shifting	Spirit Control	Spirit Possession
Ritual Site	Forest	Village	Forest
Spirit Abode	Forest, Caves	Mountains	Heaven
Spirit Sponsor	Makunaima	Pia'imà	Katú, Akwa

* The gourd used for drinking cassiri frequently mentioned in alleluia songs.

Animals in hunting magic. He also transformed both people and animals into stones and wrote *timehri* (petroglyphs) on the rocks.

By contrast, although Piai'ima is pictured as a giant anthropophage, he eventually emerges as a patron to humanity since—as his name implies—it was Piai'ima who gave men piya, that is, shamanism itself, or at least a version of it. His name thus translates as "the great or ultimate shaman." Piai'ima created the first shamans and the magical plants they use, especially tobacco. Piai'ima is sometimes known also by the name of Ataitai, a cave-dwelling cannibal forest spirit.[8] In the cosmology of the Patamuna, the kanaimà are the shamans of Makunaima, not of Piai'ima, and from this fundamental dualism of shamanic practice and the playing out of the contexts and rivalries between Makunaima and Piai'ima arises the mythopoetic model that describes the purposes of kanaimà and its unceasing shamanic warfare with the piya, or devotees of Piai'ima.[9]

Table 1 illustrates the differing ritual practices that result from this historical divergence in shamanism by laying out the basic ritual, symbolic, and sensual elements in those practices. These elements are not necessarily exclusive—piya may appear as jaguars, and kanaimà certainly perform a form of soul flight—but they are meant to suggest different fundamental logics in shamanic practice, which derive from their contrasting mythopoetic origins. (A third shamanic ritual form, alleluia, which is a critical aspect of the historical development of shamanism among the Patamuna, will be considered later, so I include in table 1 a summary of its ritual practice.) Kanaimà, then, appears as a shamanic technique that stands in strong historical and mythopoetic contrast to both piya and alleluia.

The element of plant magic in kanaimà, aside from the ritual procedures of mutilation, provides the most striking contrast with piya. This is not to say that the piya, as well as users of talen and binas, do not have copious knowledge of plant forms and magical uses, but kanaimà seems also to involve a distinct orientation to a plant spirit—Koumima, the spirit of koumi (*Araceae arum*) and mùloka (farms). This feature of kanaimà was only mentioned twice, but by senior and highly credible persons. In addition, the use of plant binas by the kanaimà is itself often clearly noted by a range of people.

A distinct and important system of magic based around the plant koumi is also suggested by Koch-Grüneberg (1979, 2:30–33), who notes that, in the Pemon myth, koumi was "blown" over Makunaima to bring him back to life after he had been killed by Piai'ima. Makunaima's dismembered body was also sewn up with koumi leaves. Furthermore, Makunaima created the stingray out of another species of Araceae, the *Caladium arborescens,* which Charles Barrington Brown mentions as the "tannier" (from the Carib and Tupi words *taya* and *taña*) with which the victim's body was rubbed down, although the term "tannier" is ambiguous and might also denote yet another Araceae, *Xanothosoma sagittifolium.* Generally, koumi is understood to be important in bodily transformation, or shape-shifting, an understanding confirmed by David Thomas (1982, 193). Koch-Grüneberg suggests that koumi magic is more recent than piya, which contradicts the information given by Patamuna kanaimàs, but nonetheless indicates the historicity of shamanic practices. However, Koch-Grüneberg does suggest that koumi magic originates as an alternative to the avian-based shamanism of the piya, the implication being that transforming into a bird, or at least wearing plumage, is not necessary for ascent of the shamanic pathway *kalawali.* Butt Colson (1966, 75–76) indicates that the Akawaio use koumi for "various food getting pursuits" and that the koumi charm (*murang*) is used by women in the farm to make things grow, and it also attracts Akumawali, the garden spirit. Women also call on Mawraima, the anteater spirit who aids the development of roots and fruits.

More broadly, at the level of plant morphology, a relationship exists among the plants used by kanaimàs: kobita (*Philodendron canaimae*), chiwi (*Zingiberidae*), and kowak (*Maranta arundinacea*).[10] The main similarities are the poisonous nature of the arum family, as well as its acrid and milky sap. The roots of the arum family are also used as foods and medicines.[11] Symbolically suggestive is the fact that these plants are usually insect pollinated, with many giving off the odor of rotten meat to attract carrion beetles and flies. Structurally notable are the similarity of the spathe and spadex inflorescence and, in the Zingiberidae, the presence of a showy flower or bract similar to those seen in tuberous roots and in pineapple and banana/plantain plants, which are common in the diet for people in this region. Both the odor of pineapple and the presence of banana leaf are, as already mentioned, connected to the practice of kanaimà.[12] The Zingiberidae most commonly have volatile oils in all the plant parts, and the genus *Maranta* contains the arrowroot.[13] These families are thought to make a morphologically very distinct botanical grouping and many genera have moved in and out of one or the other of these several families over the years. The families have some aromatic oils (*Zingiber spp.*) and are used globally as medicines, dyes, and seasonings. The root is generally used more often than other plant parts, but the various species are very identifiable from their "above-ground" morphology. The presence of colored, showy bracts or brightly colored inflorescences makes the members of these families stand out in a tropical forest environment.

For kanaimà practitioners there may exist among the plants used in their magic a systematic relationship that is also present in the myth and symbolism concerning kanaimà. While the suggestion as to the historical precedence of kanaimà over piya might possibly be reflected in differences in ritual practice, as Koch-Grüneberg suggested, it is clear that this aspect of kanaimà, as well as its relation to other forms of magic and shamanism, will need further research. Along these lines, it is helpful to compare kanaimà plant magic with a better-known system of garden magic, as described by Michael F. Brown (1986) for the Aguaruna. Brown (54–57) notes the presence of plant "souls," which can be aggressive and dangerous, particularly those souls associated with tuberous cultigens, including arrowroot and gingers, that are linked to the activities of sorcerers. Brown (106) also records that the souls of manioc plants can be extremely dangerous and may even eat the souls of or drink the blood of passing humans (see also Descola 1994, 205; Whitten 1976, 75–76). These aspects of plant magic, along with the presence in the mùloka of dangerous and life-sucking spirits, accord both with the imagery of the kanaimà as sucking, like a plant, the juices from the body of a prepared victim and with the suggestion that the mùloka is itself a preferred site for a kanaimà attack.

KANAIMÀ: SHAMANIC ORDER AND SOCIAL DISORDER

Consonant with the analyses made by Coudreau (1887, 2:236) and Koch-Grüneberg (1979, 1:170), contemporary kanaimàs do form a kind of supravillage association, although there are differences in testimony as to whether or not such organization follows ethnic boundaries. Kanaimà'san are certainly known to each other, and it is always said that if one were to kill a kanaimà'san, which certainly happens sometimes, then other kanaimà may well avenge that death. However, given the trope of "pervasive" evil that has been used to represent kanaimà in the literature—derived though it may be, to a certain extent, from general indigenous attitudes to kanaimà—one has to be careful not to overstress the regional organization of kanaimà. Coudreau and Koch-Grüneberg do seem to overstate the case, at least with respect to the current situation, and their use of the term *tribe* is also rather vague. What they report seems in fact to conflate how general accusations of kanaimà might follow the lines of political division with the fact that the regions they traveled through were, at the time, undergoing profound change. In such a context, the projection of kanaimà may have served to ward off outside incursion. The political units to which Coudreau and Koch-Grüneberg referred may also have had leaders who were in alliance with kanaimà shamans; Koch-Grüneberg (1979, 1:73, 131, 317) even mentions a famed kanaimà, Dschiawó, as the chief of a Pemon village.

Given the mythopoetic origins of kanaimà and piya, shamanic battles may take some of their motivation from the divergent political meanings of chieftaincy and shamanism. This divergence begins with the cosmogenesis of society itself, which is pictured as the divine gift of Piai'ima, through the revelation of shamanic techniques and the means of manioc agriculture. By contrast Makunaima, "a man who can command anything," although contemporary with and related to Piai'ima, begets no social order and through his malicious trickery can be understood as even inimical to such order; as such, he could be considered analogous to Odosha of Ye'kuana cosmology. In this mythopoetic context there is every reason to expect an alliance of chiefly ambition and the practice of piya against the disruptive, disordering effect of kanaimà. And, indeed, this is very much the framework for shamanic warfare, a political dynamic that may in part be responsible for how kanaimà is sometimes confused with a warrior cult. In this regard, the works by Hélène Clastres (1995) and Pierre Clastres (1977) on the *karai* (prophets) among the Tupi of Brazil seem a fruitful point of comparison. They describe the various kinds of shamanism found historically among the Tupi and in particular describe an important difference between the *paje* (piya) and karai, suggesting that this was principally reflected in their orientation to the *mburubicha* (chief) and the project of political leadership more widely. In this context the karai, as itinerant prophets and visionaries, were often inimical to the stable constitution of village life. The shamanically inspired calls of the karai to follow them to the earthly paradise of *yvy marä ey* (the-land-without-evil) literally led to the physical migrations of thousands of individuals. Pierre Clastres expresses this as a situation in which society was against, or refused, the development of centralized leadership, or the State.

From the point of view of the Patamuna tushau (village chief), the kanaimà can come to represent not just the death and mutilation of village members but the death and mutilation of the village itself (Whitehead 2001b). The body of the victim is a metonym for the body-politic of the village. Kanaimà mutilation thus can be read as a form of death that poetically renders the human hunter as divine prey by inverting the definition of "person." A real person is the possessor of an "incontinent mouth," which represents the dangerous capacities for both beautiful words and cannibalism, and a "continent anus," which stands for the control of those supremely social effluvia of sperm, menstruation, and blood. The flow of these vital substances occurs through the culturally constrained conduct of the socially constituting exchanges of war and marriage. Kanaimà mutilation reduces this person to a "thing," evident from its "continent mouth," or lack of speech, as achieved by the insertion of snake fangs into the tongue, and its "incontinent anus," or lack of sociality, as achieved by the insertion of the "magic arrows" of the armadillo or iguana tail and flexed sticks, which renders the victim physically incontinent.

More broadly, the repeated depredations of kanaimà attacks in a village locale presents the tushau with insuperable problems in his role as mediator with the outside world, both spiritually and materially, as well as in his role as a mediator of conflicts and recriminations within the village. The kanaimà thus disrupts village life and the authority of its prominent actors by perpetrating both very physical attacks on village members and even more dangerous magical assaults on the village ideals of mutuality and harmony. In this context, the piya stands as the only effective defense against the kanaimà, although Christian conversion is also held to achieve similar ends. Before the colonial suppression of collective warfare, it was precisely the role of the kwayaus (warriors) to militarily represent the political strength of the village or a kin-group. In this role they would hunt down and club to death notorious kanaimàs. Such assassinations, although they later took place with shotguns, occurred sporadically among the Patamuna up to the 1970s when changes in their relationship with the Guyanese government made gun ownership illegal without permits. Added to this has been a resurgence, among the generation born after 1960, of interest in the kanaimà, as well as campaigns of evangelism that, somewhat erroneously, sought to undermine the piya as the "agent of Satan." Since the missionary presence is now negligible, this has led to a situation in which kanaimà is perhaps more evident now than since the epidemics of 1918–19. Likewise, the presence of a mining frontier in Patamuna territory since the 1980s has provided another vector for kanaimà activity, particularly in the guise of "contract killers."

As I mentioned, kanaimà are thought of as hunting in packs, and the leader of any given group, the kanaimà'san, is in one sense the true kanaimà, the other killers merely being trained in ritual technique. The kanaimà'san kills alone on occasion, guards the pack, and fights other shamans. It is his ability to ascend to the heights of kalawali (the spirit ladder) that is most directly augmented by a kanaimà killing, for it is part of his direct relationship with Makunaima. It is the destiny of powerful shamans to become stars (*ichieri*), like Makunaima himself who became Orion, and among shamans kanaimà are the most potent of all. The starlight of the night sky is therefore a sinister reminder of the pervasive and ancient nature of kanaimà.

The benefits of kanaimà to the initiates are largely couched in terms of the dramatic nature of the enterprise of hunting and killing people, the influence this confers in daily life, and the erotic appeal it has, or is believed to have, for women. Actual practices make these categories and motives less distinct, so that it is uncertain how rigid these degrees and differences in kanaimà practitioners actually are. This also helps explain why both in the literature, as well as in my own first observations, there is confusion between, on the one hand, acts of vengeance and murder, the existence of domineering and sexually bullying characters, and contract killers and, on the other hand, kanaimà practices. Under changing political circumstances, a kanaimà killing may well be represented in any of these ways, just as such antisocial and criminal behavior can be tagged as "kanaimà." Also there is little doubt that avowed kanaimàs—and their identity is very much an "open" secret—revel in their notoriety and use it in innumerable petty ways to advance themselves materially and sexually. In the case of young men, this is perhaps the first motivation to seek initiation as a kanaimà, where it is not already part of a patrilineal tradition.

I followed one case in which, I had heard, a young initiate, Merimo, was attempting to use his proto-kanaimà status to force a girl into sex, even marriage. As I returned one day to the village, a sudden storm came over the valley wall, and my Patamuna companions and I took refuge under a large rock outcrop on the asanda (foreground in image on page 16). As the storm passed, we sat for a while enjoying the view of the valley, when from above us came the sound of someone shouting down into the valley. Merimo had not seen us, as we were exactly under the rock on which he was standing, but his words were clear: he was calling down into the valley where the girl lived, telling her she was to meet him at a certain place or "she knew what the consequences were." The meaning of this threat was doubly confirmed when we emerged from underneath the rock. He had evidently assumed that following the rain everyone else was sheltering in their houses and that there was no one else on the trail, so his reaction was to threaten us too, adding in English for good measure, "And you . . . you fuckin' white-man." At which he turned up the trail. We were all angry at both his cruelty to this girl and at his words to us. One of my companions lazily sent a few arrows in his direction to vent our frustrations—and, incidentally, nicely illustrating how the "magic arrow" of the shaman can carry the intent of its sender. This took place in 1995, and by 1997 the young girl looked quite harried and aged; although it was easy to read in a consequence I already assumed might be there, she did seem changed by the experience and the effect of Merimo's persistence. The last information I received, which I cannot completely verify, was that her parents had moved to a new village and that she had died there.

To become a kanaimà, a young man must persuade a kanaimà'san to initiate him, unless he comes from a family that counts a kanaimà among its members. It is relevant to consider, in the light of the discussion on the compatibility of forms of shamanism with the organization of indigenous political life, the destabilizing effect of male groups of cognatic kin acting as a unit in a social universe that is largely constituted through uxorilocal cross-cousin marriage. The potential this has to disrupt a system of marriage exchanges, which are usually the genealogical basis of village memberships, underlines the potential for village instability that is inscribed in what is probably the most common path for kanaimà initiation. However, obviously this is not to suggest that village authority cannot be established using patrilines, and part of the meaning of the so-called kanaimà "tribes" may relate to the fact that such villages were, if not kanaimàs to a man, at least constituted in ways inimical to the enemies who testified against them and who held very different notions about the correct constitution of village life. In turn, neither is this meant to suggest that no such accommodation between village leaders and kanaimàs could be reached—quite the reverse. Much of the close association between kanaimà and the tactics of warfare stems not only from the general role of shamans in collective warfare but also from the political uses to which the otherwise disruptive kanaimàs might be put. In this light, it is easy to make sense of testimony as to how kanaimàs aided the kwayaus in times past and how the kanaimàs were "driven there, not here," according to the regional politics of chieftaincy.

Such social and political considerations also bear on the way in which kanaimàs are considered "outside" or "marginal" figures as social actors until they are initiated. In other words, a number of levels exist within the discourse of kanaimà and simultaneously apply to the social unit and the individual, the cosmos and the shaman. Initiation ritual to some degree replicates this notion of violent paternity, since the kanaimà adept and his initiate, *kaikuci'yeribada* (jaguar-face), are conceived of as representing a jaguar and his kill. Although at first sight surprising and seemingly inconsistent with the predator/prey relationship of kanaimà to victim, this particular dyad only pertains until initiation is complete. In any case, the bonds of family and kin notoriously do not supervene that of killer and victim, nor that of teacher and pupil. In an ultimate attack on sociality, the kanaimà thus "cannibalizes" his own kin in lieu of another victim (see Charles Barrington Brown 1877, 146).

Initiates are taken into the forest, and a liana hanging from the canopy is cut at about head-height, the time of its regrowth being the time it will take to complete the apprenticeship. The initiate is taught the hunting skills of tracking, speed, and "stillness" or poise. The initiation regimen includes a highly specialized diet that is designed to enhance these skills and that therefore emphasizes foods that will make initiates light and fleet of foot, as well as sustain the mental clarity and control that makes for the most successful hunter. The initiate's diet excludes all meat except that of the dokwaru bird but includes odd items like a certain fungi that is said to aid rapid movement. The diet also involves the drinking only of "still" water—that is, water from a pool or plant leaf, not from the river, since the latter would lead the mind to "overtake itself," causing the kanaimà to lose control and risk sopanéy (madness, rage) (see also Gillin 1936, 150). Isolation in the forest itself is intended to aid the process of concentration on shamanic development of key skills, like bodily transformation (*weytupok*) and the detaching of the soul (*iwemyakamatok*), by allowing the initiate to avoid the distractions of mundane village life. A whole set of shamanic techniques also appears to be based on the use of the plant koumi, but despite repeated attempts, I could get no clear idea about this, except that it was key and a point of strong contrast with piya shamanism.[14]

Aside from learning such shamanic techniques, initiates are also tutored in the use of the landscape for the purposes of their "hunting" and so ritual cave-sites and ambush-points, as well as little-used asanda, become part of the initiate's practical knowledge of the bush. Initiates may also be called on to aid in "guarding" the bodies of kanaimàs who have gone into the forest to kill. During initiation a kanaimà'san may send his "stick" (initiate) to kill at a distance, which can lead to attacks in which some elements of ritual mutilation may occur but in which other kinds of maiming can also be involved;[15] it is this kind of attack that appears in the literature and collective memory as "uncertainly" kanaimà.

It is clearly not possible to simply reproduce here all the transcripts and notes of comments, stories, brief conversations, and lengthy interviews that I have collected with regard to the kanaimà. Although some of that material is contextually presented here in my various analyses of kanaimà, the transcribed testimony of some of the key informants needs to be presented more completely. However, neither can such transcripts be represented as some kind of unvarnished "native voice" —either by me or by those who are doing the telling. Therefore, while I herein present transcripts of interviews that include some extended consideration of a topic, I do want to emphasize that I also learned much in less-structured situations, particularly when *droghing* (trekking) between villages and other sites. I have chosen here to use either interviews in which the respondents spoke in the English language or translations that were made immediately by a bilingual Patamuna. In both cases I have preserved the syntax and vocabulary of Guyanese speech.

Killers

I have tried to collect information on the life-histories of kanaimàs and have succeeded in interviewing avowed kanaimàs. Two of those were kanaimà'san, but the others were just beginning their training (as was Merimo, who harassed the young girl from the valley). The first passage of direct speech is taken from my interview with an individual claiming the status of kanaimà'san. Although the interview was, from the point of view of the ethnographic art, not entirely satisfactory, it is important as a rare example of direct testimony from an avowed killer. Also included here are the biographies in outline of renowned kanaimàs who are currently, or were very recently, active assassins, as well as the striking testimony of the surviving relative of a reluctant kanaimà.

The Kanaimà'san

I tell you how we use kanaimà. . . . It was here always . . . always, always, always . . . even before the Patamuna came. . . . It was a thing the Kawaliyana had before.[16] . . . They used only to plant gourds,

Pirai, a *kanaimà'san*.

else they live with wild fruits in the bush. . . . Fight, they fight-fight themselves, fight everyone with *kawo'yak* [clubs]. Then the *Maionkon* [Ye'kuana] came, different from Kalitna (Karinya) and there was a big fight. . . . One was there at Kuseilapoimá, one there at Kulauyaktoi and the Maionkon were beaten back, so they [Patamuna] use kanaimà in the wenaiman [enemy pursuit] but they [Ye'kuana] took women to Venezuela who are still there. They [Ye'kuana] use a lot of piya and cause these fights. The man from Koniayatoi [one of Talinaku's initiates] was one of those kanaimàs. He had a cave up there but his enemies finally caught him up there and shot him. I was showed by [name suppressed] and I saw [name suppressed] from Sand Creek drop a man while we were working for the whites.

Piya will know when we are working, his spirit sees us, but only at night. With Makunaima you don't see us. We come invisible, fast. Piya cannot hold us back because of the way we use the corpse. It's tough work . . . it's dangerous work but we become more powerful than the piya or the alleluia. Kanaimà is more ancient than piya, more ancient than warfare. We searching for our food that is all, that is all it is. We look at someone and see something sweet to suck and all that [ritual procedures] is for food. It boosts your spirit up, up to go far in kalawali. We cut down any piya who spies on us, who trouble us with *hiawa* or *mora* in our work.[17] We can kill anyone—blacks, whites, anyone—stop them up good. This is what I will tell you of the high-science.

This is the most sustained reflection by an avowed killer on the nature of kanaimà that I was able to record. The difficulties in arranging this interview and trying to record it were but one example of the many practical difficulties that presented themselves while researching this topic. However, since kanaimà'san may also be piya'san, and since the piya do play a role in the way kanaimà killings are carried out, I have augmented this information and information collected from other kanaimàs by using piya as sources and interpreters for kanaimà shamanic techniques. It is just as difficult, and perhaps not the initial priority when interviewing a kanaimà, to gather their biographical information. However, such information is as relevant as that on shamanic techniques to a better understanding of the social dynamics of kanaimà. The following section therefore presents aspects of the life-histories of particular kanaimàs.

Kanaimà Biographies

The first individual, whom I'll call "JW," had lived in Paramakatoi and been orphaned as a boy. One night, when he was about ten years old, he was taken forcibly from his uncle and carried off to the other side of the Ireng River into Brazil "on the back of a kanaimà." He was not seen for another seven years until he came back to Paramakatoi. There are many stories of his long-range trips into the bush, and most informants will say that if "you want to work a little mischief," then it had better be a two- or three-week journey away. Informally, this does seem to set a typical range for such enterprises.[18] However, as seems to be characteristic of kanaimà biographies, sooner or later that "mischief" draws closer to home—it is JW's attack on a father and son near Paramakatoi that is related below in the narrative called *Kanaimà Hill*. Following this JW killed an Amerindian pastor, whom I'll call "GI," at Monkey Mountain in the late 1970s. As a result, a decision was taken among the kàyik (eminent men) of Paramakatoi to end JW's kanaimà career. He was shotgunned in the face.

This latter mode of execution, involving gross trauma to the head, is actually a recurring theme in tales of kanaimà killing. In earlier times, the kwayaus were said to have purposefully mashed the brains and tasted them using a club colloquially known as a "Kangai special," Kangai having been a famous warrior and killer of kanaimàs. Such clubs (taikek) were certainly used in conjunction with shotguns and were decorated with Powis feathers especially for this work. Nonetheless, local kanaimàs—and there are memories of more than one in Paramakatoi—always seem to have been tolerated for a while. Sooner or later, though, they become generally "troublesome"—that is, they foment divisions with other villages and cast something of a pall over village life generally, turning up at collective feasts and rituals to the dismay of others. Such antisocial qualities form part of the historical trajectory of kanaimà.

Two kanaimàs were also resident in the village during my time there: Merimo and his father, Pirai, who was no less prominent. Pirai was originally from Kopinan, a Patamuna settlement that has a history of warfare with Paramakatoi (Whitehead 1996c), and that history played into the events of 1992–95. It was in fact Pirai's ritual vessel that had been secreted in Kuyali'yen cave and that set in motion my first encounter with kanaimà. In response to the "troubling" of that vessel, Pirai made direct threats to the wife of Waiking, one of the men who had accompanied me, and I received a letter from Waiking a few days after my return in 1995. It reads,

6.6.95

Dear Neil,
I am sorry to disappointed [sic] by not coming today. But it is due to unforeseen circumstances. However I would like to advise you not to direct questions relating to Kanaimà or avoid mentioning names you get your information from. You can ask the captain for any assistance. I am being advice [sic] not to approach him [Pirai] myself, you can do that.

Other villagers told me that Pirai's *pegal* (bag) had been searched in the weeks before my return, when he went to relieve himself while stopping at a house along the trail into Paramakatoi. It contained both a black scorpion, spirit master of poisons, and two armadillo tails. Concerning Pirai, it was important for me to know that his wife had died after we had entered the cave and "troubled" the vessel in there. She had been killed by people from Pirai's natal village, Kopinan, where it was alleged that Pirai had killed people as a kanaimà. His wife was then killed in revenge by the victim's relatives, because they couldn't find

Robinson and Matteson Williams, Patamuna *kàyik* (eminent men).

Pirai himself. He was away "doing his work," so they took her instead. It is said that they beat her to death somewhere in the bush outside Paramakatoi.

Pirai is closely associated with another man from Kopinan, Bishop, who is well known across the whole region as an eminent kanaimà. All of the piyas with whom I spoke, as well as other kanaimàs themselves, acknowledged that he is a "really bad man." Ironically, he is named for one of the Anglican Bishops of British Guiana in the 1950s. The situation of "The Bishop" suggests something of the social milieu of kanaimà, as much as its magical and shamanic pretensions. He is also regularly mentioned, apart from his kanaimà expertise, as something of a "slick operator," having the ear of key personnel in the *backdam* (that is, with individuals who own mining operations), as well as four sons who share "his work" with him—the suggestion being that both his influence in the backdam and that fact that he has four sons "goes along with" being kanaimà. It is assessments such as these that give kanaimà an important social dynamic, regardless of whether or not the individuals themselves are actually adept.

This is no less the case with Pirai and his son, only the social dynamic here is one of marginalization, not of influence. Pirai's original outsider status as an in-marrying member of a traditionally enemy village, his own personal disfigurement, and his single male progeny combine to make his social situation marginal, no less than would the suspicion of kanaimà.[19] Added to this is the knowledge that Pirai works with Bishop as his "spotter," so that local cases of kanaimà, while not necessarily directly attributed to Pirai, are invariably seen as resulting from the kind of intelligence on particular individuals that he is passing on to Bishop. As a consequence, during 1995, there were intense discussions among the kàyik, as to whether or not this was the moment when Pirai should be shotgunned, since the death of his wife would have inevitable consequences for people in Paramakatoi. It was presumed that Pirai would make the assumption that the killers of his wife were helped by residents in Paramakatoi, as Waiking's letter to me indicates. In fact, it was not Pirai who was killed but another kanaimà'san who, I found out much later, was also believed to be responsible for my "poisoning." Whatever the truth of the latter assertion, this scenario enmeshed me firmly in the web of accusation, prompting the letter quoted above and serving to indirectly link me with the shamanic assassination of that kanaimà. The tendency for kanaimà accusations to proliferate in this way gives a good sense of the sources of its much-noted pervasiveness. Just how pervasive that actual practice may be is suggested by the following account.

The Reluctant Kanaimà

This testimony was given by someone whose uncle, "DA," was a kanaimà. According to the narrator of DA's story, DA was very much smitten by a girl from Kaibarupai and to his joy married into the family and went to live with them. DA later said that when he first arrived at his father-in-law's house he wondered why it was that the family seemed always to be out in the bush. So the family decided to show him. What he then found out was that they were kanaimàs. Even women were kanaimà in this family. They told him that "if he wanted to marry them he had to become like them as well," so he allowed himself to be initiated. They took him out deep into the forest to a small clearing. There they gave him some herbs to drink, and as the herbs took effect he lay down. He felt himself becoming "heated" so they "kept fanning him . . . slow, slow . . . they kept fanning him as they had to keep the insects off." Then they covered him with leaves, "just like a tiger hides his kill," and he lay there. "After he lay there some time he feels his spirit moved out and then he saw a woman in her farm. . . . He killed her with his hands and stopped her up. . . . He didn't really know what he was doing." However, this experience really frightened him and "then he didn't want to be part of this family anymore, even though they wanted him . . . because he was a good hunter and tracker." Feeling that his children were badly mistreated by their mother and her relatives, DA brought them back to his natal home, Kato, for a little time.

So DA was in Kato and felt safe for a while, but his in-laws eventually attacked and poisoned him. According to the narrator, in whose house he finally died, he vomited blood all the while, and his skin was covered in bruises and marks from where he had been handled.[20] The narrator alluded to other injuries but did not wish to detail them any further. After DA died, his wife, LA, took their children back to live with the kanaimà family. Unfortunately the story of killing does not end there, for both the narrator's sixteen-year-old brother, EG, and twenty-three-year-old sister, PG, were later killed by these same kanaimàs. The brother and sister had been working on their farm. On returning home from the farm, although they did not recall any attack and were not injured orally or anally, they complained of not feeling well. That same night they both developed high fevers, headaches, diarrhea, vomiting, and cramps. By the next morning they had started vomiting up some kinds of fruits or leaves.[21] Four days later, both individuals were dead.

Afterward the "kanaimà family"—who the narrator wouldn't name to me, averring that neither would they be named to the police by themselves or by anyone else—were found to be hanging around in the area of Kato, stealing as they wished from people's farms and unguardedly boasting that they had "tied a couple of cows" (i.e., killed two people). Even though the narrator's family felt that they had suffered much already for their connection to this kanaimà family, they still heard the night owl, portent and messenger of kanaimà, around their house. They heard this for almost a year, every night, until the narrator's little brother, N, died in a manner similar to deaths of EG and PG. In a sardonic touch, the kanaimà family now boasted they had also "tied and killed an *akuri* (small edible forest mammal)," presumably a reference to the little boy, who was small for his age and had beautiful, light-colored hair. As a "kindness" to his family the medical examiner recorded this death as "yellow fever," though they all knew very well what the symptoms for that would have been. In any case, the narrator's grandfather was a piya, who "fought back against the kanaimàs" in his time, so "he always knew when they were around," even if, as on these occasions, there was little he could do to stop them.

Although themes of familial revenge play into these accounts and although the purpose of revenge may in fact be served, kanaimà killings are not always driven purely by ideas of vengeance. There is another social and ritual dimension to the death of kanaimàs, which I will later discuss.

Victims

Because the facts related may otherwise seem almost incredible—to outsiders anyway—I interviewed a trained nurse on the matter of kanaimà. (The interview was originally videotaped, and a copy of that tape is now in the possession of those who helped make it.) The Nurse is a widely respected person and can speak with the authority of a medical eyewitness to many cases of kanaimà mutilations and killings. She estimates that perhaps one killing a year takes place in Paramakatoi alone. Her status as a medical witness is especially interesting for the way in which she negotiates a passage from tradition to modernity, aware of our skepticism, yet driven by the intense experiences she relates. In particular, she notes firmly that kanaimà is a man, not the insubstantial "spirit" of missionary imagination, and that the symptoms of a kanaimà attack are distinct, but must be hidden from the medical authorities. She also notes that the young as well as the old are victims, so that it cannot be that kanaimà is simply used to account for unknown diseases or causes of death, as was suggested in some of the nineteenth-century accounts. Although she has something of a privileged position as the bearer of medical services, she places herself in real danger by choosing to speak in this way. For that reason, if no other, her testimony would have to be included in this book.

The Nurse's Account

I'm a nurse-midwife for Paramakatoi village. I do have a lot of experience dealing with their various symptoms. My mother was a Patamuna and I married a Makushi man.

I can just explain what the symptoms of kanaimà are. They [the victims] have a fever, which may resemble signs of symptoms of malaria or whatever, but then they go down very fast, after this one or two bouts of this fever, they go down very fast, and they complain of a pain in a particular point, or a couple particular points in their body, and that is it. And then, after three or four days, after the *steppin* [attack] of . . . whatever, their tongues become swollen and they're not able to speak to you anymore. Their whole face is swollen. Well, they say, we say, it is because they [the kanaimà] have used a snake fang that they have taken off from the killer snake, and they prefer the fangs, and it is still poisonous, although they have taken it off the body of the snake, it is still poisonous, and they prick the tongue of the victim with the fangs and so, but of course you know a snake bite will swell up, because of the venom. And so that is how it is that their tongues become swollen and they are not able to speak to you anymore. And then if you should ask them where they've been, all they do is point and that's all, and then, they don't really live very long, within a period of five days to seven days they're gone.

Um, we had that little boy who was brought in, a four-year-old boy, who was brought in to me. In his very first day he was just passing liquid, um, blood-stained liquid. And when I checked why, the anus was just open. Their was no stricture to the anus, it was just open. And then you look just open and you could have seen right from where you were looking, to wherever. That is what happens. And they say that the kanaimà takes out the anus part. Yeah, that's what we say. But then, what I was made to understand is that they really don't take anything out as such. They take the tail of a iguana, or an armadillo. It is slender to the very end, and they push it in from the small end and put it up as rough as they can, and so they rip the strictures of the anus and that is why it is like that. They have got some diarrhea. Just diarrhea and diarrhea and diarrhea. They cannot drink.

When I have to write a report [on the death] they [the government] will never believe me. I cannot put "Killed by a kanaimà" or "Attacked by a kanaimà." If they have gotten lockjaw from these wounds, I will say that they have died of tetanus. Okay? And if they've just had diarrhea and diarrhea and diarrhea. I will say complications of diarrhea. You know, severe diarrhea. That is how I would have to put it.

I have seen cases when they have maybe some bones have been broken. I had a nephew who died on the fourteenth of September last year. Right in my mother's house. It was a . . . he took in sick . . . right, uh, okay, let's say Friday morning about three o'clock he started having a fever. Friday. And then Saturday, he was ill all through the day, fever on and off. And then Saturday evening he died. And then when we examined the body, there was another nurse together with me, we examined the body there were marks of the fingers, like this, right? Apparently they had held him from the back because these fingers were to the front, on the forearm. And there were pricks on his back, and these pricks were oozing. Okay? He had been complaining of a terrible pain to the back. Just opposite his lung, one side that is. It was to the left side, no, it was to the right side. So I said, well, well I was trying to treat him for whatever it could have been. I treated him for pain, and fever, and whatever, but then I did not know that he had been attacked. Okay. Well, after he had died we saw these marks. And then these prick marks on his back.

Cases of kanaimà are not really too many. Sometimes people die from complications of malaria, complications of gastritis, they die from severe dehydration. Elderly folks really die from anemia, gross anemia. And so. But then young people just take in like that and they die. Well I've seen cases [of kanaimà], I may have had, within the course of my being a nurse, I've probably have, um, twenty to twenty-five cases. About twenty to twenty-five cases in the last thirty years, about one a year. Their bodies have no rigor mortis. They are breaking bones and putting things up them to do this. Yes, it happens. And there are certain times in the year when we believe the kanaimà is around. Certain times in the year, not all the time. During August, that is the cutting season. Our men would normally go out in the farms, to trim down their trees, they are alone. So they wait for that kind of a time to attack the people. Most times you will find them out. Well if we don't have any people dead, then we know that isn't the season they will be around! You see, it was just shortly after August when my nephew died. Having been attacked. The kanaimàs are hunting during certain points of the year, when they can get access. Yes, that is what happens, they are out there to do their damage at a certain time of the year, most times. And then you will hear them whistling. They make a strange sound, and you know that is kanaimà sound.

We've tried to stop it. There have been times when the people have tried to report cases like this to the police. But then, the policemen are Coastlanders, they don't really believe in our own kind of beliefs.

If you learned to kill you must then kill—they have the urge to kill and it might even be a brother or sister. Even if they do, and there was an attempt made to try to get to the attackers, but they have not been successful. There have been attempts. Some people have reported to the police, that this is what happened to their family, somebody in their family, a person has died and so and so on. But then they have not really been successful because the policemen, most times, mostly, are Coastlanders and so because it is from the start, from the inception [*sic*] of the knowledge, that [they think] kanaimà is a spirit. This spirit will kill people. Okay, that is true, but then how they have the idea that kanaimà is a spirit is because the first set of people, the missionaries, the white missionaries that came, nobody really knew English, so they couldn't explain what a kanaimà was from what a spirit is, so they said kanaimà is a spirit.[22] And that is the idea that everyone is running around with, that kanaimà are spirits. So the white folks now are still thinking that . . . kanaimà is a spirit, and a spirit will not attack a human being. That is it.

Why I particularly believe in kanaimà's actions is because, when I was working in Georgetown, when I was in training and working at Georgetown hospital, I would rarely come up with these kind of symptoms.[23] That's why. And these are things you only see here and in a number of other Amerindian societies.

They had this particular village [name suppressed], that they said had these kanaimàs, . . . and whenever they came into the village, they would tell me, "Be careful, those are kanaimàs, don't um, uh, you know, be careful with them. Don't trouble them. Or don't insult them in any way that they would have to retaliate or anything. Have little to do with them. Just have little to do with them." That is what I was told. But, you know, they never really troubled me because I never really had, well, I was teaching. Which child came to my class or I had to treat the child just ordinary, just like anybody else's child. So I never really had trouble with them. I hope not to have any problems with them. (Laugh)

They go to small children because they're easy to attack. They will not defend themselves as men would defend themselves, because men walk around with guns, bow and arrows, and knives, and so on, and ladies hardly do. Well, when they're going to the garden they have their cutlasses in their hands. The children have no means of defending themselves, so they go for those.[24] That is not a brave kanaimà to attack so. . . . No, no, I wouldn't think so. I wouldn't think so at all. A lot of times we've hear that the kanaimà got stabbed here, kanaimà got shot here, kanaimà got, not really shot to death maybe, but shot here and this. Maybe that is why, you know, they really don't like to attack men, because they have their means of defense.

Encounters

Before turning to previously published Amerindian accounts of kanaimà, this section first presents the tale of a kanaimà encounter. I chose this particular tale because the events therein typify the manner of kanaimà attack, particularly the use of hunting and tracking skills in locating and attacking the victim. Furthermore, the scenario of being attacked while "on the line" (asanda) is constantly feared and referred to among Patamuna men.

This tale was told in Patamuna; I heard it from an alleluia'san, an owner of alleluia chants, while actually standing on Kanaimà Hill, on the way to Wandapàtoi, beside where the kanaimà's attack took place. The alleluia'san insisted, "The story also has an important message— it shows us that the Kanaimà is, finally, only a man and that he can be defeated by *tuwènamasen'pen* (lack of fear) and a smart trick!" This story was translated by the son of the speaker.

Kanaimà Hill

The place where kanaimà lived was the savanna they call Tendapatoi, about eight miles from Kato. But these fellows, this fellow who he want to kill, live at Kato, or it wasn't far they were living, but he was against him for some reason, as usual [with] kanaimàs. . . . And so, he said he will as usual have a little balata bleeding. . . . They never used to bleed balata large amount, a big quantity then right? They would just collect a little, dry it on the plate, dry it on the plate until they get a certain amount of balata for go down and do a little trading in town. That was the usual . . . that's before aircraft and the road and so on . . . how they get to know this river really you know the usual . . . maybe the Caribs and everybody used to run up, run up Siparuni . . . so they know that was the road to go down. So they went. He and his little son went down. Buy up his little ammunition that was necessary with the little balata money. And then balata was very cheap right? And then maybe he got . . . he was pleased with the items he got for the balatas, and he came back. How the fellow at Tendapatoi know he was coming then? Because . . . people have no kind of communication, no transmits, no radio transmit, nothing, nothing at all from Georgetown to Kato, but how did he know then he was coming that very afternoon? Anyway, the message, by people moving from along this side to go to Siparuni-Balata Landing, they meet up with that guy from Kato coming up, now. . . . They said, "They have somebody waiting on you at Kato. Either you reach home safe or not. That is you, you know man, because he really plans that this is your final trip." You know, never to be seen again. So his wife was very worried about what was going on, that they know his style . . . what type of man he is. . . . Anyway, he didn't say nothing. He said, "Okay, I will still go . . . continue the journey and come up. . . ." Anyhow then around 3.30 or 4 o'clock the kanaimà man telling his wife, "I going and hear *maam* jeering . . . and you know the maam bird is the sweet bird, is around this part."[25] Now he telling his wife he going and hear the maam jeering, he's goin to come in the night. He [the kanaimà] left Tendapatoi around 4 o'clock in the afternoon to come up to . . . and wait on him Tusenen, that is past Taruka. So you can imagine the distance where he cover . . . with the time he left there is really . . . incredible man, you know?

Anyway he did like that, he came . . . and well this man from Kato, he came up, he and his little son, he already received the message that someone is waiting on him . . . but really he thought this man was waiting on him *at Kato*. Remember there was no kind of . . . he didn't have no bow and arrow, no weapon, nothing . . . but they used to use *kulak* (blowpipes) in those days, you know . . . shoot something. The usual . . . the weapon was *kunwa* (blowpipe dart). . . . They used to make dart and soak it in curare . . . so that is why that was very useful for them. . . . So he stop and chop this blue tree and get the dart . . . the measurement he wanted . . . he bundled it in a bundle . . . so he had it with him, you know carry weight so it's heavy. . . . So he follows [the path to] Tusenen and branches off to Kato . . . he make a very smart branch off [detour], he make it by without no tracking branch and he go to the creek. OK that was the day camp. He tell his son, "Careful tonight, sometimes this man, coming." He had that suspicion in him right? He was very careful that very afternoon that he got out last, last day or last night 'cause he waiting on him, definitely. He hear this jeering dokwaru . . . dokwaru . . . and you know I already said you hear a bird different from a man, even though he tried to call, it was totally different sounding. He called. And he said, I hear something, something. Eventually the kanaimà past the track where he branched off. And he [the kanaimà] moved in front. He call again . . . no answer. Maybe he so smart that, you know, he don't call that somebody answer him so he would know directly where he moved. So he [the kanaimà] come back to the same point where the man branch off and he call again, come past back the man . . . again come back to the same point but then he pick up the man track. Then he come. So he tell his son, "I'm gonna tie you over my hammock, I underneath you." So by fright the little boy dropped asleep and tired maybe too, so he drop asleep and the big man he didn't sleep. He wait to hear what's going on. Then he hears the kanaimà man coming . . .

there he comes. He blazes fireside to keep his light and fire. Now going down . . . it was getting little . . . then he [the kanaimà] come. He [the father] pick up the same dart, the bundle what he had ready for him . . . lying there in his hammock. The poor little boy he didn't know nothing. He was sleeping, you know really tired and sleeping. So he [the kanaimà] came and see the top one [hammock] first. He peep over the top one first to see, to make sure if it was a man or a boy at the top. When he checked, it was the little boy! Now he make a reverse back to go down a little bit more, but by this time the big man was already set with his dart, the bundle. He just lashed the man on his nose and he [the kanaimà] jumped like a tiger and that tiger he run. He [the father] wake up his son now and says, "He come! Kanaimà come!" And you know they didn't sleep back for a couple hours, they tried to hear back anything, but there was no noise no more. So they said. "OK, he's dead . . . or he's run away and he can't come back no more." Early morning they wake up he said "Good let's go. . . . Pack up!" and there they went. Then they pick up the blood running from the camp to the track . . . the main road. The blood, the blood, they track the blood, they tracked the blood. Kawa . . . pass through Kawa . . . go up Kato, past Kato, that very night, and reached to Tendapatoi. He [the kanaimà] said he got accident. He hear maam jeering very well, he hear this bird going up and when he go for look up to see the bird there the branch fall and lashed his nose. All the blood was clotting inside his nose. He can't breath properly. All his face blue, blue, blue, blue, and he telling everybody this branch fall on his nose and lash him, and you know he said it was an accident he had just now. That was it, he reach back in the night.

That very afternoon then the man reached Kato and he was greeted by his wife, you know. . . the wife gave him, you know, the tale, "Man him waiting on you I'm glad you come back safe 'cause he really mean to do something to you," he said "No," he was okay, "Yeah," he said, "Everybody is alright . . . no illness . . . nothing," you know he talk out the story—right away he asked questions, "What happened? Is everybody okay around this part?," she said, "Yes! The man is there waiting on you!" . . . So really, now in the morning he said, "To be sure, go and check that very man and see how he is, what is his condition, because I lashed somebody last night and here the blood run through, and maybe it's he." "Go" or you know, "check him," he said. So in the morning now the lady go there and they make a visit a special visit, and said there, "Everybody . . . how is everybody?" and there was the man, just lying. He didn't want the lady to come and see him, but eventually she went and check the man and there was the man. All is still get blue, blue, blue, all his nose is broke up, mash up with that heavy dart, right? That was a serious lash and he died. So that was the battle between them, and you never hear nothing back about Tendapatoi since then. That is what he's saying.

What Daddy was telling me now was, JW was a man, he know himself . . . a big kanaimà in Paramakatoi. He was a lone man. You know, he never had a son or nobody. And what he tell Daddy, he says, the same question I asked, "How did he know then that he make a smart branch off from the track, in the jungle?" not to say that you will see trace back, the track, or nothing at all or any stepping or, you know, chopping bush, or anything . . . nothing at all . . . just so. How he know then? Because he can track you to a certain distance in truth. You could be a whole day of traveling, he track you, and he said you've got a broke up branch in your arm like this [in the crook of your elbow] . . . and going . . . so wherever you branch off the little sticks will move, move shake, shake. One arm twitches, or the little stick moves or . . . move . . . shake. . . . He goes back and forth until he pick up the direction where you go. . . . And all the time he going behind you . . . wherever you branch there is a stick directing him. The kanaimà will use a mask too on his face when he's tracking you. Night owl feathers. They usually mix it together, they mix the feathers, light feather. The kanaimà man himself told him that they plan this thing so neat that they disguise their face with different, different birds feather. You know the feather, it gotta be not plain it gotta be colored, it's mixed, it's mixed with different types of bird feather. . . . And every time he shakes you cannot recognize what's really going on, what is the object about, because everything is moving, feathers shaking. What he saying is a man like Johnny, he's from Kopinan. Johnny and another fellow from Kopinan too. He was a great man. He was a great kanaimà man and he himself said he shot one! He was getting threatened by somebody or some kanaimà man was tracking him too, and he fired the gun at him and when he go and check, it was the feathers cut and [that] he shot. Cut the feathers and it was the same feathers like what we pick up. It is not one, it is mixed up, together mixed, for camouflage. So that is the type of feathers, and I'm really sorry I didn't pick up all of them [feathers from the kanaimà's mask].

This account brings out many interesting features of the discourse about kanaimà, but it is also important for the direct account it gives of a particular individual. This account also reflects how kanaimàs are repeatedly represented in indigenous discourse as being fleet of foot and having superb tracking skills. It also provides additional detail on the kanaimà's methods of pursuit and style of attack.[26]

Published Amerindian Accounts of Kanaimà

I have collected additional accounts of kanaimà among the Patamuna, but other firsthand accounts have also been recorded among the Pemon, Akawaio, Patamuna, Wapishana, and Makushi over the last four decades (Foster 1993; Forte and Melville 1989; Guppy 1961). These accounts very much confirm the general analysis of kanaimà practice made here, but are also useful in providing further context to Patamuna accounts. Briefly, Guppy (1961, 171–72) records the testimony of a Waiwai man who, when a boy, had the very frightening experience of his house being assailed by a group of kanaimàs; "they never came back. But I always remember that, and that is why if ever I could meet a man who was a Kanaima, I would like to study with him, to see if it is a genuine thing." However, Henfrey (1964), who traveled through Patamuna territory a few years later, only reports kanaimà in relation to his materials collected on the origins of alleluia.

Janette Forte and Ian Melville recorded a range of "Amerindian testimonies" on many subjects and collected them into a 1989 publication. In that work there are five testimonies that mention kanaimà, three from Patamuna and two from Karinya. Notably, all the testimonies from among the Patamuna are by women. This is significant not because it in some sense "invalidates" the testimony—indeed there is testimony that women may become kanaimà—but because kanaimà is strongly inflected as a masculine performance with apparent signs of sexualized mutilation, beyond those that are ritually enjoined. Both the inexperienced and the personally vengeful are likely to exceed or embellish the required forms of kanaimà mutilation, which is recognized as either part of their training or in the fact that kanaimàs, like piyas, are susceptible to corruption of their ideal practice. However, I repeatedly observed that women were told only about certain features of kanaimà, particularly its connection to warfare and the kwayaus, but that its shamanic purposes were never so revealed. Kanaimà's persistence, since the days of the kwayaus have long since ended, may be explained by reference to other forms of masculinized aggression, particularly toward women. It must also be recognized that under some circumstances women find the notion of kanaimà attack sexually exciting, much as masochistic or violent fantasies are part of our own sexual culture.[27]

The following testimonies were given by three Patamuna women (Forte and Melville 1989). The first speaker is from Waipa village.

> Well after knowing that people from Paramakatoi say that Waipa people are Kanaima, and that their people are always dying from Kanaima, I always tell myself they stupid because they have nurses and they could easily proved whether something like that happened. But they don't try to follow up or trace what it is. So I always say most deaths are not related to Kanaima. The only time I tend to believe in Kanaima is when the whole skull is soft as if someone has beaten it out. Sometimes you find that indeed. Sometimes also the arm can turn right round in its socket which is really not supposed to be—the same thing with the leg. And sometimes the person bleeds through the nose, the eyes even, one hear all sorts of things. (113–14)

This testimony is fascinating in that it challenges the whole idea of kanaimà, in lieu of precisely the kind of statement provided by the Nurse, and because it was collected in the very village the Nurse herself discussed. However, having questioned the existence of kanaimà, the woman then goes on to delineate a number of kanaimà cases. So, the context of intervillage accusation appears to lead to a wish to deny the reality of kanaimà, at least at first.

The second woman's account (Forte and Melville 1989, 121) is brief and skeptical, but acknowledges, "The Patamuna have a strong belief in kanaima but I don't believe in those things myself." The third woman's account, however, is more revealing.

> To become a kanaima they used some binas. Some binas are gingers, some are lilies, some are from the rhizome family. They would rub some of the binas on their skins and they would drink some in order to transform themselves into kanaimas. They would also disguise themselves in the skins of tigers or anteaters and then go after the person they intended to kill. . . . I think that these binas that they use must have the same effect on them like marijuana. For instance if a kanaima is jealous of somebody doing something, if that person has more things than them, they would become so jealous that they could even kill their own families, their sisters or brothers. They could do anything when they use those binas; they have no feelings for anybody. . . . My great-grandfather was eventually killed by the villagers when they couldn't take any more killings. (130–31)

This account is particularly interesting for the emphasis given to the kanaimà's use of binas and for her claim that her great-grandfather was kanaimà, which is how she knew these things. She also gives a very contemporary reference to her account by using the analogy of binas to marijuana in order to explain the motivations for kanaimà. The shamanic dimensions of kanaimà are not necessarily evident to her.

The final two accounts come from a Warao man, who lives next to the Karinya at Manawarin, and a Karinya woman, whose friend's father was a Karinya kanaimà. These accounts are vivid, providing forceful testimony as to the details of kanaimà practice and its meaning for native people more widely. The Warao man's account (Forte and Melville 1989, 172–73), which follows, insists on the "spiritual" aspects of kanaimà, which is notably absent from the previous narrations.

> The belief in kanaima is very deep rooted among the Manawarin Caribs. They say that kanaima are people born with certain gifts or are children of kanaima who will learn the craft of kanaima and develop the ability to become kanaima themselves. The Caribs say that such a person or such a family, possessed of the ability to become invisible, let's say, and therefore are able to attack you when you least suspect that there is someone close to you. According to the Caribs, kanaima can see into the future and possess certain chants which give them supernatural powers.
>
> The belief in kanaima has come under severe attack from the evangelical churches over the last decade. The pastors of these churches say that people who believe in kanaima or dabble in this form of superstition cannot inherit the Kingdom of God. Under this sustained pressure I have noticed that the Caribs are less willing to continue with practices such as kanaima.

The Karinya woman's testimony is not unlike that of the "reluctant kanaimà," involving as it does the observation of kanaimà by a family member of the killer, who eventually consumes his own, and it also further illumines the Warao man's reference to invisibility and the relationship of piya to kanaimà in general.

> When I lived at Wallaba the daughter of this same piaiman stayed with me to keep me company. She gave me firsthand accounts of Carib beliefs in general, and especially about their strong belief in kanaima. She said that her father was not only a piaiman. He was a practicing kanaima as well and could put his knowledge and powers

to work for curing or for killing. . . . At nights . . . when her father was about to leave to perform a kanaima act, he would make himself invisible before their eyes.[28] In order to become invisible . . . her father had first to locate and kill a land camoudie (anaconda). He would then leave it to rot on the ground and on every bone of this snake a little plant would spring up without anyone having planted it there. Her father would then choose some of those plants and make a special preparation with them by putting them in some sort of oil. In addition to using this preparation he would burn other things and rub them on his body in order to transform himself into a kanaima. Of course he would repeat special chants or formulae at the same time. He'd be in front of them one minute and when they looked again he would be gone. (185–87)

She continues that the man would go as far away as the Waini or Barima Rivers to kill, returning before morning, and describes his mode of attack, which was very much in line with what has already been reported. She also adduces two additional "proofs" of his powers: the occasion when he blinded his wife for four days, then restored her sight; and the occasion when he killed her and then was himself killed because her corpse had been poisoned in anticipation of his visit. She adds that "people do not like to admit that they believe in kanaimà but they don't take chances if they can help it!"[29]

One final testimony that is helpful in understanding kanaimà was made by a Wapishana (Foster 1993, 26). His perspective is interesting because his cultural tradition places him outside the kanaimà complex. Like the Lokono, the Wapishana obviously know of kanaimà, but it is not claimed as part of their cultural heritage.

> Kanaima originally came from the Makushi Indians. It is a simple thing, a bina, just a plant. It is a man just like me, any man. Say a person [feels he has been wronged and wants to get even]. He makes a contract with the [kanaima] who kills with the plant. The kanaima travels in the wind. He takes the plant and passes it over the soles of the [seeker of revenge], from heel to toe. The person closes his eyes and in a minute he travels miles and miles with the kanaima. He hides in the farm with the kanaima and points out the man he wants to kill. . . . They attack as human beings but they wear masks on their faces; some paint their faces ugly. A lot of people appear but only one is a real person; the others are manifestations of the spirit of the plant. One by one they attack with a piece of wood with leaves tied on top.

This account reiterates the use of the bina charms and emphasizes plant magic generally, even suggesting that the plants themselves attack, led by the kanaimà as shaman carrying the yé stick decorated with leaves. One other feature of the testimonies is an insistent distinction between the symptoms of kanaimà and those of other sicknesses, kanaimà always causing vomiting. The accounts collected by Forte and Melville, as well as the Wapishana materials collected by Foster, thus broadly conform to the ideas about kanaimà expressed in the preceding testimonies. So it remains to draw out those meanings as they have been historically practiced and performed—to explore kanaimà as an indigenous category for understanding and mediating the invaders and also as a colonial category for understanding the nature of the invaded.

CHAPTER 4

Shamanic Warfare

Before it is possible to disaggregate the category of "shaman" to better appreciate the very significant differences in the means and ends of shamanic performances, the meaning of the term must, paradoxically, be extended to include both the alleluia prophets (iwepyatàsak) and the Christian evangelists. While the "shamanistic" attributes of alleluia have long been recognized (Butt Colson 1954, 1960, 1971), the idea that Christian evangelism should be considered as shamanism is more provocative. However, it allows ethnographers to do justice to native testimony that understands Christianity as another aspect of the spiritual armor that an individual may utilize. The word "armor" here is taken precisely from the native viewpoint in which evangelical Christianity, already somewhat domesticated by the alleluia movement, became a direct and effective means to counter kanaimà. This is borne out by the way in which first alleluia and then induction into Christianity were understood as potent ways to ward off the threat of kanaimà, which did not involve either the dangerous figure of the piya, who himself may anyway be a kanaimà, or a lifetime of anxious precaution to forestall the threat of a kanaimà attack.

As a result of this plurality of spirit power in the highlands, there has been more than 150 years of overt conflict between the various protagonists of kanaimà, alleluia, piya, and "godliness." These conflicts are certainly enacted in the spirit domain, for the night sky is replete with the souls of contending shamans, but they also have a very real physical consequence through the history of shamanic assassinations, kanaimà "executions," and priestly extirpations. Such conflicts are most certainly rooted in the social and political life of the village community, but the pattern of such local conflicts must also be understood in the context of broader historical changes that have occurred among the Patamuna, Akawaio, and Makushi over this period. Three closely entwined issues—the relationship of shamanism to warfare, the changes in warfare as a result of increasing external contacts, and the history of shamanic performance itself—thus warrant examination in light of each other.

SHAMANIC WARFARE, ASSAULT SORCERY, AND PROPHETIC HISTORY

Textual sources from the sixteenth century onward make copious reference to shamanism as an adjunct to warfare. This "war-shamanism" seems to have been practiced as part of piya and invariably involved the divination of the enemy's position and intentions, as well as magical assaults that delivered sickness and misfortune. Such shamanism was practiced by chiefs, for whom being *piya'san* (shamanically adept) was an important component of their overall political authority, as much as by piya who were allied with a particular chief or war-leader.[1] This style of aggressive shamanism was not any kind of substitute for military attack, but a preliminary and partner to it. As such it can been seen as the expression of a fundamental social and cultural relationship, politically sanctioned as collective antagonism, ritually evoked in shamanism, and publicly performed in rituals of vengeance—song, dance, storytelling, sacrifice—and then militarily enacted. At the same time, aggressive shamanic assault on one community by another might provoke military attack; in this respect war shamanism certainly exemplifies the way in which accusations of sorcery function to create and sustain various kinds of sociopolitical distinction (Butt Colson 2001; Im Thurn 1883; Rivière 1970). However, understanding this does not exhaust, by any means, the significance given to magical assaults, nor does it adequately interpret them, since the forms of death that result, particularly in the case of kanaimà, also express a particular poetic of violent death. The manner of wounding and killing is certainly not arbitrary, but the ritual identity of the victim often is. That the ritual identity of victims may or may not be related to their social identity in invariant ways has been the key stumbling block to a better appreciation of kanaimà's relationship to other forms of shamanism and warfare. In short, kanaimà is not war-shamanism in the sense outlined above; rather, kanaimà "goes to war" if certain historical and political conditions dictate it.

As a result, kanaimàs must be coerced or coopted in the political projects of community warfare and vengeance, but the unfolding historical circumstances of the nineteenth century gave kanaimà a special place in those chiefly projects. In essence the kanaimà was capable of performing a physical assassination, unlike the piya, and delivered it in a manner that perfectly suited a situation in which guns had become prominent. Piya assault was too generalized—it attacked communities with sickness—but kanaimà could target the kind of powerful individuals who, with an "eight or ten stand of guns" (Hilhouse 1825, 23), could muster an effective army for community terror. Assassination thus emerged as a potent military technique as evolving war culture concentrated political power in the hands of a few men, the possessors of guns. According to contemporary accounts, the leaders of such armed groups—the kàyik such as Bengi or Kosopá—and particularly their kanaimà allies, just got to be too much, "During that time there was miseries, too many at war." Into this burgeoning space of death were then inserted various ideas for a "new life," both the missionaries' gospel of peace and the mimetic voices of the alleluia prophets and singers.

An unacknowledged compact between an absent-minded Anglican evangelism of the interior and the iwepyatàsak (prophets) of alleluia (see Butt Colson 1998) then seemed set to lead the converts to that "new life," but the advent of American evangelical proselytizing in the 1940s and 1950s, followed by the end of British colonial rule in the 1960s, radically changed the historical conjuncture. The direct spiritual attacks of the Pilgrim Holiness Church on the alleluia singers and piya, and the relative neglect of the interior by the post-independence Burnham government, meant that neither the "cargo" of material development nor of spiritual redemption was ever delivered to the interior. However, with the explosion of diamond and gold mining in the Pakaraimas from the 1980s onward, there was a renewed wave of intrusions by traders and dealers, as well by the new prophets of "development" and "human rights"—for whom the kanaimàs have provided a suitable welcome. The reported florescence of kanaimà in the last two decades is in consonance with these latest intrusions, as it may have been in the initial intrusion of poor Hugh Godwin, ripped to pieces on the Orinoco.

But history is also about the future, for history *is* prophesy—words about *what has been* gain meaning only from what those words say about *the things that are to come*. In this sense the Patamuna also practice a prophetic history. The forms of Patamuna history are concerned with sustaining a Patamuna way that situates individuals and their social groups in a landscape charged with historical significance (Whitehead forthcoming) and allows them to continually negotiate the terms of being in that landscape through the action of shamanic iwepyatàsak. Prophecy thus can accommodate change wrought from the outside and sustain a set of relationships with Amerindian others—the Makushi, the Kopinan Patamuna, the Kawaliyanas, or the Karinya—in a way that gives continuity to Patamuna identities. History is not therefore just concerned with cataloging sociopolitical events; it is intimately linked to shamanic practice and prophecy. Acts of history-making include not only material, physical events but a hidden dimension of struggle for the order of the cosmos. This is evinced in the conflict between iwepyatàsak or the alleluia-san, who can remake the world through the invention of shamanic tradition, and the kanaimà, who preserve world order through the exchange of ekati (life force) with the original beings, particularly Makunaima, master of plants and animals. Thus, paralleling the history of warfare with named political and ethnic groups is a shadow war in which enemy shamans contend with each other through the use of spirit proxies.

Each shaman has a number of such familiars disguised as predators and raptors who will seek out a foe while he is ascending the spirit ladder (kalawali). If that ladder can be cut while an enemy shaman, or kanaimà, climbs it, he will die, and his pack of kanaimà-killers are left leaderless and in great spiritual danger. Such leaderless kanaimà have been reported in the literature a number of times, and they are usually killed by the kwayaus (warriors). However, a similar fate might befall an iwepyatàsak and his followers, who in turn are then physically deconstructed and, unable to resunder their bodies, are spiritually disabled by the kanaimà. In this way history may also become *embodied* quite literally in the physical presence of given individuals—that is, their very existence becomes a token of Patamuna historical vision. This is not the same as the heroic histories of kings and chiefs that cast certain lineages in a potent social role, but a recognition of the way in which individual bodies become the vehicles for hidden forces, revealed only in the transformation such bodies make into jaguars, anteaters, butterflies, and avian raptors.

Patamuna life-cycle rituals thus aim to fix and locate bodies in a cultural schema that envisions bodies as texts from which the action of the past may be read. Bodies, especially Patamuna bodies, are usually produced through the socializing forces of marriage, childbirth, and the practice of couvade, but this intent may be disrupted, a historical disjuncture may occur, when bodies not so socialized—such as ghosts, dormant bush-spirits, kanaimà shamans, or enemy shamans—intrude in the processes of what otherwise would be an almost inevitable and clearly determined path of unfolding individual and collective destiny. Individual destiny thus becomes detached from the collective by reference to these intrusive and unsettling appearances. Most recently, coastlanders such as miners and soldiers, as well as outsiders such as white-men, coming as colonial actors, missionaries, and anthropologists also appear as chaotic forces in the continuance of Patamuna life.

The Patamuna vision of history thus sees discontinuity not as evidence of progress but as evidence of external threat—first to individual persistence, then to that of a kin-group, and ultimately to the Patamuna collectively. The first white-man in the Yawong valley is recalled as a cannibal and the leader of a group of Caribs that were searching for balata and other trade opportunities, as well as the ekati of Patamuna people. But it is the killing of these outsiders, which took place at Kali'nasulatàpù, and their physical destruction that are more clearly recalled and that in Patamuna historicity represent a mimetic equalization of the power relations between themselves and those who would prey on them. The dismemberment and consumption of Patamuna bodies by the kanaimà is thus analogically seen as an attack on the body-politic as historically constituted through human action. Kanaimà assassination alludes not merely to the contingent inequalities of political or economic power but also to the negating force of those dark and hidden potentialities that threaten the humanity of Patamuna life—its sociality, its ecology, and its prophetic vision.

The power of alleluia chants to negate the kanaimà ability to locate prey is, however, closely linked to the historical moment of their invention, and as such they are seen as a contingent and evanescent practice that will also end. Indeed, when the alleluia chants and their shamanic vision return south to the land of the Makushi, from whence they originally came, this will also portend the end of all things, the end of historical time itself—unless prophetic vision can indicate a new means to sustain ekati in the face of the divine hunger of the originary beings, especially Makunaima. The writings, or texts, of Makunaima, left in the form of petroglyphs, are thus evidence for the recurrence of the possibility of prophetic vision, and as the year 2000 approached so a new prophecy was heard in the Yawong valley. Bagit Paul, once a minister in the Christian church, received a rock-crystal that enabled a vision of the apocalyptic end of the Pakaraima mountains in a great flood that would carry away all—except those who now began a path of spiritual redemption through fasting, the rejection of western medicines, and constant song. Such a vision is not without precedent. In the nineteenth century, a false prophet was reported by British missionaries to be similarly active in the highlands, preaching the end of time and the material redemption of the Amerindians. But the false prophet was also a white man and here it becomes relevant to remark that my own presence was itself testament to the imminence of radical change among the Patamuna and that my own coming was subject to prophetic vision.

THE HISTORICITY OF KANAIMÀ, 1750–1880

It seems uncertain whether kanaimà emerged from piya or represents, as some Patamuna and Makushi claim, an older, more fundamental, and therefore more powerful system of shamanic performance. Given these conflicting claims and the lack of definitive evidence one way or another, attempting to adjudicate such claims seems less important than attempting to understand why they are made. Moreover, even if one cannot descry the temporal origins of kanaimà as a shamanic category, one can provide nearly a 200-year history of its practice and interpretation. The reasons why claims as to kanaimà's relative antiquity are made then can be seen to relate strongly to the history of its practice.

Significantly, the first clear mention of kanaimà in European sources comes from the beginning of the nineteenth century and, moreover, it appears in a discussion of Akawaio warfare of that period. Brett (1881, 195) even suggests the Akawaio may have been the originators of kanaimà. This ethnological link has proved indissoluble, and the notion of kanaimà as but an aspect of Akawaio militariness remains obdurately in the literature. However, the ritual complexity of kanaimà, its claims to antiquity, and the relative powerlessness of piya to counteract or intercept kanaimàs seem to indicate rather more than that. This is not to suggest that kanaimà was not associated with warfare—quite the contrary—but the growing connection between kanaimà and warfare was a historical, not ritual, phenomenon. Kanaimà may not have developed in order to meet the changing face of armed conflict, but it certainly found an expanded social and political role as the practice of war and the bases for political aggregation were altered as a result of colonial intrusion in the nineteenth century.

The Kapohn (Akawaio and Patamuna) first appeared in the colonial record in the mid-seventeenth century, with a reference to the "Occowyes"(Scott 1925); by 1724 they were being drawn more and more into the orbit of Dutch administration, such that by the end of the eighteenth century they had become a valued part of the colonial apparatus of control among the black slave population. The name "Akawoi" (cinnamon) itself may result from the hoped-for trade in "wild cinnamon" that the Dutch West India Company sought in the Pakaraima region, as well as from the association of Kapohn groups on the Cuyuni and Mazaruni Rivers with this plant (Harris and Villiers 1911, 499). In this period the Akawaios were drawn into conflicts with the Karinya, from both the Dutch territories and from the Spanish territories and missions in the Orinoco (Whitehead 1988).

Distinct references to what are probably the Patamuna appear in 1778, as the Dutch authorities mention "a sort of bastard nation of the Acuway Indians called Arenacottes" (BGB IV, 190–92), indicating "erena-gok," or people from the Ireng River region. These references occur in relation to the Dutch trading post Arinda, at the confluence of the Essequibo and Rupununi Rivers, where the post-holder reported that a Makushi and two Arenacotte children had been brought in for sale as slaves. He added that the Arenacotte were also in the upper Cuyuni and along the Siparuni Rivers, above the Dutch post there, and that they "do business under the whites." The documents also seem to indicate that the Patamuna had encountered and captured a group of black runaway slaves. For these reasons a party of Karinya were to raid the Patamuna to recapture the slaves and also to bring in some live captives for interrogation.

However, the end of the eighteenth century represents a high-water mark for colonial administration and influence in this region. The War of Spanish Independence in Venezuela in the 1800s and the Treaty of London in 1813, which ceded all of Dutch Guiana, except Surinam, to the British, profoundly altered the position of native groups within the political economy of the region as a whole. Put simply, they became much more marginal to the progress of colonial and neo-

national political economy. The trade in forest products and their role as a "bush-police" simply evaporated as slavery was abolished and as the trade in dyes, gums, resins, and so forth dwindled away (Whitehead 1988).

It was in this context that Hilhouse (1825) wrote *Indian Notices*, as a way of suggesting both how the native population of the interior was a hidden resource and how easily the alliances of old might be resurrected if only some interest in interior development was shown. Accordingly, Hilhouse's remarks on the Akawaio and Patamuna focus on their military and economic relevance and usefulness to the colony. However, by the time that Hilhouse writes of the Patamuna directly they had already been indirectly affected by earlier contacts with the Dutch and their fleeing black slaves. (For the Patamuna, issues about black coastlanders cannot be properly separated from ideas about kanaimà and about self-representation to outsiders.)

As a result of these indirect contacts, and as Hilhouse also makes clear, guns had found their way into the interior in some numbers. Indeed, Hilhouse characterizes Akawaio warfare as having been substantially adapted to their prevalence. Patamuna oral history (Whitehead 1996c), on the other hand, indicates that it would be some time before guns became so readily available to them in such numbers. This is not surprising since it was the Akawaio's favored position in the old Dutch colonial economy that was the source of their relative military dominance, as explained by Hilhouse (Whitehead 1992). As a result, Brett (1881, 197) writes, "In former days (and possibly even now, in some instances) their [the Akawaio's] expeditions were *predatory* also. They would attack peaceful villages under cover of darkness, slay all who were able to offer resistance, enslave the defenseless, and carry off the spoil. Thus they became even more terrible to the peaceful tribes, because more subtle in their rapacity, than the formidable Caribs themselves" (emphasis in original).

In line with the relatively privileged military position of the Akawaio, and bearing in mind that the Patamuna and Akawaio were closely related as *Kapohn* (sky people), Hilhouse in turn characterized the Patamuna as "fierce," as did the Makushi.[2] However, Patamuna opposition to the "entry of white men into their country," as reported by Hilhouse, certainly has changed since then, and contemporary oral history (Whitehead 1996c) is preoccupied with their relative exclusion from regional contacts with the coast and with efforts made to correct that situation. In the eighteenth century, however, those individuals who traded with the native population were a source of much conflict both with the Dutch authorities and among the Amerindians themselves. As a result, there are a number of references to these traders being killed, often by poisoning (Harris and Villiers 1911, 231, 260).

The Akawaio may well have used kanaimà as an adjunct to other innovative military techniques, since this is the sense that Hilhouse (1825, 22) seems to give to Akawaio kanaimà, referring to it as their "nightly enterprises" and actually distinguishing it as a separate tactic from the "rapidity of their marches." The Patamuna and Makushi are no less associated with kanaimà in nineteenth-century sources, and for them it may have had a different application and derivation as a military tactic. For the Makushi, kanaimà may have been deployed as a defensive technique against the slaving predation of the Karinya, Patamuna (who sold them to the Akawaio), and the Akawaio. Nevertheless, the consequences of increasing integration into the colonial world from the mid-eighteenth century on was to intensify the frequency of raiding for slaves and to simultaneously alter the basis of communal raiding by selling the captives. So, even for those who were dominant in this system of community predation, the military consequences often were to stimulate the invention of new tactical responses of those preyed on. Such conditions applied no less to the Patamuna, who found themselves fighting not only their traditional opponents, such as the Makushi, but also the Karinya, who had brought the first "Arenacotte" to the Arinda post, as well as the Pemon and Ye'kuana from the eastern highlands. However, it is other Patamuna communities, not the Akawaio, who figure as aggressors in some of the other military conflicts narrated in these same accounts.

Patamuna oral history indicates that the practice of warfare was not at all conflated with the practice of kanaimà. Indeed there is a specific term for the "secret avenger" so beloved of the nineteenth-century descriptions: *wenaiman,* literally "a person who pursues a killer" (but also the technique of pursuit). The history of the old man who turned into a cashew tree (Whitehead forthcoming) is part of an account of just such a wenaiman. However, this is held to be quite distinct from a kanaimà, who may certainly act as a wenaiman, but could have other roles, such as assassination. Camouflage and concealment form a part of kanaimà art that relates specifically to the military wenaiman. Such wenaiman could adopt other tactics and personnel, of course. For ex-

Patamuna *benab* (houses) at Wandapàtoi.

ample, it is related that on one occasion, rather than directly pursue
Makushi raiders, the Patamuna ambushed them at a cave in the savannas that they had used previously to evade the wenaiman. By the same
token the kwayaus could adopt the appearance of kanaimàs, and it is
recalled that when kwayaus attacked they would whistle like kanaimàs.
Kàyik insist that as guns brought guerrilla tactics to the conduct of
warfare, so kanaimà came to have a definite role in war. In particular
it has been suggested that the increase in the initiation of kanaimàs in
the 1920s and 1930s was directly related to those kwayaus who went
"underground" as supplies of guns coming from Georgetown and up
the Siparuni, as well as from unnamed whites, dried up.

  A Kalitna [Karinya] raid on Wandapàtoi, in the late 1920s, is vividly
recalled, and the route of the raiding party, up Essequibo and along
the Siparuni, was an important gateway for other outsiders, such as
the balata-bleeders and missionaries, into Patamuna-land. Those who
recall the Wandapàtoi raid insist that a white man was influential in
directing Kalitna raiding. He gave out clothes and *alakapusa* (guns)
and even personally accompanied the raiders at times. He also joined
them in selecting dead bodies that they would carry off—supposedly
to eat them.[3] Following the raid on Wandapàtoi, a Patamuna encountered the returning Kalitna at a little creek in the Siparuni headwaters.

Shamanic Warfare 137

He stopped and asked them what it was that he could smell in the baskets they were carrying. They told him that he should not ask unless he was prepared to light a fire for cooking right then and there. The place where he encountered the Kalitna carrying their human cargo is known appropriately as *Abowambá* ("wrappings-of-the-arm-of-a-man"). The Patamuna man hurried on to Wandapàtoi where he saw the effects of the Kalitna raid. A wenaiman was immediately organized and pursued the Kalitna into the Siparuni valley. The site where the wenaiman finally caught up with the Kalitna is known as *Kali'na sulatàpù* ("place-where-the-Caribs-got-barbecued").

In all these external conflicts the search for, or the use of, shotguns was an important motive for raiding. Certainly the capture of women or the plunder of metal axes and knives are also cited as closely related benefits of raiding. The traditional weapons of taikek (war club), *peleuw* (bow and arrow), or kulak (blow-pipe) poisoned with *ulali* (curare) were effective enough but did not permit the kind of blanket firepower that a shotgun attack produced. According to current testimony the last *weypantaman,* or "killing fight," against the Makushi at Kulauyak-toi, was in the 1920s (Whitehead 1996c).

The apparent prevalence of the kanaimàs in nineteenth-century sources may then be related, according to the Patamuna, to the way in which the advent of gun warfare made the wenaiman an offensive as well as defensive technique. Previously the wenaiman was formed in response to raiders with the idea of a hot pursuit that might quickly and effectively avenge any injuries or deaths. As the guerilla tactics of gun warfare made smaller parties much more effective, the pursuit and tracking of those fleeing raiders became commensurately more difficult. At the same time the kanaimà was an already accomplished exponent of solitary or small group attack, so that kanaimà could just as well service the offensive in the new era of guerrilla gun warfare. Despite the military role of the kanaimàs, the kwayaus were still considered necessary for the social control of kanaimà, albeit by direct physical violence. The accounts of famed warriors and killers, such as Kosopá or Kangai, therefore often include reference to their being "big-killers" of kanaimàs.

As a result of this facility with small group or individual attacks, the shamanic abilities of the kanaimà offered specific military advantage, since a generalized assault by a piya might not meet the more immediate tactical aims of a small raiding party. For Patamuna, this was the key factor that led to the upsurge in the use of kanaimàs—they were more effective than the traditional wenaiman. Unlike the kwayaus, who offered open combat with clubs and arrows, the kanaimà made secret war, especially when the enemy had guns. So *kanaimà* came to mean "hiding . . . a secret revenge"; in this sense it is claimed as a Patamuna and Makushi word, it being pointed out that the Akawaio say *idodo* (see also Butt Colson 2001). This lexical difference may bear on the issue of how kanaimà entered into the war complexes of the Kapohn and Makushi, for both cultural and historical variation in this process is to be expected. In which case the Akawaio use of the term *idodo* may be related to the regional Cariban term *itoto*, meaning, among other things, "enemy" (see Whitehead 1988). The fact that the Akawaio use this term suggests that kanaimà was attached to their existing war complex and that it may not have originated with them, as the Makushi and Patamuna suggest. This need not be reduced to simply a case of social spacing through mutual accusation, but may also reflect the differing historical circumstances, the historicity, of kanaimà itself as responding to the military need to offset inequalities of access to guns. This does not conclusively bear on the matter of the antiquity and origins of the kanaimà complex itself, but it does show how it may yet be possible to reconstruct those beginnings if sufficient attention is given to the textual and oral histories. As a result of the character of the historical moment at which our first knowledge of kanaimà occurs, the colonial sources give an emergent picture of the kanaimà as the "secret avenger." This militarized figure then gives way, as warfare itself is suppressed by the colonial authorities, to an increasingly domesticated and sanitized figure who becomes the righter of familial and personal wrongs, the legalistic ombudsman of the wild woods. However, this embryonic Amerindian Superhero is intellectually aborted in the colonial sources by its indelible association with bizarre forms of violence and suspect behavior with regard to body fluids.

FALSE PROPHETS, MISSIONARIES,
AND THE ORIGINS OF ALLELUIA, 1750–1880

Paralleling the changes in the colonial political economy that brought the interior peoples into closer contact with the Dutch authorities, the progress of Spanish evangelization on the lower Orinoco similarly affected them. Butt Colson (1996) has researched the appearance of three ephemeral Spanish missions on the Cuyuni, Mazaruni, and Siparuni Rivers in 1756. These missions were founded with the aid of Amerindian converts from the missions on the lower Orinoco, and they inaugurated a period of spiritual change and innovation in the highlands. Butt Colson nicely characterizes this event as resulting from an "enthusiastic movement" among the missionaries and their neophytes in Orinoco who then set out to bring the "good news" to other peoples. Pragmatically, of course, the campaign to delineate between the Spanish colonies and Dutch colonies in the region influenced this enterprise, so this "enthusiastic movement" cannot be understood apart from the history of colonial conflict and the use of native proxies that was so evident throughout this region (Whitehead 1999a, 1999b, 1999c). Significantly, this enthusiastic movement acted as a precursor for the shamanic conflicts of the nineteenth century between alleluia iwepyatàsak, who then appeared as advocates of radical change to achieve a promised "modernity," and kanaimàs, who became the bearers of an antithetical "tradition." And such is the current understanding of the political meaning of those spiritual proclivities.

Inevitably, however, social control of kanaimàs became increasingly problematic against that background, since there was not perpetual war in the highlands and the opportunities and the benefits of raiding for captives or of the plunder of metals changed through time. Even though there are many examples of sustained raiding in the documentary record, it is notable that missionaries and explorers were able to pass through the highlands in relative safety.[4] Moreover, the decline in trading with the interior itself began to deprive native leaders of some of their key sources of influence and power, particularly guns. As a result, the basis of social authority, insofar as it was anchored in raiding and warfare, was itself in flux, and a social and cultural space opened up for new forms of authority to emerge. In that context, the alleluia iwepyatàsak stood in opposition to both the political authority of the tushau (headman) and the ritual authority of the piya and kanaimà. There was, then, a basis for alliance, in the nineteenth century, between, on the one hand, "traditionalist" tushau, piya, and the kanaimà'san, and, on the other hand, "modernist" tushau, piya, and their iwepyatàsak, or alleluia'san. These contending forces were, of course, imperfectly expressed through the particular actions of individuals, whose motives were certainly not necessarily phrased in these terms, but the alignment of these cultural categories in this way is perfectly evident from contemporary testimony and from the history of shamanic warfare in the region.

Kanaimà thus became increasingly centripetal in its focus, as it was directed to the locality rather than distant regions; over the course of the nineteenth century, kanaimà more and more served local political conflicts, rather than the regional political ambitions of the tushau, which had been sustained through coastal trading contacts. These political and economic conditions thus underwrote the emergence of enthusiastic movements, cargo cults, and then alleluia itself, as well as the direct missionary work that so clearly influenced the forms of native innovation—a broad message of peace and security through new forms of revelation and ritual practice was compellling to people who had clearly suffered from the upsurge in raiding and slaving that contacts with the Dutch in the eighteenth century had provoked. Added to this was the threat of direct slaving by the Brazilians, as well as by the "Spanish Indians" from Orinoco, which persisted, in the former case, through the 1880s (Riviere 1995, 171). In addition, the worsening effects of diseases such as measles and smallpox steadily undermined the overall Amerindian population. The warrior enemies of the kanaimà thus became the various kinds of shamanic opponents, even as the work of localized "revenge" sustained kanaimà influence among Amerindian communities. This is the paradox that is imprinted on attempts to explain kanaimà in the colonial literature, which for want of a historical and ethnographic appreciation of kanaimà saw only a curious and exotic form of the lex talionis. This historical conjuncture for kanaimà was then brought to a sudden, almost kanaimà-like end itself, as the pandemic of "Spanish flu" in 1918–19 cut down many thousands of Amerindians, as it did to others throughout the world. This event, harbinger of globalized modernity, was thus coeval with the "globalized" representation of kanaimà itself through the publication of Walter Roth's account by the Smithsonian Institution.

WHITE SHAMANS, 1830–1880

In 1831 an Anglican mission was founded at Bartica, inaugurating the British missionary effort in the region. This occurred almost a hundred years after the first missions of the Moravians in Surinam and

Berbice, through which the Lokono and some Akawaio were evangelized, and the entry of the Capuchin and Franciscan orders into the lower Orinoco (Whitehead 1988, 1995a). Although initial results were promising, as they would be in any unevangelized region, a measles epidemic at Bartica in 1837 (Bernau 1847, 99–100) and smallpox in the Pomeroon and Manawarin Rivers signaled the beginning of a phase of severe demographic decline of the Amerindian population, which was dealt a final blow by the global pandemic of 1918–19. Notably, Brett (1868, 145–46) thought that "the destructive sweep of this disease overcame the reluctance of the Indians to use the remedies of the civilized; and many of them consented to be vaccinated. When the small-pox had passed away the Indian congregation increased," even as "enthusiasm" for a "new life," in the face of a new form of death, filled the ranks of the departed.

Thomas Youd, replaced that year by J. H. Bernau in his missionary work at Bartica, was able to initiate his work on the Rupununi River. Youd's mission at Pirara appeared to be thriving until it was "seized" by the Brazilians.[5] The importance of this event to the course of evangelization among the Makushi was certainly profound, but it is also suggestive of some of the problems more generally facing native people at that moment. It also indicates why alliance with a government or missionary faction would have been seen as the next step toward a "new life," since the old had become insupportable under the depredations of disease and intermittent slaving by both Karinya and the Brazilian *descimientos*.[6] To the north and west of the Patamuna the Reverend William Brett had had some success in attracting a few Akawaio, by 1841, to his missions on the Moruca and Pomeroon Rivers, so it is clear that there was a growing exposure to Christian teachings. However, the "enthusiastic" nature of Amerindian commitments to the "new life" promised by these missionaries led also to developments that were not pleasing to the orthodox evangelists. Despite this Brett (1881, 198) was forced to admit that native responses to both external and internal prophets were also the basis for his own success in evangelizing the Akawaio.

Brett writes, "It was in the days [1839–40] when Joseph Smith . . . was giving the finishing touch to his Mormon imposture, and setting up his temple at Nauvoo. His fame had reached our colony. Probably in emulation of his daring example another, also named Smith, conceived the idea of establishing a spiritual dominion over the simple

Indians of the interior, with whose language he was acquainted, being the son, it was said, of a settler on the upper Demerara."[7] Brett continues that Smith made two attempts to establish his "spiritual dominion." The first was "high-up" on the Essequibo River, where, "having secretly buried a quantity of beads and other articles, near an Indian place," Smith then claimed that he had received a divine revelation of secret treasure, which he promptly found and distributed. Accordingly, "He was treated by the people with much respect." However, "after a while they *wanted more,*" and, "finding that his inspiration did not return, they put him in a little canoe and dismissed him" (emphasis in original). Smith found his way to Bartica where Bernau gave him "the report that he deserved, but would not profit by," since his "next attempt was on a much greater scale" (198–202).[8]

In the region north of Roraima, along the upper Mazaruni River at its junction with the Cako River, in the year 1845, "The Acawoios there became his dupes, and his chief agents," through whom he sent a summons to come to that place to "*see God,* be freed from all the calamities of life, and possess lands of such boundless fertility, that a large crop of cassava would grow from a single stick!" (emphasis in original). Those who did not answer the call would be destroyed in fire and flood.[9] However, "for more than a year it was perfectly successful. The Indians near the coast brought *guns and ammunition, according to the instruction given them* and numbers from every district, far and near, went off to that land" (my emphasis). In which case it would seem that this "spiritual" community was no less prepared to adopt the predatory military posture of its chief native agents, the Akawaio, who in turn were keen that their military allies, the Karinya, join with them. In particular, Brett (1881, 200) mentions a tushau of the Barahma River, Capui, who was one of the prime movers of the movement among the Akawaio, as being responsible for recruiting Karinya to Smith's cause. Brett (1868, 182) says that Kobise, a Karinya convert who had been "deluded" away, returned and gave the following account of Smith's camp: "We traveled as fast as we could for thirteen days, and at length arrived at a savannah where some hundreds of Acawoios and others were assembled. They had as yet scarcely any field provisions and game was scarce from the multitude of hunters. I was led to a little enclosed hut, from which I heard a voice commanding me to return, and fetch my friends and neighbours, as a great fire and water would come upon the whole world except that spot." Kobise also told Brett that "the

Impostor" remained hidden from view delivering his predictions by night, and that his voice sounded like that of a white person.[10] However, seeing the dancing and the cassiri drink, the making of which had exhausted the small supply of cassava they possessed, "he became apprehensive that it was a delusion of the Yurokon, or evil spirit." Brett also makes clear that the Barahma Akawaio had been trying to encourage the missionaries to settle among them to the extent that "they cleared an eligible site, and erected fifty cottages, hoping that a teacher might be sent to them" (182, 256–57). Dance (1881, 231) also mentions a similar initiative by the Akawaio at "Queah-queh" on the Curiebrong (Kuribrong) River.

However, Brett (1881, 201) continues, "The success was so great . . . that the imposture collapsed under it." As the numbers in the Impostor's camp grew and grew, so provisioning became more difficult and the camp broke up, although many continued to starve as they returned to villages where the fields had been neglected for up to a year. Capui himself was given "A document, cunningly inscribed with hieroglyphic characters . . . which he was told was a commission from Makonaima, the Almighty, to collect and send to that place all the Indians he could gather" (Brett 1868, 259). This document also had a "leaden seal" attached (Brett 1881, 202), but was thrown away in the forest by Capui since "they now attributed their delusion to the direct agency of Satan" (Brett 1868, 259).[11] Impostor Smith lived on for a "number of years," eventually dying on the upper Essequibo (Brett 1881, 202), but in the aftermath many, "were led by hunger to commit depredations on those of other tribes. This led to bloodshed and feuds, in which the Kanáima system had full scope." In 1853, the brother of Capui, "who had died in the interval," brought his "clan" to join the Pomeroon mission. Capui's son, Philip, became a key native evangelist for Brett (1881, 205–6), translating the *Apostle's Creed* and *Lord's Prayer* into Karinya and helping Brett do the same into Akawaio, as well as distributing printed versions. As a result, in 1863, many more "wild" Akawaio came to the mission in groups of thirty to seventy, including the tushau of the Cuyuni, Serrawaik, and "were followed by people of other more distant tribes," Brett (1881, 207–9) specifically mentioning the Ye'kuana, Pemon, and Makushi.

There were also native visions of redemption and material advance that competed with those of the white shamans. Brett (1868, 250–51) writes, "A Warau woman of singularly weird appearance was employed to spread a report that she had seen . . . [in] Kamwatta . . . the figure of a white man on horseback, *riding through the air,* who promised to give money and other valuable presents to her, and to all of her tribe who would assemble at that spot and dance from early morning to early afternoon" (emphasis in original). Those already baptized were excluded, and despite the efforts of the missionaries to break up the gathering, when they arrived near the place and saw the preparations, "neither the men nor the women would give the least information." There are still similar iwepyatàsak today and, in particular, Patamuna remember a false prophet from the 1950s who lived in Kouyatilina. She, like Smith, called on everyone to join her there, saying that "the Lord will not come if you keep planting."

Charles Dance (1881, 293–94) also recorded the case of a baptized Akawaio, "Christian," whose prophetic vision "for a time occasioned some excitement and trouble in the Indian mission of Muritaro." Christian claimed "he had been, like Mohammed, translated to the abodes of the 'blessed,' where, among other signs, he saw the spirits of many Indians, some of who had died, others yet alive in the body on earth. These were seated on thrones, clothed in great splendour, and enjoying perfect happiness. His commission from that blessed place was to tell all the Indians that they did wrong by renouncing the religion of their fathers and adopting that of another people; that by their apostasy they were left to the uncontrolled power and malice of evil-spirits." The nature of this vision very much underlines the spiritual vacuum into which kanaimà expanded during this period, and how conversion to Christianity seemed to answer some needs but not others. Particularly important was the notion that a moral breach with tradition invited retribution of a most traditional kind, in the form of kanaimà. According to Dance, Christian persuaded "three or four Indians of bad or questionable character, who were under sentence of excommunication," to follow his message and for their spirits to receive their "golden thrones" in his "sanctuary" after "some incantation." However, "a hint that he would have to explain his doctrine in a magistrate's court induced the man to close his prophet's chamber; and the Indians were made to read, in their own tongue, the declaration that false Christs and false prophets would arise."

Contemporary with these events in the upper Mazaruni, in the Kukenaam valley to the west of Mount Roraima, was the emergence of an Amerindian shaman prophet, Awacaipu. He founded a settlement,

Beckeranta, and called on all the Amerindians to join him there, where they would learn how they could become equals to the whites. Awacaipu had been employed by Robert Schomburgk, and in Karl Appun's (1871, 2:257–64) account he suggests that this may have inspired Awacaipu in his millennial quest for "equality" with the whites. As in other of these millenarian movements, great emphasis was put on continual singing and dancing accompanied by cassiri-beer and the renunciation of existing material goods in the hope of greater reward in the future. Like the prophet Smith, Awacaipu also handed out pieces of inscribed paper as tokens and charms, apparently sheets from the *Times* that Schomburgk had previously used for his plant specimens. Awacaipu even promised that his followers would get white skins, marry white women, and have guns instead of bows. However, what was new and sinister in the prophecy of Awacaipu, and which grimly anticipates the more recent cult activity of the Reverend Jim Jones in Guyana, was the suggestion that those who wished to attain these benefits must first die: "All who wanted to obtain these advantages would have the opportunity between that night until the one after the morrow, but those who followed this course must die during one of these three nights, at each other's hands. The night after the full moon, the bodies of those killed would rise from the dead and come down the slopes of Roraima to meet with their families, in color and disposition they would become equal to the whites, and rule over the other brown men who had not undergone this ordeal" (Appun 1871, 2:260).

Appun continues that in order to encourage the others Awacaipu immediately clubbed two or three individuals standing next to him who fell into a large cassiri container from which, as their blood and brains spread into the liquid, he drank and then offered the same to the others. There followed an "orgie" of killing that lasted three nights, claiming nearly four hundred dead. The survivors waited two weeks in vain for the resurrection of the dead and their descent from Mount Roraima in newly acquired white skins. On the fifth night after the appointed moment Awacaipu was clubbed to death by the father of Wey-Torreh, who narrated the events to Appun. Awacaipu claimed that his vision of how the Amerindians could gain equality was received directly from Makunaima, which also links this incident to the cosmology of kanaimà assault sorcery.

Although the Patamuna are not mentioned by name in any of these prophetic events, it seems highly unlikely that they would have been unaware or unaffected by them. Neither should it simply be assumed that all Amerindians were equally avid for missionary contacts. In particular Brett (1881, 210–11) mentions that the "clan of Capui" had a "blood-feud which had begun in the days of their fathers, but had then been lying dormant for many years," but that the "heathen sorcerers" revived this feud because of their opposition to Capui and the mission movement. Capui's son, Philip ("the evangelist"), was therefore a repeated target for attacks through poison or kanaimà, only escaping from a kanaimà one time by clubbing his attacker with the stock of his gun and leaving him for dead. Apparently this event and lingering disabilities due to repeated poisoning "affected the mind and conduct of Philip for a time, and probably shortened his days." Brett (1868, 269–70) also narrates the killing by kanaimàs of the brother of one of his recent converts: "they found him on the ground, with his back and neck bruised, but not bleeding," and his tongue had been pierced. Brett held this to be "in fulfillment of a threat of the heathen sorcerers, to 'kanaima' in detail all the Acawoios and others who dared to attend Christian instruction."

There is clear evidence, then, of the intention of the interior Amerindians, especially the Akawaio and likely the Patamuna, to find a way in which they could gain access to, or control aspects of, colonial society via missionaries, both official and unofficial. The case of the Impostor and that of the Warao, Akawaio, and Pemon prophets demonstrate that in part this was related to gaining access to material goods. But the emphasis given to "whiteness" or "becoming white" was also a means of performing a more fundamental transformation of encroaching modernity through a mimetic possession of its key representational trope. This is consistent with the way in which the transition from the Dutch to British administration at the beginning of the nineteenth century led to sudden changes in policy, or perhaps more exactly an absence of policy, toward the Amerindians. One of the principal and immediate effects of this was to end a system of giving customary "gifts" to favored native leaders, which provoked a visitation to the capital by one of the most powerful Karinya leaders engaged in the hinterland trade, itself an iconic interlude in Guyanese historiography.[12] Equally, the presence of various kinds of "enthusiastic" movements among the mission populations of the lower Orinoco in the eighteenth century, as well as an indigenous tradition of prophetic leadership, both in this region and across Amazonia, means that these events cannot be interpreted as materialistically motivated by a desire for colonial manufactures. Rather, as perhaps the Warao case makes clearer, access to colonial manufactures, religious ideas, and the sociocultural system that generated them had become a necessity for survival in both the material and spiritual sphere. The colonial system itself had become more invasive as it moved to delineate its various boundaries and natural resources in the interior, and the advent of missionary work brought the diseases of modernity to eat up the Amerindians—for it seemed as if the priestly shamans of the whites could assault distant communities just like the piya they actually were.[13] Given such predation at both the material and spiritual level, the search for new formulas and techniques to adapt to this "new life" was not just a question of intellectual reflection, but a pressing matter of sheer survival.

In the 1860s and 1870s the work of the British missionaries showed growing success, and by 1871 there was an Akawaio mission at Mesopotamia, the confluence of the Cuyuni and Mazaruni Rivers, manned by a black catechist, McGoggin. There were two more on the Demerara, one fifty miles below the Malali rapids, and another at Eneyuda (*Eynéh-éhutáh,* the place of misery) in 1869 (Brett 1881, 220–21). It was at that time that the Patamuna were named directly again in the sources.[14] Brett mentions that in 1876 Charles Dance baptized "some hundreds of Patamuna" who were "sufficiently advanced" in learning the Creed and Lord's Prayer. He particularly notes their spontaneous and laudable habit of family prayer. Although no funds were available, Dance recommended that a mission be placed at Curiebrong [Kuribrong].[15] Nonetheless, Patamuna kept seeking out further religious instruction and apparently visited the missionary Lobertz, stationed on the Demerara at Muritaro. Eventually Lobertz received permission to relocate to Patamuna territory itself and set up a site two days above Kaieteur falls at Shenanbauwie. Brett (1881, 234) writes,

> In a few days after his arrival, about eight hundred persons of the neighbouring clans had assembled there. The work assuming such dimensions, he sent to the bishop to ask that clergymen be sent there; and the Rev. W. E. Pierce . . . went from Bartica . . . to this, our newest in the mission field. . . . There willing people had already erected a chapel-school (ninety feet by forty-five). As he approached that building he heard "a buzzing sound, as of innumerable bees." This . . . arose from hundreds of men, women, and children, teaching and learning in

their own tongue. . . . There were never less than four hundred Indians present, and once nine hundred and sixty-seven were counted there.

In January 1881 the missionary journal *Mission Field* also reported this baptism of hundreds of "Paramuna, a tribe that has hitherto furnished few, if any, Christian converts," adding that Lobertz had, "including some 200 children . . . 678 persons under preparation for baptism." and that he "produced lists, with dates of entry of names, by which it appears that 1,376 persons have individually presented themselves as candidates for baptism. . . . Nor can any ordinary person doubt the *earnestness* of the multitude. . . . The thronging multitudes at church and the number present at schooling or catechising, *going on all day,* as well as their most reverent and devout demeanour evidence unmistakably that they are *profoundly stirred* " (1881, 15; emphasis in original). There then follows Pierce's own report (1881, 16–24), in which he makes it clear that the Patamuna had been using the pamphlets in Akawaio that Brett's native evangelist, Philip, son of Capui, had distributed in the 1860s. Among the thousand or more Patamuna were also 213 Makushis, 62 Arecunas, 37 Wapishanas, and a couple of Akawaio, which suggests that this was the first time that significant inroads had been made into those populations south of the Akawaio. However, Pierce was also much less impressed than Lobertz with the quality of understanding others that the Patamuna had derived from their Akawaio sources and "at once set [out] to prepare a very short and simple Catechism for the Macusis, Arecunis, and Wahpusianas" (1881, 20). However, as with the impromptu, if long-lasting, camp set up by the Impostor, want of food soon threatened the gathering, and with seemly haste Pierce baptized and instructed as many as feasible, as well as marrying 224 couples, though "very few were polygamists" (21). He also mentions that the Christian Patamuna who had fetched Lobertz to Shenanbauwie was named "Charley," who informed him that many more toward the Brazilian border were likewise waiting for instruction and would be prepared to journey to Shenanbauwie. Pierce (1881, 22), however, recommended that a mission station be opened at Curiebrong. In addition, Charley "sent his son, aged sixteen, and his nephew, aged fifteen with me . . . besides sending two younger sons with Mr. Lobertz" (23). As a result of all this enthusiasm the *Society for the Propagation of the Gospel* made a large grant of £520 sterling for their operations in British Guiana for 1882 (*Mission Field* 1881, 407).

Given this history of both missionary endeavor and other white prophets, it might have been expected that the Akawaio would have taken the lead in spiritual innovation, but it was the Makushis who produced the first prophet of alleluia. The Patamuna strongly insist that this was a new form of shamanism. Its appeal stemmed from the fact that it could attain all the spiritual benefits that the white-shamans proffered but did not falsely promise the material benefits that had been hoped for but never appeared. I have heard it explained by an alleluia'san as being the special "short-cut" for Amerindians, the Bible being not wrong but rather the "long way round," and so redundant.

ALLELUIA, EVANGELICALS, AND DEVELOPMENT,
1880–2000

The first certain indication of alleluia prophetism occurred around 1884, when Im Thurn in his ascent of Mount Roraima recorded "an absolutely incessant shout of Hallelujah, Hallelujah!" However, as Butt Colson (1960, 67) notes, there are no means of showing whether or not this was the alleluia known today or "one of the many religious manifestations of the period preceding it." But the interest here is not in the origins of alleluia per se, but in the way in which this and "the many religious manifestations of the period preceding it" related to kanaimà, particularly as made evident through the accounts of shamanic warfare. It has therefore been necessary to trace the history of such prophetic movements in order to understand the oral histories and accounts of kanaimà, piya, and alleluia.

In the Akawaio accounts of the origins of alleluia (Butt Colson 1960), Bichiwung, a Makushi, appears as the originator of alleluia. He traveled in the company of a priest to the coast, and possibly to England, where he had the revelation that the missionaries were actually hiding the true nature of God from the Amerindians. He was baptized but continued to fret about the deception the white people were carrying out. So, following the trail that the white people had shown him, he went to meet God. God confirmed the deception being practiced on the Amerindians and gave them alleluia instead. God also gave Bichiwung a bottle of white medicine, words and songs, and a piece of paper that was to be the Indian Bible; all of these were to be sealed in a canister. Bichiwung eventually returned to Makushi land, bringing with

PLATE I. How the Indians usually have visions of the Evil Spirit (Drake Manuscript [1590] 1996, f.III). *Courtesy of The Pierpont Morgan Library, New York. Photography: David A. Loggie.*

PLATE 11. The Skull of Kanaima. *Cover illustration for Victor Norwood's jungle adventure novel.*

PLATE III. Kanaimà *yeribada* (mask).

PLATE IV. Alfred Edwin, Patamuna *alleluia'san* (song owner).

him his gifts from God, which also included some cassava and banana plantings, as well as trade goods and a gun. He sent for his relations to come down to the coast to meet him with as many trade goods as they could assemble, which they did. All then returned to Bichiwung's home in the Kanuku mountains.

At first Bichiwung only taught his wife a little about alleluia, particularly that she should not plant or work on the Sabbath. At first she did not listen to him, and even became suspicious of incest when she found him locked inside his house with their daughter, but it was the manner of his journeying to God, which he did as he slept and his spirit went up. His wife was converted when he explained these things and so she went about preaching, too. The fame of Bichiwung and alleluia spread. This made some jealous of him, and Bichiwung was attacked three times by kanaimàs. On the first occasion he died but was resurrected by the white medicine. On the second occasion he was bodily dismembered, but his wife gathered up the body parts, placed them together, and smeared on the white medicine, and he was resundered. The third time he was again dismembered, but some of his parts were lost and the medicine was useless.

Given this entanglement of kanaimà in the roots of alleluia, it is notable, then, that the first two prophets of Akawaio alleluia—Abel and Christ—had previously been kanaimàs and that Christ may even have remained one. Abel, like Bichiwung, was eventually assassinated by kanaimàs, but, in the manner of his prophet Bichiwung, only after three attempts during which he was resurrected twice.[16] Butt Colson (1960) is quite right to closely interrogate these accounts, but it may not be sufficient to simply view these claims as part of a generalized system of envy that leads to all eminent individuals claiming to be threatened by, or actually being threatened by, "kanaimà." Particularly in the case of Christ, it is equally plausible that those shamanically adept in one sphere are likely to be so in another and that transitions from one idiom to another may not be permanent or irreversible, as current testimony would bear out.

According to current Patamuna accounts, just as alleluia had been spread from the Makushi to Akawaio people, so it was an Akawaio, called Paiwa, married to a Patamuna, who brought alleluia to the Patamuna in the period 1880–1900. The following account was made by Robinson Williams, formerly a senior alleluia singer, with the intention that it should be recorded textually by me.

How Alleluia Came

The Patamuna had a place to the west and people came from the Akawaio direction. They had a party and fell for it [alleluia] and so they went to Akawaio country to get it. There were two leaders at first, Abel and Christ, they just get inspired and sing it out. But one of the first leaders was killed by kanaimà because of jealousy of the song. They also have it with the Makushi . . . it is prophesy as well as music and it is very far different from piya which can be bad . . . the songs are not.[17] The leaders of alleluia here were Hendricks Charley [ca. 1900–1920], then John Charley [ca. 1920–1940], then George Williams [ca. 1940–1960], and then Robinson Williams [ca. 1960–1980]. . . .

Alleluia prophets said God would come to the Patamuna . . . they say he would be in the form of a book. . . . And he did. They tell us that the white men would come and that they would build the airstrip. One woman had a very strong vision of these things to come and even built a little model out of clay to show what the villages would be like in the future, though people doubted it at the time. In the end all the predictions came true, even as to where the first aircraft would land, and even as to the writing of these very words.

This testimony differs somewhat from the account of an Akawaio, Henry, published by Butt Colson (1971). There may be a number of reasons for these discrepancies, and they are not all of the same importance. Key, though, is the additional information on the transmission of alleluia to the Patamuna in the period before John Charley, which is where the Akawaio account begins. It may be possible to harmonize these accounts however, since there could have been a number of routes by which alleluia was spread among the Patamuna. In any case, the Akawaio view of their own superiority in the matter of originating alleluia songs and ritual forms might be questioned on the basis of the Patamuna account, since emphasis is put on the fact that the Patamuna "went . . . to get it," rather than being passively proselytized by their Akawaio superiors. In addition, as suggested by the description of the prophets, women seem to have a significant role, if not as singers, then as dancers and iwepyatàsak in Patamuna alleluia. Thus, for example, Lucia Edwin is named as iwepyatàsak at the time of the earliest alleluia rituals in Paramakatoi. She came from the village of Bamboo Creek (Kouyatilina) and was later known as a "false prophet" on account of her millenarian-style message. She required that believers follow her strictures, among which was the idea that "the Lord will not come if you keep planting." Another account, which refers both to Paiwa and to female prophetism, was given by Alfred Edwin, and orally translated by his son Roger, on the line (asanda) between Wandapàtoi and Paramakatoi, standing on a high hill in sight of Kukuyen as the wind blew and trees swayed as if they would fall—just as in this tale. The tale tells of prophecy and the dire consequences of ignoring these messages from the spirit side.

Taruka Alleluia Ground

There was an alleluia ground [ritual site] going to Taruka in that savanna, you know that savanna going to Taruka? That was the Alleluia ground. When you coming out from Taruka, past the Totopù rock at Akaikalakparu, they have a savanna there, right. You can view Paramakatoi from there. So, that was the ground where they used to dance Alleluia. There was an iwepyatàsak. A man named Paiwa, came from Akawaio. He settled and lived and he was a prophet for a while then. So, he predicted something. He said there will be a judgement on people. He said, "There will be a voice that you will hear that is a Satan voice," or an evil angel, or however, "You will hear it there, it can be passing and it is warning to everybody. We are going to have a get together. We are going to start to pray about that very serious matter," and so everybody did. He [Paiwa] said, "Watch! Today, gonna be a day, you are going to hear a voice, don't answer, because there will be an evil voice that pass through. Anytime someone answer that voice, there will be a great judgment on this area." He said, "Okay, don't go anywhere today, everybody will get together!" And so, one of the men, the big man said, "What? the man's saying don't go anywhere? And I have my ripe good, good bananas, ripe in the farm, I should just go and fetch them out before this voice pass," or something like that. Anyway, he did went. He and his wife went, and so, and before midday, they heard someone calling, "Arghhhhhhhhhh," one long sound. Make another one again, "Arghhhhhhhhhhh." The lady said, "What? Hear the voice," telling her husband, "Don't answer," and the man say, "What? You telling me don't answer, and there could be kanaimàs and you calling for help one one [a lot]. The man is calling for help and I would answer!" His name was Kaiwon. *Kaiwon* means fat, you know. And anyhow they call him Kaiwon. He answered the voice. He want to call again. There was no answer no more. No more sound. He called again. He tried to signal. He called the man, but there was no more voice. So he said, "What? Now I answered the voice. I shouldn't have answered this voice in truth and I fail." And suddenly, and when he come up now, there was a darkness came over and shadowed over the land. And there you heard the thunder, just thunder and shook the whole land. He [Paiwa] said, "Well now." He called everybody and he said, "Who answered this voice? Anybody went out?" and he [Kaiwon] admit "Yes," he did. He [Paiwa] said "Why you did that? I told you already no one mustn't go anywhere!" So he said, "Okay, so we gonna get together and dance alleluia, sing alleluia." So what he said again, he said, "Watch, now is the hour everybody can hold hands together in strength and ask for mercy or forgiveness or something, anyone that come with fifteen minutes left or at a late hour, don't join no more." So everybody did start dance alleluia. And then came up a heavy storm and you can hear trees falling, tumbling, tumbling. He said, "Now! Everybody hold together hand in hand and just pray to God," you know, or something, to ask for help then. So it went, it went, and that mountain, the same ridge I tell you, that range, all those going towards Taruka. There is a big landslide there from the top through the bottom. A big landslide then. All those farms and so on there that had cassava and whatever, everything just came down. Everything, all this part, going down this range here, the land just broken, all those trees just sweeping, going down, and a strong whirl-wind came. They were in the benab [house], a little benab, it shook this building, but couldn't take off the roof. And in that strong, strong wind that was coming there appear a dog, a strange dog coming in that strong wind. And he came straight to the door and *yip yip yip* start making noise and so on. And gone with the strong breeze, the dog disappeared, and so on and then the rain starts falling. The rain fall a whole night and a whole day. The next day near midday the rain stopped. But that was a terrible one, because all that was left was just broken and sliding, going down. Now, there was a voice somewhere in the valley there calling for help, but it was helpless because the land was just coming through and sweeping, going down. It wasn't like this, where we are now, it was just one clean, clean mountain-side. A lady named Susannah was living down below there. She was another iwepyatàsak right. You know she could have her own visions, too. And there was Susannah in her little benab. She had a little child, alone, no man. Anyway she had done all the alleluia praying and here were some trees coming to Susannah house! All those balata trees and big, big trees just falling. A landslide coming. You see water running dirty. They come to Susannah's house and there was a big balata tree coming and bore a path through her house. And she was on top of a little barbricot, just singing! And so all this land broke away, what

I mean to tell you is that this is the range over there, the mountain range. And when you walk in Taruka line you see where the trees grow up. Paiwa was the man who had the vision about this great judgment on this part, but not everyone listened and so they called down the bad thing on themselves. Those around Paramakatoi remember those landslides and things, and there was on a little piece of branch two little monkeys and no help because all the trees move away, right?

As well as "fetching" alleluia and having a distinct idea of alleluia ritual practice, the Patamuna also made journeys to persuade missionaries to come among them, as they have done more recently as well, as in the account that follows.[18] A more sobering note on the matter of the exact history of the routes by which alleluia spread through the highlands is the contemporary prophecy of an alleluia'san I interviewed, who suggested that, because alleluia had come up from the south to reach the Akawaio, when it goes back down to the Makushi — as it appears to be doing in terms of the reemerging "enthusiasm" for its practice—it will bring the end of days, the end of all earthly time.

The next narrative, which was again formally given in Patamuna by Robinson Williams and John Aldi, and orally translated by Matteson Williams so that I should be able to record and textualize it, is an account of how the missionaries were finally fetched and brought into the Patamuna region.

How We Fetched the Missionaries

Because alleluia is the special form of Amerindian praying to God, the Catholics and the American missionaries who came opposed the singing and dancing of alleluia, they did not understand that it is very different from piya'san, which can be used to do evil. Although the Roman Catholic missionaries had operated in Rupununi for many years, they had neglected the people of here. Bonham was the priest by the Catholic Church to minister to the people, but he was rarely seen. . . . The American missionaries of the Pilgrim Holiness Church [1940s and 1950s] were very keen to come into us and were asking to the British Government. They heard of the Patamuna people by the balata-bleeders who had been working in here at Siparuni [since the early 1900s]. It was not always good between balata-bleeders and the Patamuna . . . and many times these men pressed down [raped] Patamuna women while their husbands and brothers were away working as droghers and carrying supplies from the Siparuni head. Not all the balata men were bad like this. . . . Some helped the Patamuna to organize droghing supplies for the balata-bleeders. Sam Scipio was very important and told the Americans about the region.

The first time a white man came. . . . he was Clifton Burg and he was a missionary from the Pilgrim Holiness Church. He came around the year 1947. We [John Aldi and others] were working in the yam garden and we only glimpsed his face through the bush.[19] We all ran away not knowing who this was or what the blacks who accompanied him wanted. But then we regained our courage when we realized a white man was with them and we went out to see this strange sight. He was lying down on the ground, exhausted from climbing all the bumps and had to catch himself up a little before he could even talk.[20]

When he had recovered himself Clifton Burg told the Patamuna that God was with him, that he was an American, and that the missionaries would build a church, hospital, and school right there. At this time, only Agnes Williams knew any English, which she had learned while living at Tumutumari on the Potaro River. So Agnes translated his [Burg's] words for the rest to hear.[21] The people then held a meeting, and they agreed that Clifton Burg had a good plan. Everyone felt a little sad after he had left because they didn't know if it was going to be possible for him to come back.

So we held a meeting and we agreed to make sure this happen. Francis Williams and his wife, Agnes, together with Robinson Williams, went down to Georgetown, by Balata Landing at Essequibo, to ask that the American missionaries be allowed to work with us. We ask the bush-pilot, Teseric, but he say the Americans are no good. This really worried us as we wanted to have a school for the children and drugs, and religion was a part of that. . . . The Catholics are also against alleluia, but they did offer no clinic or school and hardly bothered to visit, so we still decided to go for it. So Agnes, Francis, and Robinson Williams decided to go ahead with their trip to Georgetown. They went with a Portuguese from Lethem, Guy Weight.

When they arrived in Georgetown they searched for Clifton Burg.[22] They stopped at the Amerindian hostel, where MacDonald was in charge at this time. Guy Weight explained the situation to MacDonald who guided them in Georgetown and arranged for an appointment with the Lands and Mines Department. Here Felix tried to help them in their request, but he was a young man without much authority and in any case was doubting their request, asking "Why Americans?" and was insisting that they had already been given a priest. So they explained that the priest never visited, that they were really in need of a hospital and school, and that the Pilgrim Holiness missionaries would be able to send people straight away.

They went back a second time, and Agnes Williams said how Kurukubaru and St. Ignatius already had a church with a school and hospital, that the blacks never gave them assistance and only raped the women, but Felix still doubted and repeated that they already had a priest. They went back a third time, but Felix still said no. So they tried someone else in the Lands and Mines Department called Lord, a big man with a bald head, who was in fact the commissioner of Lands and Mines.

Lord had already been in Region 8 as commissioner, and he said that he understood their problem but that he couldn't give permissions. So he told them to come back at "nine o'clock" for another meeting, which they did. At this meeting they were taken into a "big" white man's room. He was called Moorehead. He believed their story and saw that they felt handicapped. He referred them to the "Bush Governor," Gregory Smith, stationed at Bartica on the lower Essequibo, but they were getting concerned that they were just being passed around and they couldn't understand what was going on—even cars frightened them!

At Bartica the Bush Governor was very respected, and they went fearfully to his house, knocked on the door, and a white man came to the door (looking like you). He indicated the Bush Governor, who came up, hands behind his back, asking "What do you want?" For the fourth time, they explained the case. He said, "I promise," turned his back, and left, but the words were not understood. When they got back [to Paramakatoi], they held a discussion, but they didn't really know what "I promise" meant.

The Roman Catholic Father Bonham came with some Makushi droghers but he was told, "Too late! We have Americans coming." This was a unanimous thing, the Roman Catholics had only baptized a few.

Bonham went on to Kurukubaru and since then no Catholics have come back. Shortly after, Smith came through, with Moorehead and a doctor. He asked why the Catholics did not work there. We said because we danced alleluia and that alleluia dancers had "tails like monkeys" and would burn in Hell.

As yet the American missionaries hadn't opposed alleluia. Smith told them that they had permission to come. He asked us to show him alleluia. He said it was nothing bad and a young white man even joined in.

Then in 1949 Clifton Burg finally came and baptized them and we became Christians and then he promised to bring a teacher, Ethel Carew, and a nurse, Pinkerton. They came through Kato [airstrip] being carried, literally. This was 1950, it was still bush here but now we opened it up.

Burg said that since government not helping you I will. At first everyone went to school, even adults. Another nurse came, Higgins, and Pinkerton went home. Higgins was "rough," she wouldn't tolerate nonsense. She stayed for years and years until 1968.

In this time all the building went up. Tushau Williams, Robinson, and others were the driving force. After this they realized they needed space for an airstrip, so the tushau decided to move to Kato. Big room for an airstrip there, but a lot of people were against this, so captain suggested Taruka instead. They needed open space for the airstrip, the population was small. But Robinson was against it. Still the captain [tushau], Francis Williams, went with the teacher Carew to assess the place.

But Robinson asked, "What was the sense in moving?" So he organized everyone to cut down the bush. The women weeded and the men took down the trees, burnt it all off, and cleared it. This all happened while Francis was at Taruka. He was not pleased but said, "If he start let him do it." As the men had gone to Taruka it was mostly women who did it, moving the mud with their calabashes, digging hard laterite. It took a long time and was very hard work.

We sent a message to Teseric that they had made an airstrip. He landed a small aircraft. Nurse Higgins was very surprised. Teseric advised on improvements to the runway. Melville's benab was still in the way because it [the runway] wasn't long enough, so we knocked it down. The American assigned a pilot called Ferriman, call sign "one-six-Charlie." He suggested more improvements and brought in power saws and a generator. We decided to build the school first. At this point we are told "no more alleluia, no more strong cassiri." So people had to really follow Christianity, and it became really repressive. This was taught at school. They doubted kanaimà also, so we weren't given cassiri at other villages because we were known to be Pilgrim Holiness people. Now the school expanded, and there was constant bible reading and most of the children who are now your age [forty] went. This is the first time this has been recorded.

Maxey Walton (n.d.) provides a fascinating view of some of these events from across the cultural gulf that clearly divided the Patamuna and their would-be evangelists, revealing an important fact about the

Patamuna at that time, a fact that is not mentioned in their own narratives. He writes,

> There was something else that sent a shudder through us as we looked.
> We had been warned in advance that smallpox had been ravaging the village. . . . We had wondered . . . if we would come into contact with it. . . . Yes, there it was. Or something mightily akin to it. There were scabs in evidence on the faces of some of the children whose hands we touched in passing. Some older persons as well showed signs of the disease. And then we came to the end of the line. As we did so, we hesitated in horror at what we saw. There, sitting a little distance apart from us . . . and not to be avoided, sat an old man literally covered, like Job, from the crown of his head to the sole of his feet. The dread disease was before us without a doubt. (50)

Although the missionaries did not refuse to touch the man's hand, they felt compelled, "A moment or two later," to surreptitiously rub their hands with dirt. "That mud hand washing . . . gave us, strange to say, a cleaner feeling." Walton, like Dance, also felt compelled to write of the collective nature of the Patamuna at prayer: "They prayed, not one, but all of them. They were seemingly glad to pray at any time we suggested it" (52). Walton also mentions (53, 62) both the deceased John Charley and his younger brother, whom he briefly met. But this was not an idle tour, and Walton certainly brought "religion" for them. His first sermon to them was on the subject of "Guilt before God" (55). "We talked of lying, stealing, saying bad things. We told them too of how, though we were all guilty and worthy of sentence, yet Jesus had been willing to take our place, suffer our guilt, and assume our penalty." It was also clear (59) that medical assistance was the key to evangelical success, since the two were inseparable for the Patamuna. Walton then returned to Georgetown, after a visit of only a few days, to be greeted by the announcement of the testing of the H-bomb on Bikini atoll, commenting that, "While men plan new methods of killing each other wholesale, the Partamona Indian still waits for gospel light" (69).

When Burg returned with the Pilgrim Holiness personnel, shamanic warfare was also initiated against the piya and alleluia, but particularly the alleluia. When told of kanaimà, the Pilgrim Holiness personnel

Alleluia dancers. *Drawing by Roger Edwin.*

Alleluia dancers at Roger's Alleluia House.

simply dismissed such talk as nonsense, according to current testimony like the Nurse's. Although, unlike the Akawaio pattern of building replicas of churches in the village itself, Patamuna alleluia was always principally sung in the forest and savannas, at special sites like large trees or caves, and less often in a village setting. However, a drawing made by Roger Alfred, son of the alleluia'san Alfred, shows alleluia being danced in his "Alleluia House." As a result, although alleluia visibly disappeared from the sight of the village-bound missionaries, its discreet practice was relatively easy to continue. Some of the singers and prophets became converts and eventually pastors in the church, but accounts by both converts and alleluia singers suggest that this was often a pragmatic decision, or at least not solely based on the niceties of theological dispute. Even those who became pastors, for instance, started to compete for an audience with the alleluia gatherings; as a result, what had been a communal event rapidly became the vying of one kind of spiritual leader with another. Acquiring legitimate village space for ritual performance and its attendant proximity to the missionaries, school, and runway, was the goal. In this way alleluia was removed as a public spectacle, notwithstanding its "discreet" locations, and became more part of family life, with outsiders rarely if ever invited or made aware of alleluia performances. Thus, the event at Roger's Alleluia House in 1997 really was significant, it being the first public, village-based alleluia performance since the coming of the missionaries.

KANAIMÀ AND SHAMANIC WARFARE, 1880–2000

Through all of these events, kanaimà remained a constant. The piya were effectively marginalized by the ferocious onset of diseases such as smallpox, the measles, dysentery, and influenza, as well as by the direct assault of missionary evangelism, in which the piya was identified as the principal opponent. Thus Brett (1868, 412–13) wrote, "The system of SORCERY, inveterate and deeply rooted in the minds of Indians of every tribe, has doubtless been the greatest obstacle to their reception of Christianity. Yet some of our earliest and most steadfast converts were of the dreaded class of Piai-men. Two of them broke their marak-kas, or sacred rattles, before joining us. Others surrendered theirs in pledge of their renunciation of the practice. . . . Five of those magical implements thus came into my possession . . . some of which were hung up in the Mission-school, that the young people, by familiarity with them, might learn to despise their pretended power."

Which, paradoxically, Brett himself mimetically recognizes through the significance he gives them, even presenting two of the "dreaded instruments" to the missionary college of St. Augustine at Canterbury. He also notes that "many a life would have been thrown away under the noise, excitement, and tobacco vapour of the piai system," had not the missionaries taught the "use of *proper remedies in sickness*" (413; emphasis in original). Dance (1881, 280), in a similar vein but with brusque terseness, refers to piya as one of the "weedy entanglements of evil."

So the evangelicals of all persuasions, including those with their own personal paths to redemption, come and go but never achieve a permanent presence among the Patamuna. Constantly goaded by the tantalizing promises of a "new life," against the background of disease, slavery, and warfare, native "enthusiasm" finds its own objects and reinvents itself as alleluia. However, there is also a braiding and intertwining of alleluia and kanaimà through time, so much so that some individuals have even pursued both forms of shamanic practice. This was possibly the case with the prophet Christ, but such early prophets had been themselves kanaimà and were then attacked by kanaimàs. This interrelation is also very evident today, as in the case of *The Kanaimà Family* (presented in chapter 5), and from fact that the principal kanaimà in Paramakatoi, Pirai, is also an alleluia singer. This is difficult to explain unless one separates alleluia from the matter of Christian conversion and understands both kanaimà and alleluia as forms of shamanic technique. Just as the piya who cures may also kill, so there is no inherent conceptual contradiction between owning alleluia songs and being adept at kanaima. But there is likewise no intrinsic relationship between the two practices, so that one expects the cases of dual practitioners to be rather rare. Indeed, kanaimàs certainly kill alleluia iwepyatàsak because of the power of their songs. Moreover, conversion to Christianity appears to lead to the abandonment of piya, alleluia, and kanaimà, though the manner of such conversions suggests that defense against kanaimà can be an important factor.

The Amerindian pastor of the village visited me one rainy day, for no immediately apparent purpose, since we had barely exchanged words at that point, except on one night outside his house when he had, again for no apparent reason, begun to tell me all he knew of kanaimà—

and he knew a lot. Following both of these occasions, it occurred to me that the ambience of night and rain had allowed him to speak of things that sunlight would not. His brother was still an alleluia singer, as the pastor himself had once been, but he had come to explain why it was that he had given up those things. I was surprised to hear that, although he was a very respected pastor, it had been kanaimà that had led him to Christianity. By which he meant that fear of kanaimà, the search for some better protection in the absence of powerful piya, had led him to use Christianity to defeat the kanaimàs spiritually. He went on to tell me of how he had been followed by kanaimàs on the trail and, although fully expecting to feel the blow of the yé stick, his fervent prayer had caused them to veer off his track. Kanaimàs are keen to attack the "god-men," since people are less fearful if they have Christianity, and they are sometimes successful, as in the case of the pastor killed by the kanaimàs at Monkey Mountain.

Unlike the missionaries, who come and go, the native pastors and the alleluia iwepyatàsak are particularly threatening to kanaimàs, not only because of the continuity of their presence but also because they thus serve as tokens of alternative cosmological frameworks that defeat both kanaimà and piya by reference to their *misunderstanding* of spiritual reality. Alleluia introduces the idea of a higher and more unified spirit domain.[23] Piya, whatever the differences in ritual practice with kanaimà, is still fundamentally oriented to a world of spirit entities whose beneficence or maliciousness sets the terms for their intercession. This is why a kanaimà'san may well be also an accomplished piya, but his killers not necessarily so. This explains, in turn, why kanaimàs, or at least those engaged in the work of killing, have to be guarded—at that point, they are not themselves necessarily, nor even likely to be, piya'san. That is, the kanaimà must be guarded in the manner in which it is likely he will be attacked—not by another kanaimà, but "on the spirit side" by another piya.

I witnessed such an attack by a piya on kanaimàs who were "doing their work." The purpose of the attack was not to directly assault the killers themselves but rather to "cut down the ladder of kalawali" up which the kanaimà'san had climbed in order to protect his pack of killers. Indeed, in this regard the kanaimà'san is also responsible for "curing" them of their sopanéy (madness) after the kill, and it is at this point that his ritual knowledge for the production of maba becomes vital, literally, to the returning killers. The attack began in the manner

Kalawali (the piya'san calling down his spirit ladder). *Drawing by Roger Edwin.*

of other piya sessions, inside a small benab, which was very dark inside, although it was still possible to see a little.[24] The piya had already laid out before him three cups of tobacco juice and two anthropomorphic figurines—one made of bone, the other from a mirror—and a diamond. These were his "spirit-masters," with which he intended to assault the kanaimà'san while the kanaimà'san was guarding his band of killers. Instead of rattles, the piya held the leaves of the mora tree, said to be particularly deadly to kanaimà. His intention was to sweep the floor continuously with these leaves to stop the kanaimà'san entering from the earth below or boring under the walls. The kanaimà are said to come along the ground, not from the sky, taking terrestrial not avian forms, as is appropriate to their vegetal orientations (see also accounts of counter-sorcery in Charles Barrington Brown 1877, 139–41 and Im Thurn 1883, 336–37).

The piya'san began his attack by drinking one of the cups of tobacco juice straight down. The empty cup was then slammed hard on the little table that stood before his bench. He called to the kanaimà's spirit-doubles. As we waited, there was deep silence and then a sound like wind stirring the tress by the benab, which became more definite and punctuated as it then seemed to latch onto the thatch itself. Something then moved around the walls and up onto the roof, at which point it seemed as if the piya had balanced the bone-figurine on his hand and was moving it up and down. And then the bone figurine was gone, apparently fired through the roof from where it could then swoop back down to earth, like an avian raptor, to pierce and kill the attacking kanaimà. There was a tremendous screech and then all went silent. The arrowlike form of these figurines was therefore very appropriate to their function. However, the battle had only just commenced and within a few minutes the same noise of rushing wind returned. Once again it stopped short of the benab but then started up again at the base of the walls. I found myself silently urging the piya to drink the second cup and "warm up" another figurine before the attacker could enter. This time he sent the figure made from a mirror, which glinted in the gloom, so I again could see him balancing the piece on his hand, which he elevated repeatedly as if getting ready to launch it into the roof space. By that time the force of the shaking of the walls was quite palpable; I could see the wisps of palm leaf shaking by my left elbow where there was a small gap. Neither was I too happy to have such an inviting means of entry so close by, and as the "mirror-man" flew up, I found myself hoping that he would be as effective as the first. Thankfully he was and there was silence once again. Next came a truly tumultuous performance in which successive attempts were made by the piya to send out the last "spirit-master"—the diamond. It seemed as if more than one of the kanaimà spirits were shaking the thatch and hammering the walls. As the piya struggled to launch his last "missile," he alternated attempts to launch it through the roof with a sweeping of the floor so frenetic that I expected something to bore right up into the middle of the benab. However, the hammering and shaking abruptly stopped, and I could hear a deep exhalation of breath just outside the benab right by where I was sitting. This was followed by a heavy thud. No one moved until the piya spoke.

He told us, unexpectedly, that the kanaimà'san himself was actually dead, killed as his kalawali had been cut down by the "blades" of the diamond. He then said that we were to go to Koniayatoi Falls on Maikparu Creek and look under the cascade, where there would be a small hole or cave. In there we would find the physical body of the kanaimà, Talinaku, who would be brought there from Ulupelu. In fact, we did investigate this suggestion. I cannot offer forensic evidence, but as we approached the spot we could see birds circling and smell something truly awful, if a little sweet, and the thought of "rotting-pineapple" came into my mind. At the actual spot indicated, there was indeed a small hole under the cascade, about four feet in diameter, with something in it, but it appeared quite impossible to actually get to that spot without climbing equipment. I must confess that I in fact had no wish to get there and have remained quite shaken by this experience, the meaning of which is still not entirely clear to me.

Alleluia'san and alleluia iwepyatàsak are seen as beneficent, unlike some piya, and are culturally competent, unlike most missionaries. Moreover, the kanaimà may rely on the piya in certain circumstances. With the missionary emphasis on both attacking the "piai-system" and usurping piya role as curers through the use of "proper remedies," the cultural space for healing, beneficent piya has been narrowed, even as space of kanaimà death has opened up. The missionaries, and particularly the Pilgrim Holiness Church, also dealt a further blow to alleluia, as the oral accounts indicate. Paradoxically, then, the missionaries laid the groundwork for the current upsurge in kanaimà by their culturally inept suppression of piya and alleluia. Moreover, since the Pilgrim Holiness Church was expelled from Guyana after independence from Britain, it became yet another example of the tantalus of white Christianity in the highlands. Since then, no other missionaries have come and the ruins of their houses have become a prominent archeological feature of Paramakatoi today. The subsequent advent of a mining frontier in the highlands has again opened up the potential shamanic landscape by increasing contact with the Guyanese coast and Brazil.

Kanaimà is no exception to this. The casual violence of the mining frontier, and the repressive violence of the Burnham regime, at least after the Rupununi Incident (see next chapter), have both helped to foster a continuing relevance in the practice of kanaimà—not just as a mode of killing but also as a powerful form of cultural expression, ethnic affirmation, and route to individual eminence. The contemporary testimony that follows addresses these matters, especially as to the difference between the kanaimàs and the kwayaus, or, as it were, between magical death and its physical consequences.

The Kanaimàs and the Kwayaus

In this testimony RN discusses the kwayaus and how warfare was carried out—particularly with regard to the consequences of the grief and anger of the kwayaus, the tactics of the wenaiman, and the differences between kwayau and the kanaimà. RN also tells us about the piya man and his role in guarding the kanaimàs while they are hunting for their victims. RN's account should be compared with one in chapter 6 that narrates the attack from Kopinan that caused the wenaiman (pursuit) to kill Kasá and Kosopá, who are described here, since different individuals are given prominence in the two accounts.

> Yes, I know about the wars a long time ago, between the Patamunas, or Makushi, and Alekunas [Pemon], the day before some men went by my square [courtyard] and they were discussing about those wars which Amerindians used to do. So, when they were living not together but few here [Paramakatoi], few there, and few other side, because they want to be aware of war-men they had to live scattered about.
>
> During that time there was miseries, too many at war. Many strong men coming attacking the house. That's why they had to scatter out. Kwayaus. It happened at Tukusapilengtoi. It happened once to my grandfather when he was a little boy. Right in this area at Tukusapilengtoi, which place I have mentioned. It happened once right there. Patamuna from the Kopinan side had come to attack them. They were being an "attack team," so the war-men had to meet at the same spot and an old lady had to go running with them [carrying supplies]. In some ravine they had to stay there. In the ravine they had to stay there for one day and one night without food, being silent. You know how the small boys, when the war comes now, sometimes they would stay with their granny keeping quiet, that's how they were. They were killing only men, boys, and baby boys. They take away the women, some women, not all of them. So that happened. It was happening all over this area.
>
> Some used to do that [go to do the same to Kopinan], but not everyone. Some would go secretly and block them on the way. And that time they was hard of getting guns, but how I said before, they

used to go to Georgetown. Wygata is Georgetown, Wygata, they used to go that side and have some war. Wygata is somewhere where they would get every little thing what they need. What is being used right here now. With a war club they would fight and not with guns. With a taikek.

So now the men, not all men had a gun which they used to shoot, attack, or kill with it. One one [maybe] they had a gun but the gun is not really one that carries the cartridge, but just through the barrel they would load it . . . muzzle-loading guns. You put the powder in and you put the bullet in and *tap-tap-tap . . . kaboom!* So they had to go to war. Few of them used to go there, so my grandfather used to tell me, just a few will go and attack them. Some will go with a gun, some will go with a war club. Arrows as well. Sometimes they would have a gun, sometimes they would use war-club. Treating [making] it with a metal tip for the arrow or on the war club.

Once, there was a man right in here, he was a very old man whom I have mentioned, JI. His father's brother was a kanaimà. He was a kwayau. That's why they had to come here. His uncle had to bring him across here, so they may attack them [enemies] from here. But this is what they [kwayaus] didn't do, only his uncle used to war against those [the enemy] who were being dead by kanaimà. Kanaimà is different from kwayau. JI's uncle was a kanaimà, but he was a kwayau also.

He was using some experiments [magic], made from a bark, bush, or a herb, but I don't know how they used to make it to be as a kanaimà. It's a herb they use. Have you ever seen a ginger? Some just call it bina. It's that. But not every ginger is for an animal [for hunting]. Everything he [the kanaimà] will become like. Have you ever seen a herb too that grows in a group and he got some lumps like going from here and goes down there, some would remain here and stop the root. That is called koumi. And I would like you to have them. Ginger what is just called chiwi and I don't know the name of koumi [in English] but it's just koumi I know. And I will show you right in this village it has koumi. Right in this village it has ginger and they are the type. But it's not for attacking people, but it's for game just like tapir, deer, or Powis. But a kanaimà is also hunting other men, so he uses hunting bina. Like when a hunter goes looking for his food, or when a kanaimà goes looking for his victim, he's hunting too. So he uses his science. So that's that. And every time he uses these things, these chemicals, sometimes he may go far distance in a very fast time then come back in a quick time, too. That's the magic what he used to do.

Kanaimàs, they just kill in special way. I will tell you, my father used to tell me, not my father, my grandfather, how really the kanaimàs worked. This he learned from other kanaimà people when he was working at Mahdia [a large mining camp]. So kanaimà, he will use the same chemical as koumi and ginger, so he goes and waits for a person. Sometimes he would kill his own neighbor, his own father or mother, the chemical is making him to do that.

Listen carefully what I say. Then he would wait. Sometimes he may not be seen, he'll be in secret place . . . then the person will come . . . jump on him and say AARRHH! And like . . . after seeing that he will become a tiger and just throw him down . . . and this same koumi or chiwi, he's going to take this simply out of his mouth or anything just rub his hand . . . just hold a person . . . squeeze him up and leave him there for a while. Then he will get back, go home. After a while he's going to have pain, fever for the whole day or whole night. Then a person will get weak. Then he will feel the pain right in here or anything. Anytime when a kanaimà touch a person using the same chemical sometimes it would swell, badly swell. It will become black and blue. That's how the kanaimà will do it. They use many chemicals to do that. They do things to the mouth and put things into the back part. But some say—not me you know, I am not a kanaimà—we don't know about kanaimà. Right in this village there is no kanaimà, but the other villagers, who live in other villages, sometimes they would come and attack. So everything they do because they are working in evil. They different from the piya'san.

Now let the topic be about these attack teams or bringing war to each other. So I have heard many, many stories about them, but I think I will discuss it with you for this morning. Piya'san man will be witness for kanaimàs. Sometimes kanaimàs will become very sick when they kill people. They will become sickly, bad sickly, they will have headache. And these piya'san man now is going to work and the piya'san man will heal them up. So that's the real thing for how kanaimàs do. They have their own piya men, kanaimàs. They would walk with piya man. Even their piya man will be kanaimà.

Once there was a young wife, Asote. This is not a story, this is true to what is being seen and heard. Somewhere from the north came kanaimàs who had been in the south. There was a man who was living at Karasabai and he was a tushau [captain] and they told the young boys [who they encountered] that they are visiting the captain and they had to take the young wife with them, with themselves. And they had to climb up a high mountain, [which] had a cave. And they told them—the kanaimàs told the young boys—to wait for them right in the treetop until they return. After they went [to kill the captain] and come back they told the young boys that they didn't find the captain and that still they had to go back again and seek for him. And they had to find the captain, kill him. And they came back on the second day. And the young boys were very hungry, they were getting hungry, but there was no food. But only ginger the kanaimàs were eating. The ginger was their food when they are attack team, when they were hunting for the captain. And the young boys, now, had to ask them, "Did you see the captain?" And they said, "Yes we saw him." "Shall we go there?" the boys said. "No, we are going to return back after later morning," they said. These are the kanaimàs now and they were two and there was a piya man. Five of them, two young boys, two kanaimàs, and one piya man. The kanaimà's piya man. So the kanaimàs went back in the night [to the captain] and they were doing some magic thing. Then they came back, early in the morning, and tell those young men that they are now ready to come back. That time the kanaimàs used to carry a grater . . . graters, to grate cassava, but [they] never give any to them [the young boys]. She had to remain there [also], the young wife. In the spirit they [the kanaimàs] are going, so now they had to fall to sleep, in the spirit they had to go there. These kanaimàs would enter in every creature, a lizard, a rat, or a mouse . . . that's true. They are doing magic. They are doing magic thing. And they came back . . . shouting . . . the spirit now . . . and these human bodies were being led, but in the spirit they had to enter into the creature, and went there, and do same thing. And now the piya man who was sitting, looking at the boys, and never let any fly touch the kanaimàs. So he commanded these young men to kill them off. If a fly would touch them, sometimes they may not come back into life. So the first day they went and second day the piya man went with them. He slept . . . in the spirit, too. The two young boys were very hungry and said, "Let's go and leave them, let's go, let's leave them alone, they are doing their work." But they remained there for a moment. But as how these piya men had commanded them they did it, but they were very hungry and the piya man commanded them not to touch the body, or else he will not come back into life. But they were very hungry, so and they had to boil at [get angry with] them [the kanaimàs bodies], beat them up with a stick, roll them up from one place.

After then their spirits [of the kanaimàs] came shouting, firstly [one came] nearer, turned very near, but there was only the back of it coming. Going, coming, going back, coming back. And there it is gone, and butterflies just hum about the dead body. And it was not alive no more. The body was being chased like, and wounded, and it became a dead body. Another spirit it came now, it turned into piya man, but there was nothing but the butterflies coming, humming about the dead bodies. Then they realized [what they had done], these boys, now, so they had to run down the mountain, and return here to the village. Now these boys, they were feeling happy, because they find the village nearby, so they had to find the captain. The captain was a person who they know. So they started walking down the road towards the village and they said, "Where is captain's house?" That's how they said. The captain was the only person who used to visit them and they had to go to his house and they ask his children, "Where is captain?" But a few days ago he was being there and was being buried and they [the captain's children] had to call their mother and say, "These are the men who have killed our father," and they [the young boys] said, "No, not I, not me." So they had to gather together and they were ready to kill them, the villagers were ready to kill them [the young boys], and they said, "No, let's go and look for them. We have bodies there." They had to climb up the mountain and find the dead bodies. That they did. It's a very high mountain and a very steep mountain, right in there it has a cave.

Kanaimà and kwayau is two different. The warrior, he will be sober but he will eventually become jealous in his heart and go jump and break the door, enter into it, and just kill them. But there was not enough people in a one house village to defend themselves, just about 4 or 5. And so the kwayau will make them look fright, and they kill them. Once there was a man who I said, JI's father, when he came up from Georgetown, he met the place and there was only silence. He saw the smoke coming up from the house and the houses were being burnt up. And he shouted, but there was no answer. But a lady, an old, old lady who came out of the bush now, and she said to him, "Kwayaus have been here just now, and they have returned back." They don't used to kill the old ladies and very young ones, girls. Now he was being worried and he said to this lady now, an old lady, "I don't know why they had to left you . . . you could hardly slept when kwayaus been attacking . . . here is all these people [dead]." So he had to pick up a piece of a house, a tree, and kill her. He shouted . . . and she was then killed. And they said to their father, "Why have you killed my grandmother? Me, my sister, and my grandmother been right here and we now have to live without grandmother and mother," they said. Their father commanded them to stay there and he went back [followed the kwayaus]. He went behind the kwayaus, he had a two [barreled] gun that uses cartridge. He went right through on this trip. To Kato, he went, he went, he went, past Cheung. He went past Kurukabaru . . . Kurukabaru, yes . . . past Kamana creek. But before you meet Kopinan [River], there's a creek and it has a pool and it has a sheet rock, right there. Those kwayaus didn't only kill [the prisoners], they eat them. They did take out their . . . um . . . covering [loincloth] and put it aside one, two, three, and counting. They were naked ready to bathe now before the meat was to be finished [prisoners eaten]. They took their own war-clubs and lined them up and their coverings, lined them up also. Two lines in a row, lined up right on the sheet-rock. Have you ever heard of wenaiman? Wenaiman is a person who would guard them. Wenaiman is a person who when going [following] will attack them back, wenaiman is a person who is going behind them to attack them. So the guard now was on this side [the rear], not in front side. So he went around them, just branch out and went along. They [unawares] were sitting ready to bathe, and he now met them and said "Oh, these are Kopinan people." About seven of them were being lined up and the guard was there on the path, but the man met him from in front. Then he had to aim right and he had to get set. He fired and the next shot, he hold onto it and fire again. He fired the second time with a second gun [barrel]. Then they jumped into the water, into the pool, where they was bathing and some were getting away far. So he shouted, he was only one, but he shouted saying, "Have them! Have them there!" So these kwayaus were being afraid, they was being frightened because two times the gun was being fired, and they got frightened. So they jump into the pool anywhere, but his shots they slammed them. When he was shouting, saying "Have them right there! They are going in front! They'll be coming back!" they were thinking that they have another one [wenaiman] waiting right there waiting for them. I have another thing, another story, not this story, but the same about Kasá and Kosopá.

People [Patamuna] from Kopinan they came right on the Kowa Mountain foot, to have hunting. From there they had to hunt around, they caught some game but right at Ulupelu there was a man living, only one person. He had a neighbor and these people came as the warriors searching for a person. Then they met the man, and they had to come kill the man. After a while his neighbors got to find him dead. All of them there had beaten the man, every limb had been mashed up and they said, "We are [going to do the same] to Kasá and Kosopá." And one was an old man who was with them. After they meet there [at his house] the kàyik said, "We found an old, old howler monkey dead" and he knew that they were talking about a man. The old man came and said, "Be careful do not attack from here, do not go from here," then early in the morning Kasá and Kosopá had to travel, so the wenaiman had to go there [to Kopinan]. They were having some celebration there. They were having *Parishara* dance, they do good dance.[25] Now, as soon as they reach the Kopinan there was a lady from this area [Paramakatoi] who was being married to a man there, and everybody, everybody knew who she was. The wenaiman was now set. But Kasá and Kosopá they know what they have to do [because] they expected the wenaiman. They have climb up to the roof, house top, but inside there not outside, but inside it. Now the lady, whom I have mentioned, had to get out and pass water. The wenaiman had to meet her, and she said "Oh, that's you." They told what had happened right here [in Paramakatoi], and that is why they have to go and attack back, "And where are they?" they asked, "They were here but they have gone somewhere," she said. But they stayed there and the lady from here was dancing good now, she was feeling happy that her family has bring the attack team back so she was feeling happy and singing and dancing . . . trying to make them sweeter [Kasá and Kosopá]. So the wenaiman remain there. Now the lady went out and she said "Wenaiman is here, have your guns." She said "He's coming now get ready to shoot," then the men was ready to shoot and kill, just fire off . . . they had the guns there and keep on firing . . . but they didn't know where the wenaiman was there. Every part was beaten, mashed down with the war-club, they had to walk with war-club, they had to walk with guns. I don't how many people had to go there but I only know one person who went there, Joe's father. I saw old man Joe but his father I have only heard about. Now they mash him [Kosopá] up, they smash his head with the same war-club, and Kasá now was not being found only Kosopá was being killed this same moment. So some other war-man must have killed Kasá but I don't know who, or how it was. That's how the kwayaus were!

CHAPTER 5

Modernity, Development, and Kanaimà Violence

My father was so Amerindian. . . . he no went school, and he could kill and resurrect you in a day.—ROGER EDWIN, 1997

When Guyana became independent, the new government ordered the American missionaries to leave, but the new government did not go on helping the Patamuna people. Forbes Burnham never visited us, nor did Cheddi Jagan; only Desmond Hoyte and the Brazilian Governor [of Roraima State] came to see us in all those years.—ROBINSON WILLIAMS, 1997

These two quotations illustrate the ambiguous nature of modernity, development, and kanaimà violence in current Patamuna thinking. On the one hand, they are keenly aware of the way in which development, both now and in the past, seems to have passed them by, eluded them, and made necessary efforts to "fetch it up" from Georgetown. On the other hand, and conscious of the power of anthropology as the arbiter of "culture," the Patamuna are keenly aware of the potential for a loss of tradition, a distinct way of "being Amerindian," which, paradoxically perhaps, the ritual skills of the kanaimà and piya—death and resurrection—best express. In the face of modernity kanaimà becomes a potent symbol of continuity with the past.

For others, too, "modernity" is a much debated concept, but the idea of "modernity" employed herein is one that emerges only in opposition to the notion of "tradition." In other words, "modernity" cannot be understood apart from those social and cultural processes that in any particular situation, also give meaning and content to the idea of "tradition." In this sense "modernity" is both ancient and plural, an aspect of the continuous construction of tradition (Appadurai 1996,

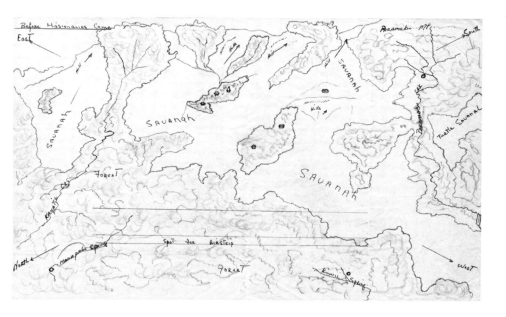

Paramakatoi before the Missionaries came and the forest was cleared, showing area designated for the airstrip. *Drawing by Roger Edwin.*

41–44; Hobsbawm and Ranger 1983). The meaning of these categories is therefore closely interrelated and historically contingent, the mutual condition of their possibility. Nonetheless, these ideas are often used and understood as if they were simultaneously the expression of a neutral or objective temporal criteria.[1] By recognizing the intimate conceptual connections between categories of "tradition" and "modernity," one is in a better position to understand the paradox of why alternative modernities emerge utilizing cultural forms that appear to be composed of the "traditional," or in the case of kanaimà, the hyper-traditional.

MODERNITIES

The expansion of industrialized capitalism in the last 150 years was a contingent historical phenomenon, bringing along with it particular notions of tradition and modernity formed largely in colonial encounter. Nineteenth-century anthropology itself had an important role to play in generating these categories via contemplation and classification of the "primitive" peoples that were encountered and reported by missionaries, merchants, and the military, and it is those notions of tradition and modernity that have been globalized to an unprecedented extent. Even if local meaning and form is given to those categories, their significance is still a matter of continuous debate for those on the point of imminent incorporation by the State. Nevertheless, how those globalized notions of modernity and tradition come to be interpreted in local contexts is not uniform, even if there are important regularities in the process of localization. As a result, local ideas of the modern and traditional may not be heavily inflected by the original content of such globalized notions, not least because the spread of industrialized capitalism has been manifestly uneven. In short, there has not been that "convergence" of modernities in the manner suggested by both Marx and Durkheim to produce a global social and cultural uniformity, but rather an explosion of alternative modernities (see Gaonkar 2001).

Patamuna experience of modernity has largely been in terms of the spread of "governmentality," the apparatus of State by which we are all rendered "citizens" (Foucault 1994). However, despite being repeatedly surveyed, classified, and converted, the systems of law, education, sanitation, and economy that were supposed to bring the Patamuna the fruits of development and progress have failed to materialize. As in other colonial and postcolonial contexts, industrial capital and western democracy have appeared wearing the differing costumes and masks of evangelical redemption, medical services, schooling, economic development, democratic rights—the full regalia of modernity, as it were. In the case of the Patamuna and other peoples of the highlands, the experiences of such successive modernities has been highly episodic and fleeting, a series of one-night shows, short runs, and rapidly folding productions. Nonetheless, the fact that the theater of modernity has been trying to establish itself in the highlands over the last two centuries means that Patamuna conceptions of the traditional and the modern are more complex and sophisticated than a simple opposition of, say, feathers and loincloths to trousers and shirts. This example is chosen quite intentionally, in the light of the earlier discussion of the semiosis of clothing, for the way in which it can reveal that in response to the repeated failure of modernity to establish itself a "hyper-traditionality" has emerged that is inimical to both external *and indige-*

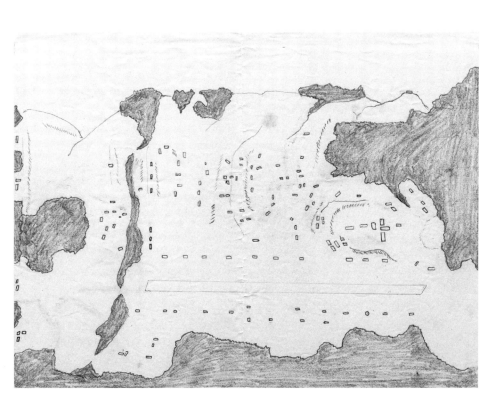

Paramakatoi after the Missionaries came, showing the missionaries compound (*center right*), the airstrip (*bottom center*), and the rim of the Yawong valley (*top left*). *Drawing by Roger Edwin.*

nous notions of modernity. Nor need this be taken automatically as a situation of "post" modernity, for the issues of governmentality that serve to give substance to the notion of modernity in the highlands and elsewhere, have not dissipated, even if they are taken as now irrelevant to the postcolonial cultural politics of Europe and the United States.

This persistence of a notion of modernity is manifested in a cultural consensus, shared by most Amerindians and other Guyanese alike, as to the relevance of these convergent, globalized ideas of tradition and modernity, those "costumes and masks" referred to above. This by no means entails any consensus over how those shared conceptions might be realized or enacted, but it does underline their coevalness. The cultural and political trajectory of kanaimà in the face of these multiple modernities in all their scene and costume changes has been violent resistance, which needs to be understood as a persistent enactment of a notion of tradition rather than some active counter-program to modernity. Kanaimà resistance has become more potent as the idea of tradition—especially "authentic," "premodern" tradition as often derived from Amazonia itself—has become widespread in modern society. Given the antimodernist rhetoric of much of the "new age" interest in shamanic tradition, perhaps kanaimà should after all be considered a truly postmodern development, an alternative traditionality in response to an indigenous modernity. Either way, designer tribalism and ethnic chic are well established cultural tropes worldwide, and the production of tradition among people like the Patamuna is likewise an issue of cultural persistence and affirmation.

The external projection of kanaimà as a cultural tradition and its meaning for practitioners and their victims have therefore become increasingly entwined.[2] Although William Brett's poem "Kànaima," Rómulo Gallegos's novel *Canaima,* and Wilson Harris's short story are works of the past, the symbolic force of kanaimà, potent enough within an indigenous poetic of violent death and already reflected in these mimetic cultural productions of outsiders, continues to haunt the modernist cultural imagination. In this sense, the kanaimà takes his place alongside the thuggee, bogeyman, cannibal, headhunter, zombie, and vampire as another ghoul in the colonial and modern nightmare of irrational, cultic violence that springs from enigmatic and atavistic cultural proclivities. This portrayal occurs in more sensationalist presentations, such as Victor Norwood's *The Skull of Kanaima* and other recent materials. However, reactions are not restricted to the cultural lexicon of colonialism or modernism, and the antimodernist search for other kinds of meaning can represent the kanaimà as a figure that is inspiring by virtue of its very cultural opacity, as in the case of Pascale Petit (1998). The following poem also reflects these aspects of kanaimà as an external symbol; it was written as a result of a conversation I had with the author.

KANAIMA MAN

Today I met a man who swore he'd seen an older truth.
Deep in the Pakaraima where the haraballi touch the sky
Sightless arrows fly—linking life to death,
And back again.

Shifting shapes and shadows
The piya stalk the night,
Stilling tongues that cry to know their fate.
Armadillo fire burns bitter to the core,
And beneath the baramalli's feet
Honey flows from lifeless veins.
Today I met a man who swore he'd seen an older truth,
Dark and deadly as the forest's night.
Cosmic circles linked to form a chain,
We feed, are fed,
Then, eaten by the Gods
Who suck the honey from our veins
And crush our hearts and skulls to dust.
So too in turn the hunters track their prey
And from the forest's floor
The spirits eat their fill.

—Leah Fraser

DEVELOPMENT AS TRADITION

Historically the Patamuna have been economically wedged between the gold and diamond fields to their north, and cattle ranching, as well as diamond mining on the Ireng and the Brazilian border itself, to the south. Contemporary with the advent of alleluia and the wave of missionary evangelism in the latter half of the nineteenth century, the first mining and ranching enterprises began in the interior.[3] Beginning in 1863–64 with gold mining on the Mazaruni—itself foreshadowed by the gold rushes of the 1840s and 1860s in the northwest of Guyana and in eastern Venezuela—gold production had soared by the 1880s. By the 1890s the Melville family, immigrants from Scotland, had also established significant ranching interests in the Rupununi region. Diamond strikes in the Mazaruni followed in the 1920s and 1950s. The Makushi to the south and the Akawaio to the north were thus in the front line of contact, but the Patamuna see themselves as having been marginal to these development frontiers. In other ways, though, the interior region overall was itself irrelevant to the colonial sugar economy of British Guiana and therefore was not a focus for investment.

With independence from Britain, the old colonial economy was almost completely nationalized by the Peoples National Congress

(PNC), but it was not run in a socialized manner, being largely exploited for the exclusive benefit of party activists and loyalists, as well as the ruling elite of the PNC. As a result, and despite the global increase in commodity prices in the late 1960s, by the early 1970s the Guyanese economy was in steep decline. This in turn led to a crash-program of development, with the aid of the World Bank, that encouraged extractive industries in the interior, such as mining and logging. This had a major effect on mining in the Mazaruni–Cuyuni region and encouraged the opening up of the Potaro and Ireng Rivers to mining activities. At the same time Brazilian *garimpeiros* began crossing the border to try their luck in Guyanese territories and have been present in Patamuna territory since the early 1990s (Roopnaraine 1996, 73).

However, both the mismanagement of the Guyanese economy and the isolation of the Rupununi region from the political culture of the coast led to the formation of a separate political party, the United Front (UF), which claimed to represent an alliance between Amerindians and white ranchers, like the Melvilles and the Harts. In 1969, claiming election fraud, the UF led a "rebellion" against the Guyanese government, seizing government offices in the border town of Lethem, an event known as the "Rupununi Incident." It is unclear what the purposes of the UF were, but the suggestion that they were colluding with the Venezuelans and contemplating a political secession led to the dispatch of government troops and a short but brutal firefight in Lethem (see also Farage forthcoming).[4]

The effect of this "rebellion" and the general weakness of government control in the interior, which it highlights, was a repression of Amerindian communities through a haphazard, if no less brutal, campaign of state terror.[5] In the view of one Guyanese commentator, "Guyana had become a land of horrors. . . . State terror had become entrenched and pervasive as a mode of maintaining the PNC power. . . . Rape, burglary, and arbitrary arrests by the security forces had become so prevalent that Indian villages became places of terror" (Premdas 1996, 61). The Amerindians were therefore cast as "demons" once again in the theater of development, seen as recalcitrant and unwilling to subscribe to the urgencies of World Bank economic planning. As a result, Amerindian communities were obstructed in attempts to make land claims, or simply denied legal titles to their ancestral territories. In addition, because of the Rupununi rebellion, a system of firearms licensing was introduced, which basically had the effect of making it im-

Calvin, Roger, Alfred (*right to left*), Patamuna *yakamana'yi* (hunters).

possible to legally possess a gun. In a context where hunting is not only a significant subsistence activity but also an important component of Amerindian identity, this has been a serious restriction. While guns are still available, for licenses are issued, illegal possession, which is much more common among the Patamuna, becomes an inevitable act of resistance. In the context of kanaimà and the traditions of the kwayaus, the possession and use of guns for political and social purposes adds another dimension to this attempt to restrict gun ownership.[6]

In 1989 a new road was planned for linking Lethem to the coast and thereby offsetting the economic and social attractions to the Brazil border and the town of Boa Vista, which is functionally much closer to the Patamuna than Georgetown. The road is still "under construction," since many sectors have simply been washed away by heavy tropical rains, but the idea of roads as key to development has led to similar activities around Paramakatoi. A road now exists from Monkey Mountain to the Brazilian border at the Ireng River, established as a result of the diamond strikes in the Ireng and Maú Rivers, as well as their tributaries the Chiung and Echilebar. In the early 1990s, the Patamuna at Paramakatoi also opened up a tractor trail to Monkey Mountain. This is now defunct, following a bad accident in which a number of people were killed when the tractor and trailer overturned. In 1997 there was a second attempt to open a route to the Brazil border, although this did not succeed either, as the route chosen was quite unworkable. As I stood one day at the head of the Yawong valley, looking south toward Brazil, which can be seen at a distance of some thirty miles, and enjoying the beautiful vista of "untamed" forest and mountain, someone asked me, "Neil, do you know what I think when I look out there?" I eagerly answered, "No," expecting then to hear of some complex cultural view of landscape and sky. He replied, "I see the lights of all the houses and a fast road running right up that side of the valley from Brazil, won't that be great?"

KANAIMÀ AS HYPERTRADITION

In this landscape of a burgeoning modernity, which wears the masks of evangelical democracy and sustained development, the practice of kanaimà has also taken a distinct guise. Kanaimàs appear as hypertraditionalists, that is, as rejecting the tokens of modernity, such as metal tools, guns, matches, and, particularly, clothing. At the same time that whites are discursively included in the culture of kanaimà, other non-Amerindians are also potential victims for kanaimà. The difference here is as much historical as it is conceptual, since whites performed the theater of development in the colonial regime, even if blacks were important supporting actors. However, with independence, the presence of blacks, or Afro-Guyanese, became the focal point for a much more general resentment against the Guyanese state. Blacks dominated, and still do, the police and Guyana Defense Force (GDF) and are important actors in the mining and logging industries. The presence of Indo-Guyanese in the interior is less, although it is growing, especially in shopkeeping, as well as mining. At the same time, the mining frontier in Brazil has steadily moved toward Patamuna territories, and Brazilians are now a prominent feature of many mining operations.[7]

In tandem with this changing face of development and modernity in the interior, kanaimà attacks have also become more explicitly directed toward blacks and Brazilians, with disputes in the mining camps themselves providing an expanded context for the operation of kanaimàs.[8] The following account—comparable to the kanaimà attack on the white manager of a balata operation—relates the killing of a black government worker. Both cases occurred in the 1950s.

The Kanaimà Family

This account describes, as in the case of Bishop, an entire family who are avowed kanaimàs. The relevant aspects of this family's history, as well as that of the people they killed, begin in the 1920s. A black coastlander, FK, was sent into the interior as a government worker, where he married an Amerindian woman, mother of the narrator of this account, DF, who is an Akawaio woman. This marriage took place despite the fact that the Amerindian woman had already been promised to the S family at Jawalla. FK lived many years in the interior and was by no means antagonistic to native ways, since he actually learned both talen magic and piya, although he balked at the final ordeals that would have been necessary to complete his training. Instead he became a Seventh Day Adventist when he was sixty and about to retire.

FK was in his garden one day when the kanaimàs came and did "their business." His wife, RK, managed to rescue him by summoning help. She tried to take him to the regional hospital, but he died en route.[9] The family who committed this deed are well known and publicly identified, rationalizing it openly to others as a need to "get rid of the black man." After his death his wife destroyed all their non-Indian articles, but then his brother in law, HK, a village captain, was also killed by the same group. RK's grandfather had fought with this family, and she had been promised to them as a way to mend the rift, but she was not willing to be part of that arrangement.

In 1968 RK's sister was killed in a kanaimà style as she unwarily made use of the forest near the house, instead of the pit-toilet, while making cassava bread with their mother. She was heavily mutilated in the throat, breasts, and vagina, and her neck was broken. Her tongue had also been pierced. The killers hung around the funeral—conducted by Alonzo Abdul, a Seventh Day Adventist minister from Trinidad—all the while boasting that she had died "in kanaimà" not "in Christ."

During the building of the Kamarang dam along one of the interior rivers, there was also an upsurge in killing, which was related to securing favorable jobs on the project. The narrator of this account, DF, also named two other killers, LW and BW, who purportedly have been responsible for a number of deaths in the past ten to fifteen years. They are both Makushis from Kwaitung on the Ireng River and were brought into the region by some Akawaio for the purpose of assassination.[10] One of these men killed DF's uncle. DF therefore suspects that one of her cousins, OK, has initiated himself in kanaimà in order to get revenge for this killing. OK is currently in jail for an unrelated murder. DF felt that the fact that her uncle had had a big role in the local alleluia movement may have encouraged her cousin to follow this course of action. In the narrator's opinion, alleluia singers, kanaimà killers, and piya men were all to some degree adept in "spirit matters," which meant there were fewer boundaries between these ritual modes than might be thought. In a similar judgement, this time on the matter of ritual eminence and gender, DF also indicates that, among the Pemon, a man she names as JI has initiated his daughter as kanaimà; she goes on to suggest that there are currently female shamans among both the Pemon and Akawaio. Certainly there are accounts of female alleluia prophets, and examples of living female alleluia prophets among the Patamuna.

Both cases, then, make an explicit connection between a kanaimà attack and the ethnic and cultural positioning of the victim. More recently, it is recounted, a Brazilian walking from Mutum to Monkey Mountain along the new road encountered five people, kanaimàs, who tried to attack him. He wounded some with his cutlass and then ran. While this was offered as an example of how an Amerindian might get a kanaimà to do a "contract killing" against a non-Amerindian, it was also explicitly stated that this would have been the work of amateur or initiate kanaimàs. Such initiates, it was added, indulge in extreme violence and mutilation that appears to have no definite purpose, which demarcates a line between such violence and kanaimà's usual ritual forms. According to the same informant, the sort of embellishment such "amateurs" use is often sexualized. They will cut off the nipples of a woman and "use" her vagina, cut off a man's "pistols" and impale him anally, as well as cutting out the tongue in a sort of reference to the usual ritual form. Such groups seem to be much more locally or family based, and they "don't mix up in kanaimà unit."

As a result of the GDF's repressive presence in the interior in the 1970s and 1980s, there are also explicit accounts of the depredations that individual soldiers made on Patamuna villages, and the issue of the rape of Amerindian women by GDF units is recalled in particular. In other contexts, however, the GDF might act in a kind of imitation of the kwayaus, physically punishing those alleged to be kanaimà at the behest of the village tushau. Among the Waiwai, the *kamara picho* (tiger-skins) all live on the "Brazil side" now, not least because all tiger-skins are chased to Brazil if they are found practicing at Gunn's Strip, the only Waiwai village actually in Guyana.[11] Kamara picho are either beaten by the GDF during routine missions, at the request of the tushau, or sometimes by the tushau himself with his staff of office, which is bestowed by the government. The particular history of the Patamuna at Paramakatoi has precluded this alliance of government and village authorities, but it does show the way in which kwayaus and tushaus might be in alliance against the kanaimàs.

Patamuna oral history actually suggests that some blacks who were associated with the Siparuni balata trade were "friends" to the Patamuna, and Sam Scipio, in particular, is recalled as being critical to bringing in the Pilgrim Holiness missionaries. Nonetheless, there is still tension about whether Patamuna with an obviously black component to their heredity are as "really" Patamuna as those with a more stereotypically "Amerindian" phenotype. This stems from the fact that, as a result of GDF rapes, many women gave birth to children who are now in their twenties and thirties, adding an aspect of intergenerational conflict to the question of Patamuna ethnic identity. As a result, accounts of attacks on blacks, even where they have married into the Patamuna, are heavily inflected with this resentment. The following account of just such an attack on RJ, a black man married to a Patamuna woman, also introduces the idea that blackness allows a potential victim a greater space and ability to resist the magic of the attack.

In 1994 RJ killed four kanaimàs, who had chased him for several hours, as they "strayed him" into the wrong part of a savanna. They kept chasing him, bringing on a light rain to confuse him. He dropped his bag at one point, but later found it on the trail ahead of him. He stooped to pick it up and walked on. At that point, he heard the roar of "baboons" (howler monkeys), but, turning to look, saw that the sound actually came from the kanaimàs.[12] As he watched, they came toward him and one of the baboons turned into a man. RJ grabbed at him, stabbing him in the chest and killing him. Another baboon then came toward him with "the leaf" (yé stick), but RJ killed him also. According to RJ's son, he then remembered nothing else, but he came down with fever and was flown out to the Georgetown Hospital. RJ was very sick in hospital, and one of the kanaimàs, who he recognized as a man called Caesar, had followed him to Georgetown. He killed Caesar in a toilet at the hospital but himself died within a few days. The fact that other kanaimàs, too, are said to operate in Georgetown and have done so since the nineteenth century is a good indication of the way in which kanaimà symbolically engages modernity through a performance of hypertradition.

Intergenerational differences have led to a situation in which some aspects of traditional knowledge are either not passed on or threatened with disappearance as younger individuals examine and evaluate the usefulness of tradition in a modern world. In the former case, talen magic, it is often complained, is not being transmitted to the younger generation, leading to a sense of incompleteness and greater reliance on standard medical procedures. Talen could be used for less serious but chronically disabling medical complaints, such as bacterial infections, bush-yaws, or headaches and stomachaches.[13] At the same time, although curing piya still practice in the region, they are becoming fewer and fewer. The rigor of training and the uncertainty as to its effectiveness, given the presence of other medical techniques, also mean that few remain who are inclined to be initiated. Indeed, one individual commented that piya was no less a part of Patamuna heritage than language use, which otherwise tends to be the primary focus of efforts at cultural persistence and revival. On the other hand, the desire to learn kanaimà is very much part of current youth attitudes.

In this situation, kanaimà can become part of an affirmation of tradition and identity, since kanaimà is itself treated by outsiders in this way. A Patamuna man put it to me like this: "Pop music and alleluia will be mixed up at a wedding say . . . and kanaimà, like alleluia, is a traditional thing. . . . That is why those boys [kanaimàs] say that wearing clothes makes you sick, it come along with the white men. . . . They even are using little sticks not stones to make the pot hangers." Kanaimà is thus assimilated to a more radical notion of Amerindian tradition, becoming a general "mindset," and everything is attributed to kanaimà activity, since this itself becomes proof of the persistence of a distinctly traditional Amerindian way of life.

Ironically, the existence of the mining frontier, it is felt, has given the kanaimàs a new and vastly enlarged scope for their activities, even as "kanaimà" itself is suspected to be less authentic than it once was. As implied by the previous accounts, some kanaimà attacks are thought to be the acting out of bully-boy youths who don't possess a sufficient understanding of the ancient magic that makes kanaimà a symbol of authenticity and potency in a world of powerlessness and shifting identities. As a result, young men that go to the mining or logging camps often come into contact with older men, kanaimàs, who try to recruit them with promises of power and money. Older men in their thirties and forties often say that they were approached by kanaimà teachers at some point in their youth.[14]

Consequently, current attitudes are ambiguous, rejecting immediate and present kanaimà as inauthentic, while still invoking old-time kanaimà as the "real thing." This also leads to analogies between kanaimà and drug-use. Indeed, the ritual substance maba is most often likened to a recreational drug, such as marijuana or cocaine. As a result, the kanaimà are pictured as "addicted" to the maba and to the killing that is required to produce it, that addiction, then, being no less a menace to society, whether Guyanese and Amerindian, than the "foreign" *narcotraficantes*. Notably, in this regard, some accounts of kanaimà, especially those that describe attacks by initiates or "amateurs" (both terms implying youth), draw a distinct analogy with "partying" or "binge drinking." I was told, for example, the story of a man who had tied up his hammock in an empty house at night, having been forced in there by heavy rain. He noticed that there was a "cassiri canoe" in the corner of the house and wondered where all the people had gone, as they must have been having a big *paiwarri* (beer festival). However, just as he was going to sleep, the kanaimà spirit sopanéylipa came, and the man realized that it was not cassiri but a kanaimà victim in the canoe. The man was thus trapped, as he didn't want the kanaimà to see him, so he watched the greedy kanaimà sucking up the maba—"*choup, choup, choup.*" There he was getting high, high, high, all by himself, drinking up the whole body.[15]

KANAIMÀ: THE SNUFF MOVIE

A carnivalesque atmosphere was apparent in the making of a film of a "kanaimà attack," itself an ethnographically revealing cultural episode for the way in which it produced a critical reflection on accounts of the kanaimà and allowed the acting out of ideas as to kanaimà ritual procedure. The movie, for which I operated the videocamera, opens with two kanaimàs preparing an ambush in the forest. We see them donning their ritual equipment of masks and tracking devices, and finding a hiding place along the trail. We hear at a distance the sounds of a group of people approaching. As they come round a bend in the trail, we see

Patamuna women at the *mùloka* (farm).

two women and a young girl. One of them stops to adjust her *warishi* (backpack) in a little clearing by the trail, a few yards from where the kanaimàs are secreted. The other two continue on. The woman finishes adjusting the straps on her warishi and begins to walk on, but she has forgotten a knife she laid down on the ground, so comes back down the trail. She recovers her knife but, a few yards farther on, out of earshot and sight of the other two, she is suddenly assaulted by the two kanaimàs. She is dragged to the ground and clubbed. They then take out their *ubi* (poison-gourd) and pour something into her throat. They pull at her arms to dislocate the socket joints and prick her along her back with a poisoned-tipped dart. On hearing the other two women returning down the trail, the kanaimà secrete themselves in dense bush once again. The woman who was attacked gets slowly up from the ground and stretches as if to relieve pain and stiffness in her back. She appears disoriented and confused, but apparently unaware of what has just happened. The three then continue down the trail toward their farm.

The actors in this drama had suggested to me that the most effective way of communicating the nature of kanaimà was to film this enactment, as it would show "what happens." The film is therefore quite revealing in regards to how kanaimà is understood to operate. First, it is women who are attacked, and this is indeed seen as sexually suggestive. In the case of this filming, the woman and one of the "kanaimàs" were actually man and wife, and it was he who dragged her to the ground, at which she was unable to stifle her giggles. This film, along with the accounts of kanaimà attacks or threat that involve sexual motives, suggests a consistent link between the construction of a violent masculinity and kanaimà. Such violent masculinity in turn relates to the way in which kanaimà families are often patrilocal—being composed of a man and his sons—and therefore unlikely to wish to abide by the more general custom of matrilocal residence after marriage.[16] The problems in getting a woman to marry into a family that so challenges the norm of postmarital residence are potentially overcome by the threat of kanaimà against the woman and her relations. This seems to have been exactly the scenario with the contemporary case of Merimo, as well as in the nineteenth-century case of Mekro and was also a factor in the history of *The Kanaimà Family* quoted above.

Second, this filming event raises issues as to the kind of reflexivity shown toward cultural tradition, which, in the light of the earlier discussion of concepts of modernity and tradition, suggests again that there is a more complex field of significance for these ideas than a simple conceptual opposition of the old and new (see Turner 1992). In short, the film becomes another example of how the traditional can be modernized and the modern traditionalized, but also shows that the medium of film allows a memorializing of culture that changes the relationship between cultural actors and their cultural repertoire. This does entail that the category of "tradition" is thereby potentially frozen at a certain moment, in a way that really is new for the Patamuna and that is also reflected in their desire for an ethnographic identity through a textual medium. In either case, there is also the possibility that textual and cinematic simulacra of kanaimà will avert its cultural force as an epitome of violent and absolute death. However, given the history of the Patamuna and other highland peoples in negotiating and capturing, through alleluia, the magical force of textual representations, the results of such filming are not necessarily negative. Indeed, the filming of a historic alleluia event led to the request that such filming be done to record the ritual practice of other alleluia'san, not to the suggestion that filming was inimical to the ritual force of alleluia, as might have been the case.

Riley (forthcoming) has analyzed one such simulacrum of kanaimà in the skits that accompany "culture shows" performed for Amerindian and non-Amerindian audiences alike. The presence of kanaimà as a representational device in these shows is highly significant for understanding the meaning of kanaimà as a token of authentic Amerindian tradition for both audiences. Kanaimà is therefore both a self-representation and an existing category of external representation. As such, it is a perfect example of mimetic representational practices among Amerindians and Coastlanders. Riley (forthcoming) describes the skits she witnessed.

> The power of the *piaiman* is shown plainly in the "skit" ceremony. He chants and beats the leaves—two definite signs which show that he really is a *piaiman*—and the *piaiman's* soul travels and goes up vertically into the air into the spirit world, shown by a leaf rising up into the air. The spirit that appears at his calling is virtually always the *kenaima*. The *piaiman* then threatens the *kenaima* with physical harm if he does not stop bothering the patient's soul. The *kenaima* then departs, showing that the *piaiman* won that round of the battle for the patient's soul. Then the *piaiman* advises the patient (also addressing the mother or care giver for the patient) what plant remedies to give to the patient to restore health. (In real life, if things do not improve by the next night, the *piaiman* will return the next evening to continue singing over the patient).

Riley adds that, in Georgetown, the kanaimà skit includes other elements, such as the inclusion of a doctor who arrives in a car. She also notes that, although the skit is "about" the piya, it is the kanaimà who steals the show and for whom the skit is named. While the context of this skit is lighthearted, the mysterious and ultimately frightening figure of the kanaimà is thereby read into the category of "Amerindian" as a defining characteristic. The power of these readings in the popular imagination is also understood by Amerindians in the highlands and is consciously exploited by them on occasion.

As kanaimà assumes these changing roles and meanings in Amerindian discourses of violent death, the global stage on which kanaimà is increasingly acted out must be taken into consideration. The persistence of kanaimà tradition into a "modern age," may not be simply dismissed as therefore anachronistic or atavistic. This has been shown in other places, such as Indonesia, Rwanda, or even Bosnia, where apparent "reversion" to traditional modes of violence and killing is shown to be very much part of the political culture of postcolonial states. In South America, Taussig (1987) has brilliantly evoked the mimetic interplay between colonial violence and the violent representation of indigenous people through colonial notions of shamanism and the savage.

In more recent anthropological thinking, traditional forms of violence, such as cannibalism, witchcraft, and head-hunting, are being reconceptualized as violent discourses as much as violent acts.[17] For lack of a culturally informed framework for interpretation, many violent contexts appear to us as frighteningly enigmatic. As a result, commentators are apt to fall back on such cultural categories as "primitive," "savage," and "tribal" in order to interpret violent events such as the Rwandan massacres, Indonesian witch-killings, or Bosnian ethnic cleansing. However, close ethnographic engagement with such situations strongly suggests that attention to the cultural meaning of violence, not just the violent act itself, is key to advancing understanding. The performance of violence, how it is enacted according to cultural codes, is therefore as relevant to understanding as is the appreciation of its sociopolitical consequences and causes.

The performance of violence in Amazonia, and elsewhere, has been increasingly the focus of a number of anthropologists over the last decade, and this approach has enabled fresh interpretations of violent practices such as assault sorcery, as well as symbolic and ritual complexes associated with warfare, such as head-hunting, torture, battlefield mutilation, and cannibalism. An interest in cultural performance thus stands in counterpoint to theoretical approaches that explain ethnographic and historical claims as to the existence of cannibal, or indeed kanaimà, practice as merely an external projection of a supposed "primitive savagery." Rather, the poetics of violence and the discourse and discursive practice to which it gives rise—that is how violence is performed—must be understood. The violence of capture, killing, and consumption of enemies is itself a ritual form understood by both perpetrator and victim, and for this reason can be seen as expressing agreement or accord over the wider issues of sociocultural reproduction, since both killers and victims participate in the same cultural quest for cosmological status. Accordingly, violence and warfare may actually represent interaction, familiarity, and exchange. In the poetics of such violence, in its autorepresentation, violence sometimes appears both appropriate and valuable, and is not necessarily understood as dysfunctional and pathological.[18] Accordingly, even careful analyses of Western forms of violence, such as of the Nazi genocide, are not necessarily relevant to the understanding of postcolonial ethnic violence, such as the genocides in Rwanda and Cambodia, precisely because "genocide" is there mediated through cultural forms with which Westerners are often unfamiliar. Unless the meaning of the mode of violence is itself understood, then the only policy option is the application of even greater violence, as in the case of Kosovo, Somalia, or, most recently, Afghanistan. Thinking of violence as a cultural form reveals that violence is often engendered not simply by adherence to globalized ideologies such as Christianity, Liberal Democracy, Communism, or Islam, but through the regional and subregional disputes whose origins are in the complexities of local political history and cultural practices. As has been argued with regard to the Patamuna, this is so even where global ideologies such as Christianity do come into play, since it is the local meaning of those ideologies that drives community and ethnic conflicts. Therefore, understanding the cultural forms of violence may reveal unappreciated sociopolitical dimensions of such cases.

There are, therefore, a number of ways in which the cultural forms of violence might be approached theoretically, as exemplified in the analysis of kanaimà here. Principally, this would mean far greater attention to the poetics of violence and the discourse that arises from it. It is the meanings of violence, not just its statistical incidence or medical features, that are of interest. For example, an examination of the cultural discourse on "cannibals" seems particularly useful and promising. The figure of the cannibal is perhaps the most historically persistent and culturally prevalent cultural icon of "monstrous violence," offering a widely intelligible symbolic summation of all that is savage, violent, and threatening. Discussion of this key symbol of human violence is also currently emerging across a number of disciplines and subdisciplines in the study of issues such as colonialism and postcolonialism, minority cultures, and the advent of modernity in traditional societies. The cannibal signifies a range of potent meanings, and both indigenous and external metaphors connected to this idea, as well as the resurgence of cannibal practice itself, are currently a strong focus for cultural studies of all kinds.[19]

As a result, analysis of cannibalism must avoid colonial-style apologetics that see it as an expression of a fundamentally corrupt and flawed human nature, but neither does anthropophagic practice need to be "deconstructed" into nothing more than a Western fantasy projected onto the unwitting "savages." Rather, ethnographic experience of ritual killing, as with kanaimà, suggests a similarly discursive nature to cannibalism. An emphasis on discourse also permits a comparative treatment of other contemporary instances of cannibal practice, since it is cultural meaning rather than social function that is thereby considered. Through this approach, ideas and actions that evoke cannibalism, both as a collective cultural expression and as an individual "criminal" pathology of serial killers, become commensurable. Such commensurability has to be derived in turn from a recognition of the mimetic and mutual meanings that cultural opposition and ethnic conflict produce, rather than the static and monolithic confrontation of primordial biologies, cultural identities, and social norms that have often been the intellectual starting point for previous examinations of such materials.[20] In such a theoretical framework, distinct ways of understanding the interplay of the imagination and the enactment of violence can emerge.

For example, by analytically emphasizing the symbiosis of antagonists, or victims and victimizers, one can see that violent discourse mediates more than difference or antagonism. This has been shown in the case of kanaimà, and such an approach also facilitates the interpretation of the apparently unrelated cultural practices of modern serial killers (Seltzer 1998, Tithecott 1997). In colonial South America, both Europeans and Amerindians shared a passionate interest in the idea of cannibalism, reflected both in the doctrinal strictures of Catholic transubstantiation and in the divine hunger of the Amerindian pantheon. It is therefore significant that cannibal practice was often carefully predicated on the way it would be read by the Europeans, as much as by other Amerindians (Whitehead 2000). The subsequent cultural meanings assigned to the cannibal trope in European usage have been thoroughly analyzed in the recent literature. Less well appreciated is cannibalism's discursive role in native thought, how that might sustain contemporary violence, as with kanaimà, and how that violence remains attuned to the mimetic violence of the Guyanese and Brazilian nation-states, whose legal and cultural proscriptions to civilize, develop, and "become modern" challenge the meaning and authenticity of native ritual violence. However, this simultaneously means that the practice of cannibalism has become a potent indigenous symbol of political autonomy. As a result, kanaimà is poetically linked to an understanding of the external meanings of cannibalism, as well as to the traditional ritual requirements of the practice.

In a similar way, the striking interdependencies of killers and victims is perhaps the most important and unremarked feature of serial killers who would "possess" their victim through a violent act: "I was always killing myself, but it was always the bystander who dies," said Dennis Nilsen, quoted in his biography, *Killing for Company* (Masters 1985). More widely, the search for intimacy through violent and dismembering possession, as well as the collecting of human mementos of such intimacies, seems to be a prevalent form of violence among contemporary serial killers in the United States. Lacking the cultural skills to form the kinds of relationship that are more usually the vehicles for intimate human contact, that lack is recovered through a direct act of irresistible intimacy—killing. Moreover, just as the notion of cannibalism played a wider cultural role in the construction of the colonial categories of conquest, such as savagery and civilization, so, too, cultural constructions of serial killers echo the monstrous excesses of the cannibal feast in the colonial imagination. This certainly suggests that much may be gained from a more systematic comparison of how ideas about internal and external violence interplay to produce cultural attitudes. The persistent fascination with both ancient cannibals in Brazil and modern cannibal serial killers thus illustrates that such cultural icons are in fact continuous with, not alien to, some of our key cultural norms.[21]

However, such exercises in the analysis of the poetics of violence would be meaningless without recognition of the institutional forms of violence that supravene and critically determine the contexts in which killers and victims emerge. It is the State, in its full Hegelian dress, that has usurped the ritual violence of both the cannibal and the kanaimà, and deployed its own forms of death in the discourse of modernity, development, and social order. In the global ethnoscape of vulnerable identities (i.e., those without a legalized ethnicity), it is the State that, like the kanaimà, can terminate and erase those identities utterly, through acts of mass assassination (genocide). Perhaps this process of violent State incorporation should be understood as a means of making a kind of modern maba, through the intoxicating consumption of industrial human labor—a State cannibalism, which echoes the plot of the movie *Soylent Green,* in which our bodies are ritually produced as labor value, profit for the consumption of the Shamanic State evident in the occult institutions of industrial capital, global finance, and the military order.

THE SHAMANIC STATE

There has been a growing literature—somewhat paralleling the literature on the resurgence of "traditional" forms of violence—that examines exactly how the state co-opts occult forces and symbols.[22] The magic of divine kingship, the apotheosis of empire heroes, and the mass human sacrifices of two world wars, of course, demonstrate that this is nothing new in the history of state building, much less in the history of the European nation-state. Nonetheless, the means by which kanaimà, or other forms of dark shamanism and assault sorcery, may play into the political culture of those nations that impinge on the zone of kanaimà—Venezuela, Guyana and Brazil—remain of interest.

Shamanism, history, and the state are the topics of Thomas and Humphrey 1996, which examines the cross-cultural validity of the category "shaman" and searches for signs of persistent kinds of relationship between shamanic practitioners and the state apparatus. Thomas and Humphrey point out (1–12) that the popular view of shamans as inherently transgressive and anti-authority is not borne out, and that the category does not transpose well, as appropriate definitions of shamanism are hard to develop, since it refers to such a variety of spiritual practices. However, the material collected in that volume does allow the editors to draw out some useful comparative observations. For instance, where shamanic traditions are divided, or even in conflict, then state hierarchies often co-opt one variety and persecute the other, encouraging the further development of radical messianism. Moreover, an underlying tension between "chiefs" and "shamans" seems to be a recurrent feature of how shamanic practice is socially expressed world-wide. In this context, the possibility exists for the marginalization of "chiefly" modes of power, such as trade and warfare, and the emergence of "shamanic-chiefs" who, by restricting ritual knowledge to a small elite, can effectively exercise political power. This might well help understand the reports of "kanaimà tribes." Thomas and Humphrey also suggest that generalized forms of shamanic practice that are widely accessible often form the basis of messianic movements. The development of alleluia, which emphasizes the inspirational capture of specific songs, seems in this light to have as much in common with the practice of talen magic as it does with the practices of the piya. Finally, the state may use shamanic practices as a context in which to define an ethnic or national identity, as in the case of President Rómulo Gallegos and his depiction of *Canaima*. Recognition of these potential roles for shamanic practice in the creation or destruction of state systems thus points to how the state can achieve authority through forms of ritual action that mimic and indicate the same sources of inspirational power that are the persistent attributes of shamanism itself—curing, killing, and a "knowledge of destiny."

The magic of modernity as enacted by the Venezuelan state has been the subject of a number of studies. The earliest analysis, made by Martín (1983, 64), suggested that popular spirit beliefs in Venezuela are part of a state ideology based on the magical forces of the political powers of national and regional authorities. This ideology forms part of and is represented in the cult of Simón Bolívar, the Venezuelan liberator and founding father of the republic. A more recent study by Fernando Coronil (1997, 1–5) argues that the state "captivates minds" by its ability to produce spectacle in the manner of a "magnanimous sorcerer," such "marvels of power" being principally those "dazzling development projects" so conspicuously absent in the realm of Venezuela's oil-poor neighbor, Guyana.[23] However, although not part of Coronil's argument, the general analysis would seem to hold for Brazil as well, particularly in its production of that national and international spectacle of progress and order—the "administrative" capital of Brasilia.[24] This implies that the magical practices of the state must be historicized as well as the practice of shamanism, since the adoption of shamanisms, or rejection of them, as a component of state ideology is in turn linked to the varieties of spiritual practice itself.

Michael Taussig, in *The Magic of the State* (1997), indicates the cen-

tral place that the potent figure of "El Indio" has in the popular practice of spirit possession in Venezuela. This obliquely underwrites the
cultural potency of kanaimà in criollo society, as reflected in the work
of Gallegos. In particular Taussig (1997, 71–72) notes the dualism of
the spirits of *bajo luz* (dark) and *alto luz* (light), suggesting that the
former are anxious to "advance" in spiritual power. As a result the
spirits of bajo luz can be openly bought and used to invade the body of
one's enemy: "One advanced in light towards the Liberator by selling
oneself as an assassin." This recalls kalawali and the shamanic battles
that occur in ascending this shamanic ladder. Taussig (127, 137) thus
sees the state as a theater of spirit possession, spirit possession itself
being part of the circulation of "value" that creates the magic of the
state. This value lies not in the source of the object nor in its exchange but in the metamorphosis and transformation of the object
through the theater of spirit possession. Accordingly Taussig (169–73)
notes that the Vicente Gomez, the dictator of Venezuela in the 1920s
and 1930s, was held to have maintained contact with the spirit-queen.
This is reminiscent of the Duvaliers in Haiti who were perceived as
voodoo *houngan* (priests), as well as of Forbes Burnham, who was associated with obeah-men and "specialists" in Guyana during the 1970s
and 1980s (Vidal and Whitehead forthcoming). In this context, the Tupian chiefs and shamans, as discussed by Hélène Clastres (1995) and
Pierre Clastres (1977), can be seen to fuse together to become kings,
then emperors, and then the Hegelian state itself. However, this script
for the development of the modern state is challenged by postcolonial
forms of statecraft that co-opt cultural forces marginalized by colonialism and Christianity, such as spirit possession, obeah, and voodoo. In
Venezuela the Liberator as the State metonymically grasps the Spirit
Queen that is metonymically America, but a criollo not indio America.
As Rómulo Gallegos depicts it, kanaimà eludes this grasp and becomes
a counterforce to the balance of spiritual and state terror. This is both
the meaning and utility of kanaimà in the forceful assertion of native
identities.

Considering violence and its cultural meanings on a global as well as
local stage must in turn lead to a consideration of how unique kanaimà
shamanism may be within Amazonia. However, kanaimà is also comparable to other resurgent forms of occult violence, assault sorcery,
and even state-led campaigns of terror, where the state itself co-opts
occult magic. Africanist work on this topic argues that magical idioms

are central to the exercise of political power. A history of particular ritual practices, then, is necessary in order to appreciate the contingency of rituals and symbols evoked as timeless or ancient and how they may have changed in response to both colonial occupation and postcolonial forms of modernity. Sorcery, at least in Africa, also benefited from colonial rule. European interest in the African occult was an aspect of achieving better control and domination of the population, and it therefore made the matter highly significant in the eyes of both colonizer and colonized. So this colonial interest itself made the occult a relevant site for both resistance to colonialism and for the invention of postcolonial political culture, in which a vast array of magical forms and techniques are currently employed. However, the issues have been framed such that it is not clear if the present use of occult ideas should be seen as a "brutal resurgence" of ancient practice or as a new invention of tradition in the face of globalizing modernity. One answer that moves beyond that stark opposition is the suggestion that shamanic innovation was as much part of prior ritual practice as it patently is of modern occult forms—which means that these processes of mystical transformation must be understood. In Africa there are currently many varieties of occult influence that leaders manipulate and use to achieve an aura of power; as much as serving as a testament to postcolonial inventions in the face of globalizing modernity, such practices must be understood according to a specifically African, or local, idiom. For example, African political leaders are often seen as the receptacles, not the owners of occult forces; this provides a strong contrast with Amazonia, where the ownership, domestication, and domination of spirit forces is also the idiom of spirit mastery.

At the same time, the involvement of the colonial state in producing and enforcing new definitions of witchcraft and sorcery only reconfirmed the centrality of secrecy, violence, and exploitation to the exercise of political power. In Amazonia, since the fifteenth century, the notion of cannibalism has likewise provided a powerful trope for the very embodiment (or dis-embodiment perhaps) of the indigenous contestation of colonial occupations. In light of the history of cannibal practice in Amazonia and the cultural politics it engendered in Europe as well, it is all the more important, as with the work in Africa, to note the distinct ways in which current practices depart from this standard motif. For it is that difference that grounds analysis of representations in the context of disjunctural histories.

Meanwhile the occult has itself gone global, and the trade in ritual equipment to service the ferment of occult innovation is itself a significant economic phenomenon. I recently made a point of visiting the voodoo shops in New Orleans to research the flow of occult materials; I found for sale there the material crafts of Amazonian Indians, marketed by the Brazilian Indian Agency FUNAI as potent fetish objects for the tourists in the French Quarter. Questioning of those who purchased such objects revealed that they do not think that such objects are ineffective but that they themselves simply don't know the techniques to bring them to life. Which brings into question the novelty of modern witchcraft in both America and Africa, in the light of the dynamic changes in occult practice of a hundred years ago, or even two hundred years ago. Providing such historical depth for understanding changes in occult practice has been very much the intent of my discussion of kanaimà here, where I have shown the connections between local practice and global change and how that can inform the shifting canvas of ethnic identification. In the context of violent struggle for political power, the responsiveness of "traditional" forms of occult assault to the vagaries of political ambition and forms of political expression suggests that "violence" itself, so often seen as the bubbling up of an old native savagery and primitiveness, has to be rethought in just the way that Africanist scholarship has so imaginatively questioned the contemporary role of the occult.

There are also many pitfalls in this analytical ambition; in particular, ritual practices must be disaggregated, and the old colonial trope of a "darkly mystical" Africa or Amazonia must be avoided. There is also a magical dimension to politics everywhere. Westerners have learned from Marx about the vampiric nature of capital and about the fetishistic ideas that mask capitalism's exploitive character. Indeed the term *vampire* itself relates to a moment and time in which capital and labor relations in the Balkans were radically changing. It may be also remembered that George Bush accused Ronald Reagan of "voodoo economics" in the 1992 primary campaign, not because he seriously was suggesting that Reagan had borrowed the Tonton Macoutes from the Duvaliers as campaign advisors, but because the operation of the market—and here even Adam Smith referred to a "hidden hand"—appeared mysterious, intelligible only to those with specialist knowledge. "Specialists" and "scientists" are thus the obeah-men of Guyanese or Caribbean political culture.

In any case, the notion of the divinity of kings, supplanted by Hegel's pronouncement of the divinity of the state, has proved a powerful source of magical legitimacy to this day; could nationalism be understood without its mystical appeal to Blood, Earth, or prophetic Destiny? And what is to be made of the film and novel *American Psycho* (Ellis 1991), which is about a "serial-killer-stock-trader" on Wall Street? This appears to neatly update the conjunction of the vampiric and cannibalistic market with a living embodiment of American nightmares. Rhetorically, one could go on—the use of astrology by Adolf Hitler and Nancy Reagan, or perhaps the more general the faith Westerners have in the notion of "secret intelligence," which, as garnered by the CIA, often proves truly phantasmagorical in its content. Indeed, the whole gallery of stock tipsters and financial specialists who provide arcane formulae for playing the lotteries of NASDAQ, FTSE, and NIKKEI, which seem no less susceptible to magical explanation and manipulation than the cultural opacity of capital relations in Africa and Amazonia. Thus, seeing magic as a mimetic and mutual production of native and colonial cultural practice has its own limits. The recognition of such mimesis in the virtual world of representations does not adequately address the wider processes of social and cultural change in the actual world of history. So, perhaps the question is less why African or Amazonian political culture is so "magical" than how it was that Western political culture used "science" and "the rational" to the same ends. Or, when did statecraft cease to be witchcraft?

Kanaimà practitioners claim a great antiquity for their ritual procedures, and the long and elaborate transformations of magical belief over the last 200 years are intimately connected to the advent of successive modernities in the highlands of Guyana. Gun warfare, evangelism, messianic redemption, cargo cults, mining frontiers, timber extraction, and now the drug trade have presented the Patamuna with a dazzling array of versions of the theater of modernity. But each show has been a short-run affair, and modernity itself could become the subject of archaeological investigation, as eroding machinery, rusting gun barrels, glassware, and tin cans burst through the rain-washed ground. In this context of multiple and successive modernities, the kanaimà have positioned themselves as hypertraditionalists, confronting a notion of modernity shared by Amerindians, the coastal Guyanese, and the World Bank alike. The magical force of kanaimà therefore not only stems from the supposed antiquity of its practice—its authenticity as a real Amerindian thing—but also from the history of kanaimà assassinations of both whites and blacks—the agents of these many modernities in the highlands. The richness of the Africanist materials therefore challenges anthropologists and historians to attempt even wider comparative studies that might enable the better appreciation of these magical particularities.

CHAPTER 6

Ritual Violence and
Magical Death in Amazonia

There are historical and cultural precedents for kanaimà in the shamanic repertoire of native groups in this region of northeast Amazonia, and there are other extant shamanic practices that also involve
assault sorcery. Comparison with these other complexes is helpful both
in understanding the ritual and symbolic meanings of kanaimà, as well
as demonstrating the importance of assault sorcery to the general ethnology of the region.

Shamanism is a subject of growing fascination for urbanites around
the globe, but it's a particular brand of "shamanism," with a media
image oriented to the supposed psychic and physical benefits that shamanic techniques can bring. This image has come about only through
a systematic sanitizing of the actual ritual practices by those who have
inspired this febrile search for personal meaning and fulfillment, for
it is surely not kanaimà that is envisaged in such cultural borrowings.
Such erasure is not only vain self-deception but, more importantly, a
recapitulation of colonial ways of knowing through a denial of radical
cultural difference and a refusal to think through the consequences of
such a denial.

Given shamanism's plurality of practice and lack of institutional
forms, anthropologists in Amazonia rightly question whether or not
the term *shaman* even describes a unitary phenomenon and have also
questioned its presence as a defined social role (Campbell 1989; Hugh-
Jones 1996). Nonetheless, the term has utility, in that the performances
of ritual specialists across the Amazon region bear a number of family
resemblances that, while not defining a distinct and bounded category
of ritual action, persistently suggest to ethnographers symbolic analogies and historical relatedness. However, anthropologists have tended
to shy away from issues connected to violence, so the "dark" side of

shamanism has not been properly examined, despite the fact that it is often integral to the efficacy of shamanism overall, since it plays a part in the origins of the cosmos, as the accounts of Makunaima and Piai'ima demonstrate. The idea that shamanism expresses a recurrent moral ambiguity—for the same abilities that cure can also kill—does acknowledge this fundamental aspect of shamanic power, but only through the representation of shamanism as a personal or individual dilemma. The deep mythohistorical presence of dark shamanism, contemporary with, if not actually preceding, the original emergence of humans and shamanic techniques, indicates that dark and light, killing and curing are complementary opposites not antagonistic or exclusive possibilities. In the same way that shamanism has been historically shaped by forces conceived of as external to the originating shamanic cosmologies, so, too, are the ritual practices of curers intimately linked to the assaults of shamanic killers and cannot be understood apart from them. The locus of these cosmological contests thus becomes the bodies, both physical and political, that are created and destroyed through the ritual-political actions of chiefs, warriors, and shamans.

Such approaches to the "mystic endowment" of society and culture are also inspired by Johannes Wilbert's pioneering study of the shamanic order among the Warao (1993, 92–125). Wilbert argues for the centrality and importance of the *hoaratu* (dark shamans) to the overall spiritual and cosmological ideas of Amazonian peoples in general, and this framework is certainly as relevant to kanaimà as it is elsewhere, such as among the Baniwa (Wright 1998). The historicity of shamanism and its mediation of colonial and national intrusion are very evident among the Baniwa, and the class of chants and evil spells comprised by *hiuiathi* (sorcery) is employed by Baniwa shamans to assail their enemies in a wide variety of social contexts. However, such chants and spells are not themselves an exclusive part of shamanic techniques, since they may be employed by anyone who knows them; such aggressive magic, for instance, is also present among the Patamuna in the form of talen, which requires no special initiation to learn and use, being primarily part of a family inheritance. Although the knowledge of such spells and chants might be general for the Warao, Patamuna, or Baniwa there is an extreme secrecy, among the Baniwa, as to who may commit acts of assault sorcery. In contrast, both the hoaratu and the kanaimà are often well-known individuals, and the kanaimàs in particular may choose to openly brag of their deeds, or purported deeds. Wright (1998) also investigates the historical nature of shamanism and millennial prophecy in the creation of notions of self and otherness and how those ritual practices relate to a broader cosmology in which shamanism comes to represent the triumph of human creativity over the destructive forces of the spirit world. This struggle is similarly represented in Patamuna thought in the contest of the primordial brothers Piai'ima and Makunaima. As with the Warao and Patamuna, the Baniwa also recognize the inevitable existence of dark shamans, *manhene-iminali,* or "poison-owners," who stand in an ambiguous relation to these destructive spirit forces and who are cosmologically connected with the existence of death in the world. Such comparisons between shamanic roles allow some provisional discrimination among the various forms of dark shamanism in Amazonia, in particular between the existence and possession of certain magical techniques (hiuiathi, talen) that may be widely known, the counter-aggression of shamans against attacks by outsiders (iupithatem, *daunonarima,* piya), and the classes of dark shamans who are initiates to a distinct system of ritual practice (hoaratu, kanaimà, manhene-iminali).

Whatever the tragedy, distress, and death that dark shamans and allied ritual specialists may perform on humanity, then, they are nonetheless an inevitable, continuing, and even necessary part of the cosmos. For these reasons, dark shamans are not simply vilified and hunted down but can become, as with the kanaimà, the source and even symbol of a potent indigenous society and culture that is capable of defending itself against the depredations of the outside world, be that a neighboring village or even the national state.

However, Amazonia generally has not stimulated an extensive analysis of witchcraft and sorcery, as in say Africa or even the Andean world. Nonetheless, a few early studies stand out: Lévi-Strauss 1967, Dole 1973, Goldman 1963, and even Napoleon Chagnon's controversial filming of Yanomamö assault sorcery in the film *Magical Death* (1973, Pennsylvania State University). But even with the appearance of more recent literature on various aspects of shamanism in general—Michael F. Brown 1985, Gow 1996, Hugh-Jones 1996, Langdon 1992, Taussig 1987—anthropological analyses of dark shamanism are far less extensive than for other ethnographic areas. Assault sorcery in Amazonia has been treated mostly in a haphazard way, with some excellent ethnographic accounts but no real regional comparisons or broader suggestions as to historical origins and processes. Assault sorcery is then subsumed under the topic of shamanism, reflecting the ethnographic reality that shamans are quite often sorcerers as well. In some societies, shamans also stand in contrast to priestlike specialists whose functions are rarely considered ambiguous and are connected to "legitimate" social reproduction in the cosmological sphere (Thomas and Humphrey 1996). As Michael F. Brown (1988) pointed out, the tendency of the literature on shamanism has been to concentrate on the morally "good" side, that is, the healing and prophetic aspects of the shaman. The "dark" side, the power to destroy or inflict harm through assault sorcery, though recognized, has received little in-depth attention. In several of the most important contributions to the South American shamanism literature in recent years (Langdon 1992, 1996; Sullivan 1988), the shaman's capacities to harness cosmic forces for the benefit of humanity receives the weight of attention. This is not to say that assault sorcery has been ignored altogether, but some of the more notable extended studies (Albert 1985; Chaumeil 1983; Fausto 2001) have not been widely read in North America (but see Whitehead and Wright forthcoming).

"Assault sorcery" is defined as a form of magical attack that results in physical harm or death to a given individual. Although the simple term *sorcery* itself has come to have the negative associations of "black magic" or "witchcraft," the addition of *assault* is intended to emphasize that various indigenous ideas of magical action clearly distinguish this category of attack from others, such as talen magic or nonmagical violence like poisoning with cassava juice or "chopping" (wounding with a cutlass). Assault sorcery itself cannot be easily separated out from other aggressive acts, and of course the conduct of warfare is also linked to the way in which techniques of assault sorcery might be deployed. Community assault by shamanic means was certainly a possible precursor for the widespread emergence of kanaimà in the nineteenth century, and although that might not have been the exact moment of its invention, the changing conditions of warfare throughout that period were certainly reflected in the practice of kanaimà. However, in considering the relationships between ritual shamanic practice and warfare, one must also examine how the conduct and purposes of warfare itself might be much more closely linked to the achievement of a variety of cultural ends than many current explanations propose.

Patamuna informants suggest that kanaimà may have originated with the Makushi, as do the Wapishana (Foster 1993). At one level, such sentiments are perhaps merely an expression of ethnic and community differentiation, but such claims, when made by Patamuna piya, may also indicate something of the historical practice of kanaimà. In the same way that alleluia was the invention of Makushi shamanism, so, too, it may be that Makushi shamans originated the key ritual and magical elements of the kanaimà complex. Given the historical links between kanaimà, the advent of gun warfare in the highlands, and the fact that the Makushi were incessantly preyed upon by others, especially the Karinya, kanaimà may have first emerged strongly at the beginning of the nineteenth century, as a defensive technique in the face of new and overwhelming military force.[1] Again, comparison with the emergence of alleluia could be fruitful, since alleluia likewise was a shamanically inspired response to rapidly changing circumstances at the end of the nineteenth century. While materials do not yet exist to answer this question definitively, closer ethnographic study of kanaimà may clarify the relationship between the various practices.

Unfortunately, the only extant anthropological materials on kanaimà among the Makushi are limited to Farabee 1924 and Riley 2000.[2] In neither case was kanaimà an explicit topic of research but Riley provides some highly interesting accounts of contemporary ideas and cultural uses of kanaimà. Her comments on the potentially harmful and secret nature of binas and other plant murang (charms) also are very suggestive for interpretation of kanaimà ritual practice (Riley 2000, 338–45). Nonetheless, in no sense has kanaimà as assault sorcery disappeared and, however such magical assaults may be interpreted, the poetical force of the invocation of kanaimà in any particular death or injury is clear evidence of the continuing relevance of the category.[3] This is reflected precisely in the use of kanaimà as a projection of, and judgment on, the authenticity of Makushi identity and of Amerindian identity more generally.

Nancy Foster (1993) reports on kanaimà in Wapishana thought, in particular how it is used "metaphorically" to define relations with others. She suggests that kanaimà functions as a "cultural diacritic," marking off the patterns of relationships between groups and individuals, and as such is more fundamental in this role than as a means of "social control," an allusion to the revenge-theory of kanaimà so beloved of the nineteenth-century authors. Foster then goes on to cite a 1986 census of a Wapishana village in which she recorded 58 percent of deaths as being attributed to kanaimà. In Foster's discussion, kanaimà is seen as three things: a plant, a "conjectural" person, and the general phenomenon of death, as attributed to extreme antisocial behavior. Wapishana accounts, as recorded by Foster, do not differ significantly from other descriptions of kanaimà practice. However, Foster does also record that kanaimà is part of the way in which relations with both blacks and whites are pictured. She quotes one man to the effect that kanaimà "is all on the part of the Indians. The white disturbs things because we have a plan, he arrives with another plan. So we drop our own plans and follow the thinking of the whites" (29). In this way kanaimà comes to represent a reaction to a "breach of the social order," an inevitable punishment for stepping outside the cultural system at the behest of outsiders, and a counterpoint to modernity as expressed in the "thinking of the whites."

It is also striking that so many deaths should be attributed to kanaimà, as this seems highly unlikely. The prevalence of such claims therefore needs a particular explanation, for the air of "unreality" about kanaimà stems in large part from such profligate attribution. The explanation may be that the invocation of kanaimà, and perhaps even some claims to be kanaimà, might in any given case be used to supply meaning to an otherwise purposeless death. This means that the broad cultural acceptance of the poetic of kanaimà works to obscure which cases are a reflection of the ritual action of kanaimàs and which are part of a thanatology that uses kanaimà to create meaning in death. This dual aspect is in turn reflected in the various distinctions made between "real" and "imaginary" kanaimà by external observers and in the fact that kanaimà is cited by participants as the cause of deaths that show no, or only ambiguous, signs of kanaimà ritual violence.

A cultural consensus thus emerges between killers and victims (or at least their kin) as to the reality of kanaimà death, in which it is accepted that not all forms of death will perfectly express the ritual action of kanaimà. The performative felicity of any given killing may thus vary widely, and a ritually "ideal" kanaimà killing may be relatively rare. This not because of the absence of the phenomenon, but because specific killers are variously adept and differently motivated, while victims are variously motivated but differently qualified, to participate in the cultural performance of kanaimà. However, they are all united by a mode of ritual performance that speaks loudly within the cultural discourse of kanaimà and that expresses a distinct poetic of violence within a cosmological theater of predatory death at the hands of divine forces. The 58 percent of deaths attributed to kanaimà in this Wapishana village may well reflect the historical condition of the Wapishana as preyed upon (like the Makushi), but very few of these attributions correspond to deaths caused by physical attack as well as shamanic assault, that is, in a "proper" kanaimà manner. The cultural purpose of kanaimà, however, must logically be to communicate its presence by the manner, the poetic, of the death spectacle, so actual or avowed killers are contemptuous of the way in which deaths are indiscriminately attributed to them. Equally, however, avowed killers may well claim responsibility for deaths that they could not have caused and for which the physical symptoms are unlike those usually associated with a kanaimà attack. Individual reasons for this may be reasonably straight-forward—a desire to impress and intimidate others—and do not take into account the outsiders' need to produce a definitive classification for "real" and "imaginary" cases.

Comparative materials on the Waiwai, introduced earlier, noted that the antisocial nature of the kanaimà was very evident in how "tiger-skins" were treated within the village of Gunns. Stephanie Huelster (personal communication) also suggests that "family magic" among the Waiwai is effective against the kanaimà precisely because it represents the solidarity of the ideal social unit against the disintegrative and lethal forces at play in the wider world (see also Riley 2000, 341). The cosiness of the benab, closed up tightly against mosquitoes and kanaimàs alike, thus perfectly expresses this ideal familial sovereignty. The notion of family magic refers to the way in which certain key magical techniques, particularly those associated with talen and the use of binas, are the property of individuals who, for the most part, pass them on only to immediate kin. This relative secrecy is also thought to enhance the effectiveness of talen and binas against kanaimà magic, which is more public in its operation and whose key elements are at least suspected and discussed by knowledgeable individuals and piya.

Peter Roe (1995, 8) also discusses kanaimà with reference to materials he collected among the Waiwai, specifically with regard to the relationship between the kanaimà and the *kamara'yenna* (jaguar-

people, or "enemies") and to kanaimà as the complementary opposite of piya shamanism, at least in its curing aspects. Both the "hyper-
natural" kanaimà and "infrahuman" kamara'yenna are contrasted and
overlapped with the human warrior in what Roe calls a "chromatic
continuum" of human/animal transformations.[4] Roe sees kanaimà as
resulting from the fact that "witchcraft takes over when warfare is
forbidden," but I maintain that it was the advent of gun warfare,
rather than its later suppression by the colonial authorities, that was
the critical context for kanaimà practice. This is also the firm opinion of Patamuna. Nonetheless, I would agree with Roe that, whatever the recent sources of kanaimà might be, its current florescence is
an aspect of native self-affirmation in the face of a colonizing modernity. Moreover, Roe notes that both the kamara'yenna and kanaimà
share an interstitial place amongst Waiwai categories of killing: the
kanaimà as the "intra-societal were-jaguar killing shaman" and the
kamara'yenna as the "inter-societal were-jaguar cannibal enemy."[5] This
insight is particularly important for understanding the relationship between kanaimà and warfare more generally, and in the particular case
of the Akawaio, it may be relevant to interpreting both the relation
of kanaimà to their war-complex in the nineteenth century, as well as
their contemporary identification of kanaimà by the term *itoto*.

Itoto is a Cariban word found throughout the region and used to des-
ignate "enemies," especially those at a distance, such distance being as
much cultural and political as geographic. *Itoto* thus expresses an unknown, unpredictable, and highly threatening kind of enemy, thereby
making an implicit distinction from "close" enemies to whom one is
likely to be tied by bonds of trade, marriage, and possibly ethnicity.[6]
Warfare among Patamuna themselves would be of the "close" conflict
kind; Patamuna warfare with the Akawaio or Makushi would be similar; but warfare with the Waiwai, Karinya, or Ye'kuana, would most
perfectly exemplify conflict with itotos. These structural distinctions
in the terminology of war and killing thus descry equivalent domains
of military and magical performance, whose intensities and modalities
change accordingly.[7] Kanaimà pertains to all of these spheres because
its origins are not in warfare, understood as a collective expression of
community. Rather, the eternal origins of kanaimà lie in the possibility
of the utter negation of community, as well as the spiritual and material
power that control of such a possibility engenders.

Audrey Butt Colson (2001) has recently revisited her field materials from the 1950s pertaining to kanaimà among the Akawaio (Butt Colson 1954) and provided a number of important insights from that perspective. The Akawaio actually use a different term for kanaimà, itoto, which Butt Colson suggests is an equivalent. It may be for the Akawaio but that lexical difference may also indicate differing origins and meanings for the kanaimà complex, connected to the way in which kanaimà, or its Akawaio expression as itoto, developed historically. Butt Colson (2001) reports that Akawaio tell the following story (*bandöng*) of the origin of itoto: "There was once a family living in their house. One night a man came and took off a leaf from the roof, entered the house and killed everyone there. After that there was Itoto" (222).

The very baldness and brevity of this tale in itself suggests that kanaimà may have had external origins for the Akawaio since there is no reference whatever to its shamanic dimensions. This is not conclusive, of course, since no one is currently researching kanaimà among the Akawaio except the Akawaio themselves, in an interesting and significant reflection of Patamuna interest in the research that was the basis of this work. Indeed, I interviewed Desrey Fox, an Akawaio who later wrote her master's thesis on kanaimà, with regard to her own personal experiences.[8] Although Fox uses materials from Butt Colson's doctoral research, as an Akawaio she obviously also represents a distinct and authoritative voice on the matter.

According to Butt Colson (2001), there are two main "methods" of itoto attack. The first, already very familiar, is the attack on the lone person in the forest or farm, but the second reflects the Akawaio tale of itoto's origins, involving the itoto's entry into the benab by night to poison the intended victim, and perhaps the rest of the household. This style of attack is rarely mentioned by the Patamuna. The possible meanings of these differing visions of kanaimà and itoto practice may in turn reflect differing historical origins for kanaimà and itoto among the Patamuna and Akawaio. This is certainly true in the case of alleluia shamanism, so the practices of alleluia are therefore different for Patamuna and Akawaio. While there are important connections, the differing ritual practices and tales of origin are direct evidence of the historicity of ritual performance, even if anthropologists cannot perfectly reconstruct the historical events that gave rise to that difference. However, gun warfare, missionary evangelism, and the mining frontier can certainly be referenced as pertinent to any attempt at such an explanation.

Colson also mentions a much more ambiguous type of attack by itoto, in which death may be caused by "daytime accidents," such as "drowning or burning by pushing his victim into a river or a bonfire."[9] The Patamuna have not mentioned such accidents to me as evidence of kanaimà, although they might certainly use allusion to kanaimà in a metaphorical sense to suggest a reason for an accident. In this sense, one might say that the piece of wood on which one stubs a toe is "kanaimà," so I never took such statements to be a serious reference to the magical action of kanaimàs, but as a poetical allusion to kanaimà as the standard source of misfortune. The idea of kanaimà as a disembodied force certainly works this way, which is why the invocation of kanaimà as an explanation of actual death, rather than just of a trivial accident, may be widespread, as in the case of the Wapishana. However, just this distinction may be drawn by others less susceptible or less motivated, thus inducing them to see kanaimà as a generalized cause of misfortune. Part of the frustration of some Patamuna with the misperception of kanaimà as being somehow unreal, was that this misperception stemmed precisely from the way in which those who were not ritually knowledgeable would make this kind of attribution for the most minor of reasons. From the point of view of the kanaimà themselves, such attributions might both occlude and enhance the force of their ritual practice; occlude it in that if everything becomes kanaimà then nothing in particular, no given death, is clearly their work; enhance it in that the very pervasiveness of the presence of kanaimà malice is a component of their social and cultural significance. However, the Akawaio do clearly see a difference between itoto attack and magical assault by a piya. The corpse of the victim of itoto is *ekilong* (black), but for those thought to have suffered an attack by talen magic or the spirits controlled by a piya, the corpse is seen as *aïmodong* (white).

The Patamuna see kanaimà attack as particularly lethal for the way in which it drives out the ekati (spirit force) of the victim, and Butt Colson (2001) has suggested an etymology for *kanaimà* that certainly matches this usage and perception. In Pemon, a language closely related to Akawaio and Patamuna, the verb *kana-ka-nepui* means to cut, sever, terminate, put an end to, chill, strike dumb, or stun—a range of meanings that certainly more than matches the key aspects of a kanaimà attack. Suffixes such as *-ima, -imï* or *-imu* add the sense of "ultimate" or "great." This leads Butt Colson to make the interesting suggestion that etymologically the word *kanaimà* implies an "ultimate terminator" (or cleaver, stunner, severer), and this seems quite persuasive. Moreover, it is easy to see how such an etymology could allow the broader sense of *kanaimà* as expressive of a thanatology in which kanaimà comes to stand for Death itself, since all deaths are pointless and untimely.

However, despite recognition of kanaimà's shamanic aspects, Colson found only a limited explanation of the motivations behind itoto. This explanation is heavily inflected with western notions of property and ownership and may have been derived from an adoption of Christian ethical systems, since the itoto is pictured as being "evil," killing out of "envy." Certainly, leaders and important men are often principal targets for attack. This may be both for political reasons or for more immediate social reasons; such men, for instance, may have many kin and affines, whose marriageable daughters constitute both a workforce and an attraction for sons-in-law. It has already been noted that kanaimà "families" often seem to be groups of fathers and sons, standing in social and political contrast to the usual norms of idealized village and household composition (Rivière 1984).

Butt Colson (2001) also notes, "The brother relationship amongst both Akawaio and Pemong is enshrined in their myth of origin relating to Makunaima and Chikï but it is noticeable that the adventurous comradeship of these heroes changed when one of them took a wife and in-law obligations led to periods of separation. These aspects of Itoto (Kanaima) require special attention" (233). This is insightful, as the Patamuna locate the origins of kanaimà in the myth-cycle of Makunaima and Piai'ima. The following is a Patamuna version of this tale of origins, told to me by Alfred Edwin and translated orally by Roger Edwin. My transcription of that recording follows.

The Man Who Got Chopped

There were two brothers alone in a settlement. The big brother had a wife and the other one didn't have none. So one afternoon they come and his wife said, "You know—let's go cut *anunto* [soursop] fruit!" When they reach toward that tree, around the tree, they stop there, she put her warishi [backpack] down and she said, "We need this cutlass to be sharpened!" So her husband take the file and start sharpening the cutlass. The big man start now and start filing the cutlass—*chop, chop, chop, chop*—all the time, right? So the lady said,

"What! What the file say? Listen to the song!" and the big man start going again—*chop, chop, chop, chop*—the lady say, "What! Chop? What it mean by that, chop?" Anyway, the big man continue—*chop, chop*—sharpening, sharpening the cutlass and then, okay, he going up and cut some fruits from there and throw them down while she's packing her warishi with them, right? So there he goes and he start to throw these fruits and so on until there was sufficient to fill that warishi. She said, "Okay—enough! You can come down now." So her husband throw the cutlass from the treetop down, and there she received the cutlass and was ready with it. The man now didn't know nothing and he just coming down. The *last* step to come down he make a stretch with his one straight leg and there the woman chopped the man's leg off clean. By the time he dropped down, remember she had already packed her warishi when he's up there, she just collect her warishi, fetch it and put it on her back and fetch it home, left him right there. Then she reach home late, and the brother-in-law, younger brother, say now, "Where's my brother?" She said, "He said he coming along . . . just around the corner there doing a little hunting and so on before night." Night came in. His brother asked again, "Where's my brother? Maybe he's on the way, coming, you know?" So it happened nobody didn't come that very night. So now she put down her warishi and she change herself, she went and lie with the man, bad lying down with the man. The man say, "What! what happened?! Usually you don't do this! You must have killed my brother!" She said, "No!" Anyway she start troubling the man and so on, the man said, "What happened with my brother?" Remember there was no torchlight and you know he was quite a bit slow that he really didn't set off yet. So he said, "I will go and see if my brother is alright, see if something is wrong with him or you know, call him or something." Anyway, he [the big brother] had to overnight. They couldn't catch [find] him and so he was crawling, and coming there, you know with one entire leg and bleeding. He was unable to reach him that very night, or afternoon rather. Now during the next morning he expected his brother. He didn't come. He got weak, the pain got beyond his control. He couldn't dare it any longer!

He couldn't go further than that! With the pain now and so he take off the coal [pupil] from his eye and like so talk to it. Simple as that! He said, "Watch! Go tell my brother I got chopped!" And this coal now eventually turned into a hummingbird and flew. And it hold onto the doorframe and started to whistle, explaining to the brother, "He got chopped!" but the bird was so tiny and speaking so fast that he couldn't pick it up. The man say, "What? What's this bird saying?"

Before he could get his attention to the bird this woman come and make noise around him and so the bird flew away. Anyway, the man who get chopped had pain again and so on. So he took out the wax from his nose and make a bird with it and said, "Watch, go . . . tell my brother I got chopped!" Anyway the bird go and the same thing happened or, you know, probably the woman had him busy or he just couldn't, you know, go see what had happened to his brother. I don't know. Now, the bird flew back again. It was so painful so he start getting his shit, you know, to make a different bird and said, "Watch, go tell my brother I cannot make it." The bird flew now, and then the bird started, this was a bigger bird, he come and talk and explain it to the man. He said, "Your wife has chopped your brother!" You know?

He said, "Whaaat!?" The bird says, "Your wife has chopped your brother! Go check him!" he said, "Listen! Listen!" So the woman come start make noise again and the bird said, "One more time!" The lady pick up a rock, tried to lash at the bird, the bird flew off and start to make one more song. "Your brother got chopped! From his wife!" He get the message. Anyway, night came in again, he crawl! The woman now have this man in a building, hugging him up, and he can't even come out because she tie up the door, and he cannot do anything, you know. Midnight! He reach home crawling and the man who got chopped said, "My brother . . . help! I cannot help myself." And the woman started hugging up this man and the man cannot get up. He [the man who got chopped] said, "Watch! If you don't want to see my face, just pass my bench and my horn . . . my horn that I blow . . . pass it though the hole!" So it happened. The woman immediately got up and push out the bench before the man does something . . . and the horn. And the woman said, "I've got this man under control." So he [the man who got chopped] decided to go. He went up to become stars. Those stars with the one side leg cut [Orion's Belt]. The horn what he had then became a fish skull, call it the head only [Pleiades]. That was his horn. And then in this same very season there will be plenty those small fish in these creeks. So when you can see those stars, well, it is also the season when that fish is present in the stream. The place where this happened is over in Brazil. This is the place they call *Wailan,* this is in Brazil, right? And how they said was they have some big rocks built like an altar, like a ladder . . . big rocks . . . that was where he started to go up . . . that's how he got up into the sky.

Now his brother was left in charge of the woman! She had a child. A baby aged like that little girl what they have over there, about eight-month baby. Okay, now it's the two of them. The woman was so proud of what she did. She was very happy after this accident passed and tried to make this man comfortable, but the brother you know, was worried, he was sad about his brother, you know, the parting was sudden and he was a real grieving man! So he said, "Okay, how would I catch this woman to be killed? What would I do to get rid of this woman? Seeing that she get rid of my brother, what a use to keep this woman with me?" So he was trying to get a point where he can catch this woman . . . to death. He said, "Okay, I spied some honey over there. I'll go and cut the honey and get it." Now the woman was feeling happy that next day going and she said, "Oh okay, I'll come and look after my farm a bit while you chopping the tree. I'll come and when you're ready, I'll come." So he said, "All right." He went and he chopped the tree about five feet up. He average, he make a little ladder for chopping tree and instead he cut the tree, setting a trap for the lady really, so he averaging it, like a little ladder here about two feet up and then she would climb. He got the honey. He workfully cut up the honey, let the honey run inside to the bottom, and then it would be plenty enough for her to come and drink. That was the smartness he was using. Now she came and she say, "You got through, you got through. . . ." He said, "Yes, I got honey there and there is plenty run inside this stump inside and you can come and have a taste of it!" She said, "Why not?" and come and climb up on the ladder and bend down to drink this honey from the stump. Remember he didn't chop down the tree completely, he just cut the top. Now she came and she climbed up the ladder and bend down to drink this honey. When she go to drink that honey he come and hold her on her head and pinned her down in the honey and she start drinking this honey—*sluurp, sluurp, sluurp, sluurp, sluurp, sluurp.* In the man's hand she turned to be a *kaykank* [armadillo]. She dropped down into the stump of the tree and got inside the dirt and inside the ground and so he left. He said, "Whaat! Why I do this, man?" He was wondering what's next to be done. Ah well, he does justice you know what I mean, so he got up, got his axe and chopped the wood with the axe and the axe went up, up, up and became a woodpecker. Before this axe went up, he sat by the same very hole and made a little seat for the baby, because remember the baby was left in the warishi there and the mother going and drink honey, and then gone. What to become of this baby now? So after he finish setting out the little baby inside the tree he then he put his axe on the tree and the axe went up to be a woodpecker. When he finish chopping this tree the axe went up to be woodpecker. He turned to be a honeydart and run! And there was the poor baby left inside the tree and start cry, cry, cry. Baby cry, baby cry, baby cry, whole afternoon, baby cry all night, baby cry, baby cry, cry, because there was no rescue no more because baby alone in the jungle. Baby alone cry, baby cry—*waa, waa, wah, wah, wahmp, wahmp, hwamp, hwamp, hwomp, hwomp*—baby crying continue, baby crying. You know, in the jungle, in the bush when you are walking you will see some leaves—*howmp, howmp*—moving by the breeze, and you might think sometimes its people moving, but really it's leaves. She became a frog in the tree hole. You remember, you usually hear it anywhere and so the baby gone to be a frog in the tree. Everybody went, axe went, the man went, the lady went, and the big man gone to be a star. All right, that's it, that's the end. Remember, the honeydart eat honey, the woodpecker like honey, so they all like honey.

This tale is obviously about many things, but in general the tensions between men and women, and how that may cut across solidarity among brothers is clearly a primary aspect of the story. The "man who got chopped" is Makunaima himself and the ambiguity of the younger brother, Piai'ima, toward his brother is patent. In this way, the tale works both at the societal and spiritual level as a narrative of the threat to fraternal solidarity caused by marriage, as well of fraternal jealousies that can lead to deadly conflict. The transformation of the elder brother and his axe into stars and of the woman, seduced by honey, into an armadillo indicates the persistent nature of this possibility. The validity of the social contract established through marriage is represented through Piai'ima's innocence of the initial intent of the woman, she being the protagonist, but is overshadowed by his failure to make any great efforts to seek out and help his wounded brother who is forced to send messengers in the form of small chattering birds, themselves associated with the presence of kanaimàs.

Issues of gender are also important in Desrey Fox's master's thesis (1997). Although she basically orients her discussion around a literature review and the ethnographic materials presented in Butt Colson's doctoral thesis (Butt Colson 1954, 296–365), she also seeks to add her own particular insights as an Akawaio woman. These are highly illuminating. First, she makes the point that kanaimà, or what she calls *iidoodoo,* has always been discussed as a separate, even idiosyncratic, aspect of Amerindian cosmology and sociology. Second, and I would certainly endorse this point, she emphasizes that divulging information "was, and still is a dangerous practice that could be fatal," as a result of which it is both difficult and perilous to study kanaimà. Fox compares the secrecy surrounding precise knowledge of the meaning and forms of the ritual procedures of iidoodoo with that exercised "in the Pentagonal Headquarters of the United States Defence establishment." Third, she argues that "Kanaimoism is the epitome of the politics of gender differentiation in Akawaio societies, it has remained a male domain" (4), and she therefore questions the ability of female ethnographers to make much progress in a study of iidoodoo. However, whatever the gender of the ethnographer, she firmly states that, "The greatest cardinal sin committed by European and other ethnographers and anthropologists lies in the definition of the Kanaimo as a mere evil spirit, monster or ghost, but never as a real person, or as an Akawaio killer" (4).

More generally, Fox correctly emphasizes the shamanic dimensions of kanaimà and in particular questions the categorical and mythical opposition of the curing piya to the killing kanaimà. Although, as with the Patamuna, the Akawaio piya in fact is important to the kanaimà as a guard for his body while his ekati is hunting, Fox sees the principal connection being the piya's role as tutor for the initiate kanaimà, which is quite unlike the Patamuna case. In short, Fox sees iidoodoo as an invention of the piya, stemming from the role of the piya in assisting collective warfare. While this may well be absolutely correct in the Akawaio case, since it explains a number of the differences between Patamuna/Makushi kanaimà and Akawaio itoto/iidoodoo, and does so in a manner that closely accords with the history of Akawaio warfare itself, it contradicts Patamuna accounts of the origins of kanaimà and its general relation to warfare. However, gun warfare in the highlands, from the late eighteenth century onward, has been a critical context for the practice of both iidoodoo and kanaimà, and there is undoubtedly much still to be learned about the relationship between them. Both Butt Colson and Fox may be premature in their conflation of the terms and associated complexes, for even if their general ethnological similarities are evident enough, it still remains to treat the issue historically, as Butt Colson (1954, 1960, 1971, 1985, 1998) has done in the case of alleluia shamanism. Fox does, however, recognize that there is some kind of relationship between changing patterns of warfare and iidoodoo, although she sees iidoodoo as having been connected to warfare well before the eighteenth century and does not make clear the distinction, found repeatedly in Patamuna accounts, between the kwayaus and the kanaimàs. Finally, Fox considers the meanings of iidoodoo in "the present day," noting in particular the inability of the Guyanese legal system to effectively cope with such killings and how its apparent secrecy leads to a sense of its pervasiveness. She also notes iidoodoo's appeal to otherwise disempowered young men and the way in which mining and development projects play into this.

Very little has been published on kanaimà among the Pemon, the neighbors of the Akawaio. David Thomas (1982) in his general study of Pemon society only alludes to kanaimà on occasion, but he does emphasize that most Pemon still believe in "Kanaima (the spirit of evil)" despite their nominally Catholic orientation. All serious illness and deaths are believed to be caused by kanaimà, and there is much fear of shamans, despite a desire for their curing abilities, because of their association with kanaimà. It is widely recognized that *taren esak* (possessors of talen chants) are unable to cure when kanaimà assault is involved, and Thomas cites a case of snakebite that demonstrated just these features. Nonetheless, kanaimà is integral to the cosmological vision of the Pemon, and kanaimàs are no less a part of the "shaman's paradise" (123, 140, 147, 166). Thomas (159) summarizes the Pemon idea of kanaimà as having a number of aspects. *Kanaima'ton* (kanaimàs) can assume animal or human forms and are the actual or final cause of all serious disease and death. The term also refers to a spirit or an embodiment of that spirit, and kanaimà is often attributed to non-Pemon. Thomas adds that, unlike for the Patamuna, the piya can "order about" kanaimà and that some piya are thought to be kanaimà. This latter idea seems to be reflected in the Patamuna notion that the piya can act as a "bodyguard" for the kanaimà when his ekati is hunting a victim. Finally, and again reflecting the discussion of kanaimà and modernity, Thomas notes that the invocation of kanaimà closely follows on a perceived breach of moral rules, understood as "the absence of normal reactions and sentiments" (165). As with the advent of kanaimà in the northwest district of Guyana following the departure of many men for the mining strikes in the Mazaruni, it is the lack or absence of correct values that allows the intrusion of kanaimà. In other words, the kinds of social relationships and moral values (or lack thereof) that are encouraged by exposure to the mining camps set the scene for vulnerability to kanaimà attack. This, in turn, is reflected in the Waiwai notion of the secure and closed nature of the family unit, with its particular and special magical defenses, which are thereby especially proof against the intrusion of kanaimà, either magically and physically. The succinct tale of kanaimà origins among the Akawaio seems also to center on the imagery of the closed family unit, disturbed only by attack through the roof of the benab—a most unusual and unanticipated form of aggression.

Sifontes (1982) complements the work of David Thomas with greater attention to the linguistics and cosmology of the Pemon, recording a number of mythic and historical accounts of kanaimà. Sifontes (31) refers to a spirit "Kanaima" who is the "bogey-man" of the Pemon and gives two accounts of the origins of kanaimà. The first suggests that the original kanaimà had no mother but that a very sick man vomited into a pot and from there the first kanaima'ton emerged. According to the second account, the original kanaimàs were the sons of Chankon, also known by the nickname "he who kills with a stick," who lives in Korume (Thunder Mountain). Significantly, in light of the earlier accounts of shamanic warfare, Chankon himself is said to have been treacherously killed at the hands of an indigenous Protestant pastor from the Roraima region, since Chankon was held responsible for causing an epidemic of catarrh. As a result Chankon's sons, the kanaima'ton, ranged across the region carrying out many killings and this caused Pemon to always carry the *marachipán,* a special kind of bladed club, for defending themselves against kanaima'ton. Sifontes (1982: 32) also records that missionaries to the Pemon saw these accounts of the kanaima'ton as referring to the historical warfare of the Pemon with their neighbors. Intriguingly, in light of the "killing" of Chankon by a Protestant pastor, the death of three Catholic missionaries at the hands of the kanaima'ton was thought to have been organized by the Adventist missionaries in Guyana.

Beyond the circum-Roraima region, the presence of kanaimà diminishes, even if it is not entirely absent. Clearly, the notion of kanaimà is known and understood by the Warao and Karinya, but it does not appear to have anything like the cultural centrality that it does for the Makushi, Kapohn (Akawaio and Patamuna), or Pemon. Although, for example, the Karinya share with these groups the myth-cycle of Makunaima and Piai'ima (Civrieux 1974), the adventures of the two brothers and their meaning and implications in the world of humans are often quite different. The earlier description of Karinya kanaimà seems to indicate as much the use of Karinya forms of snake magic (Civrieux 1974, 19–22, 109–17) as it does the use of ritual forms associated with kanaimà in the highland region. Kanaimà is also described this way in the Karinya histories recorded by the Penard brothers (Penard and Penard 1907, 1:70–77). Nevertheless, as Gillin (1936) recorded, the Karinya in the northwest of Guyana certainly encountered kanaimàs, and some appear to have been drawn into its practice by association with Akawaio. Moreover, whether or not kanaimà is part of Karinya shamanic practice, the need to defend against this kind of assault sorcery, since there is no reason that individual Karinya may not become adept in kanaimà practices, means that knowledge of the kanaimà is still important.[10]

This may also be the case for Warao of this region, but as Wilbert (1993, forthcoming) has made clear, the Warao themselves have a number of shamanic complexes, which include the hoaratu, dark shamans capable of inflicting pain and death. Moreover, as with the kanaimà, the hoaratu are engaged in a cosmic quest, not merely assassination for political gain or personal and familial vengeance. Consideration of the Warao case will therefore allow a better picture of kanaimà to emerge, as well as provide important comparative materials on the relationships between piya and kanaimà.

As with the most adept piya of the Patamuna, among the Warao the daunonarima, "Fathers of the Wooden Figurine," are also assault sorcerers. In the account of the shamanic killing of a kanaimà, reference was made to the "spirit masters" that were used to assail the kanaimà, and these effigies seem highly reminiscent of the figurines used by the daunonarima. The Patamuna piya who killed the kanaimà was certainly the most senior in a wide region and was the owner of three figurines—two shaped as men with legs together and sharp points for feet, the third a diamond in trapezoid form.[11] This arrowlike shape recalls the action of the Warao figurine's helpers, quartz pebbles that fly in triangular formation and tear into the victim like "an arrowhead." Usually this kind of assault sorcery is used to settle village conflicts or to assist in collective warfare, as with the piya, and does so in that generalized manner that made it inappropriate to the emergent era of gun warfare. As well as the daunonarima, weather shamans are also deeply feared since they are able to inflict hunger, disease, and starvation. Part of this is connected to their ability to shamanically engage the powers of Caiman, the alligator, who is the spirit-double of the assault sorcerer, or dark shaman, hoaratu. It is this association that gives weather-shamanism its most lethal aspect.[12]

Wilbert (1993, 92–125) also discusses the hoaratu at great length.

The cosmological origins of the hoaratu lie in the relations between humanity and the *Hebo* (Ancient Ones) who still reside at the cardinal points of the earth. To the west is the Scarlet Macaw, the most gruesome and violent of the Hebo. In times past the Scarlet Macaw was able to directly garner the blood of the Warao via a long tube that was projected from his terrible house of coagulated blood, splintered bone, and torn flesh over the village. Here it hovered and then plunged down, smashing into the skulls of the sleeping from whom it then sucked out the blood. This was delivered to a giant canoe from which the dark spirits could drink, not unlike the kanaimà drinking up his victim in the cassiri canoe. However, this blood tube was eventually broken, and ever after it has been the responsibility of the hoaratu to ensure that the Scarlet Macaw and his spirits do not became enraged and are appeased with a supply of human victims to replace their blood tube. So, as with a kanaimà death, to be killed by the hoaratu is to be utterly extinguished without hope of an immortality in the spirit world. The dismemberment of the Warao who dies at the hands of the hoaratu, like the mutilation carried out by the kanaimà, completely terminates and erases the individual who becomes the food and, in the case of Scarlet Macaw, the furniture of the gods.

Given the hoaratu's role in sustaining cosmological relations, it is no wonder that, just as with the kanaimà, there is a grudging acceptance of the necessity for such dark shamans. The kanaimà as shamans of Makunaima, creator of all animals and plants, are likewise responsible for ensuring that the bounty of Makunaima is balanced by a sacrifice of human nourishment that feeds Lord Jaguar and nourishes the Garden Spirit, Koumima. However, as we have seen, the fact that Makunaima shares responsibility for the cosmic order with his younger brother Piai'ima has meant that, as with the Warao, there are other forms of shamanic intercession. Unlike among Warao shamans, there seems to be an inherent tension and competitiveness involved in the relationships of the piya and kanaimà, mythically chartered by the tensions between Piai'ima and Makunaima.

Wilbert also notes the differences between novice and expert hoaratu, not just in terms of magical skills but also in physical appearance and role. The accomplished hoaratu carries the physical consequences of his dark trade and its copious use of tobacco, just as the adept kanaimà evinces the physical rigors of his craft, becoming thin and odd-smelling. The hoaratu also visits the grave of his victim to criticize the victim's stinginess and to suck the corpse's blood through a cane. The hoaratu also may be ambushed by the relatives of the victim, who shoot at him and, if he is killed, later find his body in the form of a caiman. However, in an important contrast with kanaimà, younger hoaratu are also curers, whereas kanaimà are concerned solely with death; even the older hoaratu are principally concerned with killing outside their own communities. These notions of sociality do not restrain kanaimà, which helps account for the idea of their pervasiveness, but their importance to the constitution of society is still present, even if not often recognized by all Patamuna. In the same way that the hoaratu mediate and balance the predatory forces of the cosmos, so the kanaimà ensure the continuing beneficence of the creator of plants and animals, Makunaima.

Nevertheless, the close connections that emerged between kanaimà and the changing patterns of warfare in the highlands over the last two hundred years are no less part of the current meaning of kanaimà, which in turn raises broader issues as to the role of shamanism in the social production of warfare and the cultural performance of violence.

THE SOCIAL PRODUCTION OF WARFARE

The prevalence of kanaimà shamanism across the highlands region, as well as the particular character of its ritual practice among different groups, was connected to the advent of gun warfare and its attendant slave raiding, beginning in the second half of the eighteenth century. Particularly in the periods from 1800 to 1840 and again from 1920 to 1940, in conjunction with the commencement of mining enterprises, guns came into the region and small scale raiding and individualized assassination became a part of warfare. This transition in the character and meaning of warfare was more marked in the earlier period, as the colonial authorities had a less direct influence in the interior. But in both periods warfare slipped out of community control and became much more the preserve of the kàyik and their followers, who were able to act without communal consent to a greater degree than previously. The reasons were certainly complex, but the critical factor was that warrior bodies were simply not needed in the same way. The military advantage of numbers might be outweighed by that of possessing firearms, so numbers themselves were no longer the strategic

Kulauyaktoi, a small savanna (*on the escarpment in the background*) that was the "attack point" for the Yawong valley.

issue they once had been, and gun warfare changed the way raids were conducted. In Patamuna accounts of the days of warfare, one story in particular repeated in order to illustrate this change. There is a ring of some sixty large boulders at the end of the Yawong Valley, not far from the traditional attack-point of Kulauyaktoi. At this spot, Patamunas re-count, the kwayaus from throughout the Yawong would assemble, and if their numbers were sufficient to enclose the circle of boulders, then they were ready to fight. Obviously this was not a device to actually enumerate persons in any statistical sense, but rather a way of express-ing the past collectivity of the practice of warfare. A similar story re-lates how, if the planned "attack team" was of more local composition, the warriors would surround a benab for the same purpose. Both anec-dotes emphasize a change in the social conduct of warfare, as both guns and kanaimà become critical features of the new military landscape.

By contrast in the periods from 1840 to 1920 and again from 1940 to 1980, some degree of community control over violence was, para-doxically, recovered via the practice of kanaimà at the familial level. In other words, the great emphasis given in accounts of these periods to the explanation of kanaimà as a vehicle for personal and collective re-venge against those who exceeded social norms of violence was not so much incorrect as unhistorical. While this was certainly how kanaimà functioned at these points in time, the mistake was to assume that this was the only, and continuing, reason for the existence of kanaimà. But it is clear that these were historical moments when the kàyik and other kanaimàs were being killed, rather than the slave raiding of weaker settlements and mass extermination of enemy villages. The social acceptance and political utility of kanaimà thus emerges from this historical context and is aptly expressed in the sentiment that one needs to "use a kanaimà to kill a kanaimà." These themes are well illustrated in oral accounts of warfare and in particular the account of the "end" of warfare. The battles recounted below relate to the period from 1920 to 1940.

THE TIMES OF WARFARE

From the period of 1920 to 1940, recall the Patamuna of the Yawong Valley, battles took place against the powerful wizards and fierce warriors of the Maionkon (Ye'cuana), who came across from the Caura and Orinoco Rivers, some three weeks march away in Venezuela. The Maionkon were looking to steal guns, cutlasses, and women. So the Patamuna fortified a position at Kuseilapoimá, by the planting of a *yalá* (dense hedge of bamboo). Kuseilapoimá controls the entrance to the Tusenen and Yawong Valleys. Here the Ye'cuana were "held back," although it is still said that the women who were captured by the Ye'cuana in the course of these raids are living to this day in their villages in Venezuela.

Such accounts illustrate the significance of the plunder of guns and steel tools in warfare at this time, and the Ye'kuana were also engaged in parallel fighting with the Yanomami to much the same ends (Ferguson 1995). However, the references to both shamanic battles and the capture of women suggest that the logic and meaning of warfare cannot be understood without reference to wider cultural values and practices. Thus, Ye'kuana assault sorcery via the sending of sickness and the loss of Patamuna women to the raiders are given the greatest emphasis in the telling of these tales of warfare. The plunder of metals is always a pragmatic benefit, always an element in the motivation for such raiding, but it is the history of past encounters, the sense of an unavenged or incomplete social exchange that drives the narration of events. The names of women captured, individuals killed (and by whom), and the leaders of successful raids or ambushes are far more prominent in such accounts than tallies of metals captured or possessed. Indeed, the military advantage that guns conferred was not always so much due to their mechanical effectiveness, as it was to their terrifying potential for killing. Many of those who recounted past battles emphasized, and I made a point to ask, that while shotguns were effective enough militarily, kwayaus used muzzle loaders primarily as a weapon of psychological terror, discharged to confuse and alarm an enemy, rather than with expectation that all killing might be done at a safe distance. Having fired the guns, the kwayaus then closed in to finish off everyone with clubs.

Equally, the fact that battles against both the Ye'kuana, and the Karinya also, were fought at a designated spot—Kulayauktoi—suggests that other purposes, such as community affirmation and ethnic assertion, were involved in these confrontations. Patamuna agreed that it would have been perfectly feasible for incoming raiders to bypass such battle sites, which would have allowed them to attack individual houses and small settlements in the Yawong at will. However, that this was feasible did not mean that it was considered to be a more effective method of attack, since "there would only be old women and children to kill." Nothing would have been gained against the people of the Yawong in a more collective sense. Without a body politic, manifest in the bodies of the warriors, to confront, no victory, no defeat would be possible. In this way shamanic attack on the community as a whole was understood as far more a part of the casualties of war than might have been the killing of a few individuals in their own houses, no matter what the actual tally of deaths in either case. The "life" of the Patamuna community is made manifest in the activation and performance of its sociality, so it follows that the "death" (defeat) of the community can only occur if this manifestation is attacked—this was the reason for the existence of a battleground at Kulayauktoi.[13]

It was at Kulayauktoi that the last weypantaman (killing-fight) with the Makushi occurred. The Patamuna kàyik leading the kwayaus at this time was actually born a Makushi, but he had married a Patamuna. He was known as Laiman, and his "second" was his brother, named Salaula. The Makushi kàyik, from the Kanuku Mountains to the south, was called Waila (Tapir). Salaula was killed at Monkey Mountain by Waila and his warriors in a series of Makushi raids that preceded the

Mass burial pit in Paramakatoi. Identified by Roger Edwin (*left*) and Clarence Edwin.

final battle of Kulayauktoi (see Whitehead 1996c for a verbatim transcript).

As a result of the death of Salaula, Laiman decided to hunt down Waila. Meanwhile Waila, not being satisfied with this first raid, had sent men to attack Laiman again. Waila didn't know that Laiman was already coming to the Kanuku Mountains for revenge. Laiman reached his objective in the Kanukus without delay, and it was he who found Waila and finally killed him. Laiman was "heated up" by the killing, and so his warriors asked others who they had caught in the raid if any of them was still a supporter of Waila. One of them was brave enough to say that he was a follower, so Laiman pulled his gun and "humbled the enemy" by shooting him in the face. "Never again" was the final word of Laiman and his followers. As the Makushis fled to their village with their wounded survivors, they were continuously ambushed. All of them were eventually killed "on the line" (asanda) back to their village in the Kanuku Mountains. This technique of relentlessly pursuing a fleeing enemy was, again, known as wenaiman.

This provoked a counterattack at Kulayauktoi. In military terms, Kulayauktoi was considered by both Patamuna and their enemies to be a good place to offer battle. A Patamuna village once existed there on the edge of the steep cliffs that surround the savanna on two sides. This made Kulayauktoi not only a position defensible against surprise attack but also one that offered a natural arena for combat and martial display. So, as well as the Makushi and Maionkon, the Taruma and the Kalitna (Karinya) fought with the Patamuna at Kulayauktoi. Raiding was certainly not restricted to this village alone, but such warfare was marked off from other killing fights, like those that occurred in particular villages as an aspect of conflict among Patamuna communities themselves, particularly the raid by Patamuna from the Kopinan River on the pre-mission village of Paramakatoi. The motivations present in cases such as Maionkon or southern Makushi raiding became complicated by kin ties, since Makushi and Patamuna also married each other. In this light, it needs to be remembered that the Patamuna kàyik who defeated the southern Makushi at Kulayauktoi was a Patamuna only through marriage, having been born Makushi. By the same token, the Kopinan Patamuna were much more assiduous in warring with the northern Makushi than the Makushi's immediate neighbors, the Patamuna of the Paramakatoi and Yawong Valley. In turn, the Akawaio living to the north of the Kopinan Patamuna regard the Paramakatoi Patamuna as potential itotos (enemies, kanaimàs) since they are closely associated with the northern Makushi, as in the case of the Laiman. In fights among closely related groups, there appears to have been no use of particular attacking points, like Kulayauktoi. The silent and secret surprise attack, coupled with the assault of kanaimàs, is said to have been the prevalent tactic.

The following is recounted of a raid on Paramakatoi: Patamuna from Kopinan came to raid Paramakatoi and had camped the night at the foot of Kawatùpù (Kowa Mountain). They approached Paramakatoi village from their hiding place by night, but the use of *chipa* resin torches in their approach and retreat meant that they were later tracked by the traces of dripping gum they had left. The Kopinan "team" was led by Kásá and his brother Kosopá (Sun-fish). They killed a whole household, probably some fifteen to twenty persons, and the pit where they were collectively buried can be seen in Paramakatoi to this day.

Apaiya was chosen from among the men of Paramakatoi to lead the wenaiman. The Kopinan Patamuna were tracked through Kato, Kurukubaru, and to Santa Maria, where the women accompanying the wenaiman were left. From here the Paramakatoi wenaiman hoped to

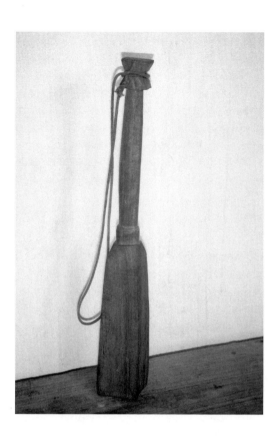

The Kangai Special,
a club for killing
Kanaimàs.

approach the Kopinan River from the north so as to allay any suspicion
that they might have come directly from Paramakatoi. At Santa Maria,
the first person sighted had been the daughter of the tushau, and she
went to fetch the tushau. They were welcomed, and they explained that
they were looking for their "friends" Kásá and Kosopá and wanted a
guide. But the tushau was suspicious of their intentions and so refused
them. However, one of the Paramakatoi wenaiman, Kangai, was very
much bent on revenge against the Kopinan raiders. He got angry at the
sight of a man from Kopinan, Wolokoto, who was in Santa Maria, and
he slapped him across the face. Kangai then jammed his gun between
the legs of the astonished Wolokoto and discharged both barrels.

This brought about the desired effect, and the tushau agreed to show
them where Kásá and Kosopá lived, so that the rest of the Kopinan
people would not be attacked. The people of Paramakatoi had already
known that Kásá and his brother Kosopá had led the original raid.

They had also heard that Kosopá had flinched away when being ritually bled after his raid on Paramakatoi and that he also had refused the *tuleneng* (hot-pepper drink). This was a true sign, a divination, to all that he had been up to "mischief" (unsanctioned violence) and that he would be killed by a wenaiman (as he was). This also nicely illustrates the way in which a breach of norms is thought to invite and, even to some extent justify, retaliation by outsiders against community members. This was also a context in which kanaimà was seen as both appropriate, and even valuable, since it regulated the overweening violence of ambitious individuals.

This is then reflected in the fact that not all those in Paramakatoi were pleased about a wenaiman raiding Kopinan, since some had married women from that place, and the wenaiman was apt to be indiscriminate in a way that kanaimà was not. In this context the name of Kápáchi is mentioned as one of those from Paramakatoi who, having married a woman from Kopinan, would have nothing to do with the wenaiman. Nonetheless the wenaiman "carried him" to Kopinan, precisely because they did not want him to betray them since preparations for the wenaiman were not secret and because his knowledge of the community was useful. While the actual raid was taking place, Kápáchi was on the other side of the Kopinan shore, dancing alleluia. He knew the wenaiman was doing its work, so he was asking for protection from God. Some say that he did manage to warn Santa Maria village that something was not quite right by shaking a small shrub in the manner of a kanaimà.

Despite the possible treachery of Kápáchi, Kangai still managed, of course, to acquire the information necessary to find the leaders of the Kopinan kwayaus. The night attack on the house of Kásá and Kosopá that followed was typical of the kind of tactics that shotguns allowed. The attack on Kásá and Kosopá began with the wenaiman setting fire to their benab, intending to club those fleeing the fire as they came out of the doorway. Often young men and boys would disguise themselves as women to make an escape in such an event, since the women and girls were not usually clubbed. However, the Paramakatoi attack team was "smart," and they began firing their shotguns directly into the benab at about the height at which the hammocks would be slung inside. Kosopá was immediately killed in the first volley of shots, but Kásá was even smarter than the attack team, for he had slung his hammock high in the roof space of the benab in anticipation of the appearance of just such a wenaiman from Paramakatoi. He made good his escape and disappeared into the Kopinan Mountains, from where he tracked the returning party and attempted to ambush them on their way back to Paramakatoi. They in turn used the "high-science" (piya'san) to jam his guns, and so were able to kill him. A terrible revenge was also taken on the occupants of Kásá and Kosopá's benab: the attack team either immediately clubbed to death the adults of both sexes; or they drove a stake up from under the victims' chins into their mouths, then used the stakes to drag them along the ground and hurl them onto a fire—a method of killing chosen precisely because it was so painful. It was meant to punish the raiders and to deter other attacks. Kangai, the most *àsà* (fierce), picked up all the children he could find, clubbed them to death, and put them on the fire, declaring them to be "bad seed."

In this period of warfare with the Makushi and others, Patamuna houses were dispersed or only collected into relatively small settlements, Paramakatoi having only a few houses at this time; but as raiding intensified, due to the influx of more and more guns from the outside, especially from Brazil, more and more households tended to concentrate into larger villages. This process was also encouraged by the activities of Christian missionaries in the region, beginning in the nineteenth century. With this process of aggregation, the politics and practical aspects of raiding changed, and the kanaimà could accomplish as much as a traditional wenaiman. It was suggested, for instance, that much of the political ill-will that still persists between Paramakatoi and Kopinan could be traced back to the Kásá and Kosopá incident of raiding. What most upsets narrators is the fact that innocent bystanders were sucked into what was seen as essentially a conflict between the kàyiks, Kásá, Kosopá, Wolokoto, and Kangai. Individual assassination of such kàyiks by kanaimà would have carried none of the community consequences that were involved in this raid; kanaimà could therefore act as the means by which political control over external violence could be reasserted in communities that contained such ambitious and violent kàyiks.[14] As a result, it is recalled that such characters were assassinated—either openly with shotguns or covertly through kanaimà, if they were not first killed by other raiders—by collective agreement. The most recent case was that of Bengi, who was also recalled as a fine exponent of many traditional Patamuna virtues.[15] However, that degree of community control established in the period after 1940 is now being lost again as the mining and development frontier has deeply affected political processes in Patamuna communities.

In this context, explanations of kanaimà through a revenge model, as espoused in the colonial literature, or through a model based on the idea of kanaimà accusations as a mode of exclusion and inclusion into a community (Butt Colson 2001) are not so much wrong as incomplete, as is evident in the fact that kanaimà is not accessible equally to all but mostly only to kàyik themselves. Since kanaimàs are both expensive to employ and dangerous even to deal with, most people would not think to "revenge" family deaths in this way. In any case, even if there were such access, many more deaths would be attributed to kanaimà since, even when warfare is suppressed, familial and individual disputes do not go away. Moreover, such familial revenge has to be mobilized as a community act and legitimized through that process. Both forms of explanation share an interest in the social structural consequences of kanaimà, but its meaning is far wider than this. In the former case, "revenge" is seen as a mechanism for maintaining "tribal" or "ethnic" distinctions; in the latter, kanaimà is seen as a cause of village fission and/or a means to more firmly integrate and thus stabilize community membership. But kanaimà is highly unlikely to originate from war or community conflict, since these do not explain why the form of kanaimà death is not militarily efficient. If the aim of warfare is to achieve a militarily effective outcome, then it is hard to see why kanaimà assassination would follow the form that it does. In short, why bother with complex mutilations if the purpose is simply to kill a given individual? The answer must be couched in terms of the cultural meanings of killing and how they connect to the cultural politics of community. In this frame of reference, kanaimà then appears as both politically and culturally effective, and this is why kanaimà can come to serve a military function. However, this happened as a result of a changing political condition (the organization of war), not a military one (the advent of guns), which explains why it has been so hard to bring together materialist and ideational models—they address different aspects of the same phenomenon, which are not distinct in practice.

Although war must be socially produced through the organization of communities and the playing out of their relationships through time, it also has a meaning greater than its social context. This is not an argument about the first causes or origins of warfare but a necessary element of interpreting any given instance of warfare. Even if an actual case of warfare does affect social structures in ways that certain models (Haas 1990; Kelly 2000; Ottebein 1994) propose, this aspect of war can't be taken as the reason why people die and, more importantly, from the point of view of anthropological explanation, why they kill. How these cultural meanings crosscut and affect the overall social organization of those who are involved is a very relevant and important question to ask, but it is not the principal question here. Rather, prompted precisely by the culturally opaque act of a kanaimà killing, anthropologists must ask not only what kanaimà achieves with regard to social structures but what it means to those who are participants in the cultural discourse of violence—the victims, killers, and observers. Such meanings are no less factors in warfare than its more tangible components such as steel tools and guns. At the same time, social structures are themselves also meaningful and the object of cultural discourse no less than the cosmology of violent acts. In sum, war is a ritual and magical act, expressing the social relations of communities and the destiny of the individual within those relationships, whether as one of the killers, one of the enemies, or one of the dead. The purposes of warfare cannot therefore be inferred from their social-structural or material consequences alone, but must also be deduced from the cultural representation of war and violence more generally. Moreover, such representation must include not just that made by "allies" but by "enemies" and "outsiders" as well.

Violence is often gendered in its conception and sexually inflected in its infliction. Sexualized mutilations to the orifices of enemies and captives has thus been a part of the cultural expression of war in all times and places (Trexler 1995). In the Americas sudden and unanticipated inequalities in military power were a repetitive feature of colonial conquest. The tactical military advantages of firearms, horses, and steel-plate armor, combined with the strategic political benefits of ferocious epidemics, sea power, and colonial military traditions, effectively guaranteed the Europeans military victory in any open encounter of massed forces. As a result, native war culture rapidly adopted appropriate tactics (Whitehead 1990a, 1992, 1996a, 1998, 1999a, 1999b, 1999c; Whitehead and Ferguson 1992)—essentially a guerrilla-style combat of sudden raid and avoidance of open engagement. This led colonial sources, in turn, schooled in the notion of "just and fit" war (Hanson 1989; Keegan 1993), to "effeminize" native war, especially in times of active conquest. The "skulking way of war" so often noted in descriptions of native fighting was therefore a matter of secret revenge, deception, poison (arrows), and cruelty. Such martial qualities were unfavorably contrasted with the "manly" conduct of face-to-face combat that served as the appropriate theater for the expression of masculine virtues—bravery, continence, and discipline. Paradoxically, at the moment of military defeat of autonomous native society, it became possible, in an expression of nostalgic remorse, to rediscover the masculine virtues of savage combat. There then occurred a "masculinization" of native war, and the wild ecstasy of the cannibal urge became a moment of premodern freedom that modern man may envy even if he does not wish to emulate. The consumption of cooked men (cannibalism) and the consumption of raw women (sexuality) also prefigures contemporary notions of a human genetic disposition that is theoretically uncovered in the agonistic context of war.

With the perspective of historical distance it is easy enough to see the subtle distortions that such ideological frameworks introduced into the representation of violence and war, but such gendered representations are still around. On the one hand, the feminine in native war has become transmuted into "ecological necessity," and warfare is thus naturalized, like gender, by being understood as an unintended consequence of a determining ecological adaptation. On the other hand, war also becomes a "biological expression" and/or "material interest," a masculine arena in which both inclusive fitness and notions of status combine to produce sexually dominant killers, a perfect masculine icon at the end of the twentieth century. However, what such theories appear to dispute is less relevant than what they really share—that is, an understanding of native warfare, whatever its enactors might say, as fundamentally the expression of "something else," be it social structures, ecological necessities, or biological eternities.

However, accounts of native warfare that derive from an actual ethnographic engagement also have the potential to reveal the way in which the symbols and rituals of war become critical to explaining particular forms of violence and killing.[16] This is because attention to meaning, as well as to form and function, allows an understanding of the multiple purposes of warfare in terms of particular cultural theories of practice. Such theories of practice in turn center on three key relational attributes: predation, reproduction, and communication.

Warfare is preeminently a relationship conducted with those other than oneself, for this is given in the very meaning of the term. However, although warfare implies a relationship with others, it is simultaneously a relationship that appears to be threatened with destruction through the very social modality that establishes it. This paradox has been resolved either by questioning the possibility for such a collective relationship in the modality of violence, thus reducing "war" to the sum of individual antagonisms, or by suggesting that war is itself socially dysfunctional but that, since it is actually only an aspect of a more deeply determining relationship between a society and its ambient environment, these negative consequences are outweighed by the positive gains made in terms of producing human spacing (though not relationships) across the landscape.

The other alternative was to examine the nature of, and ideas about, the conduct of warfare as an aspect of exchange, that is, to see the pattern of warfare as constitutive of the groups involved, not an expression of the failure of sociality among them. However, this leads to the question of how such exchange might be "balanced" through time, for if warfare is to do the work of social constitution it, logically, must allow for the survival of the defeated and put limits on the victorious, lest the relational system be reduced to a single term. This is an answer to the Hobbesian challenge; if, as was assumed, war is perpetual and widespread, how might a stable civil society be constituted other than through the overweening force of the state?

Classic structural models of warfare are therefore more concerned with delineating and analyzing patterns of persistent warfare than with examining the causes of particular conflicts. In these theories, war is modeled as a structure of a more generalized system of "exchange" in persons and things existing within one social system. In other words, warfare is not diagnostic of social distance and cultural difference but actually quite the reverse. Florestan Fernandes's (1952) analysis of Tupi warfare is an early example of this approach in South American ethnology, although it is actually anticipated by a whole series of military thinkers from Sun-Tzu ([ca. 600 B.C.] 1993) to Clausewitz (1993).

However, in the context of Lévi-Strauss's (1943) theories of exchange, which were intended to explain a wide variety of social phenomena, especially marriage and kinship, the explanatory power of such a model was greatly increased. Crudely put, war was conceived of as a form of direct exchange between counterparts in one social system that paralleled the exchanges of marriage and trade. In this way, war was brought into a unitary theory of society and culture and given a much broader function than the promotion of social cohesion or solidarity, as had been suggested by previous functionalist theory.

Warfare thus became a marker of a transition between modalities of exchange, not evidence of their breakdown in other spheres. Sahlins (1972) also contributed significantly to this model through his notion of a "scheme of reciprocities." One puzzle of viewing warfare as a form of exchange was that it became necessary to show that warfare as exchange was somehow balanced over time, for otherwise it was difficult to see how it could fulfill the role of producing what were evidently relatively stable social units through time. Sahlins therefore proposed an idea of reciprocity that allowed for different intensities in exchange relationships, ranging from the most "positive" (the exchange of food among family members) to more "balanced" scenarios (exogamous marriage or trading) to purely "negative" reciprocity (exterminating warfare). This allowed the conceptualization of war, marriage, and trade as being unified in a series of external relations; it also allowed different kinds of conflict, ranging from intervillage raiding to large-scale battles, to be conceptualized within a single framework. However, the danger was that warfare itself might become reduced to some generalized notion of exchange, with particular cultural expression and historical change being factored out as only contingently related to the more fundamental mechanism of socially constituting exchange.

The heirs to this notion of war therefore came to focus on the expression of symbolic structures in war as a way of connecting un-cognized "exchange" with the specific motivations and rituals of warriors.[17] This insight was also developed in a range of studies, particularly by French anthropologists, that emphasized the role of warfare in the symbolic as well as the material reproduction of society (in Menget 1985). These studies analyzed a number of ethnographic cases that led to a better understanding of the workings of symbolic reproduction through outsiders, which may or may not involve the actual physical destruction of others. Thus the idea of the outsider as integral to the reproduction of group identity can take less physically violent forms than warfare, or it may be a way of representing relationships, as much as conducting them. The problem was that it is manifestly obvious that the exchanges in warfare do not necessarily produce balanced reciprocating units. Rather, both before and after colonial contact, native warfare created dominant and expansive war complexes that could and did lead to highly "asymmetrical" relationships. In this context, a crucial step was taken by Carneiro de Cunha and Viveiros de Castro (1985), who recognized the "projective" and infinite character of the revenge logic of Tupian warfare and sought to locate that logic in the context of broader cultural categories, thereby fully integrating warfare into the social analysis of Amazonian groups.

Viveiros de Castro (1992) also argued that, for the Tupian Araweté, the enemy was cosmologically integral to group identity. In which case, the incorporation of enemies into the group was itself fundamental to the overall reproduction of society. The manner of such incorporation was given in an Araweté cosmology, which pictured "cannibal gods" as continually preying on the Araweté through the consumption of the souls of the dead. As a result, the mode of social reproduction itself became an analogical predation of enemies. Thus, "cannibals" become divine and enjoy longevity as immortal gods. Indigenous political theory therefore focuses on the continuous and dynamic exchange of energy between groups, not on the static confrontation of extant identities. The formal logic of exchange theory is thereby temporalized and the manner of exchange culturally contextualized.

Both Conklin (2001) and Vilaça (2000) take a similar view of Wari' cannibalism, at least as it was in the past, and their continuing emphasis on the way in which the body is central to understanding social relationships and practices is highly plausible and consonant with my own discussion of kanaimà. However, their analyses differ markedly over the issue of the ritual and emotive continuity between funerary cannibalism and other cannibalistic rites. Conklin (2001, xxiii) suggests that the Wari', "see about as much of a connection between eating their own dead and eating their enemies as we see between burying our dead and burying our garbage." But the problem is that we do see a potential symbolic connection that must then be ritually averted, just as do the Wari'. This connection is closely explored by Vilaça (2000), who concludes that, contrary to Conklin, there is a critical continuity between hunting, warfare cannibalism, and funerary cannibalism.

In general, the traditional distinction between exo-cannibalism (outside the group) and endo-cannibalism (within the group) is itself highly questionable and, one might add, it also puts into question the way both these analyses emphasize the contrast between endogenous and exogenous social status. Nonetheless, such a distinction can be useful and has proved highly productive of significant new approaches to war, as outlined here. But making this distinction also entails that less attention be given to the ways in which the structure of social opposition and complementarity may be broken down through the symbolic intimacy established between killers and victims, as well as the emotive force conveyed by the violent rituals of dismemberment and consumption. Conklin, as well as others (McCallum 1996; Vilaça 2000) certainly broach this topic in an interesting and illuminating way but only from the viewpoint of the grief and/or "love" that a close death engenders and that is then cathartically expressed in funerary cannibalism. For the Wari' this may be because, in the relation between warfare cannibalism and funerary cannibalism, death emerges from the character of group relationships, but one might also question the cross-cultural validity of an emotional category such as "love" in interpreting the emotive content present in such rituals (McCallum 1966, 70). However, a kanaimà death and the ingestion of the putrefying liquids of the victim's body that is enjoined is the very epitome of antisociality, so the relation of the victim and killer engenders a range of emotions that help interpret the meaning of kanaimà, but that do not necessarily match those experienced in Wari' cannibalism.

Kanaimà death, unlike the cannibalism of enemies, agnates, or affines, suggests only the ultimate futility of human meaning in the world by its reference to the fundamentally predatory nature of the cosmos. At one level, kanaimà is the archetype of senseless, meaningless death, precisely because kanaimà cannot be located in the production and continuation of society but rather stands in opposition to it. No shaman can repair the damage of a kanaimà attack, and the humiliating death of the incontinent and speechless victim underscores the ontological assault that has been committed. Equally, it is not just sympathetic contemplation of the victim that induces such emotions, but also contemplation of the inevitability and human origins of such malice, reflected in the insistence on the "reality" of kanaimà as actual persons. The forms of mutilation in themselves induce horror, disgust, and fear—as they are designed to do—but not just because of their physical brutality and cruelty (àsà) but also because they signal the ontological erasure of the victim. Living in a world where such things are possible profoundly affects the emotional milieu of Patamuna life, as well as those who otherwise encounter kanaimà.[18] At the same time, the emotional appeal of kanaimà stems in part from the fact that it provides an avenue of human agency in the face of cosmic malevolence. The kanaimà are but men, and the pattern of kanaimà killings may thus reflect the mundane motivations of envy, jealousy, and avarice. In this light, the inevitability of kanaimà is ameliorated by the possibility of affecting cosmic order through shamanic practice—the vision of the iwepyatàsak and the songs of the alleluia'san.

Recently Fausto (2000) has proposed greater emphasis be put on the ritual production of enemies. This is certainly consonant with my own arguments as to the meaning of kanaimà violence and creates the analytical space for integrating a consideration of the emotive force of violence with its social-structural aspects. The necessity for vengeful reciprocity itself depends on ideas as to how persons are constituted through ritual action. The key aspect of kanaimà violence that had hitherto gone largely unanalyzed was the meaning and purpose of the modes of mutilation and violence inflicted on victims. The meaning of these forms in the modality of violence are intimately connected to the ritual production of maba via the bodies of the victims. Victims must be ritually produced through violence before they can become cosmologically significant as receptacles for maba.

Nonetheless, there still remains the issue of explaining the changes in meaning and form that such structures of exchange may undergo. In the case of the Tupi, for example, the meaning and forms of cannibal ritual itself was manifestly changed by encounter with the Europeans (Whitehead 2000), as was the meaning of cultural identity and ethnic affiliation more widely (Whitehead 1996a). Moreover, such changes themselves can be seen to follow regular patterns when generated by expansive or predatory state systems. The concept of a "Tribal Zone" (Ferguson and Whitehead 1999) was developed precisely as a way of historicizing these structures of exchange and their associated ideologies. The emphasis given in the earlier chapters to the mimetic production of kanaimà, its responsiveness to the changing conditions of colonialism and modernity, and the examination of particular wars and assassinations, is therefore intended to fulfill this analytical purpose.

In addition to the need to historicize ritual practice and warfare and move beyond the constraining logics of "exchange," anthropologists must also consider modes of killing as important forms of cultural expression in their own right, not just as epiphenomena of "deeper" structural processes. In other words, war is a ritual performance as much as it is an artifact of social structures and their symbolization. In this context I want to briefly examine the structure of the cannibal *rite de passage* as an agonistic and extended process. The extension of ritual production beyond the battlefield and moment of capture was itself a key aspect of the ritual creation of the cannibal victim; it also provides a context in which to consider the emotional meanings of violence in conjunction with the social positioning of the participants, since it is through both of these means that victims and their victimizers are culturally produced.

Sanday (1986, 125–50) argues with regard to Iroquois cannibalism and torture that there are universal (Freudian/Jungian) structures of mind producing "impulses" and "urges" to eat and rape others. These emotive forces are mediated, for the Iroquois, in the rites of torture and physical incorporation, which thereby truly reveal the repressed "face of the soul's desires," the Iroquois phrase for the presence of such violent desire. Although one does not have to accept the specific way in which Sanday conducts Iroquoian dream analysis, her analysis does help illumine the individual psychodynamics of torture, especially the way in which such complexes can become part of individual subjectivity. If Iroquois warriors frequently had nightmares about capture and torture, and if the physical torture of captives was a means of preempting the torture of oneself, then any assessment of the brutality and savagery involved must take into account these motivations, as revealed in the "gentleness" with which victims were "stroked" and the victims' active participation in the ritual. In short, in order to understand Iroquois torture, one has to appreciate the internal elements of their culture, as well as making wider reference to the general and external conditions of torment and death in the seventeenth century.

The same is true when one considers Tupian rituals of anthropophagy, in particular the extended captivity of the intended victim that has often been noted as a striking element of Tupian ritual practice, a captivity that sometimes even involves the "adoption" of the victim into a household (Thevet 1953, 105, 194). This process, and how it might lead to deeper and deeper emotive engagements between victims and victimizers, is very evident from Hans Staden's account of his captivity in the sixteenth century. Indeed, Staden became sufficiently alert to the emotive meanings of Tupi cannibalism that he was able to successfully avoid being eaten and even to impress his captors with an apparent display of shamanic and prophetic competency by "curing" them of disease. The Tupian manner of ritual production precisely derived from a wider vision of the purpose of war in society as a cycle of collective exchanges through the medium of persons ritually produced as "enemies." This helps explain why cannibalism of whites was futile in these terms—they had not been ritually produced as enemies and therefore offered no possibility of reciprocation. Although whites were certainly ritually killed according to the forms of anthropophagic ritual, such killings must also be put into the historical context of intense warfare and disease that initial contacts induced, as was the case for the Iroquois (Whitehead 2000, 1993).

There are really two elements to such a ritual production of cannibal victims: the incorporation of the enemy and, at the same moment, a testing of the validity and worth of that alterity.[19] As public culture, the Tupian theater of anthropophagy was certainly a dramatization of critical social relationships, a matter of semiophagy or "signaling through eating." As the studies above suggest, this is appropriate symbolically, since cannibalism is a native Amazonian metaphor with a wide range of reference: it may represent relations with the divine and with the natural world, as well as with human enemies and affines. It also links to the primary social relationship of predator and prey and, in this form, can come to represent all other relationships, such that cannibalism may even be identified with incest. But, to avert this outcome, "enemies" and "outsiders" become integral to both social and biological reproduction. Therefore, the culinary etiquette of the cannibal feast, structured through age and gender, reflects the mediation of these categories (Combés 1992; Viveiros de Castro 1992). Cannibalism is also a ritual that proceeds from a sociopolitical theory about the constitution of society, what is necessary for its continuation, and the place that persons have in that process. Therefore, in the spectacle of anthropophagy, the social roles of gender, age, and affinity are acted out according to the cultural idioms of incorporation—both of and into the body politic. As such, cannibalism represents a perfect complicity between victims and executioners, for Tupian captives did not just share a cosmological consensus over the meaning of the cannibal ritual, but were anyway transculturated by their adoption into the group, in the manner of an affine or "pet" (Fausto 2000; Anne Christine Taylor 2001).

Just as Europeans of the sixteenth century then compared this rite to the transubstantiation of the Eucharist in Catholic ritual, so (after Foucault 1995) it is illuminating to compare the public theater of cannibal violence to the contemporary European theater of public punishment and execution. In the latter, the destruction of the bodies of the condemned was no less integral to the reproduction of society, the critical difference being that the incorporation of society took place through the symbolic exclusion of its victims. It is also significant then that European discussion of Tupian rituals put great stress on collective participation in the destructive production of the victim. This was done to illustrate the barbarity of the ritual exercise, with both commentators and illustrators on the Tupi repeatedly alluding to the participation of women and children in the cannibal moment. However, making this comparison also helps to explain why community participation was required among Tupians but not in the punishment of the European criminal—the State, not Society (after Pierre Clastres and Michael Taussig), constituted the forms of inclusion and exclusion. It is therefore striking that community participation in the cannibal moment shocked the Europeans more than the cruelties and torments themselves. But this was perfectly consistent with the notion that an inclusion, not exclusion, of the victim was envisaged in the European tradition of torture and execution as an adjunct to judicial process. Equally, the State always abrogated the right to determine community membership and deployed a monopoly of force to that end. In consequence, the mutilation of the criminal and heretic became a theatrical spectacle intended to dramatize the authority of Law and to ritualize its enforcement by the professional agents of the State. Bodies and body parts were therefore displayed as embellishments to the architecture of state power on spikes above gates, in cages on city walls, and on gibbets in sanctioned execution grounds. The destiny of the bodies and body parts of the Tupian victim was to be distributed among the community as a whole, according to the status of each member, including women and children, which thereby signaled that revenge might be made with any member of that community, that any member might be in turn ritually produced as another's victim. By extension, then, the control over this distribution of body parts by powerful leaders was, and is, a potent political power deeply embedded in cosmological ideas as to the significance of the body and sociality.

Control over bodies—both live and dead—is a way of displaying and engendering political power, and of all the modes of controlling bodies, the physical incorporation of body parts most forcefully expresses this. Such a ritual and symbolic dynamic, then, allows one to appreciate the indigenous political significance of anthropophagic ritual and to begin to understand how it was used to augment the social power of war-chiefs. Equally, the cosmological significance of the cannibal rite set up a tension between prophet-shamans, *karai,* and chiefs that implied a political opposition in their roles. Therefore, in the same way that the cannibal theater signaled chiefly power within society, the practice of cannibalism might also consciously signal a form of resistance to colonial domination. After all, it was a mutual agreement on the significance of cannibalism, as much extant European ethics, that gave the practice its highly charged political connotations in the colonial world. In this way, the "rescue" of cannibal victims by vengeful whites and the sale of those victims as plantation slaves actually did a double violence to the reproduction of indigenous society (Whitehead 1993)—first, through the commercialization of war and, second, through the resulting commodification of the captive. However, to see cannibalism in this aspect alone—as a structure and function of society, or as an act of hyperresistance to colonialism—is precisely to constrain ethnographic experience in the ways suggested earlier. But this is also the very reason why cannibalism, and even the blood-frenzy that accompanies it, cannot be reduced to some form of maniacal exaggeration of a symbolic necessity (revenge) that might be satisfied in more "civilized" ways.

These themes also emerge in considering other violent rituals of incorporation, such as among the Iroquois, and may be seen to vary according to the intensity and symbolic elaboration with which they are practiced. Iroquois agonistic torture and the ritual phases of violence in the passage of the victim from exclusion to inclusion therefore bear comparison to the Tupi case, which then enables comparison of the Tupi rite to other cases, such as the Iroquois, in terms of modes of incorporation, and suggests that the prolonged captivity of the Tupi victim was analogous to the extended torture of the Iroquois.

TABLE 2 Structural Phases in Violent Rituals of Incorporation

Subjective Representation:

Rapture—Desire—Consummation—Assumption

Objective Condition:

Capture—Torture—Death—Incorporation

(The structure of the victim's rite of passage is shown in table 2.) Indeed, the oral discourse was very similar in its content. But there are also other important factors that may explain this difference in emphasis given to the elements of incorporation ritual. As Viveiros de Castro (1992, 254) notes of Tupi cannibalism (and, I would add, as opposed to Iroquois torture), it was not a narcissistic incorporation but an alteration, a becoming. Consequently, women and children were appropriate victims for the Tupi, but for the Iroquois they did not possess those qualities that could be revealed through torture and incorporated through physical consumption of the ritually produced body. For the Iroquois, it remained to be seen if the victim's ritual performance would be worthy of incorporation; for the Tupi, the victim needed only to hold the ritual and structural status of enemy.

This contrast also applies to understanding the nature of kanaimà killing. It has been remarked before that the status of the victim is a matter of ritual indifference, any body will suffice as a potential vessel for maba, it is the shamanic ritual techniques that produce victims. However, it has also been emphasized that kanaimà has to be understood historically, that the meaning of its practice changes over time, even if the formal symbolic qualities of ritual production have remained relatively uniform over the last two hundred years. By understanding violence as a cultural performance of ritual and symbolic categories, as much as an expression of social-structural contradictions and conflicts, one can finally move beyond the sterile opposition of structure to agency. However, this can only be done through a historical contextualization of both social formation and cultural performance, such as has been offered herein for kanaimà.

Anthropologies of Violence

I want here to emphasize some of the key elements in the foregoing analyses and discussions that suggest specific new practical and theoretical issues that anthropology must deal with if it is to remain a credible source of cultural and social commentary. In particular, kanaimà shows the way in which violence may be an authentic and legitimate form of cultural expression and, as such, a potentially significant aspect of field research situations. The ambiguous attitudes of potential victims toward kanaimà—as being both a violent oppression but also a "real Amerindian thing"—expresses this conundrum perfectly. In trying to understand kanaimà, I have found that the notion of cultural performance, as much as social and political costs and benefits, is relevant, even fundamental, to interpreting the nature of the discourse. However, anthropology has traditionally resisted the idea that violence can be seen as a manifestation of cultural proclivity, for the good reason that it becomes all too easy to characterize the violence of others as a manifestation of savagery or primitiveness. This is not what I intend to suggest, and I have been careful to show that the violence of kanaimà is also closely linked to the violence of economic and political development in the colonial and contemporary eras. This interrelationship suggests that the rhetorics of antiviolence practiced in Western discourses are, whatever the sincerity of the advocates, often linked to the need to disarm and disable native militancy by reference to the overwhelming but "protective" violence of the establishment of the state. As Sorel (1999, 175) notes, "There are so many legal precautions against violence and our education is directed towards so weakening our tendencies towards violence that we are instinctively inclined to think that any act of violence is a manifestation of a return to barbarism." The suppression of native warfare and promises of a "new life" were the specific means by which such an enfeeblement was achieved in the highlands, but the imperfect nature of this process allowed kanaimà to maintain a role in shaping contemporary Amerindian identity.

The ways in which the representation and interpretation of the external collective violence of other peoples is culturally and ideologically linked to the legitimated forms of state violence and to the illegitimate violence of the criminal, both delinquent and pathological, have not often been overtly considered by scholars, although the connections between violence in foreign wars and domestic violence has certainly been much debated. The guiding theoretical principle of my study has been that the manner in which violence is enacted is not simply instinctual, psychopathological, or the result of sociocultural primitiveness ("tribalism"), but that it is also a cultural performance. The poetics of such cultural performances may be utterly enigmatic to Western cultural experience, just as the violence of domestic terrorism, school shootings, or serial killing confounds and challenges accepted cultural norms. However, such cultural performances also have an intended audience. This suggests that a more developed understanding of violence as a human capacity and its role in social and cultural relationships between individuals, communities, and ethnicities is both possible and urgently necessary. Moreover, anthropology is well situated to provide just this kind of culturally contextualized understanding.

Clearly, violence as a cultural expression is universal, but certain local cultural contexts, in which violence has an accepted, positive, and radical role in social practice, have proved particularly difficult to understand—the "ethnic cleansing" in Bosnia and Kosovo, recent witch killings in South Africa, interreligious rioting in Indonesia, the conflict between Hindu and Christian communities in India, or the ethnocide in Rwanda. At the same time, such "cultures of violence" are present within the liberal democracies, either as collective entities, such as militia, terrorist groups, and urban gangs, or as forms of apparently isolated individual expression and psychopathology, as in serial killing and school shootings. Westerners culturally represent the collective violence of others as an aspect of their sociocultural incapacity but, by contrast, see their own violence as criminal or delinquent only in an individual sense, rather than as an aspect of wider cultural patterns. Analysis of this relationship between conceptions of external and internal violence has been missing from many other studies of violence (however, see Kapferer 1988). A failure to make this link means that Westerners ignore the way in which cultural classification is fundamental to *how* acts of violence are committed, as well as represented, and this is as true for the serial killer or gang-banger as it is for the ritual assassin or agent of genocide (see Apter 1997).

By the same token, ideas as to what constitutes "violence" remain largely unexamined (see Riches 1986); we all feel that we know what it is, and it may well be that gross physical acts of harm are relatively unproblematic to identify. This is not to suggest that violence can be "deconstructed," or that with closer cultural contextualization it will be revealed as somehow less brutal or destructive. Nor is it to suggest that the ethical evaluation of violence may simply be relative cross-culturally and thus be beyond the critical analysis of the external observer. Rather, violence is also a cultural performance. However, understanding the meanings that violence may express, no less than the calculation of its material harm, is a vital part of any proper understanding. Moreover, as in the study of kanaimà herein, anthropologists must also consider how cultural conceptions are used discursively to amplify and extend the cultural force of violent acts and how those violent acts themselves can generate a shared idiom of meaning for violent death. Kanaimà has become pervasive in part because it offers a thanatology, a means of giving meaning to death, and in part because of the way in which it has entered the imagination of outsiders, especially through instances of the killing of whites and blacks. So, too, kanaimà viscerally demonstrates that how a person is killed or mutilated is not arbitrary, haphazard, or simply a pragmatic question of how human physiology may be disrupted through military science, but rather a direct cultural expression of how violence is conceived and death understood. Worldwide, the manner of killing and injury may be used to delineate ethnic difference and identity, to construct ideas of sexuality, or to assert ideas of tradition and modernity (Appadurai 1996; Bataille 1986; Bloch 1992; Das 1990; Eller 1998; Kapferer 1997; Tambiah 1996; Trexler 1995). So, while it is evident that the cultural meanings of violent acts vary cross-culturally and historically, I have intended to show how that variation affects the representation of other peoples, how it affects the form of violent acts, and the ways in which violence, such as kanaimà, itself comes to define cultural practice.

A kanaimà killing sets up a field of sociocultural significance that speaks to the immediate relations of the victim, as well as to the wider community, other ethnic groups in Guyana, and the institutional structures of the state. This cultural force is engendered not just by the vivid physicality of a kanaimà killing, but also by the way in which such acts recall the history and traditions of indigenous resistance to the colonial occupation, thereby suggesting the fragility of postcolonial nationalisms and their institutions throughout the region. This becomes all the more evident by the lack of any effective police or military response to such kanaimà killings, even when perpetrators are easily identified. This paradox stems from that fact that kanaimà violence may be a culturally enjoined and acceptable mode of political conduct, from which it follows that kanaimà could not effectively be suppressed or eradicated by simplistically treating it as a form of individual behavior that needs to be punished. Moreover, the legitimated state violence deployed to punish the illegitimate brutality of others may itself be perceived as a validation of violence as a cultural form, thus serving only to license further use of the very violence that it intended to suppress. So, sustained violent engagement with others may even go on to produce a symbiotic cultural practice (Ferguson and Whitehead 1999) such that those who would hold the moral highground are degraded through the ethical and political necessity of their own violent practices.

ANTHROPOLOGIES OF KANAIMÀ

All of these issues have weighed heavily in my analysis of kanaimà, particularly the need to make critical use of external documentation as well as contemporary testimony. I have not intended to simply make idle criticism of outsiders' attempts to grasp a confusing and exotic practice, but to draw out their styles of explanation for kanaimà, how such styles reflect colonial and current mentality, and so how to read through these sources to recover the cultural practices that stimulated these descriptions. This approach provides firmer ground for the interpretation of the contemporary testimony, which itself may also reflect the observations and sentiments recorded in the historical documentation.

Contemporary testimonies about the kanaimà have been produced from a cultural context that is neither ignorant of nor unexposed to precisely these kinds of text and their popular renderings in magazines, schoolbooks, and the like. In which case, my expectations of myself as an ethnographer, as well as the expectations and explanatory forms of those Patamuna who colluded in that ethnographic attempt, overlapped to some degree. This mutual production of the idea of kanaimà is a historical consequence of sustained contact between British colonial administration and the peoples of the interior since the mid-nineteenth century, when these texts were produced, and has become the basis for a mimetic cultural production of kanaimà that is sustained to this day. Kanaimà rapidly burgeoned into a colonial trope of interior Guyana, which brought it within the realm of the colonial imagination. As a result, the kanaimà were compared to the Shiva sects of India by Henri Coudreau and to the werewolf by William Brett, thus becoming a new version of the colonial nightmare of the shapeshifting and secretively violent colonial subject. The "Leopard-men" of West Africa, the "Mau-Mau" in Kenya, the "Thugs" of Gunga-Din, the "Hassassins" of ancient Syria, the "Zombies" of Haiti, and of course that old favorite, the "Cannibal" from Amazonia to the South Seas— all crowd the colonial imagination, vying for space in the emotive lexicon of rebellious terror and exotic horror.

At the same time, anthropological authors like Everard Im Thurn or John Gillin tried, as I have, to offer forms of cultural contextualization that allow access to the meanings that kanaimà holds for its cultural participants. Moreover, in order to avoid, one supposes, a mere celebration of kanaimà for its exoticism, most such commentators have tried to locate its origins in ideas of vengeance. This gave kanaimà a social "function" that certainly reflected its importance as a Durkheimian "social fact" about highland societies and also neatly satisfied the need for functionalist explanation. However, the appeal of the idea of law and order emerging from primitive anarchy via a rigid system of vengeance, as reflected in Im Thurn's comparison of kanaimà to the "Israelitish law of retaliation" (1883, 330), is still present in recent anthropological explanations and was taken up most obviously by David Thomas (1982) in his study suggestively titled *Order without Government*.

However, just as with serial killing in the United States (Seltzer 1998; Tithecott 1997), kanaimà turns out to be more broadly important to sociocultural reproduction than is represented in the colonial and anthropological literature. The structure of the colonial argument was that the obsessive and excessive thanatology and ritual of kanaimà distorted the actions of men, not that the action of men created a ritual and a thanatology whose meanings challenged and escaped the descriptive boundaries of the colonial lexicon. Thus, by analytically displacing kanaimà to the margins of native society, colonial commentary simultaneously dispelled the autonomous political power of native society. By making kanaimà appear more imaginary than real, colonial commentary also made a shadow of native society, which was then reinforced by appeal to the need for modernity and a rejection of tradition—"the weedy entanglements of evil." This attitude may have produced a temporarily satisfying explanation of kanaimà, but it also fundamentally misconstrued kanaimà's cultural reality. Kanaimà was not an atavistic cult that "progress" would suppress or render irrelevant, but in fact a form of dialogue with and about colonizing modernity that continues to serve a variety of cultural purposes (see also Taussig 1987).

Indeed, it may be that kanaimà emerged strongly, or even in the first place, at the beginning of the nineteenth century, as a defensive magico-military technique to ward off the new and overwhelming gun violence and slave raiding. A comparison with the emergence of alleluia is productive, since alleluia was likewise a shamanically inspired response to the changing circumstances of the nineteenth century. The materials that might answer these questions definitively do not yet exist, but closer ethnographic study of kanaimà and alleluia may clarify the relationship between the various practices. Thus, Butt Colson (2001) found only a limited explanation of the motivations behind itoto, although references in such explanations to Western notions of property and ownership seem significant in this light. Similarly, Fox (1997) considers the meanings of "iidoodoo" in "the present day," noting in particular the inability of the Guyanese legal system to effectively cope with such killings and how kanaimà's apparent secrecy leads to a sense of its pervasiveness. Both these aspects of kanaimà speak strongly to its possible origins and its history as a powerful means of resistance to external hegemony. Its appeal to otherwise disempowered young men, and the way in which mining and development projects play into this, suggest that its contemporary relevance is every bit as strong as it was in the past, if for different reasons. Thus, Thomas (1982, 165) also notes that the invocation of kanaimà closely follows a perceived breach of moral rules, understood as "the absence of normal reactions and sentiments." As with the advent of kanaimà in the northwest district of Guyana, which followed the departure of many men for the mining strikes in the Mazaruni, the lack or absence of correct values allows the intrusion of kanaimà. This was reflected in the Wai-wai and Makushi notions of the secure and closed nature of the family unit, with its particular and special magical defenses, which are then proof against the intrusion of kanaimà, either magically or physically. The brief tale of kanaimà origins among the Akawaio seems also to center on the imagery of the closed family unit that could be disturbed only by attack through the roof of the benab.

The idea that violence and retribution befalls those who have in some way transgressed social norms is also present in other ways. For example, when Kosopá was to be ritually bled after his raid on Para-makatoi, he flinched away, and he also refused the ritual *tuleneŋ* (hot-pepper drink). This was seen as indication that he had been up to "mis-chief" (unsanctioned violence) and that likely he would be killed by a wenaiman, which he then was. This shows how a breach of norms in-vites and even to some extent justifies retaliation by outsiders against community members. Moreover, kanaimà was therefore also seen as both culturally appropriate and socially valuable, since it allowed for the control of the rebounding violence of ambitious individuals. This attitude may also encourage current claims about kanaimà as a means to provoke the Guyanese state to action.

This situation is also reflected in the ever-widening meanings of kanaimà beyond the highlands, for it has become a potent sign in both Guyanese national society and beyond. Aside from the many reflec-tions of kanaimà in literature and popular culture, kanaimà has even been raised to a cosmological principle outside of the Amerindian imagination. The "evolutionist" George Gaylord Simpson (1964), lauded by both Arthur C. Clarke and Steven Jay Gould (Simpson 1996), was deeply marked by his encounter with kanaimà among the Pemon in the 1940s. Although his interests were in their classification of mammals, he refers years later to the magical force of the idea of kanaimà. Simpson (1964, 4–7) sees kanaimà as a principle of "capri-ciousness" in the world that moderns have left behind, having replaced "superstition" with an act of "faith" in science. He writes, "A world made for man is no longer the inherently hostile and evil world of *kanaima,* but that again is offset in some versions of the higher super-stition [of science] by the belief that man himself is inherently evil, or at least sinful" (7).

The paradox here is that, unlike the werewolf, the vampire, the golem-frankenstein, the cannibal, or the serial killer, who are all simultaneously victims of their monstrous condition, the kanaimà is a *man*. Even if such a man acts out of a satanically pure evil, he is still a man who has chosen to be as he is. It is this that makes kanaimà a distinct and vivid contribution to the global imagination of the forms of human malevolence. But there can be no clear end to this book, for there is no end to kanaimà. . . .

Notes

Introduction

1 "Guyana" refers to the independent country formerly known as "British Guiana"; "Guianas" is used to refer collectively to the colonial enclaves of British Guiana, Surinam, and Guyane (or French Guyana). Some writers also use "Guianas" to refer to the territories of those colonial enclaves, plus the regions of Brazil and Venezuela that lie south of the Orinoco and north of the Amazon. "Amazonia" refers to the region drained by the Amazon River, as well as the Orinoco and Essequibo and the other north-flowing rivers of the coast between the Orinoco and the Amazon.

2 The topic of kanaimà is, however, currently the subject of three different poems, two of which are published. See Brett 1880, 152–54 (quoted in chapter 2); Petit 1998, 41–55; and Fraser (quoted in chapter 5).

3 The term *Amerindian* is preferred and used by native people in Guyana and so is adopted here.

4 The Patamuna insist on correct spelling in their own language, so, accordingly, I have adopted Patamuna spellings throughout this work, including for the term *kanaimà* itself. Other orthographic forms, such as kanaima, kenaima, and canaima, are preserved in direct quotation or in referring to those usages.

5 However, I would note that Brigadier Joseph Singh, head of the Guyana Defence Force, has certainly given that organization a much more positive role in the Highlands and made it a less threatening institution to the Amerindians than it once was. He has also proven himself a true supporter of anthropological research in Guyana.

1 The Ethnographer's Tale

1 As in, for example, Evans and Meggers 1960. For a discussion of the progress in Amazonian archaeology in recent years see Whitehead 1996b, 1996c.

2   Denis Williams died in 1999. He held a unique position not just in Guyanese life but throughout the Caribbean and even internationally. Originally an acclaimed artist who shared a studio with Francis Bacon in London in the 1950s and 1960s, Denis also traveled to Africa, which inspired
both his 1963 novel, *Other Leopards* (London: New Authors), and his
1974 work on the iconography of Benin bronzes, *Icon and Image: A
Study of Sacred and Secular Forms of African Classical Art* (London: Allen
Lane). The latter heralded his return to Guyana and his commitment to
its archaeology and anthropology, which lasted until his death. I was
fortunate to have been relevant to that latter project.

3   Except through the work of Audrey Butt in the 1950s, which is discussed
in the following chapters. Dr. Terry Roopnaraine was also beginning his
field study of the Patamuna and the mining frontier at this time.

4   On 29 March 1993 the Nurse gave a verbal account of kanaimà to Denis
Williams at the Walter Roth Museum, while on a visit to Georgetown.
That document is now on file there.

5   Colonel Blashford-Snell, the inimitable director of "Operation Raleigh,"
a youth-aid program in Guyana, had also visited this cave, but in the
company of the man who was the "owner" of it and whose motives for
showing the pot to Blashford-Snell remain mysterious.

6   Professor Henry Bunn (University of Wisconsin, Madison) examined
the bone material, which he judged to be that of a female approximately
sixteen years old.

7   Paramakatoi is a particularly large village of around 1,000 people. As will
become clear from the oral historical materials in chapters 3 and 5, the
aggregation of people at this site has been closely connected to a desire
for medical treatment and schooling. The school, since many families
still prefer to live a few days out in the bush, is a boarding school and
so has dormitories, which we were using.

8   The term *drogher* is used to refer to someone who has been hired to carry
a load.

9   Johnny Roth, son of John Roth, who was the son of Vincent Roth and
brother to Walter Roth. Vincent was shot to death at the bar in Monkey
Mountain in a dispute over diamonds in the 1920s. Johnny himself was
educated in Brazil until he was twelve years old. His mother was Makushi and he has married a Makushi. He told us that he had found kanaimà
pots many times in his prospecting. I found the conjunction of the categories "Makushi," "Roth," and "kanaimà" to be an almost alarming instance of cultural overdetermination, compounded by Johnny's request
that I send him a copy of his great-grandfather's work.

10 The Amerindian Research Unit of the University of Guyana has also
done an immense amount, especially through the publications of its di-

rector, Janette Forte, to inform outsiders as to the general conditions of the Amerindian population.

11 Derek Leung (R.I.P.) was an important part of Patamuna life through his activities as a bush-pilot. I know also from direct experience that Derek was always generous in his dealings with Amerindians and in particular served regularly as an air-ambulance to take the seriously ill to Georgetown.

12 There is a "mound-complex" approximately three miles into the savanna behind Fort Nassau, some sixty miles up the Berbice River. This mound-complex is of a very significant size, with approximately 787 mounds counted in an area of less than a half-mile square. And there are many more such complexes stretching back into the savanna in the proximity of Harakuli and Blackwater Creeks. Similar complexes are reported by Amerindians to exist on the savannas between Canje and Berbice Rivers and Abary and Berbice Rivers. These mounds vary in absolute dimensions from approximately 0.48m to 1.7m in height, 4.96m to 8.25m in length, and 1.7m to 6.96m in width. Their structural and soil characteristics were analogous in each case, being composed of built-up savanna topsoil. Mound soils also contrasted strongly with the orange-red clays of the savanna subsoil. No artifacts were found within the mounds themselves, but charcoal samples were collected from three. One of these yielded a sample from the trench walls, and this sample gave a C14 date of ± 1800 BP. The mounds are concentrated around ite-palm creeks, which pervade the savanna, and where possible make use of any slight rise or undulation in the savanna floor, since the area is subject to flood in the rainy season. In Hitia, an ancient Lokono settlement site ten miles upriver from Fort Nassau, further eroded mounds were observed and associated shards collected from the deep deposits (up to 3m) of *terra preta* on which the village is situated. The area of the village is approximately a quarter-mile square. Although discussions with the older Lokono of Hitia village did not reveal any memory of the use of these mounds, we did learn that they are termed *horoman* in the Lokono language, which may be glossed as "earth-feature" or "earth-form."

13 The Lokono have a special *Yawaho* song to protect against the kanaimà. Attacks are seen as being exclusively the work of *yaku* (outsiders), usually Akawaio brought in for a specific purpose. (See chapter 3.)

14 In 1995 there was a project among the Caribs of Dominica, the Gli-Gli Project, to build an ancestral "Carib" canoe on Dominica and sail it down to the Pomeroon River as a symbol of the reuniting of indigenous peoples who had been scattered by the colonial conquest. I later learned from Jacob Frederick, one of the leaders of the project, that he had heard that I was "battling" with kanaimàs in the highlands; he averred that

kanaimà and other forms of shamanism represented the kind of traditional knowledge they had hoped they could regain as a result of the
Gli-Gli Project.

15 All Patamuna continue to use their language but are acutely aware of the
need to learn English and/or Portuguese, which in turn tends, among
the younger generation, to lead to a decline in the use of Patamuna.

16 The only other published account of kanaimà that was derived directly
from a practitioner was also achieved in this way. See Anthon 1957.

17 I suspect that in fact these were words from a special language of magical
power, as Civrieux (1974) records among the Karinya.

18 In his article on kanaimà (1957), Anthon, the son of an Akawaio, explicitly states that public knowledge as to the identity of kanaimàs is important in affecting their overall influence. He writes, "I was told that
a long time ago, Kanaimas had their establishments at far away mountains, but had to return to their villages as many suffered from lack of
food and drink. Now actually all the Kanaimas are known to their fellow-
men, which condition never existed in days gone by; so that he is now
regarded as a friend in public and a private enemy. The knowledge of
their existence among their tribes-men causes them to work as servants
as they are now known to the public" (61).

19 I should add that I had made the decision in advance of this trip to take
and use as much dried food as possible. I did not exactly fear being poisoned, though I saw no need to take such a risk anyway, but I did want to
rule out that any illness I might get could not be interpreted as another
episode of kanaimà ill-will.

20 It is a standard and widespread ethnographic fact that in Amazonia there
is no such thing as a "natural" death. Death and sickness are always the
consequence of the enmity and ill-will of others; the only diagnosis that
is of use is not the pathology itself but the identity of the person(s) who
sent it. This is not to say that the physiological and epidemiological basis
for disease and death are not understood—they are—but the nagging
questions that remain even after the medical explanation has been given
are, "But why now?" and "Why him/her and not them?" Such questions
are only susceptible to an answer that locates causation in the sociocultural network of the Patamuna.

21 I discuss the making of a kanaimà "snuff-film" in chapter 5.

22 Darell died of inoperable brain cancer on 6 March 2001, while this book
was being composed.

23 The connection between grief and rage is also noted by Renato Rosaldo
(1984) in his discussion of both Ilongot headhunting and his own experiences of death.

24 Burnett (2000: 184) also alludes to the case of Karl Ferdinand Appun,

a German naturalist who traveled in Orinoco and British Guiana in the 1860s. He died alone in 1872, Burnett suggests, "confined in the penal settlement of the colony, raving of being pursued by avenging native spirits," although the source for that notion is unclear. However, Henze (1973: 87–88) records that Appun died as a result of spilling sulfuric acid over his face. Appun had, in the last days of his life, taken to sleeping with a bottle of acid by his bed in order to defend himself against "the Indians"—presumably fearing the kind of night attack described later in this book.

25 Audrey Butt Colson (1998: 19–20), however, does not cite this passage and so interprets Davis's death as having been caused by "blackwater fever," as was reported in Davis's obituary (Boger 1911).

26 The accounts of kanaimà killings of blacks are no less important and are considered in chapter 5, but the meaning is somewhat different. Henry Roth (1950) also mentions the killing of a white man on the Demerara when he went to the outhouse, a favored spot for intercepting victims. The killers later claimed that this was an "error," as in the killing of Hashiro's father.

27 Given my own experiences in such a "safe" and "concrete" house, this detail was very much flagged by those who related the story as being relevant to me in particular.

2 Tales of the Kanaimà: Observers

1 For a lengthier discussion of mimesis and symbolic categories in the context of cultural contact see Whitehead 1997b.

2 The notion that native violence and warfare was underhanded, secret, unfair, and therefore essentially barbarous was common throughout the Americas and the rest of the colonial world. See Malone 1991 and Starkey 1998 for materials from North America. The construction of native violence as effeminized, a failure to face the enemy, or of the use of poisons as "unmanly" and illicit in that it transgressed codes and norms of western combat thus enabled a mimetic savagery on the part of the colonial and national militaries and their agents (Hanson 1989). See also chapter 6.

3 The Patamuna also tell of *yakami chalai* (warracabra tigers), unknown to zoology, which we heard at Iklantoi (Black Savanna), and there is a real fear of encountering them (see also Charles Barrington Brown 1877, 72–73). Named for the similarity of their cry to that of the warracabra bird (*Psophia crepitans*), the yakami chalai hunt in large packs. They are small—the size of a large dog—but are said to be ferocious. The Pata-

muna also say that they are usually "led" by a large *kaikuci* (jaguar, *Felis onca*). The isomorphism of men, kanaimàs, and jaguars, as well as the relation between a kanaimà'san and his killers, also can be read from these descriptions, since kanaimà sometimes hunt as "were-jaguars" and are led by a "senior" kanaimà or a were-jaguar larger than the rest, which is echoed in this account of the yakami chalai. Patamuna hunters also note the similarity of a skinned jaguar's arm musculature to that of a man, while tales of men who wear magically transforming jaguar pelts are not always clearly distinguished from tales of kanaimàs.

4 The killing of Goodwin resulted in no apotheosis, but comparison with the much-debated case of Captain Cook in the Pacific brought to light the key interpretive questions for understanding cultural encounter and the relative weakness of existing anthropological theory in dealing with them (Obeyesekere 1992, Sahlins 1995).

5 Mapoya/Opia appears in the cosmologies of the peoples of the Antilles, and the term *Opia* also suggests connections with *obeah* of the African-derived Antillean religions.

6 This was a famous French phrase for expressing the barbarity of the American "savages" in Brazil—they were without "Law, Faith, or King."

7 See also Trexler's (1995) volume *Sex and Conquest* for a wider discussion of gendered violence in the Americas and the use of a violent trope of anal and penile evisceration.

8 Both Robert Schomburgk and William Farabee did the same in their ascent of the Kuyuwini, on passing "Kanaima Mountain."

9 Robert Schomburgk (1931, 66–71) gives an extended account of his encounter with a party of Karinya who were ascending the Corentyn and who appeared to join his party. But they insisted after a certain point that it would not be possible to ascend any further. The deceptive nature of this suggestion was apparent when a party of Karinya from Surinam also joined them, boasting of their intent to raid Makushi villages in the interior and sell the captives into Brazil.

10 In fact this kind of persistent attack did have a place in Patamuna social life, but as an aspect of military revenge following a raid, termed *wenai-man* (see chapter 4).

11 Robert Schomburgk did, however, mention kanaimà in his unpublished correspondence, and this may have influenced Richard Schomburgk's later account. Robert wrote, "The hut was inhabited by 25 individuals and so small that I could not conceive how such a number could find place, much less comfort, in it. One of the young men told me through our interpreter that his father had been lately killed by a Kanaima. By this name is designated a person who, if such an expression could be used, has sworn the death of another and does not rest until his object is

accomplished. In this case poison had been administered, which they extract from a plant that according to their description resembles an *Arum*, the substance of which is a whitish colour and is said to cause [death] at an earlier or later period according to the quantity which the individual receives in his stomach" (*Royal Geographical Society*, MSS Exped.3, 1837–39, third bundle, ca. 25 October 1838). I am indebted to Graham Burnett for having supplied this quotation.

12 The following is fairly typical: on his arrival at the "Great Cataract" of the Essequibo, Schomburgk wrote, he was informed of the course of the river farther upstream and of the lake that fed the river. "They told me wonderful stories about this lake: that it was the home of an evil Spirit that lives there in the shape of a snake, *and a lot more of that stuff,*" "that stuff" being, of course, precisely the record of indigenous thought that this chapter tries to reconstruct (Schomburgk 1931, 49; my emphasis).

13 This ritual is reminiscent of the *kume* witch-finding performance practiced by Arawakan Xinguanos. Michael Heckenberger (forthcoming) writes: "The chief had explained to me that, after his son's death, the family had begun preparations for the *kume*. In preparing the body for burial, they had taken several parts (head hair, the fleshy tip of the right 'index' finger, and a small bit from thumb or palm of the left hand), to be incorporated into the kume charm." See also Carneiro 1977. The same technique is currently said by Waiwai to be their means for tracking a kanaimà and why they are not afraid of them (Stephanie Huelster, personal communication).

14 Im Thurn (1883, 19–20) also recounts that, due to his own irreverent and insouciant attitude to the spirit-being of Paiwarikaira rock, a landscape feature along the Essequibo, the piya in his party of travelers was deeply outraged. He was further humiliated by being asked to move his hammock away from that of Im Thurn at their camp that night. A respected spiritual figure among his own people, the piya undoubtedly expected to be treated with some degree of esteem, which would have been demonstrated informally by allowing him to place his hammock near Im Thurn, who was the party's leader, a missionary, and fellow "spirit master." As a result the piya threatened to kill them all. Despite this, he was allowed to prepare meals for them, even though more and more of the travelers fell sick, "in exactly the order in which the peaiman had threatened to kill us." Nonetheless, Im Thurn's expedition did finally arrive at the settlement of Arinda without anyone dying.

15 There are a number of minor sources on kanaimà, "minor" in the sense they add nothing to the existing ethnological picture derived from the key commentators discussed herein. Some of the minor sources merely use the notion of the kanaimà as a means to authenticate their own text.

These passing references are not all discussed here but appear in such works as J. Boddam-Whetham's *Roraima and British Guiana* (London: Hurst and Blackett, 1879), W. La Varre's *Up the Mazaruni for Diamonds* (Boston: Marshall Jones, 1919), and James Wickenden's *A Claim in the Hills* (New York: Rinehart, 1956). Such works are certainly part of the literary history of kanaimà but do not bear directly on the issues examined here.

16 Walter Roth (1915, 355) also noted, "I can not recall at present a single instance of Kanaima culled from the literature dealing with Cayenne, Surinam or the Orinoco region." Although he might have considered the reference in Barrère to "Chinay," he was obviously unable to include Koch-Grüneberg's materials from his multivolume ethnography, *Vom Roraima zum Orinoco* (1924). However, although Roth references the work of the Penard brothers (1908), he apparently did not read it carefully, as they do include a number of references to kanaimà among the Surinam Karinya (I, 70–74; III, 77–78), which he omits.

17 The existence of supralocal shamanic associations is known from the wider historical literature (Whitehead 1999a, 1999b).

18 The macuarie was a funerary dance performed holding whips with which the dancers in turn lashed each other's lower legs. The decoration of the whips recalls the white crane for whom the dance is named (see Roth 1924, 645–50).

19 Hilhouse (1825, 38) noted that the Patamuna sold slaves to the Akawaio and that they were described by the Akawaio as "warlike and ferocious and determined against the admission of any white person to their country." However, in general the relationship between the Akawaio and Patamuna is still ethnologically and historically obscure.

20 Dance (1881, 278) also cites three further cases of killings. The first was of Jacobus Peter who "was killed for not keeping his word respecting a debt": "A punt was at his own landing, into which he was dragged, tied, and his tongue twisted and pierced with poison, so as to swell, and be unable to enter his mouth. Before his burial, the body was poisoned by his friends, as a last retaliation against the enemy, when he should have returned to perpetrate the final act of his revenge." Dance continues that one Scapie Anthony was set on "while searching for worms for bait" by four men, who he nonetheless beat off. He was attacked "several times" after that and was finally killed some years later, but not with any signs of kanaimà. Finally, Dance notes a case in which the relatives, as with Jacobus Peter, took great pains to "poison" the corpse with *parepi* palm spines. (See also chapter 3, note 7.)

21 The frontispiece illustration in *Among the Indians of Guiana* (Im Thurn 1883) shows a seated man in full feather regalia. Im Thurn provided the

caption "A Macusi Indian in full dancing dress," but the original photograph from which this illustration is obviously derived actually appears in Jules Crevaux's *Voyages dans L'Amerique de Sud* (1883, 117), itself a compilation of materials published earlier in the travel magazine *Tour de Monde*. This apparent deception is despite the fact that Crevaux speaks warmly of his encounter with Im Thurn in British Guiana in July 1878 (Crevaux 1883, 140) and that Im Thurn brazenly claims that all the illustrations (except those otherwise indicated) are "from my own sketches" (Im Thurn 1883, viii).

22 One which I myself adopted in initial confrontations with the evidence of contemporary kanaimà killings deriving from disputes in the gold and diamond fields of Guyana and Venezuela (see chapter 5).

23 I am very grateful to Professor George Mentore (Virginia) for having alerted me to this reference.

24 This view of kanaimà is certainly part of Amerindian ideas, so I am not suggesting that Gillin is misreporting, but rather underreporting the phenomenon. See also chapter 5, note 8, for a similar account of contemporary kanaimà and how it arrived in the Barima in the 1930s, just at the point at which Gillin was doing his fieldwork. Depredation by kanaimà may certainly be seen by Amerindians as a "collective revenge" for the transgression of cultural norms, but this is not the same as the lex talionsis and its various transformations in the colonial and ethnological literatures.

25 Waugh (1934, 237; Colson 1991) apparently argued with Iris Myers (1946), a cattle rancher and amateur ethnographer of the Makushi. This argument though was a symptom of a wider disagreement as Waugh himself sought to act as an ethnographer (Waugh 1934, 31–32) in the manner of Malinowski (Waugh 1934, 174). See also Gallagher 1997, which was reproduced in the *Journal for Projects in Eschatology* 3 (1997) — a most fitting forum for debate on kanaimà.

26 Which is precisely how the Yanomami conceive of the shamanic attacks of the whites. See Albert 1988.

27 *The Skull of Kanaima* actually makes no use at all of the imagery of kanaimà killing but uses the exoticism of the word to refer to a "shrunken skull" the "size of a small orange" that is decorated with thousand-year-old inscriptions made by a "powerful witch-doctor." This talismanic object, having been stolen from a tribe who happens to occupy the site of a rich uranium deposit, then becomes the key to enabling Norwood's American and British heroes—Rocks O'Neill and Jim Trent—to outwit their Russian competitors in the South American jungle. In fact the figure of "Jacare," Norwood's bid to create an American Tarzan, is the key protagonist, and it seems clear that this work was written with

possible film-rights in mind. Norwood also wrote his own account of British Guiana, *Jungle Life in Guiana* (1964), as well as *A Hand Full of Diamonds* (1960), *Man Alone! Adventures in the Jungles of British Guiana and Brazil* (1956), and *Drums along the Amazon* (1964), recycling much of the same material for different audiences. However, Norwood's hyper-masculinity, as evidenced in these works, is curiously complemented by an interest in gender ambiguity shown in *Sex Gauntlet to Murder* (Fresno, Calif.: Fabian, 1957), which he published under the pseudonym Mark Shane and which was also released under the title *The Lady Was a Man*. Thanks are due to Terry Roopnaraine for having sent me the cover art to *The Skull of Kanaima*.

28 See Schomburgk 1836 and Burnett 2000, 181–89. Curiously both Richard Schomburgk and Marcos Vargas, the protagonist of Gallegos's novel, shared what must be considered an iconic experience of "the jungle"— both were out in a ferocious storm and find themselves in the company of a monkey that they shelter (Gallegos 1988, 228–29; Schomburgk 1922, I, 218–19).

29 Avestan Angra Mainyu (Destructive Spirit), the evil spirit in the dualistic doctrine of Zoroastrianism. His essential nature is expressed in his principal epithet—*Druj* (the Lie). The Lie expresses itself as greed, wrath, and envy. To aid him in attacking the light, the good creation of Ahura Mazda, the Wise Lord, Ahriman created a horde of demons embodying envy and similar qualities. Despite the chaos and suffering effected in the world by his onslaught, believers expect Ahriman to be defeated in the end of time by Ahura Mazda. Confined to their own realm, his demons will devour each other, and his own existence will be quenched.

30 It would have been relevant, in a wider study of the literature of the "demon jungle," to have considered Alejo Carpentier's *The Lost Steps,* The Marcelins's *The Beast of the Haitian Hills,* or José Rivera's *La Voraigne* and Darcy Ribeiro's *Maira*. Likewise, Mário de Andrade's classic novel *Macunáima* (2000), which was substantially based on his reading of Koch-Grüneberg's work, merits extended attention. However, although it is the particular poetics of kanaimà death that I am chiefly concerned with here, Lúcia Regina de Sá (1998) has made an excellent study of the effect of such indigenous texts on Brazilian and Spanish-American literature.

31 This illustration can be found at http://www.geocities.com/SoHo/4113/kanaima2.html.

32 In a related development, since the illustration is used on Orlando's Web site [www.eugeneorlando.com/kanaima.htm], the Brazilian fantasy-artist Mario Alberto has produced a visualization of "Kanaima" [www.

geocities.com/SoHo/4113/] for use in a role-playing game (RPG) created by Akritó Editora in Rio de Janeiro. Their website [www.akrito.com.br/akring.htm] describes the place of "Kanaima" in those RPG's as follows. "Lendas (Legends): In this supplement the characters are spirits of the earth that fight for the survival of the forests and waters, with which they are connected. They are Brazilian and South American legends: Iara, a mermaid that can take human form and protects the rivers and seas; Boto (Dolphin), a man that changes into a dolphin and is irresistible to women, he also protects the rivers and seas; Curupira, a human with inverted feet that protects the forests and controls animals. He or she has the power of illusion and shapeshift; Kanaima, a human whose body was invaded by the spirit of a jaguar and now has the capacity to change forms between human, jaguar and a feral half-form, but the kanaima must fight to retain his or her humanity."

3 Tales of the Kanaimà: Participants

1   The dokwaru bird is associated with the dawn, but also has a more sinister aspect through an identification with Tukulaimá, a sky-spirit who is a bringer of sickness and death.

2   Laura Rival (1996) provides some very relevant comparative information on how hunting and warfare are differently conceived among the Huaorani, which helps clarify the theory of a kanaimà killing. The Huaorani say, "We blow-hunt and we spear-kill." Spear-hunting for peccaries is a communal and relatively uncommon event; in contrast blow-pipe hunting is often daily and tends to be solitary, since monkey and bird are the prey. As a result hunting with a blow-pipe exemplifies characteristics of control, patience, quietness, and the prey is "approached" not "pursued." For a spider monkey as many as twelve darts might be needed and some thirty minutes might pass before the poison is effective. This is understood as an act of blowing, the poison being the real "killer." By extension jaguars and eagles "kill" monkey prey, but Huaorani, the human brother of Jaguar, "blow" them (*oonte go*), recalling the magic blowing (talen) of the kanaimà. Human killing is *hueno tenogui,* that is "to cause someone to die by spearing." Likewise the kanaimà, hunter of men, is disciplined and controlled in his approach to his prey, but heated by the acts of killing and mutilation that presage the production of maba.

3   It is also said that the kanaimàs will pierce the victim just below the ear, an observation that may clarify an incident I witnessed on the Orinoco at Caicara. I was in the company of the renowned Venezuelan an-

thropologist Dra. Nelly Arvelo, visiting Karinya communities along the south bank. On reaching Caicara she was contacted by two Ye'kuana who were visiting Caicara en route back to their village on the upper Caura from the goldfields in Pemon territory. They were carrying the guns of a Ye'kuana, who was known to Arvelo's ex-husband, a Ye'kuana called Simeon Jimenez. The reason for contacting Arvelo was to seek her help in legally returning those guns, as the man who owned them had been killed by kanaimàs in the goldfields. His tongue had been pierced and palm spines rammed into his ears.

4 Wassi poison is prepared from the roots of the koumi plant. See also Richard Schomburgk 1922 (1:360).

5 For the Patamuna, ekati (soul or spirit) is a property of all life-forms and this may become detached in dreams or in faints, but it also can be intentionally separated by both piya and kanaimà shamans in order to travel great distances and/or kill enemies. The physical and magical force of kanaimà attack is particularly effective because it totally drives out the ekati of the victim. In piya curing, attention is directed to aspects of this spirit force that may have been damaged or driven from the body, and it is the piya who indicates how this spirit force may be healed or recovered. In the case of kanaimà, this is precisely what the piya is unable to do because, in their own words, "of the way they use the body" of the victim. In this way, the victim, though biologically persisting, is already dead. "Death" occurs when ekati has left the body completely.

6 Hence, Sopanéy'lipa, the name of the kanaimà spirit who drinks up the body, and Sopanié'yeng, the name of a cave in the Yawong valley, which translates as "the place where spirit of kanaimà comes to suck the body after death." In oral accounts this is actually the place where kanaimàs had a stronghold.

7 However, in one case I observed, a woman was being buried when one of the mourners suggested that they place a banana leaf in the coffin. This suggestion was accepted at the time as "something traditional" and therefore a nice touch to the ceremony, but it later transpired that the individual who made the suggestion was in fact the woman's killer and was trying to facilitate his return to her grave. However, other reports (Gillin 1936, 151) indicate that banana leaves were poisonous to the kanaimà. Schomburgk (1922, I, 368) mentions that relatives of a kanaimà victim placed leather strips in the coffin to enable the dead victim to "tie the Kanaima to a tree with, should he chance to meet him on the way" as he returns to the gravesite. Dance (1881, 278) noted two cases of relatives trying to defend against the kanaimà by "poisoning" the corpse. The items used in one of the cases were put into the dead man's mouth and "consisted of (1) the parings of macaws' bills; (2) the parings of cow-

horn; (3) dog's hair; (4) scrapings from the bulb root of the *dhu turu,* and (5) another poison, the name of which did not transpire." Dance goes on to mention that another victim was "laid out naked, with a bason [*sic*] of water under it, into which the pimplers (spines) of the parepi pam were placed. The body was then washed with the water, and a portion of the spines broken and forced into the body. When laid in the grave the remaining spines were strewed over his body." This was said to kill the man who tried to taste the "juice" of the dead body. Indeed, in this case, "Nine days after the burial, the murderer dies mad; previously going to the grave every day for no ostensible purpose." "Dhu turu" is the *turu* palm (*Jessenia bataua* in Fanshawe 1996, 57; *Oenocarpus batawa* in Walter E. Roth 1924, 148, also used for blowpipe arrows) and the *paripi* palm is *Bactris minor* (Fanshawe 1996, 49).

8 Piai'ima is so named by the Patamuna and sometimes appears as the Dai-Dai in the regional literature. Ataitai is a cannibal forest spirit who lives in caves, such as one that I visited outside Paramakatoi. Here cut boards and knotted bush rope were found to the alarm of my guides, since they took this to be evidence of recent activity here by a piya acting as a kanaimà-guard.

9 See chapter 6 for a recent Patamuna version of this mythic charter.

10 I am very grateful to Stephanie Huelster for her assistance in identifying and noting the characters of these plants.

11 The members of the Araceae appear as herbs, shrubs, or epiphytes, often containing a milky juice, usually characterized as "acrid." The family contains many poisonous species and many species with adventitious roots or roots as tubers. Most taxa are found in the subtropics and tropics, with *Colocasia esculenta* (taro) and *Xanthosoma* (tanier) grown/eaten as "ground provisions." The genera *Philodendron, Anthurium, Dieffenbachia* (dumbcane), and *Monstera* are deadly poisons if ingested. Most members have a brightly colored or white spathe and spadex arrangement for the inflorescence. The Guyana–Venezuela–Brazil border area has the following numbers recorded for species: *Anthurium,* 29 (700 in neotropics); *Caladium,* 5 (12 in neotropics, may be poisonous as well); *Colocasia,* 1 (escaped from cultivation, native to tropical Asia); *Dieffenbachia,* 4 (30 in neotropics); *Monstera,* 6 (22 in neotropics); *Philodendron,* 68 (400 in neotropics, including *Philodendron canaimae,* which is endemic to the area). There are several other lesser-known genera in the family with similar morphology that are not listed here. The Penards (1907, I, plates a–d, 215–23) also noted such structural similarities and thought them significant for Karinya magic.

12 Geoffry Kite's analysis at Kew Gardens (London) of the inflorescence odors of several Amorphophallus species, including *A. titanum,* reveals

foul-smelling dimethylsulphides in groups of related species. The odors of other species were quite different; for example, the cheese-smelling *A. elatus* produced almost pure isocaproic acid.

13 The subclass Zingiberidae contain two orders: the Bromeliales, which contains the single family Bromeliaceae (with *Ananas comosus,* or pineapple), and the Zingiberales, which contains several important families in the new-world tropics: Strelitziaceae (bird-of-paradise with distinctive flower), Helioconiaceae (Helioconia with large, red, sometimes with yellow, bracts), Musaceae (banana and plantain family), Zingiberaceae (ginger family). The genus *Zingiber* contains around ninety species. The important economic "ginger" comes from tropical Asia, but there are many species in the new-world tropics as well: Costaceae (mostly new world), Cannaceae (genus *Canna* contains "purple" or "Queensland" arrowroot), and Marantaceae (sometimes called "prayer plant"). The genus *Maranta* contains "west Indian" arrowroot. The genus *Calathea* is used in basketry and in roof thatching.

14 In fact such enthusiasm for the details of kanaimà, as mentioned in chapter 1, leads either to an invitation to become adept, which is a dangerous course of action, or in my case a suspicion that such was all along my aim.

15 Roth (1915, 359) tells of a poison—*massi* (wassi?)—that, rubbed onto a stick and pointed at someone, will cause that individual to approach; but as he walks he will fall down unconscious, allowing the kanaimà, who covers him with "trisel" (*Pentaclethra filamentosa*), to do his work. This "stick" may actually refer to the initiate, metonymically alluded to as his master's killing club (yé). See also the account of kanaimà initiation given in the testimonies later in chapter 3.

16 According to oral history, the Kawaliyana were a nonagricultural group who inhabited the region before the arrival of the Patamuna. See Whitehead 1996, 2002.

17 Leaves from these trees are used by the piya to sweep out the kanaimà spirits that come to attack him during his own ascent of the star-ladder (kalawali).

18 For example, the account of Ye'kuana raids given above, shows that raiding or ritual killing occurs over distances of many hundreds of miles.

19 He has a massive trauma to the face, allegedly resulting from an attack in his youth. This is widely cited as the reason that he became kanaimà in the first place, that is, to offset the social and psychological disadvantages of his facial wounds. It is not clear whether he married before or after that incident, but his lack of offspring other than his one son is seen as somehow connected to his disfigurement.

20 I understand from medical sources that black spotting on the skin could be taken as an indication of imminent decay in the still-living body, at-

tributable to lengthy illness, not necessarily kanaimà. However, when this is not the case, the presence of "black marks" in some deaths may be used to make a post facto attribution of kanaimà.

21 Maria Moreno reports (personal communication) that an alleged kanaimà killing among the Lokono along the Pomeroon River was only judged to be so when the dying person was found to be vomiting strange leaves and stalks.

22 This is still very much the approach taken. The following account by Becky Gates [www.tagnet.org/gma/frontlin/becky3.htm], a medical Adventist missionary with the Guyana Adventist Medical Aviation Service (GAMAS), perfectly illustrates this mindset.

> One afternoon . . . I noticed a commotion down by the river. It was a boat . . . bringing a critically ill patient, a young lady in her early 20's. She was unconscious (had been for almost 24 hours), burning up with fever, her eyes rolled back and her arms and legs were stiff. . . . I grabbed my [first-aid kit] and ran up to the medical post. . . . The place was crowded with curious onlookers. Quickly I took her vital signs—everything was OK except her temp which was over 105. Her eyes were so dark I couldn't tell what her pupils looked like. She was responsive to pain. . . . After about an hour her temp had dropped to 103. During that time I heard all sorts of stories about what had happened. First I heard she was suffering from malaria—that certainly would explain the high fever. But then the auntie claimed she had recovered from malaria about a month before. . . . It seems she was about 6 weeks pregnant. Someone said she'd been vomiting steady and had gotten too weak, and had fainted away after bathing in the river, knocking her head on the floor, and had been unconscious ever since. But someone else said she became unconscious after the medic in San Juan injected her with something. Another story was that the man she was living with was not her husband and that she had taken something to make her abort. Florencia, the health worker, and I examined her carefully. We couldn't find any bruises or lumps on her head. She was bleeding vaginally. Every 10 minutes or so she would stiffen up and arch her back. We began to wonder if she was having contractions. Both of her arms had bruises that looked like someone had tried to start an IV or had given something in her vein. The villagers peeking over my shoulder shook their heads sadly. One whispered in my ear, "That's the work of Kanaima, you know!" Several others nodded in agreement. It's hard to describe Kanaima except to say it is an evil force. They tell me it is a man who can convert himself into an animal. It can go where ever it wants to by just wishing to

go there. It can do terrible things to you, but you will not remember what it does to you. Shortly afterward, however, you will die a terrible death. The Amerindians, *even our church members* [my emphasis], strongly believe in it and fear it. I began to pray earnestly that God would overrule in this situation if it could bring honor and glory to His name.

About this time she aborted the fetus. . . . [T]hey were planning to send her out on the 9:00 flight to GT [Georgetown] because she was still unconscious and was having seizures. . . . [S]he died shortly after he took off. A week later I saw Donna. . . . She told me she especially got frightened when she heard the Kanaima whistling outside her home. "You hear it?" she asked me. "I hear it whistling right now." I grabbed her hand. "Donna, let's pray. You are in the mission house right now and you don't have to be afraid because every day we ask God to surround this house with His holy angels, which are much stronger than any Kanaima." I began to pray, pleading with God to save this baby if it was His will, so that Donna and her family could experience the power of God in their lives. I couldn't stand the thought of Satan winning this round. . . . After prayer, I mixed up some oral rehydration liquid and started shooting it in his mouth with a syringe. . . . The next morning he was so much better. . . . How I praise the Lord for that victory!

23 Maria Moreno, who is conducting her doctoral research with the Lokono along the Pomeroon River, reports that she was present when the death of a villager at Wakapao was radioed in. She writes, in a personal communication,

> a man from Wakapao had been taken to Georgetown, to the hospital, to get help for his illness i.e. cramps, fever, vomiting. . . . In Georgetown he was operated upon and what was found inside consisted of leaves that were still whole (no decomposition) and sand. The man did die, during or after the operation, and that is when the radio message reached Wakapao, while I was there, informing family members of the death. People, in Wakapao, immediately responded to the news of the man's death, as having been a "kanaima death." By "kanaima death" the people meant and said themselves that "it was kanaima that killed him." In the same conversation the men and women in the house noted that in the past someone else from the community had survived a "kanaima death" by having arrived in Georgetown and been operated on soon enough to remove similar items, leaves and sand, from his stomach.

24 Maria Moreno also was told the following, which happened to a family living some distance from Wakapao village on a small island in the river. She writes, in a personal communication,

> According to the mother, on a cold, cloudy, misty day, her daughter was walking to the farm, in the back lands. This young woman was walking with her three year old daughter, even though her parents told her not to go to the farm that day, when they came upon two "white men." These two white men were a father and son team [of kanaimàs]. The younger son wanted to take the young woman with him. The father of the young man convinced the boy to leave the young woman behind, even though he kept saying that he would prefer her dead than to leave her behind. The young woman refused and the young men proceeded to take her machete and beat her with it using both sides of the machete. According to the mother, the young woman had machete marks all over her body. The event occurred on a Friday, and during the ensuing weekend the young woman had fever, vomiting, and loose diarrhea which contained leaves. She was dead by Monday. The parents never found the two men or reported the crime to the police. According to the Mom these two men, white men, were Caribs from the south who happened to be traveling through the area. The family remains on the same island, and on the island across from this family's farm there are Dutch ruins. They have never come across those two men or others like them again.

25 The maam bird is the scrub-turkey (*Tinamus subcristatus*) and is sometimes semi-domesticated. It is associated with the early morning and sometimes with Orion's severed leg (see also Walter E. Roth 1915, 173 and 1924, 556). Makunaima became Orion.

26 Terry Roopnaraine (1996), who worked with the Patamuna in Monkey Mountain, writes,

> One night, soon after nightfall at a Patamuna house near Tusenen, I heard hysterical crying coming from a smaller house outside, where a passing family was staying. I walked over to the house with Roberto, my host. Inside, we found a man sitting on a hammock, clutching his chest and weeping. Through his tears, he said that he had been walking back from the creek when he was attacked by a *kanaima*. His chest was gouged by three parallel claw-marks. Roberto suggested that perhaps the attacker had been an ant-bear (anteater) or a cat, but the man was adamant. He had heard the *kanaima* whistle. Soon he developed a high fever (I suspected a malarial attack, but he said that the *kanaima* had caused it). The following morning, we walked down the path to

the creek. The soft mud had held the man's footprints, and we could see where he had fallen, but there was no animal spoor in evidence at all. Ambivalence reigned in the household; no one seemed willing to raise the matter again in conversation. The victim left the next day as soon as he had recovered from his fever. A few days later, when Roberto and I were alone, he confided that he really did not know what had happened to the man, but that it might well have been a *kanaima* attack. I felt that this suspicion might have been there all along. Roberto owned a shotgun, and he knew I possessed a powerful torch. Had he truly believed a big cat was in the area, I think he would have been more concerned on the night for the two sheep corralled some distance from the house. (92)

Alternatively, this may have been an attack by the *massacuruman*, "something in the shape of a human form covered with hair . . . armed with the fangs of a tiger with webbed hands and feet armed with terrible claws," which is mentioned in this same region by Young (1998, 13).

27 George Mentore (personal communication) adds the following.

One of the distinctive features of what the Waiwai (borrowing from the Wapishana) would call "Kanaima" is the personal anonymity of the protagonist. The agreed upon shape-shifting capabilities of Kanaima, actually allows victims to claim ignorance about the individual identity of their attacker. That and the gender of Kanaima makes any sexual attack upon a woman appear filled with erotic mystery: "I don't know who it was, but I do know it was masculine." In a Waiwai village where all members either fall on the filial or affinal side of relations and all affinal relations remain tantamount to sexual access, many more individuals than one's spouse has legitimate (if not justified) sexual access to one. There is a joy in having sex with someone other than one's spouse and certainly with Kanaima a wonderful explanation for such sex that places all responsibility for the act in the person of the mysterious protagonist. Yes, for Waiwai women, danger is exciting. Perhaps here the danger is less in the possibility of violence and more in the mystery of the attacker. After all, the attacker could well be one's brother. And indeed, in Waiwai ideas, incest and cannibalism compute as the same thing. . . . The leading idea here has to do with the link between the jaguar, violence, and (hyper) masculinity. The erotics of it all stays steady with Waiwai ideas about death, sex, and eating.

28 This observation was made to me about another piya, as an oblique way of indicating that he was in fact a kanaimà.

29 The anthropologist Terry Roopnaraine, despite being a godparent to a Carib boy in the North-West District, where the account was collected, was stunned to find out that his adopted family had extensive knowledge of kanaimà but had never mentioned it to him until my own work in the interior prompted him to ask for himself. What he uncovered framed the remarks quoted in chapter 1.

4 Shamanic Warfare

1 Good examples of such shamanically adept chieftains were Anacajoury of the Yao and Camaria of the Karinya. Although at war they together dominated the coastal region between the Orinoco and the Amazon Rivers at the end of the sixteenth century. For example, when Camaria, "had a mind to know anything Concerning their Wars against their Enemies, he made a hole in the ground pronouncing some certain Words and then came something [Wattopa] up with a horrible thundering noise, which spake to him, and instructed him, giving him notice what their enemies were doing at that time" (quoted in Whitehead 1990b).

2 See Charles Barrington Brown (1877, 179, quoted above). Patamuna also mention the existence of "jaguar-faces" (kaikuci'yeribada) as a term to describe kanaimà initiates. In the past kanaimàs were said to sometimes have had peculiar beards "like teeth" across their chins, which seems to match the following description by Brown: "Amongst the Partamonas at the village were some men who wore curious long thin beards, arranged in a line on their chins like the teeth of a comb. This appeared strange, for Indians, as a rule, pluck out any hairs that grow on their faces" (207).

3 As a historiographical metaphor this nicely summates the predatory image that the Patamuna have of intruding traders, miners, balata bleeders, and is used with a certain irony, given that Patamuna are quite aware of the way in which Amerindians have been characterized as "cannibals."

4 Although Robert Schomburgk's ascent to the Corentyn River was stopped by the plans of a Karinya war-party to raid the Makushi for slaves, he himself was not in danger, nor was he prevented from making that ascent on another occasion.

5 The background to these events is fairly complex historiographically; fortunately Rivière (1995) disentangles the issues superbly and that work should be consulted for a more detailed understanding.

6 Basically *descimientos* were teams of slavers with some kind of military, governmental, or ecumenical authority and were charged with the task of "descending" the wild Indians from their lairs in the upper Branco and Negro in order to bring them into the labor markets of Manaus and

Belém. There are numerous references to their activities in, for example, Robert Schomburgk's account of his interior travels in these years, as there are also to a continuing slave trade by the Karinya with the Brazilians. Alexander's account (1832), redacted from the manuscript diaries of one Lieutenant Gullifer, who subsequently hanged himself, includes a rather salacious, if unlikely, description of female Makushi captives and their anthropophagous Karinya captors on the upper Essequibo. See also the accounts in Richard Schomburgk 1922 (1:288–89) and Robert Schomburgk 1931 (116, 125, 130).

7   It should not be forgotten that according to the teaching of the Church of Jesus Christ of Latter-Day Saints, an angel or resurrected being, Moroni, appeared to Joseph Smith on 21 September 1823 to inform him that he had been chosen to restore God's church on earth. Four years later Smith purportedly received plates of gold from Moroni, who, as the last of the ancient prophets, had buried them in a hill called Cumorah (near Palmyra, N.Y.) some fourteen centuries earlier. On these plates were written history and teachings about ancient American prophets and peoples; it was this knowledge that Smith recorded in the Book of Mormon, which became accepted as a holy scripture by the Mormon Church. "Amerindian prophetism" was thus mimetically produced through Western culture, even as a mimesis of that cultural production was itself being enacted in the highlands by Amerindians.

8   Richard Schomburgk (1922, 1:244) also mentions "Smyth" as having been a chief of a small Lokono settlement on the upper Essequibo, near Benhuri-Bumocu Falls, for several years. Formerly a merchant in Georgetown, he had been "banished" from the city for his "frauds and rogueries" and on the death of the old chief had managed to insinuate himself as the new leader. Following his revelation of treasure through a dream of the "Great Spirit," as narrated by Brett, he tried to prevent the development of the neighboring Waraputa mission, even destroying its provision fields at night. He also threatened to burn down the mission at Bartica, which was only forestalled by the warning given to the missionary there, Bernau.

9   Indeed a period of intense drought, followed by heavy rains, compounded the subsistence problems of those who left the camp of the "Impostor" in 1845–46, and there were also outbreaks of dysentery (Brett 1868, 184–86). Dance (1881, 229) reported that while traversing between the upper Demerara and the Essequibo he encountered the remains of a family: "Each skeleton was in its hammock, the flesh eaten, no doubt, by crows and ants."

10   This seclusion in a small benab and working by night replicates the shamanic performance of the piya and was no doubt part of the authenticity

of the Impostor for his "converts." Brett (1868, 183) also noticed this aspect of Smith's performance but saw in it a confirmation of Matthew 24: 24–26, "For there shall arise false Christs, and false prophets, and shall shew great signs and wonders. . . . Whereof if they shall say unto you, Behold, he is in the desert [the Impostor's camp]; go not forth; behold *he is* in the secret chambers [the Impostor's hut]; believe *it* not."

11 It is notable that Bichiwung, the first prophet of alleluia, was also given a text by God (see "facsimile" in Butt Colson 1998, 76). The "magical force" of text production is also discussed in chapter 1.

12 The case of the Karinya chieftain Mahanarva, whose demand for a continuation of favored status under the British colonial administration was rebuffed, thus became a metonym for the general neglect of Indian policy that had stimulated Hilhouse to write *Indian Notices* (see chapter 2 and Richard Schomburgk 1922, 1:247). Brett also invokes Mahanarva's grandson, Irai, who likewise went to Georgetown to "lay their wrongs before the Governor" and who still wore the Karinya mark of chiefly status, "a large crescent of gold, set in a frame of polished wood, which he wore on his breast" (Brett 1868, 65). See also Alexander (1832), and Robert Schomburgk's description (1931, 106–7) of a Karinya raiding party on the Corentyn.

13 Catholic Pemon converts in Venezuela held Seventh Day Adventist missionaries in Guyana responsible for having contracted kanaimàs to kill three specific Catholic missionaries—Nicolàs de Càrmenes, Maximo del Castillo, and Brother Gabino—in 1955 (Sifontes 1982, 32).

14 Brett (1881, 232) hints that they were considered all but indistinguishable from the Akawaio, which should caution us as to the apparent absence of evidence of their participation in the various "enthusiasms" of the preceding decades. He writes, "The inhabitants of the Potaro, and of its tributary the Curibrong, are chiefly of the Akawaio *race;* the Paramûna (or Patamûna) *branch of that tribe* being the most numerous" (my emphasis), which indicates that ethnographers probably can never properly distinguish the Patamuna from Akawaio in the records of this period.

15 However, in his own account of his time as a missionary in the colony Dance (1881, 227–47) mentions only Akawaio on the Curiebrong and Potaro, at the villages of Queah-queh, Waringkobai and Kurakparu. Since he does not use the term *Patamuna* or the like at all, this may well indicate merely a failure to draw that distinction. Also, he mentions baptism only in the tens not hundreds.

16 As was also the case with the missionary Thomas Youd (see chapter 2).

17 The story of one such gathering and its filming is told in chapter 1. Other contemporary alleluia singers, such as Alfred Edwin and his sons and daughters, still sing and dance alleluia today, but the repression of

the Pilgrim Holiness missionaries effectively drove the practice under-ground.

18 For example, the earliest Akawaio alleluia sites seem to have been imi-tations of Christian churches. Dance (1881, 231) describes an alleluia church at "Queah-queh," as "fifty by twenty feet, apsidal at one end, which is floored with pumpwood bark, and enclosed, with simple fur-niture, all the unskilled work of the Indians alone—the materials taken from the immediate forest, and completed with no other tools than the cutlass and axe." Of course possession of cutlasses and axes were them-selves a token of involvement with the colonial economy, so that Pata-muna alleluia sites in open savannas, caves, and under large trees provide a salient contrast.

19 An account of this journey by Clifton Burg and J. Maxey Walton of the Pilgrim Holiness Church is recounted by Walton in *The Partamona Trail* (n.d.). The date given for the journey there is June–July 1946. Sam Sci-pio, mentioned in the previous paragraph of the Patamuna account, was the principal guide and translator for the missionaries on this journey.

20 This exact event is also narrated by Walton (n.d., 37), where he refers to the narrator as "a lad of about ten summers."

21 Agnes Williams is explicitly mentioned by Walton (n.d., 45): "She was brought up under the tutorage of a deceased catechist, and speaks En-glish quite readily. She became our interpreter during our entire stay in those parts, and rendered excellent service in this respect. Her husband [Francis Williams] proved to be a fine young man who understands En-glish, but spoke little."

22 Clifton Burg, as a missionary for the Pilgrim Holiness Church, was not resident in British Guiana.

23 Butt Colson (1954, 1960) indicates that this higher shamanic plane is only inhabited by Akwa (God), U'Wi (his elder brother), and Akwalu (God's spirit). I would add that the relationship between Akwa and U'Wi is reminiscent of Makunaima and Pia'imà.

24 I had not anticipated being able to see at all, since it is more typical that no light whatsoever be allowed to enter for fear that sighting the piya as he works would cause him to fall down the ladder of kalawali and possibly also cause the observers to be blinded.

25 The Parishara dance is concerned with hunting and fishing and so repre-sents the animal and fish spirits.

5 Modernity, Development, and Kanaimà Violence

1 This point was well made by Fabian (1983) in his discussion of coevalness and its resulting denial of the validity of tradition. Sociologists, political scientists, and historians have taken up the issues of "multiple" and "early" modernities in *Daedalus* 127, no. 3 (1998) and *Daedalus* 129, no. 1 (2000), but they fail to account for the way in which modernity does not emerge as a concept sui generis but only as an aspect of tradition. Their debate is heavily dominated by examples from state or nation-state societies, but in other social contexts the meanings of modernity are no less present. However, the cultural consequences are more varied than authors in these volumes seem to realize, and the tokens of the other and early modernities they cite are still taken from the Durkheimian register, for example, the emergence of individual subjectivities, the measurement and mapping of space, and institutional innovation.

2 Kanaimà in the colonial literature and as a literary object up to the 1960s is discussed in chapter 2. Recent ethnography among the Akawaio and Makushi is discussed in chapter 6. The term *Kanaimà* does not appear in the Shorter Oxford English Dictionary in 1972 (the edition I have at hand), but it does appear in the current on-line version as "The name given by the Indians of Guyana to an evil avenging spirit." The on-line version cites the following usages from E. A. Mittelholzer's 1951 *Shadows Move among Them:* "The Genie might lure you away or a Kanaimà" (I. I. 8); and "A Kanaimà bit me. . . . He's a terrible Indian man who stalks through the jungle looking for people to attack" (xiii. 115; [http://dictionary.oed.com]). It also appears in the 1996 Oxford Dictionary of Caribbean Usage: "ka-nai-ma (ke-nai-ma) [k*ʌ*naima – kenaima] *n* (Guyn) [Amerindian] A slayer or evil one, who may be a real man or a spirit that is either invisible or embodied in a bird, reptile, or forest animal, and who is believed to be responsible for the sickness or death of somebody as an act of vengeance"—citing Im Thurn's description (1883, 332). However, no entry appears in Merriam-Webster's Collegiate Dictionary (Tenth Edition), the Cambridge International Dictionary of English, or the Cambridge Dictionary of American English, for example.

3 For an extremely useful and lucid account of the history of development in Guyana see Marcus Colchester's *Guyana: Fragile Frontier: Loggers, Miners, and Forest Peoples.* London: Latin American Bureau/World Rainforest Movement, 1997.

4 I spoke with Johnny Hart in Paramakatoi, when he came to join in the alleluia event described in Chapter 1. He was brought up in Brazil where most of the Harts still remain and views the incident as having been created by the jealousy of the government about the economic success of

the ranching operations. By 1960 there were some 50,000 head of cattle in the Rupununi, which declined to around only 11,000 in the aftermath of the rebellion.

5 As Roopnaraine (1996, 29) writes, "Many communities in the interior are literally lawless, insofar as they lack the presence of the formal structures of State law. Certainly there are police outposts, but these are staffed by officers who exercise legal authority in a fairly negotiable manner. At times, this can be extortionate, but at other moments, the flexibility allows greater individual freedom. Similarly, the formal structures of the political State are often weak in their engagements with the communities, or simply not present at all. Even in the period before the 1992 general elections, party politics was by no means a prominent topic of reflection and conversation. On occasion, the better-funded political parties chartered light aircraft for whistle-stop tours of the Pakaraimas, in efforts to drum up local support; on these trips, politicians would distribute poorly disguised bribes in the form of material goods."

6 It should be said that attempts to restrict ownership are not very successful and that there is a lively trade of guns for ganja throughout the Patamuna region. However, when walking out of Paramakatoi with certain individuals, it was necessary to conceal any guns, as those who legally possess them tend to invigilate the use of guns by others.

7 Terry Roopnaraine (1996) brilliantly evokes and carefully analyzes the anthropology of mining in the Pakaraimas, and my comments owe a debt to the careful scholarship and persistent field engagement that his doctoral thesis represents.

8 Paralleling Patamuna accounts of kanaimà during the 1970s and 1980s, Terry Roopnaraine reports (personal communication, 27 June 1997) a history of the arrival of kanaimàs in the Barima River in the North-West District during the 1930s. Either a group of Lokono or Warao, depending on who is telling it, went off to the Pakaraimas to mine diamonds following the strikes along the Mazaruni. While there, they fathered children by Patamuna women, whom they abandoned when they were ready to return to the Barima. The families of the Patamuna women, however, dispatched kanaimàs to assassinate the offenders, and kanaimàs have remained active on the Barima since (see also Gillin's account quoted in chapter 2). As Terry Roopnaraine remarks, this is a narrative not just about the historicity of kanaimà but formally links its advent to the social disorder of mining and the antisocial behaviors that such disorder induces. The individual pursuit of wealth in modern terms was the moral failure of the Warao/Lokono who went to the Pakaraimas and for whom the traditional punishment of kanaimà is to be expected as appropriate. Maria Moreno (personal communication) adds in a similar vein,

"Among the people in the house I was visiting at the time [1997] there was also a reference to the fact that the men, who had died in the past of kanaimà deaths, brought kanaimà's with them from the mining areas where they worked a good part of the year. People were convinced that there was no Kanaimà in Wakapao but that Kanaimà came searching for someone, a man, who had wronged someone in the mining areas or villages in the south."

9   According to another informant, however, the man merely suffered an accident in which he was badly burned, and he died in hospital. However, his death was "claimed" by these kanaimàs, and that is also relevant to the issue at hand.

10 They are known as *Karaiwa Makushi* to indicate their origins from Brazil, *karaiwa* being a term to indicate Brazilians in general, but used in Brazil to more often indicate "whites" or at least non-Amerindians.

11 For the Waiwai kamara picho are persons who can transform into a jaguar by using its pelt. They, like kanaimàs, are highly antisocial in their activities and also indulge in covert killings, although they do not share the shamanic associations of the kanaimà. Kamaraura was the first tigerskin. *Kamara* means tiger, and the suffix "-ra" usually indicates "not" or "no," so his name therefore means "not a real tiger" (Stephanie Huelster, personal communication).

12 I have heard one other reference to kanaimàs that is similar: it was said that they "travel like a great wind through the forest, howling like a hurricane." This is also the image used to evoke the action of *iupithatem* assault sorcery by the Wanhíwa and Baniwa shamans of the Rio Negro (Wright 1998, 174–75). The wind, *pei'cho,* is also the agent of Karinya shamanic attack (Civrieux 1974, 129).

13 One example of this situation was the case of a young man who hurt himself with his cutlass in the bush, gashing his leg deeply and losing a lot of blood. Although he managed to return to the village and was weak from loss of blood, the wound healed over. However, it became infected and turned into a serious medical problem. He was flown to Georgetown, where they offered to amputate his leg. He refused and decided to seek a bush remedy. He finally located a man who was prepared to use talen magic to cure him, which he did successfully within a couple of weeks.

14 Several Waiwai boys relate that at Bible conferences and trips to the savanna, their new young friends who are Patamuna and Makushi tell them how they have been approached by kanaimà, and some of them want to go and learn as a result (Stephanie Huelster, personal communication).

15 Terry Roopnaraine (personal communication, 27 June 1997) also writes

that "every person who told me about this set the assassination and anthropophagy [by kanaimàs] in a carnivalesque idiom; for the kanaimà, it is a festive event, a 'sport.' This is why young kanaimà, like young hawks, jaguars, and salapenter lizards, are the most dangerous. They are trying themselves out." In a somewhat more lighthearted vein, there exists a "Kanaima" cocktail: "1 Onza de Vodka, 1 Onza de Ron, _ Onza de Licor de Almendra, Pulpa de Piña, Pulpa de Durazno, Crema de Coco. Prepare en la licuadora con suficiente hielo por 20 segundos, sirva en copa de boca ancha."

16 Comparative materials from the Waiwai (Stephanie Huelster, personal communication) also suggest a link between violent/violating masculinity, sexuality, and jaguar transformation. For the Waiwai, a tiger-skin may exhibit the same kind of antisocial behavior that ritualized kanaimà killings represent. For example, Amanya, a resident at Gunn's village, after a series of accusations of antisocial behavior, like sleeping with his daughter and stealing from the farms, was finally declared to be a tiger-skin after he apprenticed with one on the savanna and then returned to Gunn's. In the village, he began to take women's panties from the clotheslines and return them "soiled." He was "enticing" women with magic and was showing his penis to women at the landing and on the trails. As a result, when the GDF came through on a routine exercise, they "beat him bad" behind the village. He then, in classic Waiwai fashion, "got away in the night" and went to Brazil, where he is still living. Recently he sent a radio message asking the tushau if he could come back to "that side" and cut a farm. The women were very afraid. A quest for power other than through village leadership, as well as "revenge" for being refused sex and/or food, is also cited as a reason to become a tiger-skin in the Waiwai case. This is usually achieved through an "accidental" death in the forest without the telltale signs of kanaimà. One example was when a group of tiger-skins, having beaten an individual, staged a bad fall from a tree to account for his broken neck.

17 See, for example, the works by Basso 1995, Combés 1992, Conklin 2001, 1997, George 1996, Geschiere 1997, Hoskins 1996, Malikki 1995, Taylor 1999, and Whitehead 2000, 2001a, 2001b.

18 There are a range of materials worldwide that substantiate this point (see note 17), but in particular Stewart and Strathern (1999) offer a comparative perspective from Papua New Guinea—where development similarly invaded the highlands on the backs of miners, loggers, and missionaries—as to the changing meanings and forms of assault sorcery.

19 See, for example, Barker et al. 1998, Lestringant 1997, Root 1996, Sanborn 1998, and Whitehead 1997.

20 See, for example, Crawford and Lipschutz 1998, Ghiglieri 1999, and Wrangham 1997.

21 In a similar vein, the idea of a mutually violent interdependency between victims and victimizers is emerging as a new and radical approach in the debate on the causes and dynamics of domestic and partner violence (Cook 1997, Moffitt 1997).

22 This trend has produced a series of very perceptive works on African contexts. For example, see Wyatt MacGaffey's *Religion and Society in Central Africa* (Chicago: University of Chicago Press, 1986); Jean Comaroff and John Comaroff's *Modernity and Its Malcontents: Ritual and Power in Postcolonial Africa* (Chicago: University of Chicago Press, 1993) and *Occult Economies and the Violence of Abstraction: Notes from the South African Postcolony* (American Bar Foundation, 1998); Luise White's *Speaking with Vampires: Rumor and History in Colonial Africa* (Berkeley: University of California Press, 2000); Birgit Meyer's *Translating the Devil: Religion and Modernity Among the Ewe of Ghana* (Trenton, N.J.: Africa World Press, 1999); Florence Bernault's special issue of *Politique africaine* (2000) on "Pouvoirs sorciers"; Rosalind Shaw's "The Production of Witchcraft," *American Ethnologist* 24, no. 4:856–76; or the work of Peter Geschiere 1997.

23 This disjuncture between Venezuelan "modernity" and Guyanese "backwardness" is nicely illustrated in the following account by the Akawaio Michael Anthon (1957).

> A Venezuelan National Guard . . . said early one morning . . . he . . . went hunting for powis. . . . On his way he imitated the said birds and a response came to his call. He tried several times and to each imitation the birds seemed to call from the farther end. . . . [H]e followed in hot pursuit, this time where the birds were calling, and to his surprise, there was a man nude and painted, wearing lots of different feathers on his head. He chased him and finally caught up with him. The Guard was not mistaken, and surely the painted man he saw was a Kanaima. Had the painted man had his gun with him, he would have taken him for another huntsman . . . but he had his poison bag and his Kanaima club with him instead. . . . The guard . . . cocked the trigger of his gun and pointed his gun at the Kanaima, but he altered his mind and took pity as the old and short Indian knelt down, his face toward the sky as if to pray for forgiveness. The Guard also spoke to him, but he did not respond. . . . Apparently this Kanaima may have been posted there . . . to capture another Indian who usually visits that particular area for hunting; but he was instead confronted with a Venezuelan Guard. As

this was the first Kanaima experience for the Guard, he was a bit scared and abandoned his hunting. He returned to relate the incident to his fellow Guards, and he said that after leaving the Kanaima a few yards away . . . he saw him making best use of his feet. Kanaimas admit that they would not interfere with any other nationality for fear of their superior strength and fighting tactics, which may bring about their defeat and identification in public, resulting in shame on themselves and their families.

This last sentiment does not appear to hold true today.

24 This magic of modernity in Brasilia is nicely rendered by Darcy Ribeiro in his novel *Maira* (1984).

6 Ritual Violence and Magical Death in Amazonia

1 It is notable that one of the few published accounts of kanaimà that derives from Karinya sources pictures kanaimà as the result of counter-raiding against precisely those highland peoples, such as the Makushi, who were themselves the subject of intense Karinya slave raiding. Significantly, in light of the discussion of Akawaio concepts of kanaimà, the Karinya also describe them with the word *itioto* (Penard and Penard 1907, 1:70–77).

2 See also Myers 1946 for a general discussion by a colonial "old-timer."

3 Riley (2000, 320–21) quotes a highly illuminating tale of a woman's "conversion" to belief in kanaimà.

The nuns taught us that there was no such thing as jumbies, kenaima or anything, only God, Jesus, Christ and Satan. But when I went back to Sand Creek . . . my father arrange it this way; he was a strong believer in *kenaima*. . . . I usually sling my hammock anywhere to show that I wasn't afraid of nothing. In the middle of the night, I wake from my sleep, I feel a pair of hands around my neck. . . . I also felt a heavy weight on my stomach. . . . Then I heard a low voice, a man's voice, speaking to me: Who are you? Why are you here? He demanded, Did I know where the village *touchau* lives? . . . He kept saying tell me where he lives, I do not believe you! I said that if he did not stop putting the choke on me that I would yell police. The voice laughed and said, there are no police around here to help you. But because I threatened to call the police, he then seem to believe me when I said that I was a stranger to the area, since if I were not, I would never have said I would yell police, because I would have known it would do no good here, that there are no police here. . . . Then he took his hands off me, suddenly he was gone—I couldn't tell if he left through a window or the door or a wall, he was so silent. . . . Since that time, I believe in *kenaima*.

4   This notion has also been developed by Viveiros de Castro (1998) as "perspectivism." Both notions are designed to escape the static oppositions of structuralism, but still address impersonal systems of symbols rather than the historical performance of such motifs. However, both authors are correct in stressing the fluidity of meaning that attaches to symbols and the critical insight that such fluctuations are systematic, involving the "point of view" of the individual expressing the meaning of a given symbol. For example, Roe suggests that the Anaconda and the Jaguar usually stand as dyadically opposite categories, such that their overlap from the Anaconda's "point of view" yields the Feathered Serpent, which partakes of the jaguar's solar domain, as reflected in the carrying of feathers not scales.

5   It should also be said that "enemies" here are actually ancestors. This is what gives a "cannibal" inflection to the imagery, since ancestors, having at death become part of a divine system of predation, are thenceforth eating of their own. Viveiros de Castro (1992) in particular has elaborated the meanings and consequences of such a predatory cosmology among the Tupian Arawété, as has Vilaça (2000).

6   Verswijver (1992, 126–87) clearly delineates the way in which Kayapó warfare is similarly attuned to the niceties of social and cultural distance.

7   Roe (1995, 9) also suggests, after Lévi-Strauss (1969), that understanding the culinary metaphors that reflect the differences between kanaimà and kamara'yenna allows a better interpretation of their ritual foods, for they are not the same. The kanaimà eats necrotic fluids cooked by the earth; the cannibal eats bodies cooked by women.

8   These appear in this volume but without direct identification.

9   This is highly reminiscent of the case of Roy Kenswil (Frederick W. Kenswil 1946), a coastlander who married into the Akawaio in the 1930s, and also mentioned to me by Desrey Fox. Unfortunately, it appears that Kenswil was the victim of "just" an accident and that the post facto claim that it was an itoto killing is unmerited. The fact of such a claim, however, is important and interesting in its own right, for reasons later discussed. See also chapter 5, note 16, which discusses the accidents that Waiwai "tiger-skins" seem to bring about for certain social purposes.

10 Terence Roopnaraine (personal communication) records that the Karinya suggest a special shotgun shell is always effective against kanaimà, even those appearing in nonhuman form. The shell is made by removing some of the standard shot and replacing it with *kariman*,

a kind of hardened beeswax. Roopnaraine recounts the following incident: A man was fishing in the night with his son, when the son fell violently and suddenly ill. At the same time, the man spotted a whistling bat. He shot it with the special load, and it fell into the creek with splash. The next day some men found a huge dead caiman, with gunshot holes in it right at the same spot (see also note 12 below).

11 Wilbert (forthcoming) describes the Warao figurine as follows: "The effigy in question is a 12-centimeter-high and 2-centimeter-thick sculpture in the round, fashioned either in the stylized form of the swallow-tailed kite's head and neck or in a naturalistic rendering of a young person of undetermined sex, wearing a neckband to which two parrot feathers are attached as wings. The shaman keeps the effigy in a small calabash bowl and basket in the sanctuary. Also stored in this container are three quartz pebbles, representing the elite of the kite's avian companions."

12 Dance (1881, 238–39) also alludes to the identification of caiman and kanaimà. He was told by an individual called "John Kanaima" or "Kanaima-Puh" that he had been traveling in the company of three others when they encountered two men who at first avoided them but then became "very gracious." Later, one of them, while approaching their camp, presumably to attack them, was seized by a giant caiman. Despite this, one of John Kanaima's companions was killed by kanaimà within the year (see also chapter 6, note 10).

13 There exist a number of such battlegrounds in the region of the Ireng River, both on the Guyana side and the Brazil side. These sites are also associated with bone dumps where the dead were left by their enemies. One such mass burial pit exists in Paramakatoi (see the account that follows).

14 Indeed, so significant is this historical moment for the Patamuna that I was offered different accounts that subtly shifted responsibilities and actions from one individual to another. The version I have given here is not therefore the only one, nor even the "actual" story as I judge it. Rather, as it is the most complete and detailed, its value lies in the way in which it illustrates the historical consciousness of the Patamuna.

15 For example, Bengi is remembered as an eminent runner of the kakú—a foot race through the mountains at the end of which the runners must pass a line of men to get at the copious quantities of cassiri beer that the women of the "enemy" village have prepared for them. Access to the beer is then virtually equivalent with access to those distant and thus eroticized women, who laughingly pelt the runners with manioc peelings as they struggle with the women's line of defenders.

16 This is no less true of small-scale conflicts than it is of the "world wars"

and "colonial actions" of Europe and the United States. The literature here is potentially vast but recent works by Abler (1999), Seed (1995), and Shapiro (1997) illustrate the kinds of studies that are relevant. However, some theorists hold an a priori commitment to explaining human behavior in certain ways so that, whatever the relevance of cultural meaning to explaining particular motivations, such meaning is seen as ultimately derivative from the preexisting and universal biological or ecological conditions of human existence.

17　See, for example, Albert 1985, Ales 1993, Chaumeil 1983, Descola 1993, Lizot 1994, Otterbein 1985. The work of Otterbein is discussed in Whitehead 2001a.

18　The "melancholia" of the sixteenth-century Karipuna was connected to their sense of oppression by the dark spirit, Mapoya, as were the "fear" and "hate" that characterized Karinya attitudes towards Wattopa, or Tupi attitudes to Aygnan. Although Henfrey (1964) suggests that the Patamuna are "Gentle People," their apparent passivity relates not to some moral precept but rather to the condition of existence in a predatory cosmos. "Don't trouble it, just don't trouble it" is a key phrase, recurring in conversations about the places of the dead or the presence of kanaimà, and is a token of that "oppressive nightmare" (Richard Schomburgk) that haunts the imagination of the Patamuna and other highland peoples. In an urban South African context, Adam Ashforth (2000) provides a recent memoir of his friend *Madumo: A Man Bewitched,* in which the emotional meanings of the encounter of magic and modernity are forcefully depicted (see also Stoller and Olkes 1987).

19　Significantly the Greek word for 'torture,' *basanos,* also carried the implication of a 'testing,' as in the proofing of precious metal content.

Works Cited

ABBREVIATIONS

BGB   British Guiana Boundary (*Arbitration with the United States of Venezuela*. 7 vols. London: Harrison and Sons [1899])
BL   British Library
ADD   Additional Manuscripts
Sloane   Sloane Manuscripts

PRINTED WORKS

Abler, Thomas S. 1999. *Hinterland warriors and military dress: European empires and exotic uniforms*. Oxford: Berg.

Albert, Bruce. 1985. *Temps du sang, temps des cendres: Représentation de la maladie, système rituel et espace politique chez les Yanomani du Sud-Est (Amazonie brésilienne)*. Ph.D. diss., Laboratoire d'Ethnologie et de Sociologie Comparative, Paris.

Ales, Catherine. 1993. Violencia y orden social: Conflictos y guerra entre los Yanomami de Venezuela. *Folklore Americano* 55:75–106.

Alexander, J. E. 1832. Notes of two expeditions up the Essequibo and Mazaroony Rivers in the years 1830 and 1831. *Journal of the Royal Geographical Society* 2:65–72.

American Bible Society. 1966. *Wakù Itekale Mak Nùmenukapù (The Gospel according to Mark in Patamuna)*. Kingston: Bible Societies.

Andrade, Mário de. [1928] 2000. *Macunaíma: O herói sem nenhum caráter*. Belo Horizonte: Livraria Garnier.

Anthon, Michael. 1957.The Kanaima. *Timehri* 36:61–65.

Appadurai, Arjun. 1996. *Modernity at large: Cultural dimensions of globalization*. Minneapolis: Minnesota University Press.

Appun, Karl Ferdinand. 1871. *Unter den tropen Wanderungen durch Venezuela, am Orinoco, durch Britisch Guyana und am Amazonenstrome in den jahren 1849–1868*. 2 vols. Jena: H. Costenoble.

Apter, David. 1997. *The legitimization of violence.* New York: New York University Press.

Arens, William. 1979. *The man-eating myth.* New York: Oxford University Press.

Ashforth, Adam. 2000. *Madumo: A man bewitched.* Chicago: University of Chicago Press.

Augé, Marc. 1995. *Non-places: Introduction to an anthropology of supermodernity.* London: Verso.

Bachinger, Katrina E. 1986. Shedding the skins of *Kanaima* in the commonwealth short-story. In *The story must be told,* edited by P. O. Stummer. Würzburg: Königshausen and Neumann.

Barker, Francis, Peter Hulme, and Margaret Iversen. 1998. *Cannibalism and the colonial world.* Cambridge: Cambridge University Press.

Barrère, Pierre. 1753. *Nouvelle relation de la France equinoxiale.* Paris: Piget, Damonneville and Durand.

Basso, Ellen. 1995. *The last cannibals: A South American oral history.* Austin: University of Texas Press.

Bataille, Georges. 1986. *Erotism: Death and sensuality.* Translated by Mary Dalwood. San Francisco: City Lights Books.

Bernau, John Henry. 1847. *Missionary labours in British Guiana.* London: John Farquar Shaw.

Bloch, Maurice. 1992. *Prey into hunter: The politics of religious experience.* Cambridge: Cambridge University Press.

Boddam-Whetham, John Whetham. 1879. *Roraima and British Guiana.* London: Hurst and Blackett.

Boger, E. C. 1911. Memorial service for Elder O. E. Davis. *Advent Review and Sabbath Herald* (November 1911):23.

Breton, Raymond. 1665. *Dictionnaire Caraibe-Francois.* Auxerre: Gilles Bouquet.

Brett, William Henry. 1881. *Mission work in the forests of Guiana.* London: Society for Promoting Christian Knowledge/E. and J. B. Young.

———. 1880. *Legends and myths of the aboriginal Indians of British Guiana.* London: William Wells Gardner.

———. 1868. *The Indian tribes of Guiana.* London: Bell and Daldy.

———. 1851. *Indian Missions in Guiana.* London: George Bell.

Brown, Charles Barrington. 1877. *Canoe and camp life in British Guiana.* London: Edward Stanford.

Brown, Michael F. 1989. The dark side of the shaman. *Natural History* (November):8–10.

———. 1986. *Tsewa's gift: Magic and meaning in an Amazonian society.* Washington, D.C.: Smithsonian Institution Press.

———. 1985. Shamanism and its discontents. *Medical Anthropology Quarterly* 2, no. 3:102–20.

Burnett, D. Graham. 2000. *Masters of all they surveyed: Exploration, geography, and a British El Dorado.* Chicago: Chicago University Press.

Butt Colson, Audrey. 2001. Kanaima: Itoto as death and anti-structure. In *Beyond the visible and the material.* Edited by Laura Rival and Neil L. Whitehead. Oxford: Oxford University Press.

———. 1998. *Fr. Cary-Elwes S. J. and the Alleluia Indians.* Georgetown: University of Guyana.

———. 1991. Obituary: Iris Myers. *Anthropology Today* 7, no. 3:19–20.

———. 1985. Routes of knowledge. *Antropológica* 63/64:103–49.

———. 1971. Hallelujah among the Patamona Indians. *Antropológica* 28:25–58.

———. 1966. Akawaio charm stones. *Folk* 8/9:69–81.

———. 1960. The birth of a religion. *Journal of the Royal Anthropological Institute* 90, no. 1:66–106.

———. 1958. Secondary urn burial among the Akawaio of British Guiana. *Timehri* 37:74–88.

———. 1954. The burning fountain from whence it came. *Timehri* 33:48–60.

Campbell, Alan Tormaid. 1989. *To square with Genesis: Causal statements and shamanic ideas in Wayãpí.* Edinburgh: Edinburgh University Press.

Carneiro, Robert. 1977. Recent observations on shamanism and witchcraft among the Kuikuru Indians of central Brazil. *Annals of the New York Academy of Sciences* 293:215–28.

Carneiro de Cunha, Manuela and Eduardo Viveiros de Castro. 1985. Vingança e temporalidade: Os Tupinambás. *Journal de la Société des Américanistes* 71:191–208.

Cerulo, Karen. 1998. *Deciphering violence: The cognitive structure of right and wrong.* New York: Routledge.

Chaumeil, Jean-Pierre. 1983. *Voir, savoir, pouvoir.* Paris: EHESS.

Civrieux, Marc de. 1980. *Watunna: An Orinoco creation cycle.* Edited and translated by David M. Guss. San Francisco: North Point Press.

———. 1974. *Religión y Magia Kari'ña.* Caracas: Universidad Catolica Andres Bello.

Clastres, Hélène. 1995. *The land-without-evil: Tupí-Guaraní prophetism.* Urbana: University of Illinois Press.

Clastres, Pierre. 1977. *Society against the state: The leader as servant and the humane uses of power among the Indians of the Americas.* New York: Urizen Books.

Clausewitz, Carl von. 1993. *On war.* New York: Knopf.

Comaroff, John, and Jean Comaroff, eds. 1998. *Occult economies and the*

violence of abstraction: Notes from the South African postcolony. Chicago:
American Bar Foundation.

———. 1993. *Modernity and its malcontents: Ritual and power in postcolonial
Africa.* Chicago: University of Chicago Press.

Combés, Isabelle. 1992. *La Tragédie cannibale chez les anciens Tupi-Guarani.*
Paris: Presses Universitaires de France.

Conklin, Beth. 2001. *Consuming grief: Compassionate cannibalism in an
Amazonian society.* Austin: University of Texas Press.

Cook, Philip W. 1997. *Abused men: The hidden side of domestic violence.*
Westport, Conn.: Praeger.

Coronil, Fernando. 1997. *The magical state.* Chicago: Chicago University Press.

Coudreau, Henri A. 1887. *La France équinoxiale.* 2 vols. Paris: Librairie
Coloniale.

Crawford, Beverly, and Ronnie D. Lipschutz, eds. 1998. *The myth of ethnic
"conflict": Politics, economics, and "cultural" violence.* Berkeley: International and Area Studies, University of California–Berkeley.

Crevaux, Jules. 1883. *Voyages dans l'Amérique du Sud.* Paris: Hachette.

Dance, Charles Daniel. 1881. *Chapters from a Guianese log-book.* Georgetown, Guyana: Royal Gazette.

Das, Veena, ed. 1990. *Mirrors of violence: Communities, riots, and survivors in
South Asia.* Oxford: Oxford University Press.

Descola, Philippe. 1994. *In the society of nature: A native ecology in Amazonia.* Cambridge: Cambridge University Press.

———. 1993. Les affinités sélectives: Alliance, guerre et prédation dans
l'ensemble Jivaro. *L'Homme* 33, no. 2/4:171–90.

Dole, Gertrude E. 1973. Shamanism and political control among the
Kuikuru. In *Peoples and cultures of native South America,* edited by D. R.
Gross. New York: Doubleday/The Natural History Press.

Drake Manuscript. [1590] 1996. *Histoire naturelle des Indes.* Foreword by
Patrick O'Brian. New York: W. W. Norton and Company.

Duclos, Denis. 1998. *The werewolf complex: America's fascination with violence.* Oxford: Berg Press.

Eller, Jack David. 1998. *From culture to ethnicity to conflict: An anthropological perspective on ethnic conflict.* Ann Arbor: University of Michigan Press.

Elliott, Delbert, Beatrix Hamburg, and Kirk Williams, eds. 1998. *Violence
in American schools: A new perspective.* Cambridge: Cambridge University Press.

Ellis, Bret Easton. 1991. *American psycho.* New York: Vintage Books.

Evans, Clifford, and Betty Meggers. 1960. Archaeological investigations in
British Guiana. *Bureau of American Ethnology Bulletin* 177. Washington:
Smithsonian Institution.

Evans-Pritchard, Edward Evan. 1937. *Witchcraft, oracles, and magic among the Azande.* Oxford: Clarendon Press.

Evreux, Yves d'. 1985 *Voyage au nord du Brésil: Fait en 1613 et 1614.* Paris: Payot.

Fabian, Johannes. 1990. *Power and performance.* Madison: University of Wisconsin Press.

———. 1983. *Time and the other: How anthropology makes its object.* New York: Columbia University Press.

Fanshawe, D. B. [1946] 1996. *The Fanshawe/Boyan glossary of Arawak names in natural history.* Georgetown: University of Guyana.

Farabee, William Curtis. 1924. *The central Caribs.* Philadelphia: University Museum.

———. 1917. A pioneer in Amazonia: The narrative of a journey from Manaos to Georgetown. *Bulletin of the Geographical Society of Philadelphia* 15, no. 2:57–103.

———. 1915. The Amazon expedition. *Museum Journal* 6, no. 1:1–54.

Farage, Nádia. Forthcoming. Rebellious memories: The Wapishana in the Rupununi uprising, Guyana, 1969. In *Histories and Historicities in Amazonia,* edited by Neil L. Whitehead. Lincoln: University of Nebraska Press.

Fausto, Carlos. 2001. *Inimigos Fiéis: História, guerra e xamanismo na Amazônia.* São Paulo: Editor da Universidade de São Paulo.

———. 2000. Of enemies and pets: Warfare and shamanism in Amazonia. *American Ethnologist* 26, no. 4:933–56.

Ferguson, R. Brian. 1995. *Yanomami warfare: A political history.* Santa Fe: SAR Press.

Ferguson, R. Brian, and Neil L. Whitehead, eds. 1999. *War in the tribal zone: Expanding states and indigenous warfare.* 2d ed. with new preface. Santa Fe/Oxford: SAR Press/James Currey.

———. 1992. *War in the tribal zone: Expanding states and indigenous warfare.* Santa Fe: SAR Press.

Fernandes, Florestan. 1952. La guerre et le sacrifice humain chez les Tupinamba. *Journal del la Société des Americanistes* XLI, no. 1:139–220.

Forte, Janette, and Ian Melville, eds. 1989. *Amerindian testimonies.* Georgetown, Guyana, printed for the authors.

Foster, Nancy F. 1993. Kanaima and Branco in Wapisiana cosmology. In 'Cosmology, values, and inter-ethnic contact in South America' (ed. T. Turner), *South American Indian Studies* 2:24–30.

Foucault, Michel. 1995. *Discipline and punish: The birth of the prison.* 2nd ed. New York: Vintage Books.

———. 1994. *The order of things.* New York: Vintage Books.

Fox, Desrey. 1997. *A critical restudy of the Kanaimo/iidoodoo within the*

Akawaio "Kakpong" society of Guyana. Master's thesis, Department of
Sociology and Anthropology, University of Kent.

Gallagher, Donat. 1997. Acrimonious anthropology. *Evelyn Waugh
Newsletter and Studies* 31, no. 1:5–6.

Gallegos, Romulo. 1984. *Canaima.* Translated by Jaime Tello. Norman:
University of Oklahoma Press.

———. 1935. *Canaima.* Barcelona: Araluce.

Gaonkar, Dilip P., ed. 2001. *Alternative modernities.* Durham, N.C.: Duke
University Press.

George, Kenneth M. 1996. *Showing signs of violence: The cultural politics of
a twentieth-century headhunting ritual.* Berkeley: University of California Press.

Geschiere, Peter. 1997. *The modernity of witchcraft: Politics and the occult in
postcolonial Africa.* Charlottesville: University Press of Virginia.

Ghiglieri, Michael Patrick. 1999. *The dark side of Man: Tracing the origins of
male violence.* Reading, Mass.: Perseus Books.

Gillin, John. 1936. *The Barama River Caribs of British Guiana.* Papers of the
Peabody Museum, XIV (2). Cambridge, Mass.: Peabody Museum.

Goldman, Irving. 1963. *The Cubeo Indians of the Northwest Amazon.*
Urbana: University of Illinois Press.

Gow, Peter. 1996. River people: Shamanism and history in western Amazonia. In *Shamanism, history, and the state,* edited by Nicholas Thomas
and Caroline Humphrey. Ann Arbor: University of Michigan Press.

Grillet, Jean, and François Bechamel. 1698. *A journal of the travels . . . into
Guiana in the year, 1674.* London: Samuel Buckley.

Guppy, Nicholas. 1961. *Wai-Wai: Through the forests north of the Amazon.*
Harmondsworth: Penguin Books.

Haas, Jonathan, ed. 1990. *The anthropology of war.* Cambridge: Cambridge
University Press.

Hanson, Victor Davis. 1989. *The Western way of war: Infantry battle in
classical Greece.* New York: Knopf.

Harcourt, Robert. 1613. *A relation of a voyage to Guiana.* London:
W. Welby.

Harlow, Vincent T., ed. 1928. *The discoverie of Guiana, by Sir Walter Ralegh.*
London: Argonaut Press.

Harris, Charles Alexander, and John Abraham Jacob Villiers. 1911. *Storm
van's Gravesande: The rise of British Guiana.* London: Hakluyt Society.

Harris, Wilson. [1964] 1995. Kanaima. In *Concert of Voices,* edited by V. J.
Ramraj. Peterborough: Broadview.

Heckenberger, Michael. Forthcoming. The wars within: Xinguano witchcraft and the balance of power. In *In darkness and secrecy: The anthropology*

of assault sorcery and witchcraft in Amazonia, edited by N. L. Whitehead and R. Wright. Durham, N.C.: Duke University Press.

Henfrey, Colin. 1964. *The gentle people.* London: Hutchinson and Company.

Henze, Dieter, ed. 1973. *Enzyklopädie der Entdecker und Erforscher der Erde.* Graz: Akademische Druck un Verlagsanstalt.

Hilhouse, William. 1825. *Indian notices.* Printed for the author.

Hobsbawm, Eric, and Terence Ranger. 1983. *The invention of tradition.* Cambridge: Cambridge University Press.

Hoskins, Janet, ed. 1996. *Headhunting and the social imagination in Southeast Asia.* Stanford, Calif.: Stanford University Press.

Hugh-Jones, Stephen. 1996. Shamans, prophets, priests, and pastors. In *Shamanism, history, and the state,* edited by Nicholas Thomas and Caroline Humphrey. Ann Arbor: University of Michigan Press.

Hulme, Peter. 2000. *Remnants of conquest: The island Caribs and their visitors, 1877–1998.* Oxford: Oxford University Press.

———. 1986. *Colonial encounters: Europe and the native Caribbean, 1492–1797.* London: Routledge.

Hulme, Peter, and Neil L. Whitehead, eds. 1992. *Wild majesty: Encounters with Caribs from Columbus to the present day: An anthology.* Oxford: Oxford University Press.

Humboldt, Alexander von. 1907. *Personal narrative of travels to the equinoctial regions of America.* London: George Routledge and Sons.

Im Thurn, Everard. 1883. *Among the Indians of Guiana.* London: Kegan, Paul, Trench, and Company.

Kapferer, Bruce. 1997. *The feast of the sorcerer: Practices of consciousness and power.* Chicago: University of Chicago Press.

———. 1988. *Legends of people, myths of state: Violence, intolerance, and political culture in Sri Lanka and Australia.* Washington: Smithsonian Institution Press.

Keegan, John. 1993. *A history of warfare.* London: Hutchinson.

Kelly, Raymond C. 2000. *Warless societies and the origin of war.* Ann Arbor: University of Michigan Press.

Kenswil, Frederick W. 1946. *Children of the silence: An account of the aboriginal Indians of the Upper Mazaruni river, British Guiana.* Georgetown, Guyana: Interior Development Committee.

Kirke, Henry. [1898] 1948. *Twenty-five years in British Guiana, 1872–1897.* Georgetown, Guyana: Daily Chronicle.

Koch-Grüneberg, Theodor. [1924] 1979. *Del Roraima al Orinoco.* Translated from the German by Federica de Ritter. 3 vols. Caracas: Ediciones del Banco Central de Venezuela.

Langdon, Jean. 1996. *Xamanismo no Brasil: Novas perspectivas.* Florianópolis: Editora da UFSC.

————. 1992. *Portals of power: Shamanism in South America.* Albuquerque: University of New Mexico Press.

Laudonnière, Rene. 1591. *Histoire notable de la Floride.* Franckfort am Mayn: Dieterich Von Bry.

La Varre, William Johanne. 1919. *Up the Mazaruni for diamonds.* Boston: Marshall Jones Company.

Léry, Jean de. 1990. *History of a voyage to the land of Brazil.* Edited by Janet Whatley. Berkeley: University of California Press.

Lestringant, Frank. 1997. *Cannibals.* Berkeley: University of California Press.

Lévi-Strauss, Claude. 1969. *The raw and the cooked: Introduction to the science of mythology.* Vol. 1. Translated by John and Doreen Weightman. New York: Harper Row.

————. 1967. The sorcerer and his magic. In *Magic, witchcraft, and curing,* edited by John Middleton. New York: Natural History Press.

————. 1943. Guerre et commerce chez les Indiens de l'Amerique de Sud. *Renaissance* 1:122–39.

Lizot, Jacques. 1994. On warfare. *American Ethnologist* 21, no. 4:845–62.

MacGaffey, Wyatt. 1986. *Religion and society in central Africa.* Chicago: University of Chicago Press.

Malikki, Lisa. 1995. *Purity and exile: Violence, memory, and national cosmology among Hutu refugees in Tanzania.* Chicago: University of Chicago Press.

Malone, Patrick M. 1991. *The skulking way of war: Technology and tactics among the New England Indians.* Lanham: Madison Books.

Martín, Gustavo. 1983. *Magia y religión en la Venezuela contemporánea.* Caracas: Ediciones de la Biblioteca Universidad Central de Venezuela.

Masters, Brian. 1985. *Killing for company: The case of Dennis Nilsen.* London: Cape.

McCallum, Cecilia. 1996. Morte e pessoa entre of Kaxinawá. *Mana: Estudos Antropologia Social* 2, no. 2:49–84.

Melville, Pauline. 1997. *The ventriloquist's tale.* London: Bloomsbury.

Menget, Patrick, ed. 1985. Guerre, sociétés, et vision du monde dans les basses terres de L'Amerique du Sud. *Journal de la Société des Américanistes* 71:129–207.

Meyer, Birgit. 1999. *Translating the devil: Religion and modernity among the Ewe in Ghana.* Trenton, N.J.: Africa World Press.

Mission Field. 1881. *The Mission Field: A monthly record of the proceedings of the Society for the Propagation of the Gospel.* London: G. Bell and Sons.

Moffitt, Terrie E. 1997. *Partner violence among young adults: Summary of a presentation.* Washington, D.C.: U.S. Dept. of Justice, Office of Justice Programs, National Institute of Justice.

Myers, Iris. 1946. The Makushi of British Guiana: A study in culture contact. *Timehri* 27:16–38.

Norwood, Victor. 1951. *The Skull of Kanaima*. London: Scion.

Obeyesekere, Gananath. 1992. *The apotheosis of Captain Cook: European mythmaking in the Pacific*. Princeton, N.J.: Princeton University Press.

Orlando, Eugene. 2000. Kanaima. In *Life on Victoria's street: An anthology of Victorian short stories and novellas*. [www.eugeneorlando.com/kanaima. htm]

Otterbein, Keith. 1994. *Feuding and warfare: Selected works of Keith F. Otterbein*. Langhorne, Pa.: Gordon and Breach.

———. 1985. *The evolution of war: A cross-cultural study*. New Haven, Conn.: Human Relations Area Files.

Penard, Frederick Paul, and Arthur Philip Penard. 1907. *De menschetende Aanbidders der Zonneslang*. 3 vols.Paramaribo: H. B. Heyde.

Petit, Pascale. 1998. *Heart of a deer*. London: Enitharmon Press.

Pierce, W. Edward. 1881. Report of W. E. Pierce to the Bishop of Guiana. *The Mission Field* (January 1881):16–24.

Premdas, Ralph Rikhinand. 1996. Race and ethnic relations in Burnhamite Guyana. In *Across the dark waters: Ethnicity and Indian identity in the Caribbean*, edited by D. Dabydeen and B. Samaroo. London: Macmillan.

Ralegh, Sir Walter. 1997. *The discoverie of the large, rich, and bewtiful Empyre of Guiana by Sir Walter Ralegh*. Edited, annotated, and transcribed by Neil L. Whitehead. Exploring Travel Series, vol. 1. Manchester: Manchester University Press; American Exploration and Travel Series, vol. 71. Norman: Oklahoma University Press.

Reichel-Dolmatoff, Gerardo. 1996. *Yurupari: Studies of an Amazonian foundation myth*. Cambridge, Mass.: Harvard University Press.

Ribeiro, Darcy. 1984. *Maira*. Translated by E. Goodland and T. Colchie. New York: Vintage Books.

Riches, David, ed. 1986. *The anthropology of violence*. Oxford: Blackwell.

Riley, Mary. Forthcoming. Guyanese history, Makushi historicities, and Amerindian rights. In *Histories and historicities in Amazonia*, edited by Neil L. Whitehead. Lincoln: University of Nebraska Press.

———. 2000. *Measuring the biomedical efficacy of traditional remedies among the Makushi Amerindians of southwestern Guyana*. Ph.D. diss., Department of Anthropology, Tulane University.

Rival, Laura. 1996. Blowpipes and spears: The social significance of Huaorani technological choices. In *Nature and society, anthropological perspectives*, edited by P. Descola and G. Pàlsson. London: Routledge.

Rivière, Peter G. 1995. *Absent minded imperialism: Britain and the expansion of empire in nineteenth-century Brazil*. London: I. B. Tauris and Company.

————. 1984. *Individual and society in Guiana: A comparative study of Amerindian social organization.* Cambridge: Cambridge University Press.

————. 1970. Factions and exclusions in two South American village systems. In *Witchcraft, confessions, and accusations,* edited by M. Douglas. A.S.A. Monographs 9. London: Tavistock.

Roe, Peter. 1995. *Myth material cultural semiotics: Prehistoric and ethnographic Guiana-Antilles.* Paper presented at the 94th Annual meeting of the American Anthropological Association, Washington D.C.

Roopnaraine, Terence. 1996. *Freighted fortunes: Gold and diamond mining in the Pakaraima Mountains, Guyana.* Ph.D. diss., Department of Anthropology, University of Cambridge.

Root, Deborah. 1996. *Cannibal culture: Art, appropriation, and the commodification of difference.* Boulder: Westview Press.

Rosaldo, Renato. 1984. Grief and a headhunter's rage: On the cultural force of emotions. In *Text, play, and story: The construction and reconstruction of self and society,* edited by Stuart Plattner. Washington, D.C.: American Ethnological Society.

Roth, Henry. 1950. The Kanaima. *Timehri* 29: 25–26.

Roth, Walter E. 1924. *An introductory study of the arts, crafts, and customs of the Guiana Indians.* 38th annual report of the Bureau of American Ethnology, 1916–17. Washington: Smithsonian Institution.

————. 1915. *An inquiry into the animism and folk-lore of the Guiana Indians.* 30th annual report of the Bureau of American Ethnology, 1908–9. Washington: Smithsonian Institution.

Sá, Lúcia Regina de. 1998. *Reading the rain forest: Indigenous texts and their impact on Brazilian and Spanish-American literature.* Ann Arbor, Mich.: UMI Dissertation Services.

Sahlins, Marshall David. 1995. *How "natives" think: About Captain Cook, for example.* Chicago: University of Chicago Press.

————. 1972. *Stone age economics.* New York: Aldine.

Sanborn, Geoffrey. 1998. *The sign of the cannibal: Melville and the making of a postcolonial reader.* Durham, N.C.: Duke University Press.

Sanday, Peggy R. 1986. *Divine hunger: Cannibalism as a cultural system.* Cambridge: Cambridge University Press.

Schomburgk, Robert H. [1841] 1931. *Travels in British Guiana and on the Orinoco during the years 1835–1839.* Edited by O. A. Schomburgk. Translated by Walter Roth. Georgetown, Guyana: Argosy.

————. 1836. Report of an expedition into the interior of British Guiana. *Journal of the Royal Geographical Society* 6: 226–84.

Schomburgk, Richard. [1848] 1922. *Travels in British Guiana 1840–1844.* Translated by W. Roth. Georgetown, Guyana: Daily Chronicle.

Scott, John. [1669] 1925. *The discription of Guyana.* In *Colonising expeditions* to the West Indies and Guiana, 1623–1667, edited by V. Harlow. London: Hakluyt Society. BL Sloane 3662, ff. 37b–42b.

Seed, Patricia. 1995. *Ceremonies of possession in Europe's conquest of the New World, 1492–1640.* Cambridge: Cambridge University Press.

Seltzer, Mark. 1998. *Serial killers: Death and life in America's wound culture.* New York: Routledge.

Shapiro, Michael J. 1997. *Violent cartographies: Mapping cultures of war.* Minneapolis: University of Minnesota Press.

Shaw, Rosalind. 1997. The production of witchcraft/witchcraft as production: Memory, modernity, and the slave trade in Sierra Leone. *American Ethnologist* 24, no. 4:856–76.

Sifontes, L. Barcelo. 1982. *Pemonton Wanamari.* Caracas: Monte Avila.

Simpson, George Gaylord. 1996. *The dechronization of Sam Magruder: A novel.* Introduction by Arthur C. Clarke. Afterword by Stephen Jay Gould. Edited and with a memoir by Joan Simpson Burns. New York: St. Martin's Press.

———. 1964. *This view of life: The world of an evolutionist.* New York: Harcourt, Brace and World.

Sorel, Georges. 1999. *Reflections on violence.* Cambridge: Cambridge University Press.

Starkey, Armstrong. 1998. *European and Native American warfare, 1675–1815.* Norman: University of Oklahoma Press.

Stedman, John G. 1988. *Narrative of a five years expedition against the revolted negroes of Surinam.* Edited by Richard and Sally Price. Baltimore: John Hopkins University Press.

Stewart, Pamela, and Andrew Strathern. 1999. Feasting on my enemy: Images of violence and change in the New Guinea highlands. *Ethnohistory* 46, no. 4:646–69.

Stoller, Paul, and Cheryl Olkes. 1987. *In sorcery's shadow.* Chicago: Chicago University Press.

Sullivan, Lawrence. 1988. Icanchu's drum: An orientation to meaning in South American religions. New York: Macmillan.

Sun-Tzu. [ca. 600 B.C.] 1993. *The art of war.* New York: Morrow.

Tambiah, Stanley. 1996. Leveling crowds: Ethnonationalist conflicts and collective violence in South Asia. Berkeley: University of California Press.

Taussig, Michael. 1997. *The magic of the state.* New York: Routledge.

———. 1987. *Shamanism, colonialism, and the wild man: A study in terror and healing.* Chicago: University of Chicago Press.

Taylor, Anne Christine. 2001. Wives, pets, and affines: Marriage among the Jivaro. In *Beyond the visible and the material,* edited by Laura Rival and Neil L. Whitehead. Oxford: Oxford University Press.

Taylor, Christopher. 1999. *Sacrifice as terror: The Rwandan genocide of 1994.* Oxford: Berg Press.

Thevet, André. [1575] 1953. *Le Brésil et les brésiliens: Le français en Amérique pendant la deuxième moitié du XVIe siècle.* Edited by S. Lussagnet. Paris: Presses Universitaires de France.

Thomas, David John. 1982. *Order without government: The society of the Pemon Indians of Venezuela.* Urbana: University of Illinois Press.

Thomas, Nicholas. 1994. *Colonialism's culture: Anthropology, travel, and government.* Princeton, N.J.: Princeton University Press.

Thomas, Nicholas, and Caroline Humphrey, eds. 1996. *Shamanism, history, and the state.* Ann Arbor: University of Michigan Press.

Tithecott, Richard. 1997. *Of men and monsters: Jeffrey Dahmer and the construction of the serial killer.* Madison: University of Wisconsin Press.

Trexler, Richard C. 1995. *Sex and conquest: Gendered violence, political order, and the European conquest of the Americas.* Ithaca, N.Y.: Cornell University Press.

Turner, Terence. 1992. Defiant images: The Kayapó appropriation of video. *Anthropology Today* 8, no. 6:5–16.

Verswijver, Gustaaf. 1992. *The club-fighters of the Amazon: Warfare among the Kaiapo Indians of central Brazil.* Gent: Rijksuniversiteit te Gent.

Vidal, Silvia, and Neil L. Whitehead. Forthcoming. The shamanic state in Guyana and Venezuela. In *In darkness and secrecy: The anthropology of assault sorcery and witchcraft in Amazonia,* edited by Neil L. Whitehead and Robin Wright. Durham, N.C.: Duke University Press.

Vilaça, Aparecida. 2000. Relations between funerary cannibalism and warfare cannibalism: The question of predation. *Ethnos* 65, no. 1:83–106.

Viveiros de Castro, Eduardo. 1998. Cosmological deixis and Amerindian perspectivism. *Journal of the Royal Anthropological Institute* 4, no. 3:469–88.

———. 1992. *From the enemy's point of view: Humanity and divinity in an Amazonian society.* Chicago: University of Chicago Press.

Walton, J. Maxey. n.d. *The Partamona Trail.* Foreign Missionary Office of the Pilgrim Holiness Church.

Waterton, Charles W. 1825. *Wanderings in South America.* London: J. Mawman.

Waugh, Evelyn. 1934. *Ninety-two days.* London: Duckworth.

Wrangham, Richard W. 1997. *Demonic males: Apes and the origins of violence.* London: Bloomsbury.

Whitehead, Neil L. Forthcoming. *Histories and historicities in Amazonia.* Lincoln: University of Nebraska Press.

———. 2001a. A history of research on warfare in anthropology: Reply to Otterbein. *American Anthropologist* 102, no. 4:834–37.

———. 2001b. Kanaimà: Shamanism and ritual death in the Pakaraima mountains, Guyana. In *Beyond the visible and the material,* edited by Laura Rival and Neil L. Whitehead. Oxford: Oxford University Press.

———. 2000. Hans Staden and the cultural politics of cannibalism. *Hispanic American Historical Review* 80, no. 4:721–51.

———. 1999a. The crises and transformations of invaded societies (1492–1580): The Caribbean. In vol. 3, part 1 of *The Cambridge history of Native American peoples,* edited by F. Salomon and S. Schwartz. Cambridge: Cambridge University Press.

———. 1999b. Lowland peoples confront colonial regimes in northern South America, 1550–1900. In vol. 3, part 2 of *The Cambridge history of Native American peoples,* edited by F. Salomon and S. Schwartz. Cambridge: Cambridge University Press.

———. 1999c. Native society and the European occupation of the Caribbean Islands and coastal Tierra Firme, 1492–1650. Chap. 7 in vol. 3 of *A general history of the Caribbean,* edited by C. Damas and P. Emmer. London: UNESCO Publications.

———. 1998. Colonial chieftains of the lower Orinoco and Guayana coast. In *Chiefdoms and chieftaincy in the Americas,* edited by E. Redmond. Gainesville: University Press of Florida.

———. 1997. Monstrosity and marvel: Symbolic convergence and mimetic elaboration in trans-cultural representation. *Studies in Travel Writing* 1:72–96.

———. 1996a. Ethnogenesis and ethnocide in the settlement of Surinam. In *History, power, and identity: Ethnogenesis in the Americas, 1492–1992,* edited by J. Hill. Iowa City: University of Iowa Press.

———. 1996b. The Mazaruni dragon: Golden metals and elite exchanges in the Caribbean, Orinoco, and the Amazon. In *Chieftains, power, and trade: Regional interaction in the intermediate area of the Americas,* edited by C. H. Langebaek and F. C.-Arroyo. Bogotá, Colombia: Departamento de Antropología, Universidad de los Andes.

———. 1996c. *An oral history of the Patamona, Yawong Valley, Guyana.* Georgetown, Guyana: Walter Roth Museum.

———. 1996d. Searching for paradise? Recent research in Amazonian archaeology. *Journal of Archaeological Research* 4, no. 3:241–64.

———. 1995a. Ethnic plurality and cultural continuity in the native Caribbean: Remarks and uncertainties as to data and theory. In *Wolves from the sea: Readings in the archaeology and anthropology of the Island Carib,* edited by Neil L. Whitehead. Leiden: KITLV Press.

———. 1995b. The historical anthropology of text: The interpretation of Ralegh's *Discoverie. Current Anthropology* 36:53–74.

————, ed. 1995c. *Wolves from the sea: Readings in the archaeology and anthropology of the Island Carib.* Leiden: KITLV Press.

————. 1993. Native American cultures along the Atlantic littoral of South America, 1499–1650. *Proceedings of the British Academy* 81:197–231.

————. 1992. Tribes make states and states make tribes: Warfare and the creation of colonial tribe and state in north-eastern South America, 1498–1820. In *War in the tribal zone,* edited by R. Brian Ferguson and Neil L. Whitehead. Santa Fe: SAR Press.

————. 1990a. Carib ethnic soldiering in Venezuela, the Guianas, and Antilles: 1492–1820. *Ethnohistory* 37, no. 4:357–85.

————. 1990b. The snake warriors—sons of the tiger's teeth: A descriptive analysis of Carib warfare: 1500–1820. In *The anthropology of war,* edited by Jonathan Haas. Cambridge: Cambridge University Press.

————. 1988. *Lords of the Tiger-Spirit: A history of the Caribs in colonial Venezuela and Guyana, 1498–1820.* Dordrecht-Providence: Foris Publications.

Whitehead, Neil L., and Robin Wright, eds. Forthcoming. *In darkness and secrecy: The anthropology of assault sorcery and witchcraft in Amazonia.* Durham, N.C.: Duke University Press.

Wickenden, James. 1956. *A Claim in the Hills.* New York: Rinehart and Company.

Whitten, N. 1976. "Sack Runa. Ethnicity and Adaptation of Ecuadorian Jungle Quichua." Urbana: University of Illinois Press.

Wilbert, Johannes. Forthcoming. Elements of Warao shamanism and sorcery. In *In darkness and secret: The anthropology of assault sorcery and witchcraft in Amazonia,* edited by Neil L. Whitehead and Robin Wright. Durham, N.C.: Duke University Press.

————. 1993. *Mystic endowment: Religious ethnography of the Warao Indians.* Cambridge, Mass.: Harvard University Press.

Wittgenstein, Ludwig. 1953. *Philosophical investigations.* Trans. G. E. M. Anscombe. Oxford: Blackwell.

Wright, Robin. 1998. *For those unborn: Cosmos, self, and history in Baniwa religion.* Austin: University of Texas Press.

Young, Matthew French. 1998. *Guyana: The lost Eldorado.* Leeds: Peepal Tree Press.

Index

Acoori, 31

Afghanistan, 192

Africa, 44, 197–201, 204, 245, 248, 283 n.18. *See also* Azande; Niger; Rwanda; Songhay

Akawaio, 4, 15, 52, 53, 54, 55, 62–63, 66, 69, 70, 71–73, 75–76, 84, 123, 128, 133–36, 139, 142, 143–45, 147–53, 155, 161, 179, 183–84, 209–12, 216–20, 250, 256 n.18, 260 n.19, 273 nn.14, 18, 280 n.1

Aldi, John, 155–56

Alleluia. *See* Shamanism: allelluia

Aluatatupu, 16, 21

Akaikalkparu, 21–22, 153

Amazonia, 7, 9, 52, 147, 178, 191, 197–201, 202–43, 248, 253 n.1

America(s), 197, 232; North, 205; South, 8, 13, 14, 26, 36, 84, 191, 193, 205. *See also* United States; Western culture

Amerindian(s), 1, 2, 7, 24, 32, 37, 38, 41–47, 52–55, 62, 63, 66, 69, 72–74, 76–84, 87, 88, 108, 118, 123, 128, 131, 133, 136, 139, 140–47, 149–50, 155, 156, 162, 174, 180–82, 185–87, 190–91, 193, 197, 200–201, 206–7, 233, 236, 244–45, 249–50, 253 n.3, 254 n.10

Anai, 56

Andes, 204

Animals, 65–66, 73, 77, 97–99, 131, 221, 250

—*birds* (and feathers), 51, 77, 90, 91, 92, 95, 100, 111, 122, 131, 164–65, 213–14, 216; goatsucker (kururukuru), 51; kite (kumalak), 97; macaw (arara), 221; night-owl (bokoboko), 88, 114; powis (dokwaru), 64, 92, 107, 111, 120, 168, 263 n.1; scrub turkey (maam), 120–21, 269 n.25

—*fish*, 70, 90, 98, 214; stingray (tsiparu), 98, 100

—*insects*, 21, 101, 113; ants, 96; bees, 148; butterflies, 96, 131, 170–71; flies, 101, 170; scorpions, 98, 111

—*mammals*: acoori (akuri), 114; anteater (tamanak), 23, 90, 96, 101, 124, 131; armadillo (kayank), 93, 104, 116, 179, 215–16; baboon (aluata), 155, 157, 172, 185; jaguar (kaikuci), 46, 60, 63, 64, 65–66, 67, 68, 69, 75, 76, 80, 85, 90–92, 96, 99, 106, 114, 121, 124, 131, 169, 184–85, 208–209, 257 n.3, 277 n.11

—*reptiles*: crocodile (caiman), 74–75, 220, 222, 281 n.10, 282 n.13; iguana (iwo), 93, 104, 116, 170; snakes, 31, 59, 61, 75, 80, 85, 89, 93, 98, 103, 116, 126, 218, 219

See also Hunting; Landscape; Plants; Shamanism: weytupok; Spirit beings

Anua-Naitu, 74–75

Anthropology, 7, 9, 11–13, 15–17, 35, 36, 69, 76–83, 132, 174–76, 191, 202, 204, 206, 210, 217, 232–33, 235, 244–51; and archaeology,

Anthropology (*continued*)
11, 12, 18–19, 24, 50, 79, 166, 200, 253 n.1, 255 n.12; and ethnography, 7, 11–40, 47, 83, 88, 108, 109, 128, 141, 189, 193, 204–6, 216–17, 233–36, 242, 244, 248–49; and ethnology, 78–79, 206–22, 217; Royal Anthropological Institute, 69; Royal Geographical Society, 56; Smithsonian Institution, 141; Walter Roth Museum, 11, 12, 19, 24, 27, 31, 35, 79. *See also* Burials; Roth, Walter; Williams, Denis
Antilles, 49–50
Appun, Karl, 146, 256 n.24
Arawak. *See* Lokono
Asanda. *See* Landscape: path
Asote, 169
Arawété, 236
Azande, 44

Baniwa, 203–4, 277 n.12
Barahma River, 143, 144
Barima River, 126
Bartica, 141–43, 148, 156
Barrington-Brown, Charles, 69–72, 100
Beckeranta, 145–46
Berbice river, 25, 73, 83, 142
Bible, 98, 150, 158
Blackness, 109, 134, 135, 148, 156–57, 182–87, 201, 207, 246
Boa Vista, 181
Body, 14–16, 40, 42, 49, 51, 59, 64, 66, 70, 72, 73, 76, 77, 60, 81–83, 92–97, 94, 100, 102, 103, 107, 116–18, 126, 131–32, 137, 139, 145–46, 151, 166, 170–71, 187, 195, 197, 203, 211, 217, 221–23, 225, 240–43; and soul (ekati), 66, 94, 96, 99, 100–102, 131, 132, 211, 217–18, 264 n.5. *See also* Cannibalism; Clothing; Shamanism: iwemya-kamatok; Shamanism: weytupok; Shamanism: wulukatok; Violence; Warfare
Bolívar, Simón, 196–97

Bosnia (Balkans), 191, 199, 245
Brazil, 4, 17, 22, 23, 34, 82, 103, 110, 142, 149, 166, 174, 179, 180–82, 184–85, 194–96, 199, 214, 230, 258 n.9, 271 n.6, 277 n.10
Breton, Raymond, 49
Bry, Theodor de, 50
Burials, 18–20, 26, 49, 59–60, 61, 64, 67, 74, 82, 94–97, 109, 126, 187, 211, 221–22, 264 n.7. *See also* Cannibalism; Shamanism: maba; Vampires
Burnham, Forbes, 130, 166, 174, 197
Burro-Burro River, 71
Bush, George, 199

Cabunie, 70
Cako River, 143
Caliban, 85
Cambodia, 192
Cannibalism, 14, 17, 43–44, 49, 50–54, 60, 65, 66, 68, 69, 73, 85, 87, 99, 102, 103, 107, 132, 137–38, 172, 178, 191–95, 198, 200, 233, 236–43, 248, 251, 281 n.5. *See also* Burials; Headhunting
Canterbury, 162
Capui, 143–44, 147
Carib, 4–5, 100, 139, 209. *See also* Akawaio; Karinya; Makushi; Patamuna; Pemon; Taruma; Waiwai; Ye'kuana
Caribbean, 27, 199. *See also* Dominica; Haiti
Caroni River, 84
Caura River, 224
Chieftaincy. *See* Men: tushau
Children, 20, 26, 58, 61, 66, 81, 84, 93, 94, 108, 110, 114–18, 120–22, 123, 125, 132, 134, 149, 154, 156, 158, 159, 167, 169–71, 185–87, 214–16, 225, 229–30, 240–41, 243, 249, 277 n.15
Christian, 104, 128, 133, 142, 145, 147, 149, 158, 162–63, 166, 183, 192, 197, 212, 230, 245. *See also* Missionaries

Christmas, 20, 26

Clothing, 46–47, 74, 137, 176, 182, 186

Colonialism, 13, 14, 15, 37, 38, 42, 43–46, 52–57, 63, 68, 69, 71–73, 82–84, 87, 92, 104, 134, 139–41, 143, 147–48, 175–87, 191–94, 197–200, 203, 209, 222, 231–33, 236, 238–39, 242, 244, 247–49. *See also* Modernity; Western culture

Cook, Captain, 39, 258 n.4

Cosmology, 1–2, 40, 47–50, 62, 65, 78, 80, 84, 98–100, 102, 106, 131, 146, 163, 179, 192, 203–5, 208, 216, 218–22, 232, 236–38, 242, 250–51

Cotinga River, 58

Coudreau, Henri, 57, 73, 80, 102, 248

Crevaux, Jules, 76, 260 n.21

Criminality, 5–6, 27, 29, 43, 45, 59, 71, 74, 76–87, 105, 176, 193, 241, 245, 248, 258 n.6, 276 n.5. *See also* Revenge

Culture, 1–2, 11, 14–16, 23, 27, 29–30, 32, 35, 37, 39–47, 50, 54–55, 60, 69, 71–72, 82–83, 86–87, 103, 124, 126, 129, 131, 139–41, 148, 158, 166, 174–78, 182, 186–87, 189, 191–95, 197, 201–2, 204–9, 211, 219, 224, 232–48, 250; performance, 2, 8–9, 37, 46–47, 50, 60, 68, 71–72, 83, 129, 166, 175, 187–94, 198, 206, 208–10, 222, 232–35, 239, 243–46; political, 84, 180, 191, 195, 197–200, 247; semiotics, 2, 47. *See also* Anthropology; Colonialism; History; Ritual practice; State; Warfare; Western culture

Cuyuni River, 4, 134, 140, 144, 148, 180

Dell, Floyd, 82

Demerara River, 63, 68, 75, 83, 143, 148

Demons. *See* Spirit beings

Development, 8, 38, 83, 119, 130, 135, 174–201, 218, 244, 249, 275 n.3; World Bank, 180, 200. *See also* Guyana: government; Resource extraction

Devil(s). *See* Spirit beings

Disease, 23–27, 31, 35, 39, 42, 48, 51, 58, 69, 77, 80–81, 104, 115–16, 121, 127, 130, 141, 142, 148, 159, 162, 169, 186, 218–20, 224, 232, 240, 256 n.20. *See also* Medicine; Shamanism

Dominica, 27, 255 n.14

Droghers, 21, 108, 156

Durkheim, Emile, 176

Dutch West India Company, 38, 47, 53, 134–36, 139, 141, 147

Echilebar River, 72, 181

Edwin, Clarence, 34

Edwin, Roger, 33–34, 153, 174–75, 212

Essequibo River, 4, 38, 52, 56, 70, 134, 137, 143, 144, 156, 157

Europe, 9, 46–47, 54, 55, 62, 63, 66, 83, 85, 133, 176, 193, 195, 198, 217, 232–33, 238, 241–42. *See also* Colonialism; Western culture

Evans-Pritchard, E. E., 44

Farabee, William Curtis, 80–81

Farms (mùloka), 31, 91, 100–102, 114, 117–18, 126, 153–54, 183, 188, 210

Fraser, Leah, 178–79

Gallegos, Rómulo, 84–85, 178, 196–97, 262 n.28

Gender, 58, 61, 83, 93, 98, 105, 123–24, 184, 189, 212–18, 230, 232–33, 240, 246, 258 n.7, 270 n.27. *See also* Men; Women

Gillin, John, 44, 79, 81–83, 248, 261 n.24

Globalization, 8, 101, 141–42, 175–78, 191, 195, 197–201, 262 n.31

Godwin, Hugh, 39, 46, 65, 130, 258 n.4

Gomez, Vicente, 197
Graves. *See* Burials
Gravesande, Storm van's, 38
Guns. *See* Warfare
Gunn's Strip, 185, 208, 222–25
Guiana, British, 46, 57, 66, 76, 77, 80, 82, 112, 149, 179
Guyana, 4, 11, 12, 24, 26, 27, 29, 32, 36, 37, 47, 53, 78, 79, 83, 87, 108, 147, 166, 174, 179–80, 182, 185, 187, 195–96, 199–200, 218–20, 247–48, 250, 253 n.1, 279 n.23; coastlanders, 117–18, 132, 135, 183, 190; Georgetown (Wygata), 11, 25, 26, 29, 35, 64, 68, 118, 119, 137, 156, 159, 168, 171, 174, 179–81, 185–86, 190; government, 5–7, 11, 12, 29, 35, 83, 104, 117–18, 130, 134–35, 142, 174–77, 182–85, 197, 218, 247, 249–50, 253 n.5, 276 n.5; highlands, 1–7, 27, 41, 73, 85, 128, 133, 136, 140, 166, 176, 179, 182, 189–90, 201, 217–18, 222, 245, 248, 250. *See also* Burnham, Forbes; Colonialism; Development; Guiana, British; Rupununi River; State

Haiti, 197, 199, 248. *See also* Caribbean
Harris, Wilson, 85–86, 178
Hashiro, 22, 24–27. *See also* Lokono
Headhunting, 43, 178, 191. *See also* Cannibalism; Burials; Mutilation
Hilhouse, William, 53–55, 61, 62, 76, 135, 136, 260 n.19
Hindu, 245
History, 27–28, 39–42, 73, 91, 111, 128, 130–39, 140–41, 147, 175, 182, 185, 189, 191–92, 195, 198, 201, 203–6, 210, 217, 223–24, 233, 238–39, 243, 246–47, 249, 282 n.14
Honey. *See* Shamanism: maba
Houses (benab), 4, 14, 19, 21, 22, 31, 34, 39, 59, 74, 85, 88–89, 123,

154, 158, 164–65, 173, 183, 187, 208, 210, 212, 214, 218–19, 221, 223, 225, 227, 229–31, 240, 250. *See also* Society
Humboldt, Alexander von, 54, 56–57
Hunting, 46, 66, 72, 90–92, 97, 98, 103, 104, 105, 107, 114, 117, 119, 122–23, 143, 167, 168, 179, 204, 217, 240, 257 n.3, 263 n.2

India, 73, 245, 248. *See also* Hindu; Shiva sects
Indonesia, 191, 245. *See also* Headhunting
Ireng River, 4, 11, 17, 72, 73, 110, 134, 179–81, 183
Iroquois, 239–43. *See also* Cannibalism; Torture
Islam, 145, 192

Jawalla, 183
Judaic law (of retaliation), 44, 77, 248

Kaibarupai, 113
Kaiteur Falls, 148
Kamarang dam, 183
Kanaimà. *See* Shamanism
Kanaimà Hill, 52, 119
Kanuku mountains, 151, 225–26
Kapohn. *See* Akawaio; Patamuna
Karasabai, 169
Karinya (Carib), 48–49, 51–55, 62, 71, 73, 79, 81–82, 109, 119, 123, 125–26, 131, 132, 134–38, 142–44, 147, 206, 209, 219–20, 225, 227, 256 n.17, 258 n.9, 260 n.16, 271 n.16, 273 n.12, 277 n.12, 280 n.1, 283 n.18
Karipuna, 48–50
Kato, 4, 11, 114, 119–21, 158, 172
Kawa, 121
Kawaliyana, 108, 131, 266 n.16
Kayapó, 36
Kilgour, Duncan, 27
Killing. *See* Violence: killing
Kinship. *See* Marriage; Society

Kobise, 143

Koch-Grüneberg, Theodore, 38, 57, 79–80, 100–102, 260 n.16, 262 n.30

Koniayatoi, 109, 166

Kopinan, 4, 31, 32, 111, 112, 122, 131, 167, 172–73, 227–30

Kosovo, 192, 245

Koumi (Araceae). *See* Plants: koumi

Kouyatilina, 145, 152

Kowa Mountain (Kawatùpù), 4, 8, 13, 172, 227

Kukenaam, 145

Kulauyaktoi, 109, 138, 223, 225–27

Kuribrong River, 144, 148, 149

Kurukabaru, 11, 156, 157, 172, 227

Kuseilapoimá, 224

Kuyali'yen (Macaw cave), 18, 23, 97, 111, 254 n.5

Kuyuwini River, 81

Kwatin, 183

Landscape, 4, 12, 37, 39, 58, 81, 84, 131, 136–37, 161, 166, 182, 223, 234, 262 n.30; cave (yen), 12, 17–20, 58, 97, 99, 107, 109, 111, 137, 161, 166, 169–70; forest (yek), 4, 11, 14, 21, 25, 31, 38, 49, 59, 61, 64, 65, 66, 68, 72, 80, 84–85, 89, 90, 99, 101, 107, 109, 110, 112, 113, 114, 119–22, 132, 134, 144, 161, 171, 175, 177, 179, 182, 183, 187, 210; path (asanda), 4, 14, 16, 21, 89, 105, 107, 119, 153, 226; savanna (toi), 4, 11, 17, 22, 85, 90, 119, 137, 143, 153, 156–58, 161, 175, 177, 185, 227. *See also* Body; Development; Resource extraction; Shamanism: karawali; Spirit beings

Latex. *See* Resource extraction

Laudonnière, Rene, 50, 51

Lethem, 27, 34, 156, 180, 181

Leung, Derek, 25, 35, 255 n.11

Lokono (Arawak), 11, 13, 19, 20, 52, 65, 68, 69, 73, 75, 142, 255 nn.12–13. *See also* Hashiro

Lycaon, 66. *See also* Animals: mam-

mals; Shamanism: weytupok; Werewolf

Macona-Ura, 74–75

Madness, 84. *See also* Shamanism: sopanéy

Magic, 2, 8, 32–33, 41, 43, 49, 50, 63, 80–82, 84, 91, 94–95, 97, 99–102, 104, 105, 112, 127, 129, 161–62, 167, 168, 170, 183, 185, 186, 189, 195–244, 249–50, 256 n.17, 264 n.5, 265 n.12, 273 n.11, 277 n.13, 278 n.16, 280 n.24; charms (bina/murang), 91–92, 100, 124–27, 168, 206, 208; spells (talen), 41, 80, 81, 91, 100, 183, 186, 196, 203–5, 208, 211, 218, 263 n.2, 277 n.13. *See also* Animals: reptiles; Plants

Mahaica River, 11, 26

Mahdia, 35, 169

Makushi, 2, 4, 15, 20, 22, 38, 52, 56, 58, 59, 60, 70, 71–73, 77, 78, 80–81, 85, 86, 95, 96, 115, 123, 126, 128, 131, 134, 135–39, 142, 144, 149–52, 155, 157, 167, 179, 183, 206, 208, 209, 217, 219, 225–27, 230, 250, 258 n.9, 260 n.21, 272 n.6, 277 n.14, 280 n.1

Malinowski, Bronislaw, 82–83, 261 n.25

Manawarin River, 125, 142

Marriage, 2, 5, 103, 105, 106, 132, 189, 209, 212–16, 235, 240. *See also* Society

Masks. *See* Shamanism: masks

Marx, Karl, 176, 199

Mazaruni River, 4, 70, 134, 140, 143, 145, 148, 179–80, 218, 250

Mead, Margaret, 82–83

Medicine, 25, 26, 35, 38, 63, 86, 94, 101, 114–15, 133, 142, 151, 162, 166, 176, 186, 190, 192, 254 n.7, 266 n.20, 267 n.22, 277 n.13. *See also* Disease; Nurse

Melville, Pauline, 86

Mekro, 73–75, 189

Men, 29, 49, 50, 61, 80, 81, 89–90, 98, 103, 105, 119, 123, 125, 145, 189, 212–16, 233, 238; kàyik (eminent men), 5, 8, 39, 112–13, 130, 137, 155, 172, 212, 222, 224–25, 230–31, 282 n.15; tushau (headman), 31, 56, 85, 91, 102–4, 129–31, 140–41, 143, 144, 158, 169–71, 183, 184–85, 195–96, 203, 228, 271 n.1. *See also* Gender; Warfare: kwayaus

Mining. *See* Resource extraction

Misseyari, 59

Missionaries, 4, 5, 8, 16, 17, 27, 33, 38, 43, 44, 47, 57, 62, 63, 65, 68, 69, 76, 86, 104, 110, 115, 118, 125, 128, 130, 132, 133, 137, 139–61, 166, 174–77, 183, 200, 210, 219, 227, 230, 273 n.13

—*Adventists, Seventh Day,* 183, 219, 266 n.22, 273 n.13; Abdul, Alonzo, 183; Gates, Becky, 267 n.22

—*Anglicans,* 112, 130, 141; Bernau, John Henry, 60–63, 93, 142, 143; Brett, William Henry, 13, 44, 63–69, 76, 94, 96, 142–44, 147, 148, 161–62, 178, 248; Dance, Charles, 73–76, 98, 145, 148, 159, 162, 260 n.20; Im Thurn, Everard, 44, 63, 69, 76–79, 150, 248, 259 n.14, 260 n.21; Jones, Archdeacon, 68; Lobertz, Rev., 148–49; Philip (Akawaio), 144, 147, 149; Pierce, Rev. W. E., 148–49. *See also* Anthropology; Capui

—*Catholics,* 82, 155–57, 193, 218–19, 241, 273 n.13; Bonham, Father, 155, 157; Davis, Pastor, 38, 257 n.23; Youd, Thomas, 38, 62–63, 68–69, 86–87, 142

—*"False" prophets,* 139–50; Awacaipu, 145–46; Jones, Rev. Jim, 146; Smith, "The Impostor," 142–47, 149, 272 nn.8, 10

—*Moravians,* 141

—*Mormons (Joseph Smith),* 142, 272 n.7

—*Pilgrim Holiness Church,* 33, 130, 155–61, 166, 185, 273 n.17; Burg, Clifton, 156–57, 159; Walton, Maxey, 158–59

See also Bible; Shamanism; Ritual; Spirit beings

Modernity, 8, 38, 83, 85, 115, 140, 141, 147–48, 174–201, 209, 233, 238–39, 246, 249, 262 n.31, 275 n.1, 279 n.23. *See also* Anthropology; Colonialism; Globalization; Missionaries; State; Tradition

Monkey Mountain, 22–25, 36, 110, 163, 181, 184

Moruca River, 142

Muritaro mission, 145, 148

Mutilation, 1–2, 5, 14–15, 40, 44, 45, 48–51, 57, 61, 64, 67, 68, 70, 75–77, 78, 80, 90, 92–96, 100, 103, 107, 114, 115, 116–17, 123, 124, 129, 147, 151, 169, 183–84, 188, 191, 211–16, 221, 232, 237–38, 241, 246

Mutum, 184

Myers, Iris, 83

Myth. *See* Cosmology; History; Poetics

Nazi, 29, 192, 200

Niger, 36

Norwood, Victor, 84, 178, 261 n.27

Nourage, 51

Nurse, 13, 15–16, 24, 25, 93, 115–18, 124, 161, 254 n.4. *See also* Medicine

Occult. *See* Magic; Shamanism

Orinoco River region, 39, 46, 47, 65, 134, 139, 140, 142, 147, 224

Orlando, Eugene, 87

Pakaraima mountains, 4, 7, 12, 36, 45, 130, 134, 178

Paramakatoi, 2–5, 11, 13, 17, 19, 21, 25–34, 36, 110–13, 115, 122, 124,

153, 155, 157–62, 166, 167, 173, 181, 185, 227–30, 250, 254 n.7

Parishara dance, 173, 274 n.25

Patamuna, 2–8, 11, 15, 17–19, 21, 22–23, 25, 27–29, 31–33, 35, 38, 41–42, 52–54, 58, 62, 71–73, 76, 80–81, 88, 95–96, 98, 99, 100, 104, 105, 108–9, 112, 115, 119, 123–24, 128, 130–39, 142, 146–52, 155–62, 167, 172, 174, 176, 178, 179, 181, 184–86, 189, 192, 200, 203–4, 206, 209–211, 217–18, 220, 222–31, 238, 248, 253 n.4, 256 n.15, 260 n.19, 273 n.14, 277 n.14, 282 n.14, 283 n.18

Pemon (Arecuna /Taulipáng), 52, 73, 74, 79, 80, 100, 102, 123, 136, 144, 146–47, 149, 167, 184, 211, 212, 218–19, 250, 273 n.13

Penard, F. and A., 220, 260 n.16, 265 n.12, 280 n.1

Petroglyphs (timehri), 21, 99, 132–33, 153

Pirara, 142

Pischaukó, 80

Piya. See Shamanism

Plants, 15, 64, 80, 89, 91, 96, 100–102, 107, 108–9, 113, 114, 127, 131, 134, 136, 168–69, 206, 221–22, 229, 265 n.11; arrowroot (kowak), 91, 101; Arum (genus), 59, 101, 124, 258 n.11, 265 n.12; banana (plantain), 101, 151, 153; coca/cocaine, 32, 187, 200; ginger (chiwi), 91, 101, 124, 168–69, 170, 266 n.13; kanaimà plant (kobita), 91, 92, 94, 101; koumi (Araceae), 58, 91, 93, 94, 97, 98, 100, 107, 168–69; manioc/cassava, 4, 20, 22, 49, 75, 102, 143, 144, 151, 154, 170, 183, 187, 205, 221; marijuana, 124–25, 187, 200; mora, 109, 164, 266 n.17; pineapple (akaikalak), 26, 94, 96, 101, 166; tannier (taya, taña), 70, 100; tobacco (kawai), 97, 162, 164–65, 221. See also

Animals; Magic; Poisoning; Shamanism: maba

Poetics, 2, 58, 65–69, 78, 85, 91, 99–100, 102–3, 129, 178–79, 192, 194, 206–8, 211, 245, 253 n.2

Poisoning, 21, 22, 25, 27, 31, 38–40, 51, 55, 58–64, 69–72, 74–79, 86–87, 113–14, 116, 136, 147, 188, 204, 210, 233; curare (ourali, ulali), 64, 120, 138; massi, 79, 266 n.15; poison-gourd (ubi), 188; wassi (wassy), 58, 91, 94, 264 n.4. See also Plants

Pomeroon River, 36, 65, 79, 142, 144

Portugal, 55, 156

Posey, Darell, 36–37, 256 n.22

Potaro River, 4, 85, 156, 180

Prophecy. See Shamanism: iwepyatàsak; Missionaries: "false" prophets

Prussia, 57, 60

Puruni River, 70

Puwa, 11, 23

Ralegh, Walter, 46

Reagan, Ronald, 199

Reagan, Nancy, 200

Resource extraction: diamonds, 23, 164–66, 179, 220; gold, 130, 179; latex (balata), 39, 119, 132, 137, 154, 155, 156, 182; mining, 4, 104, 112, 130, 132, 166, 169, 179–82, 186–87, 200, 210, 218, 222, 249, 276 nn.7, 8. See also Colonialism; Modernity; Slavery; Warfare

Revenge, 13, 42–45, 50, 53–60, 62, 64, 65, 68, 70, 71, 73–79, 81–82, 84, 88, 90, 92–94, 96, 97, 102, 105, 111, 115, 126, 136, 138–39, 141, 144, 207, 220, 223–24, 231, 233, 236, 238, 241–42, 248. See also Criminality; Shamanism: kanaimà; Warfare: wenaiman

Rio Branco, 38, 52, 73, 79

Rio Negro, 73

Ritual, 1, 27, 28, 30, 32, 41–42, 46–

Ritual (*continued*)
50, 54, 59–61, 62, 64, 68, 74, 78,
82, 88, 91–102, 107, 109, 123, 125–
26, 128–29, 133–34, 140, 141, 152,
155, 161–62, 184, 187–89, 193,
196, 198–200, 202–43, 248–50.
See also Cosmology; Poetics;
Missionaries; Shamanism; Spirit
beings
Roopnaraine, Terry, 36–37, 254 n.3,
269 n.26, 271 n.29
Roraima Mountain region, 4, 38,
66, 68, 74, 79, 98, 143, 145–46,
150, 174, 219
Roth, Henry, 81–84
Roth, Johnny, 23, 253 n.9
Roth, Walter, 13–14, 23, 44, 76,
78–79, 83, 141, 260 n.16. *See also*
Anthropology
Rupununi River, 38, 83, 134, 142,
155, 179; incident, 166, 180, 275
n.4. *See also* Guyana: govern-
ment
Russell, Bertrand, 82
Rwanda, 191–92, 245

Sand Creek, 109
Santa Maria, 227–29
Saxon, 44, 77
Schomburgk, Richard, 45, 56–61,
77, 81, 84, 90, 258 n.11, 262 n.28
Schomburgk, Robert, 45, 56–57,
59, 81, 84, 146, 258 n.9, 258 n.11,
259.12, 271 n.6
School, 20, 71, 84, 148–49, 156, 158,
174, 176, 254 n.7. *See also* Children
Scipio, Sam, 156, 185, 274 n.29. *See
also* Blackness
Sexuality. *See* Gender
Shamanism, 5, 8, 36, 41, 43–44,
47, 52, 57, 60, 73, 77–81, 83, 97–
100, 104, 105, 106, 107, 112, 123,
125, 127, 128–73, 184, 191, 195–
96, 202–5, 209–10, 217, 218, 220,
237–38, 240, 249
—*Akawaio* (itoto/ídodo), 139, 210–
12, 216–18, 227, 249, 280 n.1

—*dark shamanism,* 5, 28, 35–36,
46–53, 195, 202–5, 208, 220–21;
assault sorcery, 2, 5, 8, 9, 28, 32,
39, 42, 46–52, 63, 76, 81, 129–33,
146, 163–66, 191, 195, 197, 202–12,
220, 224–25, 261 n.26, 277 n.12,
282 n.11; obeah/obiah, 69, 197,
199; sorcery, 36, 44, 49, 67–70,
73, 100, 129, 147, 161, 203, 205;
voodoo, 197–99; witchcraft, 2,
15, 16, 44, 191, 199, 209, 259 n.13
—*alleluia,* 5, 8, 9, 25, 27, 33–34, 63,
73, 91, 100, 109, 119, 123, 128, 130–
32, 139–41, 150, 163, 166, 173, 179,
184, 186, 189, 196, 206, 210, 229,
238, 249, 273 n.17, 274 n.18
—*alleluia'san:* Abel, 151–52; Bichiwung, 63, 150–51, 273 n.11;
Charley, Hendricks, 149, 152;
Charley, John, 152, 159; Christ,
151–52, 162; Edwin, Alfred, 33–
34, 153, 212; Paiwa, 151, 153–55;
Williams, George, 152; Williams,
Robinson, 151–52, 155–56, 158,
174
—*iwemyakamatok* (soul flight), 107,
151, 165, 170–71, 212–16
—*iwepyatàsak* (prophet), 8, 33, 47,
63, 73, 91, 103, 128, 130–33, 139–
42, 145–48, 150–55, 162–63, 184,
196, 200, 238, 240, 242; Awacaipu, 145–46; Edwin, Lucia, 152;
Paul, Bagit, 133; Susannah, 154
—*kalawali* (spirit ladder), 42, 80,
100, 104, 109, 131, 163–66, 197,
214, 266 n.17; Wailan, 214
—*kanaimà,* 1–2, 4–9, 11–17, 19, 20–
33, 36–141, 144–45, 147, 150–51,
158–71, 174–244, 246–51, 275 n.2,
280 n.3
—*kanaimà'san:* Bishop, 31, 112–13,
183; Caesar, 185; Dschiawó, 79,
102; Emewari, 28–29; Pirai 19,
21, 22, 24, 28, 32, 110–13, 162, 266
n.19; Talinaku, 109, 166
—*maba* (ritual food), 15, 42, 90–

91, 96–97, 163, 179, 187, 195, 215, 237–38, 243. *See also* Burials
—*masks,* 36, 106, 122, 126, 187
—*piya, piya'san,* 5, 8, 28, 41, 43–45, 48, 49, 51, 57, 60, 61, 63, 64, 69, 70, 73, 74, 76–77, 79, 80, 81, 91, 99–102, 103, 104, 107, 109, 112, 115, 123, 125–26, 128–30, 133, 138, 140, 148, 150, 152, 155, 159, 161–67, 169–71, 174, 179, 183–86, 190, 196, 204, 206, 208, 209, 211, 217, 218, 220, 230, 259 n.14
—*sopané y* (spirit madness), 68, 95, 107, 163, 169, 187, 264 n.6, 272 n.10, 274 n.24
—*tchak-tchak* (marakka), 161–62, 164
—*weytupok* (shapeshifting), 49, 65–66, 69, 75, 78, 80, 85, 91, 96, 100, 102, 107, 124, 126, 136, 170–71, 179, 209, 212–16, 222, 277 n.11. *See also* Animals; Vampires; Werewolf
—*wulukatok* (resurrection), 151, 170–71, 174
—*yé* (ritual stick), 93, 96, 104, 107, 126, 163, 185, 219
—*yeribada* (initiates), 79, 93, 97, 104–9, 113–14, 123, 137, 184, 187, 217, 221, 266 n.15, 271 n.2; Merimo, 105–6, 108, 111, 189
See also Magic; Missionaries; Ritual; Spirit beings; State; Warfare
Shapeshifting. *See* Shamanism: weytupok
Shenanbauwie, 148–49
Shiva sects, 73, 248
Siparuni River district, 22, 39, 119, 134, 137–38, 140, 155, 156
Sky (kak), 86, 128, 135, 164, 178, 182, 263 n.1
Slavery, 38, 53, 55, 134–36, 141, 162, 206, 222, 224, 249, 258 n.9, 271 n.6
Smith, Adam, 199
Smith, Gregory, 157

Smith, Joseph. *See* Missionaries: Mormons
Society, 4, 16, 44, 50, 53, 55, 56, 65, 74, 78, 79, 81, 90–91, 102–7, 109, 111, 112–13, 117, 124, 126, 128–33, 136, 139, 140–41, 151, 161, 169, 171, 182–87, 189, 191–92, 203, 205–9, 211–12, 218, 222–25, 230–46, 249–51. *See also* Culture; House; Modernity; Revenge; State; Village; Warfare
Society for Propagation of the Gospel, 149
Somalia, 192
Songhay, 35–36
Sorcery. *See* Shamanism
Soul. *See* Body: and soul
Spain, 46, 134, 139–40
Sparry, Francis, 46
Spirit beings, 1–2, 5, 16, 21–22, 42, 48–49, 51, 52, 57, 60, 64–66, 75–77, 80, 81, 84, 85, 91, 98–100, 115, 118, 126, 131–32, 144, 145, 153, 164–65, 193, 197, 198–99, 204, 217, 220–21, 236, 259 n.12, 262 n.29; Ataitai (forest cannibal), 99, 265 n.8; Aygnan (forest demon), 48–49, 283 n.18; Canayi (kanaimà), 52, 61; Chankon (kanaimà), 219; Chinay (corpse-sucker), 52; Kaagerre (forest demon), 49; Kaikuci'ima (jaguars), 97, 221; Katú, Akwa (God), 5, 63, 98–100, 125, 143, 145, 150–52, 154–56, 159, 229, 274 n.23; Koumima (gardens), 91, 96, 100; Maku-naima (plants/animals), 80, 98–100, 103–4, 109, 131–33, 144, 146, 203–4, 212–16, 219, 221–22; Mapoya/Opia (darkness), 48–49, 258 n.5, 283 n.18; Mawraima (anteaters), 101; Odosha, 98, 103; Piai'ima/Chiki (piya/ men), 80, 98–100, 102–3, 203–4, 212–16, 219, 221, 265 n.8; Setan/Makui

Spirit beings (*continued*)
(the Devil), 42, 46, 51, 52, 69,
76, 98, 104, 144, 153, 251; Totopù (caves), 21, 153; Wanadi,
98; Wattopa (oracles), 48–49, 271
n.1, 283 n.18; Yalock (poisons),
76; Yurokon (evil), 144; Yuruparí
(evil), 48–50. *See also* Animals;
Body: and soul; Missionaries;
Shamanism: alleluia
Staden, Hans, 241
Stars (ichieri), 104, 214, 216; Orion
(chopped leg), 104, 214, 269 n.25;
Pleiades (fish skull), 214
State, 44, 74, 103, 176–77, 204, 238,
241, 244–45, 247; Hegelian, 194,
197, 200; Hobbesian, 43, 234;
magical, 8, 84, 196–97; shamanic,
195–201; terror, 8, 180, 197, 241,
245; *See also* Guyana:government
St. Cuthbert's, 26
Surinam (Dutch Guiana), 134, 141

Taruka, 21–22, 120, 153–55, 158
Taruma, 227
Tendapatoi, 119–22
Teseric, 156, 158
Torture, 191, 239–43, 283 n.19. *See
also* Body; Poisoning
Tradition, 8, 46, 115, 140, 174–87,
246–47, 249. *See also* History
Treaty of London, 134
Trinidad, 183
Tukusapilengtoi, 167
Tumutumari, 85, 156
Tupi, 48–50, 100, 103, 236–43, 281
n.5, 283 n.18. *See also* Arawété;
Cannibalism; Torture; Wari'
Tusenen, 120, 269 n.26

Ulupelu, 166, 172
United Kingdom, 7, 12, 16, 20, 26,
27, 38, 43, 44, 46, 47, 53, 55, 60,
62, 71, 87, 105, 108, 118, 133, 134,
141, 147, 148, 150, 155, 166, 179,
248. *See also* Guiana, British
United States, 12, 26, 31, 35, 47, 78–
79, 130, 155–58, 174, 176, 194, 200,
217, 248
Uraricoera River, 80

Vampires, 44, 52, 102, 178, 199,
221–22, 251. *See also* Burials
Venezuela, 4, 80, 84, 109, 134, 179,
180, 195–97, 224, 279 n.23
Vengeance. *See* Revenge
Village (uten), 1–4, 11, 19–23, 29,
31–32, 34, 35, 37, 38, 53, 54, 56,
59, 70–72, 75, 78, 79, 85, 91, 94,
99, 102–13, 115, 118, 124, 128, 135,
144, 152, 158–59, 161, 162, 168–71,
180, 183, 184–85, 204, 207–8, 212,
220, 224–27, 230–31, 235. *See also*
Paramakatoi; Society
Violence, 1–2, 8, 9, 14, 17, 27, 29,
36–37, 39, 43, 55, 62, 65, 68, 70,
73, 74, 84–85, 88, 93, 98, 106,
124, 129, 139, 166, 174–201, 221,
223, 229–30, 233, 236–39, 241–42,
244–47, 257 n.2, 258 n.7; killing,
1–2, 5, 7, 14–15, 17, 26, 27–29,
31, 36, 38, 42–43, 46, 52, 55, 57,
59–63, 65, 68, 70, 73, 74, 76–80,
88, 90–92, 97, 107 104, 105, 107,
108–15, 110, 111, 114–15, 124–26,
128–32, 136, 138, 146, 151, 162–
73, 183–85, 187–89, 191–92, 196,
201, 207–11, 217, 219–20, 222,
230–33, 237–38, 241, 243–45, 247,
249, 260 n.20, 263 n.2, 269 n.24;
serial killers, 69, 192–94, 200,
245, 251; snuff movie, 187–89;
victims, 1, 7, 14–15, 26, 30, 32,
39, 42, 46, 55, 59–60, 63–68, 76–
78, 80–81, 88, 90–94, 100, 104,
107, 111, 115–23, 126, 167, 187–89,
192–93, 207–8, 210, 220–22, 232,
237–39, 241–44, 269 n.26. *See also*
Body; Criminality; Shamanism;
Shamanism-kanaimà; Warfare

Waiking, 17, 21–28, 30, 111, 113
Waini River, 126
Waipa, 124

Waiwai, 52, 61, 86, 123, 184–85, 208–9, 218, 250, 270 n.27, 277 nn.11, 14, 278 n.16
Wallaba, 125
Wandapàtoi, 3, 119, 137–38, 153
Wapishana, 52, 83, 86, 123, 126, 127, 149, 206–8, 211
Waraputa, 56, 58
Warao, 52, 73, 125, 144–45, 147–48, 203–4, 219–22
Warfare (weypantaman), 9, 13, 27, 36, 38, 42–43, 51, 52–53, 54, 55, 62, 76, 99, 102–3, 104, 106, 109, 123, 128–73, 192, 196, 205–6, 209–10, 217, 222–45, 249, 257 n.2, 282 n.13; blowpipes (kulak), 120–22, 188, 263 n.2; bows and arrows (pàlau), 59, 61, 72, 104, 105, 118, 120, 138, 139, 146, 165, 168, 178, 220, 233; claymore mine, 29; clubs, 51–52, 70, 77, 109, 111, 138, 139, 146, 147, 168, 172–73, 187, 219, 225, 228–30; cutlass, 74, 90, 118, 184, 205, 212–13, 224–25, 232; guns (alakapusa), 46, 60, 62, 73–75, 80, 104, 110–11, 113, 118, 119, 122, 130, 135, 137–39, 140, 143, 146, 151, 167, 168, 171–73, 180–82, 200, 206, 209–10, 217, 220, 222–26, 229–32, 249, 276 n.6, 281 n.10; H-bomb, 159; kwayaus (warriors), 52–53, 103, 104, 110–11, 123, 130, 131, 136–39, 167–73, 184, 203, 209, 217, 220, 222–31, 235, 238, 239, 242, 246, 250; wenaiman (attack team), 109, 136–39, 167, 172–73, 223, 226–30, 250; yalá (defensive hedge), 224. See also Body; Men; Shamanism; Violence
Wari', 236–37
Watunna, 98

Waugh, Evelyn, 82–83, 261 n.25
Wayana, 52
Weather, 220, 269 n.24; rain (konok), 105, 154, 162, 181, 185, 187, 200; wind (asetun), 126, 153–54, 165, 277 n.12
Weight, Guy, 156
Werewolf, 44, 66, 67, 86, 251. See also Animals: jaguar; Shamanism: weytupok
Western culture, 29, 42–43, 133, 192–93, 200, 212, 244–46, 249. See also Colonialism; Culture; Europe; United States
Whiteness, 15, 21, 38–40, 44, 45, 53, 63, 70, 74, 80, 83, 86–87, 105, 109, 118, 132–38, 141–66, 182, 186, 201, 207, 240, 242, 246, 269 n.24. See also Medicine
Williams, Agnes, 156–57, 274 n.21
Williams, Denis, 12, 31, 35, 254 n.2
Williams, Frances, 156, 158
Wittgenstein, Ludwig, 16
Women, 38, 49, 61, 66, 72, 78, 81, 86, 90, 93, 98, 100–101, 105, 106, 108, 113, 114, 123–26, 138, 145, 151, 155–56, 167, 169, 171, 183–85, 187–89, 212–16, 224–25, 229, 233, 241, 243

Xinguanos, 61, 259 n.13

Yabiku, 22, 24
Yanomami, 80, 224, 261 n.26
Yawong River valley, 4, 16, 17, 21, 28, 32, 33, 132–33, 182, 223–27
Ye'kuana (Maionkon), 52, 84, 98, 103, 109, 136, 144, 209, 224–25, 227, 263 n.3, 266 n.18
Young, Matthew French, 83
Yuruari River, 84

Zuruma River, 58

NEIL L. WHITEHEAD is Professor of Anthropology at University of Wisconsin–Madison. He is the author of *Lords of the Tiger Spirit: A History of the Caribs in Colonial Venezuela and Guyana, 1498–1820* (1988) and has edited numerous works, including *Beyond the Visible and the Material: The Amerindianization of Society in the Work of Peter Riviere* (2001, with Laura Rival); *The Discoverie of the Large, Rich, and Bewtiful Empyre of Guiana, by Sir Walter Ralegh* (1998); and *Wild Majesty: Encounters with Caribs from Columbus to the Present Day: An Anthology* (1992). He is the editor of *Ethnohistory.*

Library of Congress Cataloging-in-Publication Data
Whitehead, Neil L.
Dark shamans : kanaimá and the poetics of violent death / Neil L. Whitehead.
p. cm.
Includes bibliographical references and index.
ISBN 0-8223-2952-2 (cloth : alk. paper) —
ISBN 0-8223-2988-3 (pbk. : alk. paper)
1. Patamuna Indians—Rites and ceremonies.   2. Patamuna Indians—Death.
3. Makushi Indians—Rites and ceremonies.   4. Makushi Indians—Death.
5. Violent deaths—Guyana—Paramakatoi Region.   6. Shamanism—Guyana—
Paramakatoi Region.   7. Witchcraft—Guayana—Paramakatoi Region.   8. Ritual
abuse—Guyana—Paramakatoi Region.   9. Paramakatoi Region (Guyana)—Rites
and ceremonies.   I. Title.
F2380.I.P3 W45   2002
299'.84—dc21   2002003192